D1720715

László Almásy's most daring Mission in the Desert War

Operation Salam

László Almásy's most daring Mission in the Desert War

Operation Salam

Kuno Gross / Michael Rolke / András Zboray

Foreword by

Dr. Rudolph Kuper

in co-operation with

Saul Kelly

belleville

"His sense of honour as a sportsman, aviator and driver were beyond frontiers.

He had an overwhelming love of the desert, especially the Libyan Desert."

Statement about Almásy given by *Oberstleutnant* Franz Seubert, "Angelo", to Jean Howard[1].

---

1   Letter of Howard to New York Times, 1996, Köln/Archive Kuper

The Authors

Kuno Gross

Born in 1965 in Switzerland, Kuno worked in the construction business in Libya for eleven years. During this time he travelled the desert extensively and became more and more interested in the history of the Desert Campaign of WWII.

Michael Rolke

Born in 1951 in Heidelberg, Germany, Michael studied in Heidelberg and Freiburg and works as a teacher in Oberkirch. He has been visiting the Sahara since 1988, trying to solve historic questions about travellers and explorers.

András Zboray, FRGS

Born in Budapest, Hungary, in 1964. Parallel to his business career in aviation, András organised numerous expeditions into the central regions of the Libyan Desert, primarily in search of prehistoric rock art sites. He translated Almásy's Hungarian language writings into English.

Front cover: Desert landscape of the Great Sand Sea, Almásy at the Yabsa Pass and "Inspektor".

© Kuno Gross, Michael Rolke, András Zboray / 2013
© 2013 belleville Verlag Michael Farin | Hormayrstrasse 15 | 80997 München. All rights reserved. All text by the authors; illustrations by Kuno Gross, color photographs by Kuno Gross unless otherwise stated.

Design & typesetting: Heidi Sorg & Christof Leistl, Munich
Printing: Druckerei Steinmeier, Deiningen

ISBN 978-3-943157-34-5

www.belleville-verlag.de

Contents

Dedication

This book is dedicated as a monument to László Ede Almásy, sportsman, aviator, and one of the greatest desert explorers of the 20th Century.

It is also dedicated to all those who love unhindered travel in the desert, and still dream to find one day the hidden oasis of Zerzura.

A Sooty Falcon *(Falco concolor)* flying above the hills near "Finger Point" on the route from the Gilf Kebir to Ain Dalla.

Acknowledgements

National Archives, London, UK

Churchill Archives, Churchill College, Cambridge, UK

Imperial War Museum, London, UK

Das Bundesarchiv/Militärarchiv, Freiburg and Koblenz, DE

The Almásy Family, Bernstein for their kind permission to publish Almásy's Salam diary and to use passages of his book *Rommel seregénél Libyában*.

Dorothea Auer, Embassador of the Republic of Austria in Tripoli, Libya, for her kind assistance.

Karin und Manfred Blume for the photos of *Sonderkommando Ritter*.

Brendan O'Carroll for his assistance regarding the Long Range Desert Group.

Ian Chard for the provision of his father's photos of Cairo and the careful and very valuable review of the manuscript.

Roberto Chiarvetto for his never ending assistance in all matters during the research.

Peter Clayton † for his help and advice.

Urs Ernst, Festungsmuseum Reuenthal (Switzerland), for his assistance regarding German weapons.

Tim Farnden for the photographs of his late grandfather Leonard Elsey's journey to Kufra.

Peter Gierlach and Ragnar Otterstad for their assistance regarding the *Agentenfunkgerät SE.99/10*.

Titan Honner for information and photographs about Almásy in Graz 1949.

Jean Howard (Alington) †, for the provision of her transcribed and corrected version of the Salam diary.

Saul Kelly, Author of **The Hunt for Zerzura** for the permission to use and quote parts of his outstanding book.

Stefan Kröpelin for his assistance and the provision of the Eppler photographs.

Rudolph Kuper for his invaluable assistance, writing of the foreword and the contribution of correspondence and documents.

Selina Küst, Stadtarchiv Karlsruhe, for finding out von Steffens whereabouts after the 1970's.

Dal McGuirk for the provision of photographs of German equipment and the original photographs of Operation Salam.

Rolf Munniger for the photographs of his late father.

Franz Nitzsche, "Rheinpfalz", Ludwigshafen, for his assistance regarding the Kaps reports.

Jonathan Pittaway for his always available help and assistance.

Walter Rummel, Landesarchiv Rheinland-Pfalz, Speyer, for helping to find information about Eppler's postwar life.

Oskar Seubert for the provision of the photos of his late father.

Dimitris Skatsilakis for the photos of *Kampfgeschwader 26*.

Michele Soffiantini for his contribution regarding the Italian maps.

Francois De Wet for the information regarding the 15 Squadron, South African Air Force.

Uncounted other persons who gave small hints, advice and encouragement while doing the research for the book.

"… and had many stories to tell"

by Dr. Rudolph Kuper

"… and had many stories to tell". This is all we get to know from Ralph Bagnold, the leading figure among the small group of early explorers of the eastern Sahara when he describes his memorable last encounter with Almásy[2]. In the 1930s both had been searching for the lost oasis of Zerzura, the 'holy grail' of the Libyan Desert – and by doing so they had opened up its vast limitless expanse.

Bagnold described in detail the luxurious banquet on occasion of the inauguration of the Egyptian Desert Institute in december, 1950 in the Abdeen Palace in Cairo, to which "a number of old friends had been invited". Besides Pat Clayton he gives special mention of "László Almásy, a Hungarian desert enthusiast we had known before the war, who had lately served in Rommel's staff against us" (and who was just appointed the Director of the new institute). Incredibly: Bagnold, founder of the Long Range Desert Group, and Almásy, who was able to go past them in a bold operation, were exchanging their experiences over a glass of wine only six years after the war!

Unfortunately none of the stories had been passed on, so it was up to Kuno Gross, Michael Rolke and András Zboray to gather all the details in this book, which goes beyond already published material to finally give an objective and complete picture about Operation Salam and especially about the man who stood behind it.

Once before such an attempt had been started by Jean Howard, who as a young woman was a member of the radio interception services, the "Code and Cypher School" in Bletchley Park during WWII. Transcribing captured radio messages, she caught the trail of Operation Salam, and after the War she embarked on a search for the mysterious man behind it. Unfortunately at the time few listened to her and her Almásy biography was never published. Jean Howard seems to have been especially fascinated by Almásy. Although they never met in person, she followed his short remaining life intensively after the war, and left no doubt in a conversation I had with her in 2004 together with Stefan Kröpelin about her sympathy for the man who had caused a lot of trouble to her colleagues. This became obvious when prompted by the film *The English Patient*, a defamation campaign started in the international press that by far surpassed the improper phrase "a Nazi but a sportsman" in the otherwise well-meaning obituary in the "Geographical Journal"[3]. Neither his close relationship to the Jewish writer Richard A. Bermann (alias Arnold Höllriegel), nor his assistance given to several Jewish friends in Budapest during the war fits the image of a "Nazi spy". Consequently in repeated public statements Jean Howard vehemently defended Almásy in whose integrity she had no doubt.

He was also portayed by Hans Rhotert as an honest character when in 1963 we spent several months together exploring rock art sites close to the oasis of Ghat in Southwest Libya. Over many long evenings Rhotert spoke about the Frobenius expedition of 1933, which took him in the company of Almásy to the Gilf Kebir and later to the Wadi Howar at the southern edge of the Sahara. Several personal letters from the estate of Hans Rhotert, dealing with the question of first discoveries between Frobenius and Almásy after the end of that journey, prove Almásy's straight-forwardness, and his fair and friendly attitude towards Rhotert. The last part of the 1933 expedition leading to Wadi Howar was a very strenuous one that lasted – due to a shortage of supplies – only a few days during which the members of the expedition had to forfeit their own cigarettes to keep chain smoker Almásy in a good mood. Apparently the sacrifices were worthwhile, since it were the rich archaeological findings of 1933 that prompted the start of the Cologne University researches in 1980 concerning the prehistoric settlement of the Eastern Sahara in this part of the Libyan Desert.

During the Second World War, Rhotert was in charge of the logistic preparations of the special *Abwehr* unit "Sonderkommando Dora" which mainly consisted of scientists and had the task to survey and explore the southern parts of the desert in Libya[4]. Here he met Almásy once again, who told him about the story of the successful Operation Salam but only seemed to be unhappy at not having received the "Knight's Cross" of the "Iron Cross" for this exceptionally brave operation. Nothing was mentioned of the inglorious end of the two agents in Cairo.

With Johannes Willy Eppler, alias Hussein Gafaar, one of the two agents, Almásy seems to have had a rather aloof relationship. The two characters were much too different. While Eppler in his book about the operation showed some appreciation for the leader of the expedition, he also made himself his immediate deputy in the rank of a captain. Almásy however did not spare any friendly words calling Eppler "one of the untidiest fellows I ever had under my command". It is not hard to imagine his judgement were he to have known about the loose living of the two agents in Cairo! Strangely, a completely different side of Eppler emerges from a notebook that was found in his estate, which he began while in solitary confinement in Maadi near Cairo. The book contains a hand-written encyclopaedia from A to Z with hundreds of entries in small tidy block letters on 270 pages, ranging from aviation technology to the gods of ancient Egypt. This was obviously an attempt of a prisoner isolated from the outside world to retain some form of sanity. There is a remarkable entry on page 94 under the letter H: "HITLER, Adolf born 20 April 1889, illegitimate son of a maid, adopted by his stepfather, volunteered in 1914 (to World War I) … becomes dictator on 30 Jan 1933". Perhaps another sign of the free abandon of the author who did not fully consider the potential consequences if possibly released earlier and under different circumstances.

3   Murray, *Ladislas Almásy (obituary)*
4   Kuper, *Hans Rhotert (obituary)*

Jean Howard called Eppler a "story teller" and justly so. Stefan Kröpelin and I found him sympathetic and entertaining after surprisingly he had made contact with us in 1997 because of an article in "Die Zeit" magazine. At his home in the Alsace he showed us a convincingly designed page from a diary of the private Munz (actually sergeant), – probably the last time he tried to fool someone with his spy stories. In a neat typescript, with the correct date of 18 May 1942, it describes the visit of *Salam* to the "Cave of Swimmers" in Wadi Sora. The rest of this diary was not available, and neither was it two years later when Eppler visited us in the Cologne Institute. While obviously much of it was made up, the central part of the text seemed realistic:"The rock pictures are beautiful as if finished only lately. People, appearing to be swimming and animals. For us ordinary soldiers completely amazing. Something like that in the middle of this dumb desert!"

For Almásy, Wadi Sora was certainly of special importance. Previously he had been there on an exploration journey with his wartime Long Range Desert Group opponent Patrick A. Clayton, and on the later Frobenius expedition of 1933 he discovered here the paintings of the "Cave of Swimmers", which became the central setting for the love story of the "English Patient". Amusingly Clayton's son Peter later recalled that his mother and Lady Dorothy Clayton (the real-life character of the female lead-role in the movie) made constant fun of Almásy behind his back, who appeared as a rather odd character to them.

Nevertheless the picture of László Almásy is incomplete without his role in the exploration and study of the Libyan Desert and its history. Although this present book is mainly dedicated to his military achievements during Operation Salam, also this enterprise was closely related to his love of the desert and its exploration. Certainly obsessed by the passion of many other adventurers and explorers he, however, also had the reasoning ability to put his observations into a general context of environmental and cultural change and to anticipate in a visionary manner what later was confirmed by archaeological findings and more than 500 radiocarbon datings[5]. At a time when the humid period in the Sahara still was regarded as corresponding to the Ice Age of the North, he writes: "evidently the Libyan Desert of today offered then – 8,000 to 10,000 years ago – living conditions for herders and hunters who lived at the foot of the Gilf Kebir, at Uweinat and in southern Libya as well as in Nubia."[6] He concluded that with progressing desiccation the shepherds were pushed out from the savannah, and "there is no doubt that the prehistoric people which created these pieces of art continued to develop their culture along the Nile". Having said this, however, he warns with (for an amateur explorer) remarkable caution: "… we are far from being able to form a firm opinion on the relationship between the pyramids of the Pharaohs and the rock pictures of the Desert Mountains."

This last assessment is valid up to the present day, and points at the same time to one of the central problems for ongoing archaeological research in the Libyan Desert. The answer to many historical questions still lies hidden among the vestiges of human presence littering the surface of the desert sands and gravels. Due to constant wind erosion, the desert is like "archaeology in reverse". Instead of becoming buried, all left-behind objects remain on the surface, with few decades

---

5   Kuper & Kröpelin, *Climate-Controlled Holocene Occupation in the Sahara: Motor of Africa's Evolution*
6   Almásy, *Ismeretlen Szahara*

old rubbish lying beside palaeolithic tools, an open book of history for those able to read it.

Unfortunately this fragile evidence is in great danger from thoughtlessness among the steadily growing number of desert tourists, whose violation of the cultural and natural heritage is often encouraged by the indifference and negligence of their local guides. Much of what remained intact for thousands of years is obliterated in an instant by driving across ignorantly, being collected for souvenirs or as items to be sold, or even by pure vandalism. Losing their context the information we could gain from these remains is irrecoverably lost. Also mineral exploitation, especially the oil industry, often destroys vast areas with little regard for the invisible but lively ecosystems or for archaeology that, where written records are lacking, is the only source of history. This comprises evidence up to our days and it can be hoped that this book, with the story of "Purzel" and the remains of *Räuberlager* will not only contribute to a correct picture on Operation Salam and its participants, but will also create some awareness and respect to the so-called "modern rubbish" of recent history that is an integral part of the archaeology of the desert, forming the last chapter in a story that began hundreds of thousands of years ago.

Introduction by the authors

This book is the result of a multi-year collaborative research effort by the authors, following the trail of László Almásy, partially in the musty gloom of remote document archives, but also in a very real sense, in the scorching sands of the Libyan Desert. Our objective was to give a complete and balanced account of the activities of Almásy in North Africa during the Second World War, culminating in the daring Operation Salam which succeeded in delivering two German spies to Egypt across the vast Libyan Desert, practically under the nose of the enemy. The three authors all had deep but very differing personal affiliations with parts of this story.

Michael first heard about Almásy's explorations in the Egyptian Western Desert and his daring raid in 1942 to Assiut on meeting with Rudolph Kuper, prompted by another historical project related to the Desert Campaign of WWII. During some later research, he accidentally found Almásy's *Salam* diary in the Imperial War Museum, London, which was later given to Michael Farin to be included (in German) in the annex of the 1997 re-publication of Almásy's desert writings titled *Schwimmer in der Wüste*.

Some time later Michael received some photos from Ottokar Seubert for the other project which unexpectedly contained many of Operation Salam. In the 1990ies he was able to make telephone contacts with Eppler and Sandstede, and the latter provided an unedited excerpt of his memoirs dealing with Operation Salam.

The aforementioned 1997 reprint of Almásy's 1939 *Unbekannte Sahara* (Unknown Sahara) was one of the first books Kuno read about the exploration of the Sahara desert or the North African Campaign of the Second World War, with its dangerous missions in the deep desert. It was press reactions to *The English Patient* and a linked review about the just re-published book which grabbed his attention. Seeing the actual movie some years later, he became convinced that the real story of Almásy was much more fascinating than what was presented on the screen in 1997. Following the film, where Almásy was depicted as a tragic lover and hero, it did not take much for the "true story of the English patient" to surface in the press: suddenly he was described as an "ugly Nazi spy and homosexual". Obviously, the idea was to present him in the worst possible light compared to his movie *alter ego* in the *English Patient*. One thing is certainly true: he was a mysterious person and even after several years of painstaking research, it is still not clear whether he really was a spy – or for which side.

In the meantime, to some extent also prompted by the media hype surrounding the *The English Patient* movie, András made his first deep desert ventures to the remote

Gilf Kebir plateau and the mountain of Uweinat deep within the Libyan Desert. These legendary locations were explored by a small group of desert enthusiasts including Almásy, Bagnold and Clayton in the nineteen thirties, who later found themselves on opposing sides in the same desert during the War. Initially András' objectives were simply to visit all the prehistoric rock art sites reported by these early explorers, but this grew into an ongoing systematic rock art survey lasting more than ten years, which resulted in the finding of hundreds of new sites. While his interests were primarily related to rock art, related research in the British archives revealed a number of documents dealing with the wartime activities of Almásy and the other explorers.

In 2001 András came accross the correspondence between Brigadier Bagnold and Jean Howard from the mid-1970ies relating to Almásy and Operation Salam among the Bagnold Papers in the Churchill Archives, Cambridge (which also contain two 1935 letters from Almásy to Bagnold). Jean Howard used a neat printed letterhead with a Knightsbridge address and a telephone number. Taking the chance, András called the number on the way back from Cambridge to London, and a suspicious female voice answered. Doing away with the niceties of introduction or greeting, she immediately asked "How did you manage to find this number ? It is not listed anywhere!" On hearing the explanation she was clearly pacified, for the answer was "Oh, all right then, I am Jean Howard, would you like to come over for a cup of tea?" The rest of the afternoon was spent in her Knightsbridge apartment among the immense piles of books and papers, talking about Almásy, the Enigma transcripts, Ralph Bagnold, Yugoslavia, the Zerzura Club, Eastern Europe and Almásy again … Before parting, Jean gave a copy of her transcript of the *Salam* diary to András, in which she had corrected many of the translation errors contained in the version she obtained from Bagnold (identical to the one found by Michael in the IWM). It is this version of the *Salam* diary which is reproduced in full in this book.

During this time Kuno was living and working in Libya, and his attention turned to the rich scatter of WWII relics in the deserts of Libya, and the history of the units behind them, like the LRDG. This culminated in the 2009 publication of *The Incident at Jebel Sherif*, a small episode of the Desert War, during which Major Patrick Clayton, leader of the daring LRDG raid on Murzuq and companion of Almásy on earlier expeditions, was captured by the Italian *Compania Autosahariana di Cufra* at this remote location deep in the desert.

In late 2008 Almásy's book *With Rommel's Army in Libya* was to be released in German language, and Kuno offered assistance to the publisher to identify the names and the locations in that book. His interest was re-awakened and he started to re-read the books dealing with Almásy and Operation Salam. It soon became very clear that much of the story remained to be told. Authors such as Eppler[7] and von Steffens[8] were telling a lot, but not only the truth. Even the book *Schwimmer in der Wüste* which contained Almásy's diary for Operation Salam and some of the intercepted W/T messages brought up more questions, since the interpretation of some of these W/T messages did not match other known facts. In the meantime, many related files in the British National Archives were made public and more information was available for research than ever before.

7   Hans Eppler, one of the Spies brought to Egypt by Almásy during Operation Salam.
8   Hans von Steffens, Staff Seargant with Operation Salam.

Meanwhile Michael read Ondatje's book *The English Patient*; while the book itself was intended as pure fiction, much of the surrounding publicity took the whole context of the book's action as fact, misusing the name of Almásy. Reading other books, e.g. Eppler's *Rommel ruft Kairo* and von Steffens's *Salaam*, many contradictions were found, which became the first and strongest motivation to remove the myths and legends that were making the story of Operation Salam so confusing and still do today.

It was at this point that the interests of all three authors converged, all of them feeling that it was time to find out the truth, to correct the historical picture of Operation Salam and of Almásy himself. Of course they were aware that it was probably not possible to write such a story correct to the very last detail. The available documents leave large gaps, but to a great extent they could rely on their own desert travel experiences, the principles of which are the same today as they were in 1942.

One thing did change since Almásy's time – where unhindered free travel was possible then, now there is a border between Libya and Egypt, impermeable not because of any physical barriers, but because of the bureaucracies on both sides of the invisible divide. When they started to plot the route of Operation Salam on the maps the idea came up to re-trace it one day. While they have succeeded in parts, completing the entire route remains a dream. A dream as it was to find the lost oasis of Zerzura by Almásy.

The main content of this book is based on Almásy's diary of 15 to 29 May, 1942 which describes the middle part of the desert journey. Unfortunately the rest of his diary is not available – possibly was not even written – so the story before 15 and after 29 May had to be extracted and inferred from other sources. Piecing together the available information, combined with the three authors' knowledge of the Libyan Desert and of the particular regions crossed by Operation Salam, allowed the scripting of a quite precise sequence and a vivid tale. The aim was to complete the fragmentary story left behind by Almásy based on verified sources and to give the reader a good impression of what probably happened in those days.

Much had already been written about the subject, but unfortunately, none of these authors were in possession of the full picture, and more than one of them had the intention to make himself appear more important than he ever was. It is the nature of such stories, in particular if they are sensational ones, that much is manipulated, interpreted or sometimes invented freely. It was not easy to disentangle factual information from personal views and to avoid unsubstantiated comments or interpretations. It was not the authors' intention to provide just a further version of the story of Operation Salam and Operation Kondor but to take all available information and to extract what is, in their best assessment, closest to reality.

To provide the reader with a chance to compare and establish his own, possibly different, conclusions, references are provided to all sources, and footnotes explain statements and deductions where it was deemed necessary and helpful.

It is to be noted that more documents will probably appear in the course of time. Most important would be the personal file of Almásy, compiled by the British Security Service (MI5), to which several references exist in other released documents. It is said to have been destroyed during a "house keeping" review, however as personal files of much less significance have been retained and released to the public, it is suspected that it still remains locked away in the inaccessible Security Service archives …

Another more awkward issue confronted the authors. Taking into account that the mission was organised and carried out by the German Military Intelligence (the *Abwehr*), Almásy was accused in a number of recent publications of being a German spy and even to have been a Nazi, not to mention his sexual preferences. Inevitably the "legend" contained much myth, nonsense and outright lies.

Indeed it would be wrong to ignore all this and try to pretend that Operation Salam was something like a recreational journey through the desert during wartime. To avoid any misunderstanding, the authors wish to emphasise the following:

Almásy was a Hungarian nobleman, having grown up in the old Austro-Hungarian Empire and therefore practically "by birth" a Hungarian monarchist. There is a wide distinction between such a patriot and what is commonly understood as a "Nazi"; he never was a member of the NSDAP (the Nazis) or any similar party or organisation in Hungary. A number of his friends and travel companions were of Jewish origin, and there is some evidence that he helped some Jewish acquaintances hide or flee Hungary towards the end of the war.

Almásy was suspected by the British of spying for the Italians before the Second World War, then for the Germans. It is true that in the pre-war years many German (and Italian) agents were present in Egypt as they were in most other countries of interest. The famous air races of the 1930s were also used to gain aerial intelligence of potential enemy installations. To what extent such intelligence was helpful a few years later is a completely different subject. That Almásy gathered any intelligence for the Germans in the pre-war years was never proven; most probably he did not. There are however some episodes which one may consider as intelligence gathering by Almásy, for example when he handed over photographs of the Italian installations at Kufra to … the British in 1934!

Working for the German Military Intelligence (*Abwehr*) did not automatically make one a spy in the derogatory sense and it was certainly not necessary to be an active "Nazi" or to sympathise with Hitler: a famous example is the fate of the commanding officer of the *Abwehr*, Admiral Wilhelm Canaris[9]. An interesting statement in the post-war interrogation report of Thomas Ludwig (Theodor Levin), member of AST (*Abwehrstelle*) Istanbul from 1941 to 1944 provides further evidence: "With Admiral Canaris one could work with a good conscience … he would never demand of an *Abwehr* officer anything which his conscience would forbid him to do. Canaris stressed this at any meeting of *Abwehr* officers and constantly forbade, in the severest terms, any 'murder organisation' under his command."[10]

Nevertheless, although Operation Salam was comparable to many quite similar missions carried out by the Long Range Desert Group, it was under the control of

---

9   Whilst in the earlier years, Canaris was an admirer of Hitler and his ideas; he turned after a visit to a Concentration Camp in 1937 and from then on supported the resistance against the regime. See chapter "Other Persons of Interest" / *Admiral* Wilhelm Canaris.

10   TNA, London, KV 2/2652, Security Service Personal File series, Thomas Ludwig

military intelligence and not of the *Panzerarmee Afrika*, and thus it is not wrong to call it a "spy mission".

Finally, a war remains a terrible crime against humanity and one should constantly keep this in mind while reading a book dealing with a small sequence out of this war – no matter how fascinating and relatively benign this sequence might be.

Regarding Almásy's sexual habits, the authors did not find any relevance to the story of Operation Salam. This subject is therefore deemed a completely private one which shall not receive any further attention in this book.

The aim of this project was from the beginning to write a memorial for a great desert explorer and an account about a fascinating desert journey. If this helps the reader to find the final truth about Almásy, that will be an added bonus.

PART 1
EARLY MISSIONS

Beda Fomm, 90 kilometers south of Bengasi at
the *Via Balbia*. Here the remnants of the Italian
10th Army capitulated to O'Conners troops in the
afternoon of 7 February 1941.

The first phases of the Desert War in North Africa

The beginning of first phase of the Desert War in North Africa was fought by Italy against the British and her allied Forces. After the Italian defeat and withdrawal, the Germans entered the theatre with the famous *Afrikakorps* under *Generalleutnant* Erwin Rommel. Since the German military intelligence service, the *Abwehr* was already present in Libya long before the first regular units arrived, this period of the Desert War will be described in brief to give the reader a better understanding of the situation.

Italian attack and defeat

The hostilities in North Africa started shortly after Italy had declared war on 10 June 1940. Only four days later, the British Army's 11th Hussars, with assistance from elements of the 1st Royal Tank Regiment, crossed the border from Egypt into Libya and captured the Italian Fort Capuzzo. On 13 September 1940 Italy launched the 200'000 strong 10th Army stationed in Libya on an invasion of the British protectorate of Egypt, advanced and set up defensive positions near Sidi Barrani well inside Egypt along the Mediterranean coast. The Italian Marshal Rodolfo Graziani, Governor-General of Libya, then decided to order a halt and not to continue further towards Cairo unless the situation of his supplies was improved.

After the Italian army had stopped its advance, the Allied Forces launched their counteroffensive, Operation Compass, in December 1940. It took the Italians by complete surprise and they had to withdraw back into Libya suffering serious losses. The Allied Forces pursued the Italians, and after brief fighting they took the strongly fortified cities of Bardia and Tobruk. The advance was fast and at Beda Fomm, some 90 kilometres south of Bengasi, the Italian army was completely destroyed. The exhausted Allied Forces continued their advance unhindered until the small fort and village of el-Agheila, where they came to a halt.

While it may only be considered as a minute episode in the context of the general North African situation, some events played out in the deep southern deserts of

Libya had a major impact on our main story. In the summer of 1940 the soldier and desert explorer, Ralph Bagnold, through a series of fortuitous coincidences, was given the opportunity to form a small vehicle dependent desert-raiding unit which became known as the Long Range Desert Group. Several of the early desert companions, Patrick Clayton, William Kennedy-Shaw, and Guy Prendergast joined the unit which was mostly manned by New Zealanders seconded from their respective units. After the first sorties in the autumn of 1940, the LRDG was ready for a bigger punch. Following Bagnold's successful diplomacy in teaming up with General Leclerc's forces in Chad, a daring attack was planned and implemented led by Patrick Clayton on the Oasis of Murzuq on 11 January 1941, some 2'000 kilometres inside Libyan territory, deep behind Axis lines. While the attack itself caused relatively insignificant damage and casualties, the implication that the British had the means to strike unnoticed so deep inside Libya created substantial concern among German and Italian commands, and resulted in the diversion of valuable resources from the northern action. While Clayton was captured on the return journey at Jebel Sherif by an Italian unit[11], the Free French capitalised on the success of the Murzuq operation, and made a successful raid on Kufra, capturing the oasis from the Italian garrison on 28 February 1941. For the remainder of the North African campaign Kufra remained in Allied hands despite the repeated turn of odds along the Mediterranean coast, to be used as a base for LRDG operations deep behind enemy lines.[12]

El-Agheila, the remnants of the famous Italian fort, where Rommels advance units chlashed for the first time with their British counterparts on 24 February 1941.

German involvement and a new advance

Since during Operation Compass the Italian 10th Army was destroyed, fresh Italian troops together with German troops, the *Deutsches Afrikakorps* under *Generalleutnant* Erwin Rommel, were rushed in to stabilise the situation and build up a new front in western Libya, to prevent a complete loss of the Italian possession. At the same time the Allied Forces, who had just defeated the Italians, were withdrawn from the Western Desert. Due to the situation of the war in Greece, the British government decided to withdraw a big part of its forces from Libya and Egypt to assist the Greeks. Only weak and inexperienced forces remained to hold the line.

Although Rommel's troops were to help holding the line and to install a "blocking force", he immediately advanced with reconnaissance units towards el-Agheila and soon it became a full-scale offensive move in March 1941 which, with the exception of the strongly defended fortress of Tobruk, could push the Allied Forces

11   Gross, Chiarvetto, O'Carroll, *Incident at Jebel Sherif*
12   Kennedy Shaw, *Long Range desert Group*

back into Egypt. In fact, both sides were then back to their positions as they were before the start of hostilities. Then, the Allied Forces fought back with a small attack called Operation Brevity, to push the Axis forces back across the border, but this did not succeed. Shortly thereafter this was followed by a larger offensive, Operation Battleaxe, with the intention to relieve the siege on Tobruk. It also failed.

The interception and deciphering of coded German W/T messages

At the outbreak of the War, the Radio Security Service (RSS or MI8) at Hanslope Park started to monitor suspected German agent radio transmissions, first to screen possible enemy transmissions from the UK mainland, but with the help of enlisted radio amateurs, the service was soon extended to cover Europe and the Mediterranean regions to monitor all suspected German intelligence traffic. The messages intercepted by RSS were transferred to Bletchley Park – officially called the "Government Code and Cipher School" (GC&CS) – for deciphering and analysis. During World War Two, thousands of people worked at decrypting enemy W/T messages which were intercepted by the RSS, other listening stations and field units. The most important achievement was the breaking of the code of the supposedly impenetrable ENIGMA cipher machine,[13] which was used extensively by all German forces including the *Abwehr*. The intelligence reports produced from these most secret messages, known by the code name ULTRA, was of crucial assistance to the Allied war effort. Although so many people worked there, the ULTRA secret only became known to the public in the 1970s.

In early 1940 the German hand enciphered radio traffic code was broken, and a section was set up at Bletchley Park, named after the section head Oliver Stratchey, to report and analyse what was confirmed to be Abwehr radio traffic. This Intelligence Section Oliver Strachey (ISOS) produced daily reports on the deciphered and translated messages from 14 April 1940 onwards, but was also responsible for the intelligence analysis and the production of ULTRA reports to various allied commands to act upon the captured intelligence. ULTRA reports were sent to a select group of intelligence officers (eg. Head of SIME – Security Intelligence, Middle East) who were instructed to destroy them immediately after reading (hence none survives in archives), and were only to convey information to tactical units that would not compromise the source of the intelligence.

While most of the *Abwehr* traffic with field agents was hand cipher, the *Abwehr* also used the Enigma – G312, a smaller than a standard Enigma cipher machine with four rotors, principally for communication between *Abwehrstellen* (AST). This code was broken in late 1941 by the team lead by Dillwyn Knox, and Intelligence Section Knox (ISK) was formed to produce the *Abwehr* Enigma reports from 25 December, 1941.

13 The "cracking" of ENIGMA was actually not done at Bletchely Park by the British but in 1932 by the Polish mathematician Marjan Rejewski. In the same year, a German named Hans-Thilo Schmid gave the keycode to the French and the British – only they did not understand how to use it. The British code cracker Dillwyn "Dilly" Knox had still not succeeded when in July 1939, with war imminent the Polish handed over all their knowledge to the French and the British. Still the key for the *Reichsmarine* was not in Allied hands – but this problem was solved when the British captured the German U Boot U.110 intact.

The work of decoding and translating *Abwehr* messages was done in Huts 6 and 3 (as the workload increased, the original Bletchley Park Mansion was outgrown, and a series of wooden barracks, known as 'Huts' were erected on the mansion grounds). Hut 6 was responsible for deciphering the messages, while analysts in Hut 3 (including Jean Alington) were responsible for translation, indexing and intelligence analysis.

Contrary to what is commonly believed, the deciphering of the captured messages was far from being instantaneous. The *Abwehr* decrypts were only a small fraction of the volume of deciphered messages, the majority originating from the *Wehrmacht, Luftwaffe* (both processed in Huts 6 & 3), and the *Kriegsmarine* (processed in Huts 8 & 4). Depending on the War situation, some sources had priority over others, with lower priority messages taking days, sometimes weeks after transmission and capture to be deciphered and translated.

In the case of messages related to Operation Salam, substantial delays in deciphering were caused by the realization in mid-May that an attack by Rommel is imminent, and top priority was given to messages originating from H.Q. *Panzerarmee Afrika*. It is also evident that the intercepted messages were not deciphered in their capture order, but rather haphazardly, for reasons unknown.

While the deciphered messages were invaluable to the war effort, the neatly ordered and numbered messages which survived in the ISOS and ISK reports are at present a wealth of historical information, confirming events, times, dates and places for which there is no other reliable historical source. They are so important to understanding and following the story of events presented in this book that the full text of all messages which have a bearing on Almásy's activities in North Africa are reproduced in full in **Appendix 2.**

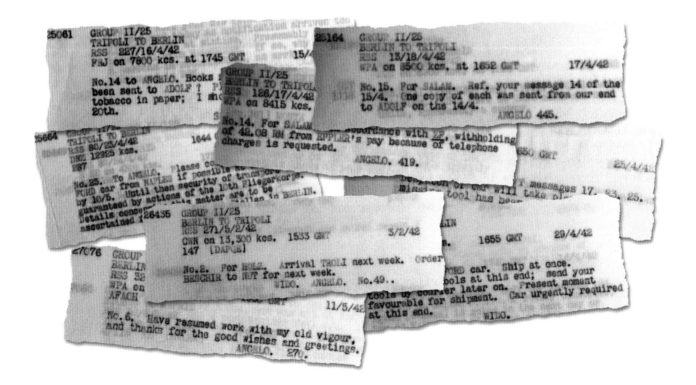

Secret missions of the *Abwehr* in North Africa

As it was the case all over the world during the Second World War, German military intelligence, the *Abwehr,* was present in North Africa. It is the nature of a secret organisation that much fewer facts are documented about its activities than for normal fighting units of the army. The significance of such clandestine activities are very often greatly over-estimated, and sometimes are not much more than just a "fairy tale". This chapter will concentrate on verified operations and missions where Almásy was involved, as in *Sonderkommando Ritter* and *Sonderkommando Almásy*.

Major Wittilo von Griesheim, commanding officer of *Abwehrstelle Tripolis* with the codename WIDO. *[Ottokar Seubert]*

Early presence of the German *Abwehr* in North Africa

Not much is known about the activities of the *Abwehr* in the early stages of the Desert Campaign, but the R.I.S. Report "German Espionage in North Africa"[14] gives a patchy insight of British intelligence based on intercepted German messages.

While nothing is reported about any *Abwehr* setup near the front line in the eastern part of Libya, a W/T network called WIDO has been recognised with its centre near Tripoli and connections in Tripolitania and in the Fezzan. WIDO was the codename of *Major* Wittilo von Griesheim of *Abwehrstelle Tripolis* who was reporting to ANGELO in Berlin. The latter was *Major* Franz Seubert of *Amt Ausland Abwehr I H-West 3*. His W/T station was first based east of Tripoli, up the escarpment of the Jebel Nefusah at Nalut (Call sign NUT) but later on shifted to Zuara, the border town to Tunisia on the shore of the Mediterranean, since von Griesheim was also involved with the management of supply traffic coming to Libya from Vichy-French Tunisia. Von Griesheims's assistant was a certain *Wachtmeister* Holzbrecher (callsign HOLZ). Also *Wachtmeister* Hans von Steffens, who later on became a member of Operation Salam, was employed as W/T operator at Nalut and most probably as well at Murzuk in the Fezzan. Unfortunately for British intelligence, von Griesheim hardly used W/T messages but obviously sent his reports in written form via air courier to Berlin. The wireless transmitter was only used for administrative matters or in cases of great urgency. Von Griesheim maintained W/T transmitter sta-

Major Franz Seubert at *Amt Ausl./Abw I H-West 3* in Berlin was the overall leader of Operation Salam. His codename was ANGELO. *[Ottokar Seubert]*

14   TNA, London, KV 3/74

Almásy in the uniform of a Hungarian airforce captain with *Major* Ritter in Berlin. Studying the maps for the planned ventures.
[Karin & Manfred Blume]

(From left to right) *Major* Ritter, *Hauptmann* Fischer, *Major* Meier-Peterling, *Hauptmann* Almásy.
[Karin & Manfred Blume]

(From left to right) *Major* Meier-Peterling, *Hauptmann* Almásy, *Leutnant* Raydt.
[Karin & Manfred Blume]

tions at Ghadames (callsign GHAS), at Mizdah, at Ghat and at Murzuk. While there is evidence that he was also in contact with the Italian SIM (*Servizio Informazioni Militari*), it was concluded, mainly from the form of the messages sent from Murzuk after the LRDG attack on the fort and the airfield on 11 January 1941, that German staff manned the stations.

Beside the connection to Berlin, *Abwehrstelle Athen* (Call sign ADOLF) was also in direct contact with WIDO. It was recognised that von Griesheim not only maintained contact via W/T transmitters but that he paid several visits to his stations by car and even by plane, and that via Arab agents he was collecting not only information from the south of Libya but from French Tunisia and Algeria as well.

Meetings in Budapest and Vienna[15]

Major Nikolaus Ritter was in charge of espionage operations against Britain and the United States of America in *Abwehrstelle Hamburg, Abteilung I L*. He visited Budapest in September 1939[16], only shortly after the outbreak of the Second World War, to find a meeting point for his secret agents outside Germany. It was there that he was introduced to a certain Captain Almásy of the Hungarian Intelligence Service[17]. From then on, Ritter visited Almásy frequently at his home when he was in Budapest, where he enjoyed many pleasant hours listening to the stories Almásy had to tell about his life and expeditions in Africa. He recognised that Almásy was practically living in his African memories and recollections, and as an intelligence person he grasped the hints that Almásy had good and influential relations with high-ranking Egyptians, including General el-Masri Pasha, the former Chief of Staff of the Egyptian Army.

Almásy, who was very keen to return to Egypt and to the desert, as recalled by *Major* Ritter, said more than once: "If ever it should be the case that you have something to do in

15   Based on a postwar letter of Seubert to Buchheit and on Ritter, *Deckname Doktor Rantzau*

16   It is to be noted that Hungary only joined the *Dreimächtepakt* on 20 November 1940 and had only declared war on Yugoslavia in April 1941, then on the Allies following Pearl Harbor on 13th December 1941(Typical of how seriously this was taken, the US did not even bother to respond and declare war until the middle of 1943).

17   TNA, London, KV 2/88, Final Report on Ritter. However; it is to be noted that no Hungarian sources suggest any involvement of Almásy with Hungarian intelligence. Should this have been the case, it would have undoubtedly been used as evidence by the prosecution during Almásy's post-war trial.

Egypt, where I could be of help then let me know – I know the land and people like my own pocket."

Major Franz Seubert, who was responsible for North Africa and the Middle East in *Abwehr Abt I H West,* had assembled several acknowledged specialists and advisers for these areas, among them members of the circle around the Great Mufti of Jerusalem, Mohammed Amin al-Husseini, and also the former Prime Minister of Iraq, Raschid al-Gailani. However, none of these specialists was familiar with the situation in Libya and the North African desert, so Seubert was delighted when he was made aware of Almásy and his competence in the subject. *Major* Seubert and Almásy met in Vienna in the famous Hotel Sacher where they agreed that Almásy would be seconded to German Military Intelligence, the *Abwehr* by the Hungarian Air Force[18]. Further, to allow Almásy to liaise on the same level of authority with his German counterparts, he was allowed to wear the rank and the uniform of a *Hauptmann* of the German *Luftwaffe* with all rights and duties. However, he was given the right to refuse any task that he thought would be against his conscience[19].

Mil.-Geo. and Almásy's involvement

As soon as he was seconded to the German *Abwehr* and before any involvement with *Sonderkommando Ritter* and later Operation Salam, Almásy at first worked as an adviser on the equipment and feeding of troops in the desert, at the General Staff of the German Army; he was then working at the *Abteilung für Kriegskarten und Vermessungswesen (IV. Mil.-Geo.)*[20] at the *Heeresplankammer* of the *OKH* to assist them with his highly valuable knowledge of Egypt and the south-eastern regions of Libya.

Militärgeographische Beschreibung von Libyen and *Nordost-Afrika*. Almásy contributed to both of these during the early period of WWII.

IV. Mil.-Geo. had the important task of providing illustrated handbooks for each country the *Wehrmacht* had a strategic interest in. Such booklets included information about the geography, locations and cities; they were literally "travel guides" for the military: attached were overview maps, road descriptions and city maps. Particular attention was paid to strategic needs and any possibilities for the resupply of armies. Equally important were the descriptions of the climatic and sanitary conditions which one might find in each country. Further subjects were industrial development and installations, such as factories, bridges, harbours and airports, and the nature of the population. The country was normally split into regions which were defined by rivers, mountains or other natural boundaries.

Militärgeographische Beschreibung von Ägypten – Bildheft (1942). This pictorial booklet contains a number of Almásy's own photographs which he took during his expeditions to the desert.

18   Almásy was a reserve officer in the Hungarian Air Force. His transfer orders were presented by *General* Waldemár Kenese, the Commander of the Air Force. To complete the picture, Kenese was previously the Commander of the Szombathely airfield where Almásy lived in the Twenties, and the two men would have known each other well, possibly even being friends. It is entirely conceivable that the transfer was arranged at Almásy's personal request, contrary to him being "ordered" to join the Germans as he claimed in his war crimes trial.

19   This information is given in a letter of the former *Major* Seubert to Gert Buchheit (filed in Bundesarchiv Freiburg, date unknown).

20   Department for military maps and surveying

Photos of the Yabsa Pass between Kharga and Assiut. The same road was used by Operation Salam in 1942.

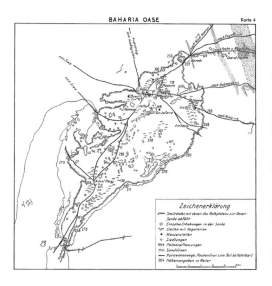

Sketch of Baharia Oasis.

And – typical for a "travel guide"– a small dictionary of the local language was included.

Mil.-Geo. (Militärgeographische Betrachtungen[21]) were classified and had the marking *"Nur für den Dienstgebrauch"*(for official use only) with the remark that they should be treated with care so as not to fall into unauthorised hands. Many of the *Mil.-Geo.* were further marked as *"Entwurf"* (draft), which underlined the preliminary nature of them. Fighting units were requested to provide corrections and proposals for improvement.

The following issues were printed on the northern parts of Africa:

Mil.-Geo. Nordost-Afrika   28.11.1940 (Egypt and Libya)
Mil.-Geo. Libyen   29.01.1941
Mil.-Geo. Tunis   10.10.1941
Mil.-Geo. Franz.-Westafrika   31.01.1942
Mil.-Geo. Ägypten   20.06.1942
Mil.-Geo. Franz.-Marokko   10.11.1942
Mil.-Geo. Algerien   10.11.1942

Almásy is mentioned by name in *Mil.-Geo. Nordost-Afrika* and *Mil.-Geo. Libyen*, page 23 as an expedition leader, and he gives advice on special driving techniques, navigation and equipment for the desert. Among the illustrations, several of Almásy's photographs can be recognised, and sometimes he may even be seen in person. The picture book *Ägypten* which was printed in June 1942 definitely bears Almásy's "fingerprint", since it contains many photographs which were taken duirng his desert journeys.

Aufklärungskommando Nordostafrika or *Sonderkommando Ritter*

Aufklärungskommando Nordostafrika was renamed *Sonderkommando Ritter* when its commanding officer *Major* Nikolaus Ritter was discharged from *Abwehrstelle Hamburg* and posted to *X Fliegerkorps*. It was the ill-fated predecessor of *Sonderkommando Almásy*[22].

Increasingly frequent differences of opinion between Ritter and the *I L Gruppenleiter*, *Major* Brede, with the latter's assistant, *Major* Busch intervening, culminated in December 1940 with the notice of Ritter's impending transfer to *X Fliegerkorps* in North Africa[23]. *Oberst* Piekenbrock later confided to Ritter that Busch, who was himself anxious to become *I L Leiter Abwehrstelle Hamburg*, had requested his transfer. However, Ritter, who had already unsuccessfully applied several times to be released for active service, was not displeased with the prospect, especially when he learnt that he was to command the *Aufklärungskommando Nordostafrika* where he could expect spectacular enterprises.

By the end of January 1941, Ritter handed over the responsibility of *Ref I L Hamburg* to *Major* Wenzlau and prepared himself for his forthcoming African adventure. Captain Almásy, whom he had previously met several times in Budapest, still had many excellent connections in Cairo and was most willing to join the *Kommando*. He was instrumental in securing a promise of collaboration from the new Hungarian envoy to Egypt, Bárdossy. With both of them Ritter discussed his future plans in Budapest in the course of January 1941.

The tasks set to Ritter's *Kommando* were to attempt to get the dissident Egyptian General el-Masri Pasha into German hands, as originally suggested by Almásy and approved by *I L Berlin*, and to place secret agents in Egypt. Furthermore they were tasked to assist the Ic of *Deutsches Afrikakorps* through Almásy on specific questions about the desert and Egypt, since Almásy had considerable flying and driving experience in this area.

Major Nikolaus Ritter.
[Karin & Manfred Blume]

22 Text based on Kelly, **The Hunt for Zerzura**; Ritter, **Deckname Dr. Rantzau**; Almásy, **Rommel Seregénél Libiában** and TNA documents (individual reference is given).
23 TNA, London, KV 2/88 Appendix D to FR28, Ritter

(From left to right)
Hauptmann Almásy,
Major Ritter and the
commander of the
airfield.
[Karin & Manfred Blume]

Catania Airfield, Sicily. Almásy standing next to
an Italian Macchi C.200 Saetta (Lightning) fighter
aircraft of the *72ª Squadriglia, 17° Gruppo,
1° Stormo.*
[Karin & Manfred Blume]

The vulnerable Junkers Ju 52 are flying low over
the surface of the Mediterranean.
[Karin & Manfred Blume]

Ritter extensively studied books and information on the scene
of his future operations, collected a series of maps and made
other arrangements for his new enterprise. With *Major* Trautmann, who ran the *Abwehr* communications centre at Wohl-
dorf, he selected four likely W/T operators to maintain communications with Hamburg and Berlin.

In early March 1941 the *Kommando* left Germany for Taormina, Sicily, where they reported to the HQ of *X Fliegerkorps*
and Ritter set up his headquarters at the Hotel Diodoro. An
intermediate W/T station was established to maintain communication with *Abwehr* HQ in Germany and Ritter's designated HQ at Derna in Cirenaica. *General* Geisler, the commanding officer of *X Fliegerkorps*, promised his support for
Ritter's *Kommando*. It was then decided that Almásy should
obtain the uniform of a *Hauptmann* of the German *Luftwaffe*[24]
in order to avoid any questions by the *Afrikakorps* or even the
British in case of being captured.

Ritter kept the group as small as possible, with himself as the
commanding officer and *Hauptmann* Almásy as the second in
command. *Oberleutnant* Theo Blaich[25] and *Leutnant* Günther
Raydt were employed as pilots (Raydt, who was inexperienced,
was subsequently transferred back to Germany). The W/T
operators were named Deppermann, Brinkmann and Wichmann[26] the name of the fourth is not recorded. The *Kommando*
was equipped with two aircraft of its own, a four seater Messerschmitt Bf108 "Taifun" (which was actually privately owned
by its pilot, Theo Blaich) and a Fieseler Fi 156 "Storch". Heinkel
He 111 aircraft for long distance flights were placed at the disposal of Ritter by KG.26 (*Kampfgeschwader* 26).

In May 1941 the HQ of the *Kommando* transferred to Derna,
Libya, leaving at Taormina only a W/T detachment to maintain
daily contact with Derna, Cairo, Hamburg and Berlin. Reports
of operational interest to *X Fliegerkorps*, especially movements
of enemy ships and aircraft, were received from Ankara, from
France and from the Gibraltar area.

24   The uniform was indeed German, but Almásy was permitted to retain
        his Hungarian Air Force markings, something that was changed
        only after a skirmish with Italian Military Police in Libya on account
        of the non-standard uniform. (Source: Almásy's testimonial during his
        war crimes trial, People's Court documents, National Archives,
        Budapest).
25   Theo Blaich, a former farmer in the Cameroons, was an experienced
        pilot. He joined Rommel's forces with his privately owned Messer-
        schmitt Bf.108 "Taifun" and became famous later on with his *Sonder-
        kommando Blaich* in 21 January 1942, when he bombed Fort Lamy
        in French Tchad in a daring raid with a Heinkel He 111.
26   Wichmann was later to be a member of *Sonderkommando Blaich*
        when he flew the plane in the attack on Fort Lamy in January 1942.

Ritter entering a Junkers Ju 52 transport aircraft for the flight to North Africa.
[Karin & Manfred Blume]

Sonderkommando Ritter leaving Tripoli. Standing in front of the 1934 Ford Model B (UK) are (from left to right) Wahrlich, (unknown), Busekros, Hassan, Giuseppe, Blaich and Depperman.
[Karin & Manfred Blume]

L'arco dei Fileni – Marble Arch. Mussolini's triumphal arch near R'as Lanuf.
[Karin & Manfred Blume]

Sonderkommando Ritter at rest somewhere between Bengasi and Derna. (From left to right) Busekros, Blaich, Deppermann, Hassan, Wahrlich, Giuseppe. *[Karin & Manfred Blume]*

Ritter's quarters at Derna were at the *Collina Duazza* near to the hospital and the road to Bengasi. A captured CMP truck is in the foreground.
[Karin & Manfred Blume]

On orders received from Berlin, Ritter reported to *Major* Stoltmann, from *OKW IH West*, at Rommel's HQ. He was to interrogate 1'100 Indian POW in camps at Derna and Barce and select from among them 50 to 60 of more than average intelligence for eventual training as propagandists. Ritter selected these men, of whom the majority were Sikhs, and they were then flown via Tripoli to Germany.[27]

Besides the Germans and the Hungarian Almásy an Egyptian cook was found, and an Italian driver who preferred to stay with them rather than to return to his original unit. Since no complaint from his superior in Tripoli ever reached Ritter, the man was kept and proved to be very useful. Since the unit was directly subordinated to the *OKW* nobody in Libya could give them any orders or instructions. This resulted in a degree of jealousy, maybe even mistrust from other units.

The following chapters portray the missions of *Sonderkommando Ritter*.

27 Germany was assisting the Indian resistance movement under Subhas Chandra Bose against the British occupation and formed a *Legion Freies Indien* beside many other activities to support them.

Text labels within aerial photograph:
← Strasse nach Bengasi
Lazarett
Derna Bach
Hotel Derna
Casa Mia
Badestrand
Auf Grund gesetzter Frachter

Lazarett

German aerial photograph of Derna.
The location of Ritter's quarters is near
the top of the photo (see enlargement).
[Kuno Gross]

A German water treatment facility 50 kilometers west of Tobruk. *Sonderkommando* Ritter's Ford standing in the background.
[Karin & Manfred Blume]

A courtyard in the old city of Derna in 1941.
[Kuno Gross]

The same courtyard in the old city of Derna (from a different angle) in 2003.

The road climbing the escarpment of Derna towards the airfield of Martuba.
[Kuno Gross]

The first clandestine flight to Egypt

The second *Gruppe* of *Kampfgeschwader* 26 (ll/KG26) had just received a new commander, *Hauptman* Kowalewski, and in his place *Hauptmann* Friedrich Müller was appointed 6. *Staffel* leader. The unit had moved from Catania to the airfield of Comiso, Sicily, and was continuing its bombing raids against the British-held island of Malta when Rudi Schmidt and the crew of his Heinkel He 111[28] were called to the *Gefechtsstand* in mid February 1941.[29]

The crew was informed that they had been chosen to carry out a special mission, and were introduced to a gentleman from Berlin, who told them that they were to fly three people to a particular location in Egypt, far behind enemy lines. During the briefing, they were instructed on the precise route with aerial photographs and maps. They were to fly first from Sicily to Bengasi in Libya, refuel there and continue the flight into Egypt, where it was planned to reach the target location by about midnight. After the planes had landed, the secret agents would leave on foot and the planes could return to Bengasi.

After all had been discussed to the last detail, the crews prepared their planes, received the latest weather forecast for the region and made their calculations for the flight. At about 17:00 they were ready for departure. They had not yet had the time to go back to their quarters and tell their comrades about the mission ahead, when the said gentleman from Berlin arrived by car with the two secret agents. They did not carry much luggage, only some sort of rucksack. Everything went very quickly. The three passengers took their place in the plane and then they taxied to the take-off point.

After three hours of undisturbed flight across the Mediterranean Sea, they landed at Bengasi's Benina Airport at about 20:00. A fuel bowser was ready for them. The crew was not allowed to leave the plane while refuelling went on and after only about 20 minutes they taxied to the start of the runway again and took off to their mysterious flight into the night.

The sky was clear and thanks to the full moon, they even had sight of the ground. At first, they followed the coastline east and then, near the El Alamein railway station that was later to become famous, they changed direction southeast until they could recognise the Nile delta. The waypoints marked on their maps and photographs fitted perfectly and soon they could re-

28 German standard two engine bomber.
29 Based on Schmidt, **Achtung – Torpedo los!**, TNA, WO 208/5520, Detailed Interrogation Report of Eppler about *Major* Ritter and a letter written by Ralph A. Bagnold to Jean Howard.

cognise the city of Cairo. A huge brightly illuminated complex was the POW camp marked on their map. Once it was passed they turned west for a few minutes, dropped down to barely 100 metres and followed the contours of the ground. Their timing was off but they did not yet see any sign from the ground. No lamp and no flash. They flew a wide left turn and then suddenly they saw the light. The beam of the lamp gave the direction for landing and they hoped that the wind direction had been considered. Now they had to act quickly – but with due care. Another left turn was flown and the W/T operator, Heinz Brückner, kept the light under observation. It seemed that all was as it should be, and they attempted this dangerous landing on unknown ground. Nobody knew if the enemy was waiting for them …

They touched down near the lamp and it was not a smooth landing. Soon the plane came to a standstill. When the plane stopped, the three passengers left in a hurry. The crew saw them running away from the plane and waving a last good-bye, then they busied themselves getting airborne again. Their view was limited but thanks to the clear sky and the full moon they could see for some hundred metres and took off again in about 600 metres. To avoid attracting the enemy, they flew as low as possible on a northwest course, to reach the coast and follow it eastwards. Schmidt and his crew were happy that everything had worked fine and they flew back to Bengasi, where they landed again at about 03:00. After another refueling, they decided to fly straight on and were back at Comiso in the early hours of the morning.

One of Schmidt's passengers was a Hungarian. His name was *Hauptmann* Almásy of the *Sonderkommando Ritter*.

The mission was kept secret and officially it was declared a reconnaissance flight. Much later, when Schmidt and his crew were garrisoned in Greece, they learned that another crew of the 4. *Staffel* had flown a similar mission about four weeks after them; they were not taking secret agents to Egypt, but recovering them.[30]

View down to the city of Derna from the top of the escarpment.

Catania. Almásy , Ritter and *Leutnant* Haller (?) in front of the control building of the airfield. *[Karin & Manfred Blume]*

30 This account matches with what Ralph A. Bagnold wrote to Jean Howard in a letter (at Churchill Archives). He met Almásy in December 1950 on occasion of the founding of the Desert Institute in Cairo, to which both Bagnold and Clayton were invited. Almásy claimed to have flown in to near Cairo on a Fieseler Fi 156 "Storch", landing behind the pyramids, and riding a motorcycle into town. He suggested to the incredulous Bagnold that they go out together to check the tyre marks of the aircraft and the motorcycle. However, the Fi 156 had a maximum range of 350 kilometres and this leads to the conclusion that the plane had been mistaken for the He 111 that was actually used. Further, it must be considered that Almásy had a known tendency to 'colour up' his stories The solo flight with a "Storch", and a motorcycle ride into town, sounds much more dramatic than being just a passenger on a He 111 and being picked up by local helpers.

Preparing for the first flight to Egypt: The Heinkel He 111 H4 of II/KG 26 at Catania airfield.
[Karin & Manfred Blume]

Passing oil storage tanks in low flight over the desert.

Aerial photo of Martuba airfield located on top of the escarpment at Derna. It was one of the most important Axis airfields during the desert war.
[Kuno Gross]

Night flight

The detailed interrogation report of Hans Eppler, one of the two spies captured in Cairo[31], confirmed this second flight when he reported that Almásy told *Major* Ritter in May 1941 that he had recently flown to Egypt to bring back two Hungarians from a landing ground about 40 kilometres from the Pyramids of Gizeh. The eventful return flight from Egypt is told by Almásy himself.[32]

Easter Sunday 1941. Two Heinkel He 111 of *Kampfgeschwader* 26 were ordered to bring back secret agents from Egypt to Libya. This time the flight started in the late afternoon so the passengers could be picked up in daylight. They had just started the return flight when the sun went down and within minutes it became dark. The two planes flew low above the ground to avoid being detected by the enemy until it became completely dark, then they went higher. Almásy noted how the pilot relaxed after the high tension of recent moments was released. He could not see the other members of the crew and the passengers who were sitting in their positions behind him. Nobody spoke. Only the even hum of the two engines was to be heard.

The altimeters indicated 600 metres when he saw the second plane on the right below them. The other's task was to escort them and to cover their return in case an enemy plane should attack them. Then, slowly the escort plane disappeared into the darkness until he could see it no more. They flew by the compass, following a course Almásy had calculated on the map. It would take about 5 hours to arrive back at Derna. Slowly they climbed to 2'400 metres which was considered the best altitude for their engines, where their fuel consumption was at its lowest.

Eleusis Airfild (Athens) in May 1941. A Heinkel He 111 H4 of *Kampfgeschwader* 26 and several other planes in the background.
[Dimitris Skatsilakis]

The flight was uneventful until all of a sudden the rear gunner addressed Almásy from behind his glass screen and remarked that the escort plane could be seen again: "Right behind us, slightly higher than we are. About 100 metres away."

Then the message came that the escort plane had its navigation lights on! Almásy was angry since he had ordered that there were to be no lights, even the pilot's cabin lights were to be dimmed. They were still above enemy territory and therefore transmitting on the radio was also forbidden. But now, in this critical phase, this fool switched on the red and the green navigation lights. He ordered the W/T operator to switch on but only to receive in case the other plane sent a message. Maybe they wanted to inform him of something important and had switched on the lights for this reason. He hoped that they did not have engine trouble or were running out of fuel. But there was no message from the other plane. Almásy calculated their position and saw that they would come close to Mersa Matruh where the enemy anti-aircraft defence was known to be strong. Possibly they could even encounter night fighter planes in this area.

31   TNA, London, KV2/1467 Detailed Interrogation Report on Eppler
32   Based on Almásy, ***Rommel Seregénél Libiában***, chapter "Night Return". From the ISOS transcripts it appears that the purpose of this flight may have been to get MARTIN/JOSKA out.

Then another message came from the gunner, saying that the escort plane could not to seen any more. Obviously it had switched off the lights and stayed back. Almásy relaxed again.

Sometime later, when they were just taking their meagre dinner, they spotted a blazing fire on the ground below them. Barracks and buildings were in flames. It was not clear to Almásy what it was, but he guessed that the withdrawing Allied Forces had set fire to their supply dumps at either Sollum or Bardia. He took the map and concluded that they must have reached Sollum, near the Libyan border. They corrected their course accordingly. But then he was not so sure. Was it really Sollum? Was it Bardia or even Sidi Barrani? He could do nothing but trust his calculations and follow the course shown by the compass. Since the pilot did not feel tired, Almásy did not have to relieve him, so he went back in the fuselage to have a short sleep. He only woke up when he sensed from the reduced noise of the engines that the plane was descending and the crew was preparing for landing.

Eleusis Airfild (Athens) in May 1941.
A Heinkel He 111 H4 of *Kampfgeschwader* 26. The torpedos are hanged underneath the fuselage.

[Dimitris Skatsilakis]

Then the lights of the airbase flashed on and the pilot made a perfectly smooth landing after which the lights were immediately switched off again to avoid attracting enemy planes. When they left their plane, about a dozen people came marching towards them. One of them Almásy recognised as the pilot of the escort plane. They had obviously arrived before them. Now everybody was relaxed, hands were shaken and they congratulated each other on the successful completion of a dangerous mission. The others were surprised and protested vigorously when Almásy's crew mentioned the escort plane's switched on lights. Within minutes it became clear that the escort plane had taken a more southerly course and that they have never climbed higher than 2'000 metres. The plane which followed them was not their escort plane but one of the enemy's that had probably flown to Mersa Matruh and switched on their navigation lights shortly before landing!

Flight Routes
June 1941

Legend:

- ⭕ Oasis / Town
- ⭕ Landing Ground
- ⭕ Place / Location
- ✈ "Op, el-Masri" 7 June 1941
- ✈ "Op. Condor" 17 June 1941

Kilometres 80 40 0 80 160 240 320 400

Miles 80 40 0 80 160 240

This map of the reconstructed flight routes is based on *Übersichtskarte von Nordost-Afrika 1:5'000'000; Gen St d H. Abt f Kr-K u Verm Wes (II), 1941.*

Dreiecksrechner, System Knemeyer DR2 manufactured by C. Plath in Hamburg in 1941. This instrument was widely used by *Luftwaffe* crews for navigation.

Plan el-Masri

The best-known operation of *Sonderkommando Ritter* was the attempt to lift the former Chief of Staff of the Egyptian army out of his country and bring him to Germany, to help raise open resistance of the Egyptians against the British administration in Egypt[33]

During a visit by *Major* Ritter to Budapest in September 1940, Almásy informed Ritter that his old friend, the Chief of Staff of the Egyptian Army, General el-Masri Pasha, had been intrigued out of his position. The British suspected him to have secret contacts with the Italians since he refused to cooperate with British forces. El-Masri Pasha was the idol of the young officers surrounding Gamal Abdel Nasser, including Anwar el-Sadat and Hussein Zulficar, who later called themselves the "The Society of Free Officers" when they overthrew King Faruk in the 1952 revolution. Almásy told Ritter that el-Masri Pasha and his nationalist fellows were all hoping for a German victory against the British who had occupied their country, and that they were convinced this would mean the liberation of Egypt from colonial rule.

Theo Blaich standing in front of *Sonderkommando Ritter's* Fieseler Fi 156 Storch.
[Karin & Manfred Blume]

The idea of bringing el-Masri Pasha out of Egypt fascinated *Major* Ritter and when Almásy confirmed that he thought it was possible, the operation started to take shape in Ritter's mind. If available in Berlin, el-Masri Pasha could help the German General Staff to organise uprisings in the Arab world, mainly in Egypt. However when Ritter approached Admiral Canaris with this, he was told to forget about the "silly idea". Just one month later, Admiral Canaris changed his mind and ordered Ritter to meet Almásy in Budapest to work out the details of the operation. Almásy was absolutely sure that the operation was feasible – although Ritter had the feeling that it was more the desire to go back to Egypt that gave Almásy his conviction[34]. Due to the progress of the war – the Italians had attacked British Forces in Egypt from Libya – direct contact with el-Masri Pasha was not possible for the Germans, so they used the new Hungarian legation envoy, Bárdossy, to smuggle an

33   Based on Kelly, *The Hunt for Zerzura*
34   Ritter, *Deckname Dr. Rantzau*

Abwehr wireless set into Egypt in January 1941. With this W/T set available, they could not only establish direct contact with el-Masri Pasha, but also receive general intelligence like weather reports, information about Allied troop movements and other news from Egypt. Weather reports were vital for the German *Luftwaffe* and its operations in the Mediterranean area.

When Ritter reported to Rommel at the end of April, he learnt that the latter doubted that Operation el-Masri would work and was more interested in getting precise weather reports. By this time, Ritter's unit was based at Derna, and they were in daily contact with the Hungarian legation in Cairo, where the envoy Bárdossy had employed a capable W/T operator with the codename MARTIN.

Through MARTIN, arrangements for the planned escape of el-Masri Pasha were made. While el-Masri Pasha at first had insisted on being picked up by a German submarine, Ritter had convinced him that the waters of Lake Berello in the Nile delta were much too shallow, and in the end it was agreed to use an aeroplane. Next, Ritter had to obtain suitable planes. Together with *Oberleutnant* Blaich in his "Taifun" he flew to Athens to meet *General* Geisler and his chief of staff, to persuade them once more to provide two He 111 and their crews for Operation el-Masri. On the same occasion, Ritter picked up a full set of British maps of Egypt and bordering countries which had been found in the luggage of a British officer fighting in Greece and was left behind during their general retreat.

By the end of May the two He 111 arrived at Martuba airfield near Derna and the crews were familiarised with the planned operation. El-Masri Pasha had received all the details of the plan and confirmed them to Ritter. The meeting point proposed by Almásy was the so-called "Red Jebel", a hill not far southwest of Cairo at the track leading to the oases in the desert. At this location, el-Masri Pasha was told to place a big cross of white fabric as a landing mark for the incoming planes. One plane would land to pick him up while the other would circle above for protection. The date for the mission was set for 5 June 1941 but on the evening of 4 June, a message was received from Cairo that el-Masri had had a minor car accident, and so the operation had to be postponed.

Finally, in mid-afternoon on 7 June the two He 111 took off from Bengasi Benina and flew over the Jebel Akhdar in Cirenaica towards Egypt. They were planned to be at the meeting point at 18:00, after a three-hour flight. Ritter had received orders from Berlin which prevented him from joining the operation personally. He waited

Left: Theo Blaich pointing at a hole caused by an enemy bullet on the rudder of his Taifun. *[Karin & Manfred Blume]*

Right: *Castel Benito* Airfield. Theo Blaich inspecting his privately owned Messerschmitt Bf 108 Taifun. *[Karin & Manfred Blume]*

at the base in Derna, sitting by the W/T operator. It was agreed that the planes would send a message at 19:35, once out of the most dangerous zone. At quarter past eight the message had still not been received and Ritter started to feel worried. He felt responsible for his comrades and feared trouble with *X Fliegerkorps* if the planes did not return. Finally, at quarter to nine the leading plane made contact. They had already reached the area of Tobruk. Ritter took his car and drove up the escarpment of Derna to the Landing Ground of Martuba where he found that nothing was yet ready for the coming night landing. Preparations had scarcely been completed when the first He 111 arrived and circled low over the landing ground. The lights were switched on and the plane made a good landing.

Almásy jumped out and reported to Ritter, who had approached the plane: they had flown first at low altitude deeper into the desert, to avoid enemy planes, and then had gone up to several thousand feet. Approaching the "Red Jebel", they found that el-Masri Pasha had not laid out the agreed white cross. They thought that he might be delayed and, after checking their fuel reserves, decided that they could circle and wait for about half an hour. They were looking out for any sign but nothing was to be seen, so they flew along the track towards Cairo. When it became obvious that el-Masri Pasha was not around they had to turn and fly back. The pilots were angry because of the failed operation, but Almásy was sure that something serious must have happened to prevent el-Masri showing up.

The next morning they received a W/T message from Cairo, revealing that the British had most probably put el-Masri Pasha under house arrest.

Portrait of the former Chief of Staff of the Egyptian Army, Abdul Aziz el-Masri Pasha. The photo was taken in the 1940ies.
[H. Eppler via Archiv Kröpelin]

The former Chief of the General Staff of the Egyptian Army had made another attempt to flee just before the failed attempt by Almásy and the *Abwehr*[35]. A Middle East Intelligence Centre (MEIC) Summary of 22 May states that Aziz el-Masri Pasha tried to escape on the night of 16/17 May, possibly to Syria en route to Iraq, in an Egyptian Air Force plane with two officers, Hussein Zulficar Sabri and Abdul Moreim Abdu r-Ra'uf. But the aircraft made a forced landing only 16 kilometres from Cairo. El-Masri and his companions returned to Cairo by car and had since disappeared.

The British Ambassador to Egypt, Sir Miles Lampson, informed the Foreign Office on 19 May 1941 that the "Egyptian Government had issued an official communiqué stating that acts committed by Aziz el-Masri Pasha and two flying officers constituted an offence against Egypt's safety and security. An award of 1'000 Pounds was to be paid to anyone who assisted in securing arrest of one or all three and that anyone harbouring them or helping them to escape would be severely punished".[36]

Lampson eventually cabled to the Foreign office that he had been informed by the Egyptian Prime Minister that el-Masri Pasha and his two companions had been arrested on 6 June. They had been hiding in a suburb of Cairo.

35   TNA, London, WO208/1560, Appendix to MEIC Summary 513, 22 May 1941
36   TNA, London, FO 371/27430/J1551/18/16, Lampson to FO, tel.1410, 19 May 1941

The distinctive glazed cockpit-section of a Heinkel He 111 of *Kampfgeschwader* 26. *[Bundesarchiv Koblenz]*

A Heinkel He 111 of *Kampfgeschwader* 26 flying over Greece. The aircraft is carrying a heavy bomb underneath the fuselage. *[Bundesarchiv Koblenz]*

Sonderkommando Ritter sitting on a captured Morris Commercial PU 8 cwt in front of their quarters at Derna. (from left to right, standing) Blaich, Ritter and Almásy. (Sitting on truck) Busekros, Klein, Hassan, Mühlenbruch, Wahrlich, Depper-mann. Raydt, the second pilot seems to have left the group at this point. The insigna of the British 2nd Armoured Division can be seen on the mudguard of the truck. *[Karin & Manfred Blume]*

Operation Kondor

It is quite confusing, but the Germans had two *Operation Kondor*. It is not known why the same name was used a second time very shortly after the first such operation ended in complete failure. The first *Operation Kondor* was the last mission to be executed by *Sonderkommando Ritter*.[37]

Since *Plan el-Masri* had failed and there was no chance of getting him out of Egypt any more, *Sonderkommando Ritter* had to concentrate on its second task: To take German agents to Egypt. On 27 May Ritter reported to *Abwehr* HQ in Hamburg: "Everything in order here. Imminent success in sight."[38] This message was intercepted by the British as well as another one to Berlin, saying "Operation Hassan fixed for 1/6". Hassan, however, obviously did not know the address of his rendezvous with the contact in Cairo and by 31 May 1941, Berlin HQ had sent a message to Libya, suggesting that if he does not remember the address, he should go to the Pension Monclair, Rue Malika, Farida 33 in Cairo and there meet Mrs. Lisel Plested. She was married to a British man who did not know about his wife's activities, and the time was to be chosen so that her husband was not at home. Suddenly, on 2 June, Ritter sent a message to Berlin that he would arrive there on 5 June and that Operation Hassan had to be postponed to 12 June.[39] Unfortunately, the reason for this postponement of Operation Hassan which was planned for 1 June is not reported and in fact, it never took place.

37   Based on Kelly, *The Hunt for Zerzura* and Ritter, *Deckname Dr. Rantzau*
38   TNA, London, HW 19/7 ISOS.5798
39   TNA, London, HW 19/8 ISOS 6299

Ritter travelled to Berlin to arrange the next mission and another message was intercepted by RSS, saying that from 12 June 1941 two Heinkel He 111 aircraft would be ready for a special mission. Among their crew was *Oberleutnant* August Leicht. On 11 June Ritter was still in Berlin and informed his HQ in Derna about the delay in his return. He said that he should be back in Libya between 13 and 15 June and requested Almásy to inform *Ic Afrikakorps* that he would bring several Intelligence Officers, among whom was Hansjoachim von der Esch[40] who had been seconded from the *OKW* directly to Almásy. Von der Esch had spent a long time in Egypt in the prewar years and took part in several expeditions with Almásy[41]. It seemed that soon it would be like old times again. No more messages were intercepted until 20 June when Almásy reported to Berlin that Operation Kondor had failed terribly.

Coming from Berlin with Ritter were the V-men who had volunteered to go to Egypt after *Admiral* Canaris had given permission for the new operation. The group consisted of *Sonderführer* Keller and seven other men. Among them were the agents Klein and Mühlenbruch, both of whom spoke fluent Arabic. They were to be taken to Egypt first. The others should follow in subsequent operations. In his memoirs, Ritter described Klein as a Hamburg Jew, a stocky man, dark-skinned with black hair and cunning brown eyes, about 40 years of age. He had served as an *Unteroffizier* in the First World War and moved to Egypt afterwards. He had returned to Germany only shortly before the outbreak of the Second World War[42]. Ritter wrote in his memoirs that there was something about Klein what made him not trust him but he felt very differently about the second agent, Mühlenbruch. He was just the opposite of Klein: tall, slender and blonde with honest blue eyes and a forthright manner. Mühlenbruch had operated a boat along the Palestine coast before the war and wanted to go to Haifa, where he was not known as a German. Klein was expected to operate from Alexandria.

The great task was to enter enemy territory unnoticed and it was decided to enter Egypt from the south, where they would be least expected. There was discussion as to whether a camel caravan should transport the agents or if they should parachute from a plane. The caravan seemed to be the safest way.

40   TNA, London, HW 19/8 ISOS 6458
41   Von der Esch, ***Weenak – die Karawane ruft***
42   Nothing can be excluded, but it sounds fairly strange that a Jew would come back to Germany just before the outbreak of the Second World War. However, it is reported that on several occasions the Abwehr employed Jews even during World War 2. This was a method used by *Admiral* Canaris to bring them out of Germany, and obviously, the *Abwehr* seems to have beeen a much more liberal place than most other German organisations of that time.

The agents Klein (l.) and Mühlenbruch (r.) sitting in the Back of a Volkswagen Typ 82 in front of their quarter at Derna.
[Paul Carell]

Oberleutnant August Leicht (far right), *Oberleutnant* Haller (left) and two unidentified members of the crews of the two He 111.
[Karin & Manfred Blume]

Sonderkommando Ritter under the wing of a Heinkel He 111 which was at their disposal from *Kampfgeschwader* 26. On the left, Theo Blaich, then Almásy (with the back against the Camera) and Ritter with the outstretched right arm.
[Karin & Manfred Blume]

View from a low flying Embraer 170 in the evening light. This may give an impression on the view the pilot of the Heinkel He 111 had.

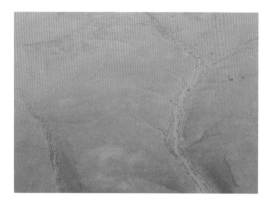

View of the desert from a plane flying at an altitude of about 1000 meters above ground.

Approach to Bengasi-Benina airfield.

But a caravan would take weeks and was therefore not suitable. Flying them in was more dangerous since the planes could easily be detected, but to study the best possible flight route was what Ritter had Almásy for. The first task was to find a suitable landing place, as parachuting had been already excluded. The area of the Nile Delta[43] was not suitable, since it was under constant surveillance by the British. Almásy proposed a spot near the caravan route from Deirut to the Farafra oasis, about 100 kilometres away from the Nile. There a hill grew out of the otherwise flat desert, and the plane could easily land and take off again on a strip of hard *serir* sand[44]. To drop off the two agents was one thing, for them to cover the remaining 100 kilometres to the Nile another; the solution was thought to be a motorcycle, which could be stowed in the plane and driven by one of the agents.[45] To prevent the motorbike from revealing the identity of the V-men, a suitable model by an Italian manufacturer was found, which was in common use in Egypt at the time. Ritter had managed to get the same two He 111 and the same crews assigned from KG.26 as had been used for the el-Masri mission. To allow them to carry more fuel, the agents and their motorcycle, the planes were stripped of all unnecessary equipment.

By 13:00 on 17 June 1941 all was ready and the group left their HQ at Derna for the landing ground of Martuba, up the escarpment. In the first vehicle were Ritter, Almásy, the W/T operator Winter, a pilot and an observer and in the second Blaich with the other crew. Klein and Mühlenbruch were riding their motorbike. The higher they went up the serpentine roads, the hotter the air became, and near Martuba the air was as always full of dust from the many airplanes taking off. The two Heinkel He 111 were ready for the mission. While Ritter was giving the crew their final instructions, a mechanic approached and informed him that one of the tyres of the lead plane was not in a good shape, it would not be advisable to land with this plane on an unknown strip. Unfortunately a

43 Ritter writes about the "upper Nile" in this occasion. However, the "upper Nile" would be in Sudan and it is most probable that he mistook the expression here – for some unknown reason.

44 With first hand knowledge of the terrain it is considered extremely unlikely that this area would be suitable for landing and take off. The top of the limestone plateau is completely unsuitable for landing an aircraft – even though it appears flat from above, the surface is very rough and stony, the best one can do with a *Landcruiser* is 20–25 kph. The authors could not conclusively identify the possible landing zone, maybe it was intended to be somewhere farther north, possibly around the Fayum depression. *Serir* is a totally flat and featureless form of the sandy desert.

45 Perhaps this is the source of Almásy's 'improvement'of his story to Bagnold noted earlier. It is amusing to make the connections and see the elements of truth emerge in what initially appeared to be a partly made-up story.

spare tyre was not available and Ritter could not wait for one to be flown in. He rightly feared that if he waited for a new tyre, the aeroplanes would be ordered back to Greece and he would have to postpone the operation for an indeterminate period.

Klein and Mühlenbruch had to get to Egypt now. Ritter decided to change the planes. He, the two agents and *Oberleutnant* Leicht would fly in the other plane while the one with the damaged tyre would not land but remain in the escort role. Obviously there was some quarrelling about the decision to let the more inexperienced pilot fly the plane to make the landing. However, Ritter was of the opinion that the crews had better stay with their own planes and not change over. Almásy did not agree with this decision at all and insisted on his rights as a Hungarian Officer – he refused to obey Ritter's orders and did not take part the operation. *Oberleutnant* Blaich, the second to have considerable experience of off-field landings, albeit with a much smaller plane, stepped out as well[46]. Since both these officers were no longer available for the operation, Ritter decided to take part in the flight himself, although Berlin had forbidden him to do so.

Ritter boarded the plane and sat on the frame between the inexperienced pilot and *Oberleutnant* Leicht. To avoid enemy planes, they first flew southeast at a low altitude, but when confronted with the *ghibli* they had to climb to 4'000 metres to avoid the dust. Their first landmark was the oasis of Giarabub about 380 kilometres south of Tobruk. *Oberleutnant* Leicht had to navigate very carefully since there were few notable landmarks to help. Ritter could hardly imagine that they would find a small area of hard *serir* sand in the vastness of the desert. The estimated time of arrival was 17:30. The sun was already at their back and the shadows on the ground started to lengthen. The instruments showed nothing alarming and the sound of the engines was even. *Oberleutnant* Leicht was unceasingly calculating and plotting their route on the map. After nearly five hours of flight, he touched Ritter's arm and pointed ahead: a single hill rising out of the flat plain. About 115 kilometres north of this point was the landing zone chosen by Almásy. Not long and they would have reached their target!

While the escort plane stayed circling at 3'500 metres, the pilot flew the Heinkel with Ritter and the two agents down to about 600 metres and prepared to land. There was not much time left as the sun was already low. They had only a few minutes to find the landing zone. When they saw it, they threw a smoke grenade to find the direction of the wind. Ritter went to the back of the plane to instruct Klein and Mühlenbruch to prepare for the landing. The pilot made the approach with Ritter, who had neither a seat nor a safety belt, holding on to the fuselage frame. All of a sudden, the pilot broke off the approach! Leicht asked angrily, why, while the pilot turned to make another attempt. He was very nervous, and when Leicht told him to land, he answered that he could not do so because there were too many rocks. Leicht shouted back that these were not rocks but only normal stones which just seemed bigger due to the low sun and long shadows.

---

46   Ritter in his book does not mention that Almásy and Blaich both bailed out of the operation. The information was provided by Hans Eppler's interrogation report. It is assumed that Almásy had told Eppler during Operation Salam.

But it was too late; the pilot lifted the plane up and turned back westwards. There was no chance of a third attempt.

Ritter was now aware that the decision not to change the pilots had been the wrong one. Leicht proposed that the two agents should parachute, but then they would have had to walk for a hundred kilometres. Ritter decided that they would not survive such a march and refused. The plane was already up at 1'000 metres and the sun just dipped below the horizon. It was clear that the operation had failed and nobody wanted to speak on the way back to Derna. The flight in the darkness went well and was uneventful, there was enough fuel for another 45 min-0utes when the W/T operator received the message that they were not allowed to land at Martuba, as the airfield was under enemy air attack. They were instructed to divert to Bengasi-Benina. 300 kilometres more to go to Bengasi; the fuel would hardly be enough. Then the rear gunner recognised enemy planes behind them and gave the alarm. The pilot automatically went down in a curve to evade them. Nothing was to be seen. Then one of the instrument needles started to shake wildly. The pilot checked everything and found that there was something wrong with the synchronization of one of the engines. The variable pitch controller of the left engine was out of order and they were practically flying on one engine.

Ritter with the broken right arm standing in front of the Junkers Ju 52 which will fly him out to Athens. Note the Phänomen Granit 25H ambulance truck (Kfz.31) and the Ford Sedan which belonged to *Sonderkommando Ritter*. *[Karin & Manfred Blume]*

They had to land urgently. There was no chance to continue the flight to Bengasi. The only airfield near them was Martuba which was under attack. Fuel now remained for only 30 minutes – not even enough to return to Martuba. Bailing out was also out of the question because of the rocks of the Jebel el-Akhdar below them, so Ritter ordered the pilot to try to make an emergency landing on the shore of the Mediterranean, since he guessed that it could not be far. Although the observer, *Oberleutnant* Leicht had now taken the lead, the young pilot was completely lost. Leicht ordered him to go down and switch on the landing lights. But all they could see was water; they had already crossed the coastline. The W/T operator was told to send a distress call, then all electrical devices were switched off and the plane ditched hard into the sea.

On impact some of them were injured. Ritter had a broken arm, Leicht broke some ribs and Klein bruised an arm. Along with them, the uninjured pilot, the mechanic and the radio operator managed to get out of the plane before it sank. Mühlenbruch had been crushed to death by a crate and disappeared into the depths of the sea with the plane. Fortunately they were able to get the life raft out of the plane and inflate it. After nine hours in the water they made landfall on the Cirenaican coast between Derna and Barce, but they were not yet safe, as they had nothing to drink. They walked inland for a long time, suffering from thirst when finally they met an Arab shepherd, who took them to his family's camp. They learnt that the nearest place was Barce, some 17 kilometres further away. This was too far for them and they started to bargain with the Arabs for their donkeys. Negotiations were still in progress when three Fieseler "Storch" of the *Wüstennotstaffel* were seen approaching. Signals were laid out with sheets belonging to the Arab family and the planes managed to land directly on a flat spot nearby. They were safe.

When he was flown to the hospital at Derna, where his broken arm was put in cast, Ritter learnt that the second plane had made it safely to Bengasi-Benina. He was very depressed because he felt responsible for the failure of the operation. He argued with himself that he should have persuaded Almásy to join in, and to switch the pilots. But it was too late; they had lost one of the precious planes – not to speak of the life of Mühlenbruch who had become a good comrade. Ritter felt that his lucky star had left him.

Before Ritter and Leicht were flown to Kiphissia near Athens by a medical aircraft, Ritter handed over the command of his small unit to Almásy. Ritter hoped to be taken to a hospital in Berlin from where he might assist Almásy and Blaich. He did not waste much time, since on 27 June 1941 the RSS intercepted an urgent message ordering Almásy to come to Berlin to discuss their most ambitious plan: The penetration of Southern Egypt with vehicles through the desert![47] However it appears that the *Abwehr* by this time lost faith in Ritter's abilities, and by mid-July he was relieved of all duties related to operations in Libya and the Middle East. Nevertheless the plan itself was not forgotten, nor was Almásy as the only person able to carry it out.

Ritter sitting in a chair, awaiting the transport back to Europ by the Junkers Ju 52.
[Karin & Mandfred Blume]

47   TNA, London, KV 2/88, Appendix D to FR 28, Ritter

PART 2
OPERATION SALAM

The Marabout and the cemetery of Sidi Rezegh.
Fighting took place here from 19 November to
3 December between the 8th Army and the Axis
forces, with very heavy losses on both sides, during
Operation Crusader.

The Desert Campaign in late 1941/early 1942

After the defeat of the Italian 10th Army by the Allied Forces, in the second week of February 1941 Germany had sent a "Blocking Force" under *Generalmajor* Erwin Rommel which soon became famous under its name *Deutsches Afrikakorps*.

Rommel did not stay behind the Italian defence lines in Tripolitania as originally planned, but immediately attacked the now weak enemy and pushed forward to the border with Egypt. After two inconclusive battles in May and June, the Axis and Allied forces both started to prepare for an offensive. The Allied moved first, and launched an attack, codenamed *Crusader*, on Axis positions on 18 November 1941. This phase of the Desert Campaign and the results of the Allied offensive are especially important for Operation Salam since they delayed its start for a considerable time.

Operation Crusader and the Axis withdrawal to el-Agheila

In the second half of November 1941, both opponents were getting ready to attack but the commander of the Allied Forces, Sir Claude Auchinleck, started the offensive a few days before Rommel's planned attack on Tobruk, disrupting the preparations of the Italo-German units. The aim of Operation Crusader was clear: to destroy the Axis armour between Bardia on the Egyptian border and Tobruk, to push back the Axis forces to the border of Tripolitania, and so to relieve the besieged garrison of Tobruk.

From the night of 17/18 November 1941, the 8th Army under General Cunningham started crossing the border to Libya. German and Italian units were taken by surprise, but managed to achieve some early successes. Nevertheless, at the end of the first day of the Allied attack, Rommel still did not have a clear picture of what was happening, and did not accept that he was facing a full-scale enemy offensive.

The following five days marked a crisis in the battle which eventually saw the Axis forces defeat the Allied armour at Sidi Rezegh, while suffering heavy losses themselves. Following this victory, Rommel started to move towards the border of Egypt in order to cut off the Allied forces. On Tuesday 25 November 1941, GOC 8th Army, General Cunningham, decided to abandon the battle and to withdraw his troops into Egypt. Only the personal intervention of General Auchinleck, who then replaced Cunningham with his deputy chief of staff, Major General Neil M. Ritchie, prevented this withdrawal, and the fighting continued.

Tobruk, Perimeter Post S12. The eight month long siege of Tobruk by the Axis forces was finally lifted on 7 December 1941.

After heavy fighting, by 2 December, the losses of the both forces were very heavy, and a growing supply crisis forced Rommel to order a withdrawal to the Gazala line in the west on 7 December. The siege of Tobruk, which had lasted for some seven months, was lifted. On the same night, the United States of America entered the war.

XIII Corps attacked the new position almost immediately, and on the morning of 15 December 1941, the Germans recognised that a strong enemy tank formation was advancing towards el-Mekili and that their own weak forces could not avoid being surrounded. Rommel had to make a further withdrawal to the west. Axis forces were ordered to occupy a new defence line in the area of Agedabia – Saunnu, with the aim of eventually moving back to the line of Mersa el-Brega – Marada Oasis, for a final stand in defence of Tripolitania. This new defence position had the benefit that the supply line from Tripoli was considerably shorter and could not be cut by the enemy.

Tobruk. Sunrise over the harbour bay.

Fortunately enough for the Axis, on 19 December 1941 the first large convoy since October arrived with reinforcements of tanks, artillery and supplies. Nevertheless, at this stage the Axis forces were much too weak for a real counterstroke and the withdrawal continued. Rommel was once more at the very same point from where he had begun his first offensive in spring 1941.

A German helmet found in a *Sebkha* near Benghazi.

On 5 January 1942, another convoy with substantial supplies reached Tripoli. Axis medium tank strength had now risen but was still too weak to stand a major enemy thrust. The British command considered the Axis too weak to launch any sort of offensive for a long time. However, successful Axis intelligence gathering indicated that the Axis forces could briefly expect to be superior to the Alllied Forces in Cirenaica. Rommel planned a new offensive. This was kept secret from almost everybody, not even *Comando Supremo* was informed.

Rommel attacks

On 21 January *Panzergruppe Afrika* attacked. Surprised Allied troops were pushed back quickly and the next day, Agedabia was again in Rommel's hands. Four days later Msus was re-taken and Rommel decided to re-direct his forces towards Bengasi to secure the port and prevent any enemy counterattack from this direction. Rommel's rapid and unpredictable movements forced the Allied Forces to withdraw further towards the Gazala line, not knowing how weak the enemy actually was and how difficult was their supply situation. On Thursday 29 January 1942 the city of Bengasi was again in the hands of Italo-German forces and Rommel continued his advance east without a break.

Derna was reached on 4 February and the Bay of Bomba immediately thereafter. Then, before the defensive positions of the Gazala line, Axis troops met fresh Allied troops, and it was no longer possible to take Tobruk in the same stroke. On 5 February, Rommel, who led the attack personally, had to recognise that his rapid advance had to be halted. The advance stopped on the Gazala line for four months which both sides used to reinforce their troops and to resupply.

From January onwards, due to the neutralisation of Malta by the German air force and the weakness of the Royal Navy, more Axis convoys were able to reach the shores of North Africa. *Panzerarmee Afrika* – as it had been designated since 21 January 1942 – received more and more supplies, mainly fuel and ammunition, as well as new tanks and artillery.

Both opponents were keen to launch the next attack and the British Prime Minister, Winston Churchill urged General Auchinleck to attack as soon as possible to help relieve Malta from the severe air attacks it was undergoing. But on Tuesday 26 May 1942 at exactly 18:30, Operation Theseus, the Axis attack on the Gazala line was launched. South African reconnaissance units had discovered the enemy forces on the morning of the 26th, but none of their messages reached General Ritchie and his staff and so the Allied Forces were not aware of this development. In the moonlight the motorised units of *General* Rommel reached the area of Bir Hakeim which was outflanked to the south by the *Afrikakorps* and the Italian mobile corps. British commanders still believed that this was not the main attack which was expected to take place in the middle of the defence line.

Left: *Panzerregiment 5* advancing towards the fortress of Bir Hakeim. *[Rolf Munninger]*

Right: Smoke columns on the horizon give evidence of shot up vehicles. *[Rolf Munninger]*

The Allies were not alone in misinterpreting the situation. Rommel had underestimated the enemy's strength around Bir Hakeim and guessed that he was facing only one infantry division and two tank brigades. He did not know that the position of Sidi Mufta had been fortified and had not considered the deep minefields which went south until the last of the "boxes" at Bir Hakeim.

During 27 May heavy tank battles took place and, when Rommel thought he had won the battle, the fighting became even fiercer. An Allied counterattack brought him very close to a defeat and at dawn, *Panzerarmee Afrika* was in a most precarious situation.

Oberst Wolz reports to Rommel and General Gause. In the background rommels Opel Blitz 3 ton bus. *[Rolf Munninger]*

Thursday 28 May 1942 was a critical day for *Panzerarmee Afrika* as the enemy had realised the situation and was concentrating his forces to destroy the dispersed Axis units piecemeal. Despite this, Rommel stuck to his original battle plan and ordered his tank units to continue to march north. *General* Crüwell was to break the Gazala line and open a route for the supply columns.

German ammunition containers littering the area near Bir Hakeim

Friday 29 May 1942 began badly for the Axis forces but towards the evening Rommel had regained control over his units. The next day, Rommel managed to attack again but his tanks ran into an unmarked minefield which caused 11 losses. While General Ritchie was convinced that the Axis has suffered a severe defeat, Rommel was regrouping his units.

In the morning of 1 June 1942, *Stukas* flew heavy attacks on the defence position of Sidi Muftah. The same evening Rommel gave orders to attack the Bir Hakeim "box" which was held by the Free French 1ˢᵗ Brigade under General Koenig. Attacks against Bir Hakeim on 2 June 1942 had no success: the Free French and the Foreign Legion stood firm, while two strong British tank columns came against Rommel's forces. The Allies thought to force a decision, but none of the British commanders was given overall command for the attack and so cooperation between units was not good at all. The Allied Forces' counteroffensive of 4 June 1942 failed to develop and was destroyed by the Axis.

After Bir Hakeim was taken on 10 June 1942, Axis units immediately attacked again and continued to advance. British command was still not unified and could not agree co-ordinated countermeasures. From intercepted W/T messages, Rommel was fully aware of the enemy's disorder and made best use of it during the subsequent tank battle which lasted for several days. British tank units suffered severe losses and were forced to withdraw.

On Sunday 14 June 1942, General Ritchie gave orders to abandon the garrison of Tobruk and a hasty withdrawal towards Egypt followed directly. Tobruk was not prepared for defence as for the previous siege, not even the old defence positions were ready and the garrison was tired and exhausted.

On 19 June 1942, Rommel launched his decisive move and attacked the defence line of Tobruk from the east. During the night his engineers cleared lanes through the minefields and in the morning of 20 June 1942 *Stukas* flew heavy attacks on the outer perimeter ring of defences with devastating effect. Shortly after 08:00, the first *Panzer* broke through the line and pushed directly towards the harbour, where they arrived in the late afternoon. "Fortress Tobruk" was now split into two parts and by evening one third of it was in Axis hands. On the morning of 21 June 1942 Rommel accepted the capitulation of Tobruk.

The old fortress of Bir Hakeim which was bravely defended by the Foreign Legion and the Free French under General Koenig against a far superior enemy.

Prelude to Operation Salam

Compared to other operations and in particular to the setup of the *Long Range Desert Group* which was done in about six weeks, preparations for Operation Salam took quite a long time. Obviously the *Wehrmacht* and the *Abwehr* were not prepared for behind-the-lines operations in the North African desert; László Almásy could not count on any experienced assistance. He had to deal with a number of unexpected events and delays, and since the party intended to return behind their own lines, they had to wait for the front line to advance sufficiently close to the Nile valley.

March 1941, evaluations

A travel guide for Bengasi and Tripoli publisehd by the C.I.T. In 1938.

When war broke out in North Africa, the *Abwehr* was not prepared for this theatre. To cope with these expected new demands, they began to look for suitable personnel to act as advisors or even possible agents. Candidates included Hans Eppler and Hans-Gerd Sandstede, both of whom had spent a considerable part of their lives in Africa.

It so happened in March 1941 that Hans-Gerd Sandstede was sent to Berlin on secondment to *Abwehr 1, Fremde Heere West*, to prepare for a mission in Africa[48]. Much time passed and nothing materialised, so he managed to get a posting to the *Heeresplankammer* and was employed revising maps of East Africa and Egypt. Three months passed and he realised the risk of being posted to a front-line unit in Russia. Luckily he had met another soldier with a similar problem, Hans Eppler. Since both of them had lived in Africa (Eppler even had an Egyptian step-father) and since they knew that the *Abwehr* was in need of agents for North Africa, they approached the relevant authorities and were accepted for transfer to *Abwehr 1*. Eppler and Sandstede were then introduced to their duties as secret agents and W/T operators.

While the *Abwehr* was finding suitable personnel, in North Africa, the Ic of *Panzergruppe Afrika, Major* von Mellenthin, was busy building up his organisation. Under

48   Based on Sandstede, unpublished memoirs

his command was *Rittmeister* Hoesch in the role of *Nachrichtenbeschaffungsoffizier* (NBO)[49] who, on 21 August 1941, informed his superior that agents to be deployed to the Nile Delta should be equipped with W/T stations, to allow them to stay in permanent direct contact with Panzergruppe Afrika. He was sent to Berlin by plane the next day to discuss the situation with *Amt Ausland/Abwehr, Abw. I H West*. He met *Major* Seubert on 1 and 2 September 1941 to discuss the following possibilities for the transport of the agents to Egypt:

1. Dropping by parachute in Egypt.

2. Dropping off and later picking them up again by airplane.

3. Employing László Almásy, the desert specialist, to bring them by motor vehicle to the mid- Nile area bypassing Kufra to the northeast.

4. Deploying via Turkey, Syria and Palestine or from Crete by fishing boats.

5. Official "in-channelling" of Egyptians and Europeans via Portugal, the unoccupied zone of France, South Africa, Abyssinia and Port Sudan[50].

On 3 September 1941, Hoesch met the Adjudant of *Abwehr, Amt II* in relation to the deployment of V-men from *Regiment z.b.V. 800 Brandenburg* which was subordinated to *Amt II*; then, the following day, he met *Major* Sensburg of *Abwehr-Leitstelle Athen* and agreed upon close coordination in forthcoming operations.

After Hoesch had met the Ic of the *X Fliegerkorps*, on 10 September 1941, they discussed with Almásy the possibilities of transport by motor vehicle. On 15 September 1941 he again met *Major* Seubert, who then assigned *Hauptmann* Pretzl as the liaison officer between *NBO* and the *Abwehr*. After several meetings with the recruited V-men, on 22 September he reported back to HQ in North Africa[51].

The small practical guide with city-map for Tripoli published in 1939 by U.C.I.P.I. *(Unione Coloniale Italiana Pubblicità Informazioni Soc. An.).*

On 1 October 1941, the *NBO* commando of *Rittmeister* Hoesch (consisting of him, *Oberstleutnant* Nordhaus, *Leutnant* Häusgen, *Leutnant* Heymanns and three cor porals – among them Munz and Beilharz, who were later to take part in Operation Salam[52] – three soldiers and a W/T troop of four operators) arrived at HQ *Panzergruppe Afrika*. It took some time to recruit more agents, all of them Libyans to be used only for "short range" work. As fate would have it, on the night of 7 to 8 October, enemy bombers attacked the camp of the *NBO* and his commando with disastrous results. *Rittmeister* Hoesch and *Leutnant* Heymanns were killed and *Gefreiter* Buse was slightly wounded[53]. This was just the start; by 14 October the whole commando was out of action as *Oberleutnant* Nordhaus, two corporals and

---

49 Bundesarchiv Freiburg / Militärarchiv, RH19 VIII – 47; Tätigkeitsbericht der Abteilung Ic in der Zeit vom 15.8. – 31.8.41

50 Bundesarchiv Freiburg / Militärarchiv, RH19 VIII – 47; Tätigkeitsbericht der Abteilung Ic in der Zeit vom 1.9. – 30.9.41

51 Bundesarchiv Freiburg / Militärarchiv, RH19 VIII – 47; Tätigkeitsbericht der Abteilung Ic in der Zeit vom 1.9. – 30.9.41

52 TNA, London, KV 2 / 1467, Defence Security Office Egypt 19 October 1942

53 Bundesarchiv Freiburg / Militärarchiv, RH19 VIII – 47; Tätigkeitsbericht der Abteilung Ic in der Zeit vom 1.10. – 31.10.41

two soldiers fell ill from malaria and had to be taken to the field hospital[54]. Neither Eppler nor Sandstede were unhappy when they learned that an enemy bomb had killed *Rittmeister* Hoesch, who wanted to drop them into Egypt by parachute[55].

Professor Pretzl, promoted to *Hauptmann*, took over responsibility for the mission and training in W/T and other technical matters went on. Although Pretzl did not persist with the idea of dropping the two spies by parachute, his idea of taking them to Egypt by *S-Boot* was no more favoured by the two. But since it was not their decision, they had to wait and see what was going to happen. When their training was nearly complete, Pretzl decided to pay a visit to his family in Vienna on 28 October before the start of the mission. The plane Pretzl was travelling in crashed, killing him. While this further fatal accident brought the mission to an early halt, the two spies spent a happy and carefree time in Munich before they had to return to Berlin. In the meantime they were paid a considerable salary of 3'600 *Reichsmark* a month and received as many ration coupons as they wanted. Despite this comparatively high salary, at the end of the month they were already short of cash[56] due to their excessive life style.

July to October 1941, Almásy on sick leave [57]

While the wheels were already in motion in Berlin, Almásy became ill at the beginning of July, apparently while still in Libya, and never made it back to Berlin as Ritter ordered him. It is not clear what illness he was suffering of, however various forms of dysentry was a common problem among forces of all sides operating in Libya. In any case, Almásy was flown out (probably from Derna) to Athens, to spend some weeks there in the Officer's Sanatorium. Following his discharge he received eight weeks recreational leave, which he spent in Budapest. At the end of his leave Almásy was ordered to report back to *Amt Ausland* in Berlin, which he probably did around the end of October.[58]

Some sources appear to contradict this, suggesting that Almásy was in Paris on the 20th October recruiting Mohsen Fadl for what was later known as the *Pyramid Organisation* spy ring in Cairo, and subsequently met Fadl in Berlin and Istambul during the course of November. This was based on the assumption by British intelligence that a certain Graf von Meran, apparently the control officer of Fadl, was „undoubtedly identical with Count Almassy" (*sic*).[59] However this was the case of a mistaken identity, Graf von Meran was later revealed to be an SD officer[60], and the *Pyramid Organisaton* was entirely an SD affair with no connections to Almásy or any Abwehr operation.

---

54   Behrend, *Rommels Kenntnis vom Feind im Afrikafeldzug*, page 116 ff
55   Sandstede, unpublished memoirs
56   Sandstede, unpublished memoirs
57   Based on Kubassek; *A Szahara büvöletéeben*
58   Statement made by Almásy during his War Crimes trial in 1942. This was corrobated by Zsolt Berencsy (interviewed by Kubassek in Sweden) who as a boy lived in the same house as Almásy, listening to his stories about Africa during the long hours spent in the basement air raid shelter during the USAF raids on Budapest in 1944.
59   TNA, London, KV 2/1463, Pyramid Organisation
60   TNA, London, KV 2/2652, Thomas Ludwig

10 November 1941, planning and preparations in Germany

By 10 November 1941 Almásy had met Eppler and Sandstede and had been introduced to them as their new mission leader. Both looked very favourably on Almásy's idea of taking them to Egypt by motor vehicle instead of by plane, by parachute or by sea. They held a long discussion and it seemed that there was a good common understanding between them from the outset. Both spies very much appreciated Almásy's lack of the military formality common among German officers. *Fähnrich* Hans Entholt[61] joined the group but was considered rather as a "special type" by Gerd Sandstede[62].

Allied Forces launched Operation Crusader on 18 November 1941. After the offensive which had forced Rommel's troops out of Cirenaica and back to el-Agheila by 15 January, not only were the Italians and the Germans weak and exhausted, but the Allied Forces had also suffered great losses in men, weapons and materials. The need to have agents in Egypt grew once more, to ensure that first hand information from the other side of the front was received. The *Abwehr* was required to set up a network of agents in Egypt who could report by wireless the intelligence they had gathered. After the previous attempt by *Sonderkommando Ritter* to fly spies to Egypt had failed, Almásy's idea of transporting the spies by motor vehicle was now definitely the preferred one. Two spies and their W/T equipment were to be transported from the area between el-Agheila and Agedabia in Libya, through the desert to Assiut on the Nile, south of Cairo. Having accomplished their mission, the vehicles were to drive back to their own lines. The route covered a distance of approximately 1'200 kilometres each way as the crow flies. After certain doubts were overcome, *Admiral* Canaris, the head of the *Abwehr*, finally gave his approval. While it became Almásy's task to evaluate the best practical route, *Major* Seubert gave *Wachtmeister* Hans von Steffens the duty of organizing all the logistics. Von Steffens was a recent *Abwehr* recruit in Libya, whom Seubert had personally chosen on account of his tough military bearing and his experience with the French Foreign Legion.

Serious preparations for the forthcoming mission had started now and everybody was busy trying to obtain the equipment and materials needed for the long journey to Cairo. They had an old truck, which they drove from one place to another in the bitterly cold city of Berlin to collect the items ordered. As Almásy advised the group, he reckoned on a three-week journey from Tripoli to Assiut. There were many things to consider and prepare, for example the rope ladders needed if a vehicle were to became stuck in soft sand. Naturally no such equipment was available in Berlin so it had to be designed, manufactured and tested first.

---

61   From surviving letters held by the Almásy family in Bernstein, it is clear that there was a close relationship between Almásy and Entholt.

62   Sandstede, unpublished memoirs

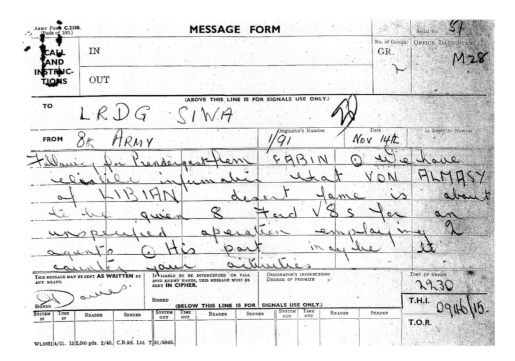

The telegram sent from HQ 8th Army to HQ Long Range Desert Group at Siwa, warning of Almásy's presence in Libya. *[Imperial War Museum, LRDG/WBKS Papers 3 Serial 51]*

14 November 1941, a telegram

Almásy's activities in Libya did not go unnoticed by the British intelligence. On 14 November 1941 8th Army sent a telegram[63] to HQ LRDG which was then located at Siwa with the warning that Almásy might be setting up an operation against the activities of the LRDG.

"Following for Prendergast from FABIN. We have reliable information that VON ALMÁSY of LIBIAN desert fame is about to be given 8 Ford V8s for an unspecified operation employing 2 agents. His part may be to counter your activities."

It is not known who FABIN was, but the content of the telegram appears to be related to a later visit by Almásy to army HQ in February 1941, where he got the final approval to obtain eight vehicles. We do not have any information on the source of this intelligence, there is no record in the ISOS or ISK transcripts of any such intercepted messages. However it does appear that some news of the preparations for Salam leaked out through some other sources. No confirmation exists from available documents whether any LRDG patrols were made aware of Almásy's expected activities. However, since Almásy has already left Libya in early July, and the new mission was not to start for several more months, there was no possibility of the LRDG finding any trace of Almásy at this time[64].

63   London, IWM, LRDG Papers, W.B. Kennedy Shaw 3, Serial 51
64   David Lloyd Owen, Commander of Y patrol, mentioned to his son Christopher that LRDG patrols were instructed not to intercept Almásy during Operation Salam. Based on the documentation available on Operation Claptrap, it seems rather that the LRDG was not aware of Operation Salam until it was too late to intercept. It is therefore presumed that Lloyd Owen's statement refers to the telegram of 14 November 1941, or other earlier intelligence about Almásy, rather than Operation Salam.

Preparations

Once *Panzerarmee Afrika* had advanced east again, Operation Salam received the "green light". The group was still in Germany, so nothing could yet be prepared in Libya, and many weeks were needed to obtain and prepare the vehicles and to test the wireless transmission equipment.

24 January 1942, Almásy returns to Libya[65]

After the unexpected new attack by Rommel's troops launched eastward from Agedabia on 21 January, the time seemed ripe to start Operation Salam. This was the moment Almásy had waited and worked for. It was the best chance to obtain approval from the higher authorities and to travel to Libya to arrange matters. Preparation of the equipment in Germany was still under way but Almásy left it in the hands of Hans von Steffens and the others. He departed at once for Tripoli via Rome by fast train on 22 January 1942. With Almásy was only Hans Entholt who had worked with him before.

While Almásy continued the journey to Tripoli, Entholt remained in Rome and when Almásy arrived at Tripoli by plane on 24 January 1942, Rommel's *Panzerarmee Afrika* was already near to Msus, which was taken from the enemy the next day. The Allies expected the German columns to continue their thrust towards el-Mekili, but they turned north and advanced towards the important Cirenaican harbor city of Bengasi. The rapid advance made Almásy very optimistic about his coming venture. The further east the frontline reached the shorter the distance he needed to cover to deliver the two spies to the Nile valley.

The officer version of the *Luftwaffe* tropical field cap as it was carried by Almásy. *[Dal McGuirk]*

Army tropical field cap – *Afrikamütze*, as it was called by the German soldiers . *[Dal McGuirk]*

65   Based on Eppler, *Rommel ruft Kairo* and von Steffens, *Salaam*

29 January 1942, Bengasi taken[66]

To continue his arrangements, mainly to obtain transport, Almásy had to drive to Cirenaica, where there was the best chance of obtaining vehicles, many recently captured from the enemy. The Ford cars and trucks he intended to use for his mission were thought better suited to desert use than available German vehicles, and furthermore such vehicles would be essential to prevent the Allies from recognising the column as enemy straight away. He was preparing to travel east over the next few days in the same staff car from his previous sojourn in Libya.

Left: Bengasi, *Piazza 28 Ottobre.*

Right: Bengasi, Governor's Palace

Bengasi, the Cathedral with its two distinctive domes.

Hans Entholt arrived at Tripoli that day and was received by Almásy at the Italian seaplane base, next to the Mehari hotel on the eastern coast of the city, where he came ashore by small motor launch. His car was under repair at the FIAT workshop in Tripoli but was ready just in time for Almásy to pick up. Hans Entholt had worked with Almásy in Germany when he was preparing the *Militärgeographische Angaben über Nordostafrika* for the Army General Staff.

66   Based on Almásy, **Rommel Seregénél Libiában**, chapter "From Tripoli to Benghazi"

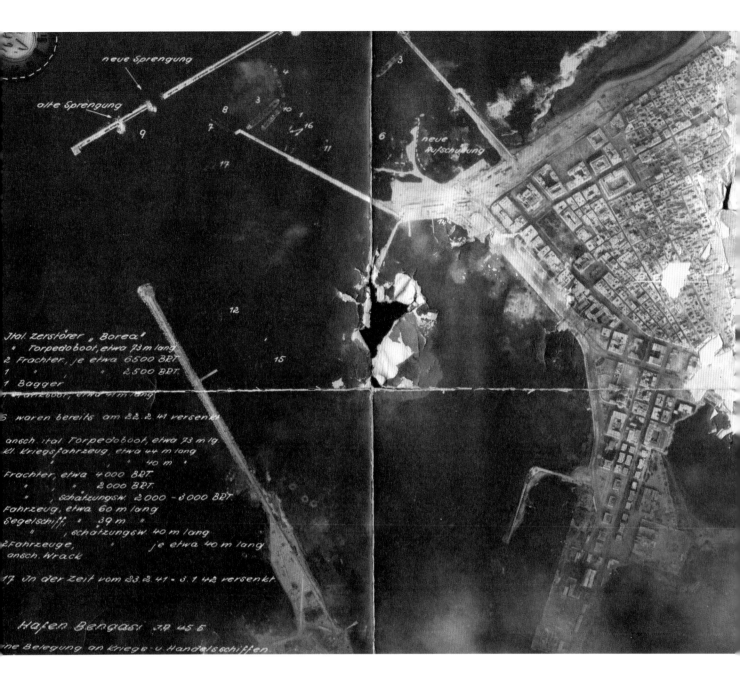

Within the aerial photograph, the following handwritten annotations are visible:

neue Sprengung

olte Sprengung

Ital. Zerstörer „Borea"
„ Torpedoboot, etwa 73 m lang
2 Frachter, je etwa 6500 BRT.
„ „ 2.500 BRT.
1 Bagger

waren bereits am 22.2.41 versenkt

ansch. ital. Torpedoboot, etwa 73 m lg.
Kl. Kriegsfahrzeug, etwa 44 m lang
„ „ 40 m „
Frachter, etwa 4000 BRT.
„ „ 2 000 BRT.
„ „, schätzungsw. 2.000 – 3.000 BRT.
Fahrzeug, etwa 60 m lang
Segelschiff, „ 39 m „
„ „, schätzungsw. 40 m lang
2 Fahrzeuge, je etwa 40 m lang
ansch. Wrack

17. in der Zeit vom 23.2.41 – 3.1.42 versenkt.

Hafen Bengasi 7.9. 45 5
ine Belegung an Kriegs- u. Handelsschiffen

neue Aufschüttung

German aerial photo
of 1942 showing the
harbour installations
at Bengasi.

Gebhardt von Walther, the German Consul in Tripoli,[67] was host to Almásy in those days and they met for dinner at the *Grand'Albergo*[68] on the *Lungomare* in Tripoli. With them were Hans Entholt and a German *Major*[69] who intended to travel to Cirenaica with Almásy the following morning. After the excellent meal – Almásy wrote that it was camel meat and not beef as the others believed – the Consul was called to the telephone and came back full of excitement. He said that: "Rommel has re-taken Bengasi!" Von Walther wanted to go along as well, but since there was no available driver, it was decided that he would travel with Hans Entholt.

67 Almásy mentions him as Seppel von Walther. His correct name was Gebhard von Walther but since he used the callsign SEPP in his W/T messages it might have been some sort of a nick name. "Seppel" would be the diminutive of the German name "Joseph".

68 Today's hotel el-Kebir (Grand Hotel) is a construction of the early 1980s. The old hotel no longer exists.

69 The name of this German *Major* is not known. Possibly *Major* Wittilo von Griesheim but there is no further proof for this assumption.

30 January 1942, journey to Bengasi[70]

Almásy, along with the German *Major* and his W/T operator, left Tripoli for Bengasi in the early morning of 30 January 1942. They followed the coastal asphalt road, the *Via Balbia*[71], passed Tagiora, Homs and Misurata. Their car could maintain a high average speed, but since all the supply columns for the fighting in the east used the 5.5 metre wide asphalt ribbon, they were considerably slowed. A truck column usually consisted of a maximum of 20 vehicles, which had to remain close together and on the right side of the road, to allow faster vehicles to pass them. Many such columns had to be overtaken on the 1'000 kilometre journey from Tripoli to Bengasi and by then the thousands and thousands of heavily loaded trucks had considerably damaged the asphalt.

By late evening they reached the imposing structure of the *Arco dei Fileni (Arae Philaenorum)*[72] which marked the border between Tripolitania and Cirenaica. They passed the 31 metre high stone-gate and continued east, until they reached the small village of el-Agheila with its famous fort. This was where Rommel had started his first advance in March 1941 and again in January 1942 after he had to withdraw as a consequence of Operation Crusader. There was no hotel available but the three travelers found adequate accommodation in a building of the Italian fort. 750 kilometres were already done and another 250 were to be driven the next day.

The first C11ADF obtained by Almásy – "Consul". The vehicle does not yet have a roof rack, roof hatch and also the MG mounts are not yet there.
[Ottokar Seubert]

70   Based on Almásy, **Rommel Seregénél Libiában**, chapter "From Tripoli to Benghazi"
71   Literally "Balbo's street". Named after the former Italian Governor for Libya, Italo Balbo.
72   Known as "Marble Arch" by the British, the arch was built by Balbo when he was governor of Libya to celebrate the completion of the coastal asphalt road. It commemorated the classical story of the Fileni brothers who preferred to be buried alive than to betray their country. It was declared open by Mussolini on the evening of 15 March 1937 in a Hollywood-style ceremony. The structure survived the war but was blown up in 1973 by the Libyan Government.

Arco dei Fileni – Marble Arch. Mussolini's triumphal arch at the mythical border between Tripolitania and Cirenaica. Almásy standing next to his Station Wagon, "Consul".
[Ottokar Seubert]

They continued towards Bengasi on 31 January 1942, and started to see signs of the recent fighting. There were destroyed tanks and trucks in the Agedabia area, and Italian sappers were removing the mines which were buried everywhere.

All of a sudden, they recognised a small black dot on the eastern horizon, approaching very fast: an enemy plane was searching for targets along the road. They could not immediately leave the asphalt due to the minefields on both sides, only after driving on for some distance to where the minefield ended. Fortunately they were not the targets the pilot was heading for. He attacked an Italian truck column moving just a few kilometres ahead of them.

Upon reaching Bengasi, they asked for the HQ of the *Panzerarmee Afrika* which was to be found outside the town, among the trees of a former Italian agricultural installation. Almásy was happy to meet many faces familiar to him, people he had worked with in Derna the previous year. The main subject of discussion was naturally the unexpectedly rapid advance of Rommel's army and the recent victories over the Allied forces. Almásy was informed that he would have to wait for some days in Bengasi before receiving the vehicles he had been promised by the deputy of the GOC *PzAA*. While talking in the casino, the General Officer Commanding, the newly promoted *Generaloberst* Rommel arrived in his dust covered Horch Kfz.15 staff car. He received Almásy for a few minutes and asked to be kept informed of the latest status of Operation Salam.

The location of the HQ was not a good choice. The RAF bombed it during the night, and since the Allied Forces had previously used the area as an ammunition dump the attack had a severe effect. One of the wounded was *Fähnrich* Hans Entholt who had arrived that evening from Tripoli with the German Consul.

Almásy moved into the town, to the *Grand Albergo d'Italia*[73]. But again it was not a lucky choice as the building was hit by a bomb the following night.

On 6 February the Ic of the *PzAA* general staff, *Major* Mellenthin, arrived in Tripoli from a period of convalescence in Germany, and replaced the *Ia* who was on leave. *Major* Zolling took over Mellenthin's duties as the Ic on a temporary basis[74].

Left: Marble Arch survived the war but was blown up in 1973. The lines of its foundation were still visible in 2009.

Right: The parts of one of the reliefs which were placed inside the arch are kept at the archaelogical area of Sultan, 50 kilometers east of Sirte.

Left: The sign of the airfield of Agedabia.
[Kuno Gross]

Right: Agedabia. 160 kilometres south of Bengasi.
[Kuno Gross]

Left: An Allied field cemetery in the Cirenaica. Almásy standing in front of the Muslim graves of victims of the recent battle.
[Dal McGuirk]

Right: Hans Entholt at the same cemetery.
[Dal McGuirk]

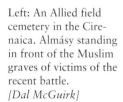

73   This hotel does not exist any more. Its place is occupied today with a nondescript building for offices and apartments.
74   Bundesarchiv Freiburg/Militärarchiv, RH19 VIII – 65; Tätigkeitsbericht der Abteilung Ic in der Zeit vom 17.2. – 28.2.1942

Bengasi, the cathedral
with its distinctive
domes in the back-
ground.
[Kuno Gross]

7 February 1942, completion of preparations in Germany[75]

The remainder of Almásy's group had continued their preparations and the purchasing of equipment in Germany, while the Italo-German army had taken Derna
and advanced further east, when Rommel realised that his troops were too weak
and too exhausted to continue and ordered a halt to resupply.

Almásy himself was at the Army HQ for discussions about the planned operation on
7 February and obtained approval for eight vehicles, to be provided by the *O. Qu*
(*Oberquartiermeister*) from transport captured during the recent advance[76].

By 10 February 1942 Eppler and Sandstede had run extensive trials with the newly
developed W/T equipment at Stirgau. The tests were passed successfully. Meanwhile,
Feldwebel Beilharz and Munz had joined the group and finally, on 17 February
1942, all equipment and baggage was mustered and stowed into a railway carriage
to be transferred to Rome and Napoli on 19 February. It seems that their equipment
was quite heavy and bulky; full five tons had to be stowed.[77] The equipment previously prepared by the *Nachrichtenbeschaffungsoffizier* (NBO) who had been
killed, was ordered to be handed over to Almásy.

75 Based on the Sandstede's unpublished memoirs and on von Steffens' *Salaam* as well as on the
    interrogation protocols of the captured spies
76 Bundesarchiv Freiburg / Militärarchiv, RH19 VIII – 65; Tätigkeitsbericht N.B.O vom
    7.2. – 28.2.1942
77 Von Steffens, *Salaam* p.107

28 February 1942, the group arrives in Tripoli[78]

On 20 February the German part of the group had arrived in Rome[79], stayed there for 8 hours and then continued to Napoli. Since the army in North Africa needed all available planes and ships to supply the fighting troops, it was very difficult to obtain transport. Almásy had to fly back from Tripoli to Rome to arrange the necessary permissions but it was only on 27 February that two Junkers Ju 52[80] transport planes were made available for them. Due to the danger from enemy fighter planes on Malta, they could not fly directly from Napoli to Tripoli but had first to fly to Trapani in Sicily. Bad luck struck at once, the undercarriage of one of the planes was damaged upon landing, and it had to be exchanged for another one. Next day they continued from Trapani to Sousse, Tunisia. They flew very low over the water until in sight of the Tunisian coast, to evade the fighters. Finally they landed safely at Tripoli airport, located some 30 kilometres to the south at *Castel Benito*[81]. Almásy, Entholt and *Unteroffizier* (NCO) Munz who had recently joined the mission greeted the arriving group on the airfield. Except *Unteroffizier* (NCO) Aberle, who was already with *HQ PzAA* in Cirenaica, the whole crew was now assembled in Tripoli.

Left Page: *Luftnavigationskarte in Merkatorprojektion, 1:2'000'000, Nr. 2425 Mittleres Mittelmeer.*

Unloading had to be done very quickly to release the planes for another transport flight[82] and the equipment was transferred to the accommodation in Tripoli provided by the *Luftwaffe*[83]. The accommodation was a spacious and comfortable Italian villa, located in one of the new quarters of the city in the *Via Cesare Billia*, just a few hundred metres south behind the Governor's Palace[84]. While a *Luftwaffe* staff-unit was responsible for food supplies, *Fähnrich* Entholt proved to be a successful cook and even Almásy insisted on cooking *Reisgoulasch* to a recipe from his mother.

Before the group arrived, Almásy had already completed much of the preparation in Tripoli and was keen to move on. *Wachtmeister* Hans von Steffens, who had previously spent some time in Libya for the *Abwehr* and was in charge of all W/T communication for Operation Salam, noted his disagreement with the way Almásy was acting. Obviously he felt himself to be the real leader of the operation and had difficulties to accept Almásy, but he had even more difficulty with the rather unmilitary behavior of the two spies and some other members of the group. The coming conflict was already obvious at this early stage.

78   Based on the unpublished memoirs of Gerd Sandstede and von Steffens, *Salaam*, plus W/T messages intercepted by British intelligence. By this time the British were not only able to decipher the Abwehr hand-cypher, but also the German high grade machine cyphers, and had developed the organizational capability to process the high volume of captured information in a timely manner. From this point onwards there is a transcript of practically all sent and received Salam messages in the National Archives, London.
79   TNA, London, HW 19/94 ISOS 26386, Berlin to Tripoli, 20 February 1942
80   Standard German tri-motor transport plane. These planes were slow and vulnerable to enemy fighter attack.
81   Castel Benito, today Qasr Bengashir, is still the main airport of Tripoli.
82   Very often the crews of the Ju 52 had to make several such dangerous trips per day.
83   The German air force did not only provide the accommodation but also the food, clothes, compasses and machine guns for the group.
84   The villa is still standing and was positively indentified in January 2012.

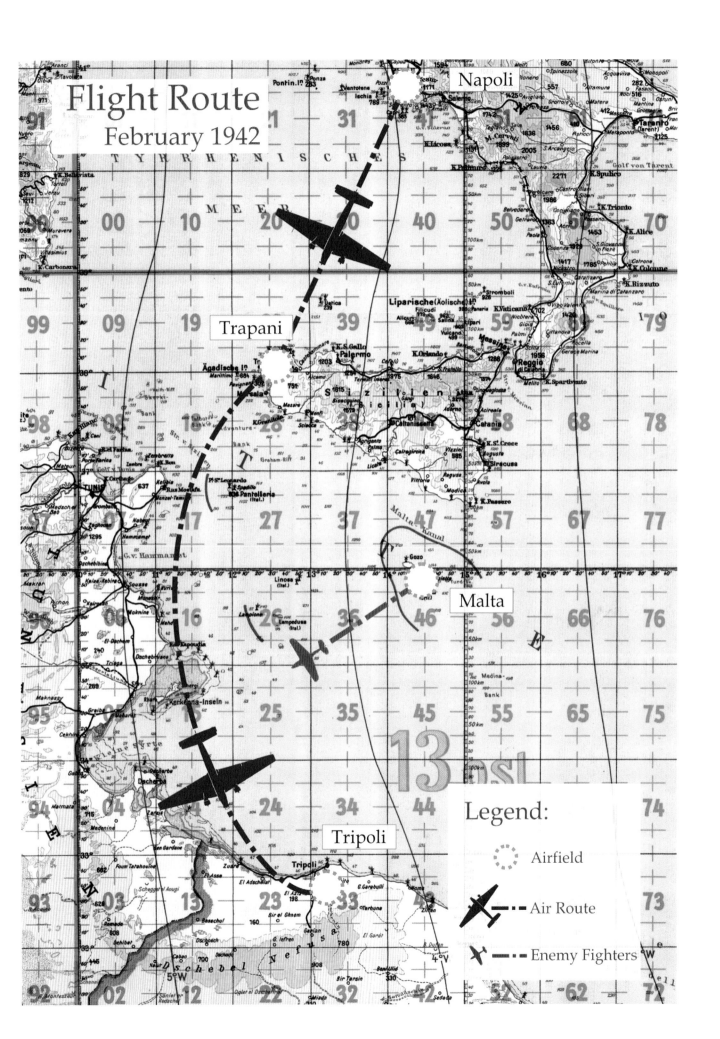

Flight Route
February 1942

Napoli

Trapani

Malta

Tripoli

Legend:

- Airfield
- Air Route
- Enemy Fighters

Hauptmann Almásy

Feldwebel Beilharz

Wachtmeister von Steffens

Unteroffizier Munz

Unteroffizier Wöhrmann

Obergefreiter Körper

Gefreiter Sandstede

Schütze Eppler

The personnel of Operation Salam now consisted of 12 people:

- *Hauptmann* Almásy, the overall leader of the mission;

- *Feldwebel* Beilharz;

- *Wachtmeister* von Steffens, responsible for logistics and W/T operations;

- *Fähnrich* Entholt;

- *Unteroffizier* (NCO) Munz and

- *Unteroffizier* (NCO) Aberle as drivers;

- *Unteroffizier* (NCO) Wöhrmann; driver and W/T operator;

- *Obergefreiter* Körper as driver and mechanic;

- *Gefreiter* von der Marwitz and

- *Gefreiter* Weber as W/T operators;

- *Gefreiter* Sandstede and

- *Schütze* Eppler.

The Airfield of Castel Benito south of Tripoli where the men and equipment of Operation Salam arrived on 28 February 1941. The aircraft are a Caproni Ca. 133 on the left and the Ca. 309 as the second from the right. The biplanes in between are wrecked Fiat CR.32 fighters.
[Dal McGuirk]

1 March 1942, preparations in Tripoli[85]

Despite the long period already elapsed, the operation was still far from ready to start. Over the first few days, supplies had to be stored properly in the villa in Tripoli and equipment had to be checked carefully. The three Ford C11ADF Station Wagons Almásy had obtained, two nearly brand-new vehicles from Bengasi and one from Tripoli, had to be properly maintained and overhauled to make sure that they would not cause problems during the long journey through the desert. Almásy had already arranged for some modifications on the single vehicle to be equipped with a machine gun. Special attention was paid to the engines and the suspension and long test-drives were made to evaluate the actual fuel- and oil-consumption of the vehicles. It was found that the fuel-pump gave problems at high temperatures. Fortunately Körper, who proved to be a highly skilled mechanic, solved this problem.

Tripoli, the Red Castle seen from the *Lungo Mare Conte Volpi*. Note the sailship on the right edge of the photo and the mythical wolf on the column.
[Dal McGuirk]

85   Based on Sandstede, unpublished memoirs and von Steffens, *Salaam*

A representative Italian building at the *Via Lombardi* near to the *Piazza Castello*.
[Dal McGuirk]

Tripoli in times of war. The entrances are protected by stone, sandbags or wooden structures.
[Dal McGuirk]

Tripoli. View from the upper floors of the Grand Hotel towards the harbour basin and the East. The distinctive tower of the Waddan Hotel can be seen in the centre of the photograph.
[Dal McGuirk]

Von Steffens, who was in charge of logistics soon complained that not everybody in the group participated in preparation work, and that Eppler and Sandstede in particular thought such work beneath them. However, Almásy did not intend to bother himself with such issues. Beilharz seemed to sympathise with Eppler and Sandstede and Entholt had other priorities as well. It is no wonder that the situation became worse and worse between von Steffens and that particular faction of the group and one day, when Almásy was away, it nearly ended in open mutiny against von Steffens. Only Almásy's return and especially the pacifying intervention of *Major* Wittilo von Griesheim, the Commanding Officer of *Abwehrstelle Tripolis*, could reconcile everybody again, but it was now clear that the operation would suffer from bad relations among the participants.

Without trying to judge who was right or wrong, most probably the two secret agents were not really aware of what awaited them, and were mentally already in a cool bar somewhere in Cairo. Although the two were no doubt a "special package" in all respects, von Steffens' attitude towards the others did nothing to ease the situation but exacerbated it[86]. Furthermore, it may be concluded that von Steffens, who with Almásy probably had the most desert experience, and was very active in preparing the enterprise, became increasingly conscious that he was not considered the most important person.

12 March 1942, testing the wireless telegraphy equipment[87]

Nearly two more weeks had passed and Operation Salam was still at its beginnings. The required number of vehicles had still not been received[88], when time was found to start serious testing of the W/T sets, newly developed by the workshop at Stahnsdorf. W/T communication with *HQ PzAA* had already been started and to their surprise it was either bad or did not work at all. The W/T sets were checked and found to be in good order, so the problem had to be somewhere else. Since

86   These difficulties in Tripoli were not described by Sandstede in his diary but were detailed in von Steffens's book *Salaam*. Though there were certainly conflicts, probably von Steffens exaggerated them in a quite dramatic way. These details are not quoted here.

87   Based on Sandstede, unpublished memoirs and on von Steffens's, *Salaam*

88   It can be assumed that the HQ PzAA did not give Operation Salam. such a high priority as it was stated in the books by Eppler and von Steffens, and that it was therefore fairly difficult for Almásy to obtain equipment, vehicles and assistance required for the operation.

View from the
Grand Hotel along the
Lungomare towards
the Red Castle.
[Dal McGuirk]

The main entrance to the castle of Tripoli.
[Dal McGuirk]

perfect long-distance communication was vital to the operation, serious testing of the several sets was carried out. One set was set up in Tripoli, another one with Eppler and von der Marwitz was at Misurata, some 200 kilometres to the east, and the third, operated by von Steffens and Wöhrmann, was placed even further east. While Wöhrmann could communicate with von der Marwitz without problems, the other two W/T stations could not be reached at all. Consequently another dispute came up in the evening, when von Steffens accused the others of working on the wrong frequency while they insisted they did everything as ordered It cannot be ruled out that they had been playing a trick on von Steffens, but since it was also difficult to contact HQ *PzAA*, and the whole operation suffered from communications difficulties throughout, there is no proof of it.

The triumphal arch of Marcus Aurelius in the northern part of the *Medina Kathem* of Tripoli. The minaret of the Gurgi-mosque can be seen in the backgorund.
[Dal McGuirk]

18 March 1942, to HQ *Panzerarmee Afrika* and obtaining the trucks[89]

It was already in the second half of March when at last Almásy was informed that three CMP Ford F8 *Flitzer* had been earmarked for his enterprise and were ready in Cirenaica to be taken over from the *Fallschirmjäger* of *Kampfgruppe Burkhardt*. He ordered von Steffens to take Sandstede, Eppler and Körper with him to bring back the new vehicles. Almásy himself intended to drive to Bengasi and then to Mameli to negotiate further matters with *HQ PzAA*. Von Steffens had planned to use this chance to test their W/T sets again, this time to a distance of more than 1'000 kilometres. Wöhrmann was to remain at Tripoli and man the W/T station there. A first test was done after about 200 kilometres at Misurata. The antenna was erected quickly and the connection was fine; von Steffens was surprised by Eppler's unexpected professionalism. About half way between Bengasi and Tripoli, at el-Agheila, a further test was done but despite all efforts, they were not able to contact Wöhrmann in Tripoli. They decided to drive on to Bengasi and to try once more from there. Again there was a very good connection to Tripoli. Since Wöhrmann stated that he was trying to call them as well, they suspected that their W/T sets had a "dead zone". This was confirmed during further testing on the return journey; their SE.99/10 sets did not work properly at ranges between 250 and 600 kilometres.

The photo probably shows a villa in the neighborhood where Operation Salam resided during the preparations in Tripoli. The exact place and the persons on the photo could not be identified.
[Dal McGuirk]

89   Based on Sandstede, unpublished memoirs and on von Steffens's, *Salaam*, plus intercepted W/T messages

This photo was taken from the roof terrace of the villa where Operation Salam was accommodated in Tripoli. The domes of the Governor's palace are visible in the background. This was the key photograph that enabled the location of the villa.
[Dal McGuirk]

Building across the *Via Cesare Billia* as seen from the villa of of Operation Salam.
[Dal McGuirk]

View over the city of Tripoli, probably taken from the roof terrace of the villa.
[Dal McGuirk]

Instead of staying the night in Bengasi, they carried on for another 160 kilometres and drove to *HQ PzAA* at Mameli. There they learned that their three trucks were still with *Kampfgruppe Burkhardt* some 30 kilometres back at Marawa. They decided not to drive there during the night but the following morning in daylight. The *Fallschirmjäger* were not very pleased to hand over three of their rare captured vehicles to another unit, but had to obey the order.

Although Operation Salam was prepared in all secrecy, something must have leaked out. Part of *Kampfgruppe Burkhardt*[90] had occupied Gialo oasis since February, when it had been re-taken from the enemy. They had recently been relieved by the 3th platoon of the 2nd *Gebirgsjägerkompanie* of *Sonderverband 288* and moved to Marawa. Before being released, they were given a rather strange task: to do a reconnaissance to the east to find out about terrain conditions for a planned operation. A *Hauptmann* of the *Fallschirmjäger* put two and two together and came up with an accurate guess. It must have become clear to him that von Steffens and his men were members of the group intended to execute this secret mission. He told von Steffens that the available Italian maps were definitely wrong and that instead of plain *serir* about 50 kilometres to the east of Gialo endless ranges of high dunes were to be found.

90   *Fallschirmjäger Lehrbataillon* under Major Burkhardt

The cars of Operation Salam parked on the empty plot of land adjacent to the villa serving as their residence on *Via Cesare Billia*.
[Dal McGuirk]

The villa with the distinctive balcony still stands, in substantially the same state as when it accommodated Operation Salam in 1942.

Five of the six vehicles of Operation Salam parked on the empty plot of land. Note the inscription *Via Cesare Billia* left of the iron entrance gate. *[Dal McGuirk]*

The iron entrance gate is still in place today as it was in 1942. Only, the neighbouring plot of land is overbuilt now.

The main entrance of the Salam villa in 2012.

The buildings across the corner are also still the same.

With the necessary papers signed, the trucks were handed over to von Steffens and the others. It was already 11:00. They thought they could save some time by taking the direct road from Barce via Tocra to Bengasi instead of driving via el-Abiar up in the hills. They were quite surprised to meet a German roadblock just after coming down to the coastal plain, and were informed that the area they had just crossed had not yet been cleared of the enemy. Since the return to Tripoli could not be made the same day, they stayed the night near Agedabia.

On 20 March the group was back at Tripoli[91]. Preparations continued at the a same slow pace, and on 25 March they were told that a fuel dump was to be established at Gialo oasis by a supply unit of the *Panzerarmee*. On 27 March, the Intelligence Officer of *PzAA* was informed that the vehicles were expected to be ready in about nine or ten days and that Almásy had planned to come to HQ with his own car at the end of the month on 30 or 31 March. The question was put whether fuel had already been sent to Gialo[92]. The word used in radio messages for fuel was "Sprit", a term which is literally used in Germany for "fuel". The British translators misinterpreted it as a codename for another W/T station of the *Abwehr*.

91   Bundesarchiv Freiburg / Militärarchiv, RH19 VIII – 68; Tätigkeitsbericht der Abteilung Ic in der Zeit vom 1.3. – 31.3.1942
92   TNA, London, HW 19/30 ISOS 26524 (Tripolis to IC), 27 March 1942

5 April 1942, air attack on Gialo[93]

Almásy travelled from Bengasi to Umm er-Rzem to where *HQ PzAA* had been moved from Mameli, to deliver *Gefreiter* Weber, assigned to join *Unteroffizier* (NCO) Aberle as the W/T operator of SCHILDKROETE, the station to receive messages from SALAM and later KONDOR. Once back at Bengasi he did not return directly to Tripoli but drove down to Gialo, planned as their "jump off base" to Egypt. There, on 3 April, the regular courier plane brought an Italian priest who intended to hold mass on the coming Easter Sunday. This was one of the very few changes to the daily routine of the Italian garrison at Gialo who had been there without relief since February.

Left: Rommel's HQ at Mameli, 30 kilometres south of Cirene in March 1942. The HQ was established in an abandoned house of an Italian settler.
[Rolf Munninger]

Right: The HQ at Mameli. Rommel giving last instructions before leaving for a vacation.
[Rolf Munninger]

The mass was celebrated in the positions of 2rd Company in the usual manner; a simple field-altar beneath the palms, spent artillery cartridges holding palm leaves to left and right, and the Italian flag over the altar. The Commanding Officer of the company and a young soldier assisted the priest and nearly all ranks attended the mass. It was a peaceful moment in this remote oasis, to where the war had brought them.

After mass, walking through the village, Almásy heard the distant sound of an approaching aircraft, and soon spotted an incoming German Junkers Ju 52. He had been expecting this plane, bringing more fuel supplies for his planned operation. After circling the oasis at low level it landed at the nearby airfield. The crew consisted only of the pilot, the W/T operator and a gunner, and the plane was full of long-awaited supplies, including Almásy's jerrycans.

Almásy, his company and the crew of the aircraft were invited to Sunday lunch at the Italian officers' mess. The food was excellent. The red wine lifted everybody's mood and soon they started toasting and singing. Only a few minutes later, the sirens of an air alert brought them abruptly back to the reality of war. Almásy left the building and assembled with his men at their vehicles, standing outside the *Presidio* under some trees.

Two white dots were seen circling high above the Oasis. If it were only one, it would probably have been just a reconnaissance plane, but two of them meant something else. The pilot and gunner of the Junkers took a motorcycle and drove off towards the landing ground, but the others stayed near their vehicles under the trees. For about a quarter of an hour nothing more happened, the two enemy planes just kept on circling. The Italian soldiers were still busy driving the villagers into their houses

93   Based on Almásy, ***Rommel Seregénél Libiában***, chapter "Easter Sunday"

Two Bristol Beaufighter Mk.IC of No. 272
Squadron RAF in flight over Malta.
[Imperial War Museum, CM 005109]

Bristol Beaufighter Mk.IC, T3316 M of No. 272
Squadron RAF parked at Idku airfield in Egypt.
[Imperial War Museum, CM 001129]

Bristol Beaufighter Mk.IC, T3314 M of No. 272
Squadron RAF at Idku airfield in Egypt running
up its engines.
[Imperial War Museum, CM 001127]

when the two planes made a sudden steep dive. Using his field glasses, Almásy recognised them as Bristol Beaufighters, ground attack planes rather than bombers.

It was not clear who started shooting first, the planes or the guns of the garrison. All machine-guns and light anti aircraft guns of the Italian garrison and the German *Gebirgsjäger* joined in. Almásy got in a shot with his machine gun when one of the planes flew low over the *Presidio*. Suddenly it was quiet again; the two planes turned away and flew off eastward. It was all was over as quickly as it had started, but the men remained on alert and kept their weapons ready.

Soon afterwards the FIAT staff car came back to the *Presidio* and a body was taken out of the vehicle and into the building. It was the Junkers-gunner. He had been killed in the fight with the attacking planes. Almásy learnt that both the gunner and the pilot had reached their plane before the two Beaufighters attacked, and manned two machine guns to try to defend their precious plane. While the gunner was firing on the Beaufighter, a bullet hit and killed him. At the same time the *Gebirgsjäger* platoon had taken up position around the area and returned fire with machine guns and other infantry weapons. The Ju 52 was ablaze but they could see that each of the withdrawing enemy planes was trailing smoke. German losses, beside the gunner of the Ju 52, were the second in command of the *Gebirgsjäger*, *Feldwebel* Dussler, and another soldier who was seriously injured.[94]

6 April 1942, prisoners of war[95]

That evening, when Almásy was invited for dinner at the house of Hadj Taher, a noble of the oasis, he was told the story that a month back a British motorised patrol of three trucks carrying nine white men had kidnapped a 16 year old youth who had gone to Bir Buttafal to get water with his old father. Since the only camel with them was shot by the patrol, the old man had to walk back the 30 kilometres to the oasis. Almásy promised to drive to the place and to look for any traces of the incident. When he walked back to his accommodation, he heard Italian soldiers talking about the enemy planes; one of the planes had been seen to come down, although it did not seem to have crashed.

Early the following morning Almásy left the oasis in the direction shown to him. Soon he passed the soft sand surrounding the oasis and found a good drivable surface of *serir*. After about 10 kilometres they could make out an object at the horizon. The vehicle was stopped carefully to avoid breaking through the hard surface of the *serir*. Through the field glasses they recognised an aircraft standing on its wheels. They approached the plane very carefully from two directions to avoid possible machine-gun fire. Once they had reached the plane, they could see that it had been hit by many bullets but there was no blood in the empty cabin so they assumed the crew got away unhurt. The location of the force-landed plane was only 16 kilometres off Gialo but obviously the crew did not intend to surrender to the enemy and had decided to walk to the tiny oasis of Gicherra some 45 kilometres to the Northeast, where there was no Italian garrison. It was fairly easy for Almásy and the two other cars to follow the footprints of the two-man crew of the Beaufighter and once they had reached the oasis, children

95   Based on Almásy, ***Rommel Seregénél Libiában***, chapter "Easter Sunday"

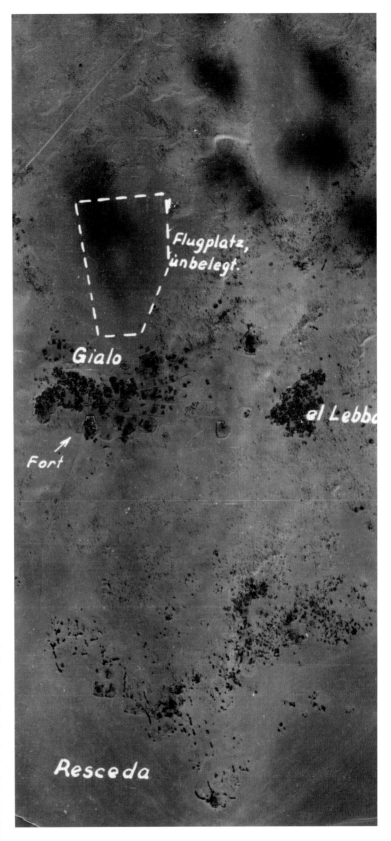

Aerial photograph of Gialo taken by the Germans in 1942 *(Bildstelle X Fliegerkorps).* *[Kuno Gross]*

approached them and gave away the house where the exhausted British airmen were resting after their long march. They were taken prisoner and brought back to Gialo where they were handed over to the Italians as prisoners of war.

The second Beaufighter was discovered some 120 kilometres away from Gialo by one of the *Ghibli* reconnaissance and liaison planes stationed at the oasis. The crew had obviously had time to send an emergency message and to inform a ground party of their location. Traces seen by the crew of the *Ghibli* revealed that they had been rescued by one of the enemy's desert patrols.[96]

Gicherra oasis where the crew of one of the force landed Beaufighters was captured.

Serir. Nothing can hide and the force landed plane was visible from far away.

96   ORB (Operations Record Book) of 272 Squadron confirms Almásy's account, providing the following information: A Beaufighter of 272 Squadron that had taken off from LG.05 at 12h05 on 5 April had failed to return from an attack on Gialo aerodrome. It made three attacks, destroying an unidentified aircraft on the ground. Last seen after the third run by a Maryland who then lost sight of the Beaufighter but then immediately saw an aircraft burning on the ground. A/C T4839 with the code BT-K made an emergency landing and the crew Fg Off George M Gee and Sgt John B Gill were both taken POW. This plane actually belonged to 252 Squadron but might have been 'borrowed' by 272 Squadron.

The *serir* between Gialo and Gechirra. An endless flat plain of sand.

Aufkl. Gr.122
2.(F)/122
F 69/43 V. 25.1.43. 12²⁵
Flgzf. und Beob.:
Lt. Straßmair

Hafen TRIPOLIS
M = 1:12400
Karte 1:1,000000

1 = Frachter etwa 9500 Brt. (ansch. auf Grund)
2 = Fracht- u. Fahrg. 9500 -"- (leichte Schlagseite)
3 = -"- -"- 6700 -"-
4 = Frachter etwa 3400 -"- (ansch. Deckzerstörung)
5 = ansch. Spezialfrachter etwa 4000 Brt (3.T. unter Wasser)
6 = Frachter (Maschachtern) -"- 5200 -"-
7 = Frachter -"- 11000 -"- (ansch. auf Grund)
8 = Frachter gekentert
Im Hafen noch verteilt Schuten, Prämen, Leichter und
sonstige kl. Hafenfahrzeuge, 3.T. auf Grund
9 = gesprengte Kai und Anlageanlagen
☐ = Zerstörungen.

Schiffssperre

Bildstelle 2.(F.)/122

10 April 1942, *Admiral* Canaris in Tripoli, further preparations

Almásy only returned to Tripoli shortly before the visit of the Commanding Officer of the *Abwehr*, *Admiral* Canaris, who had arrived by special flight from Germany on 10 April[97]. He was on a tour to inspect his *Abwehrstellen* in North Africa, together with *Oberst* Piekenbrock, *Oberst* Maurer, *Oberstleutnant* Helfrich and several high-ranking officers of the Italian army and the Italian intelligence service[98]. Wittilo von Griesheim and Almásy were asked to be at the office at 15:00 to report to Canaris on their sphere of work[99].

German aerial photograph of Tripoli harbour taken on 27 January 1943 (shortly after the Axis forces had withdrawn by 2(F)/122 (long range reconnaissance unit). Although the photo has been taken after Almasy and his group had arrived in Tripoli it gives a very good impression how the city looked like. *[Kuno Gross]*

97   TNA, London, HW 19/30 ISOS 25357
98   TNA, London, WO 208/5520, Interrogation Files, Consolidated Report about Eppler and Sandstede of 6 August 1942
99   TNA, London, HW 19/30 ISOS 25330

Tripoli, the old city. View from the (partially land-filled) harbour bay.

Tripoli, the Waddan hotel. This distinctive complex was planned by the Italian architect Florestano di Fausto and built in the year 1935. Today it is standing in the shadow of a giant newly built hotel.

Tripoli, the "new" old city. The old Italian buildings still dominate the view, although many have been replaced by modern ones.

They also visited a POW camp at Misurata and on 14 April, Canaris left Tripoli by car to Tunis via the coastal road and paid a visit to *Abwehrstelle Zuara* which was located directly on the route[100]. On the same date, another message was received from Seubert (going by the code name ANGELO) in Berlin: he confirmed that he could supply Eppler and Sandstede (PIT and PAN), with several cases of tobacco as previously requested[101]. On 15 April, Tripoli informed Berlin that the codebooks had been received and that SALAM planned to leave Tripoli on 20 April. In addition, three cases of tobacco in paper were ordered[102]. Tobacco was clearly the code used in the messages for money[103]. The books were copies of Daphne du Maurier's novel **Rebecca** which were to be used to encode and decode the messages following the *Abwehr's* book code. A set of these same books were also sent to *AST* Athens in order to eventually provide for another communications station for the two spies once they have reached Cairo. Appartently the process was not well coordinated, as deciphered Enigma traffic between Berlin and Athens revealed that Athens initially received the books only, but was not briefed on the transmission schedules or call signs to be used during Operations Salam and Kondor. Even when the schedule was sent, Athens seems to have had no idea what purpose the schedule served.[104]

While from their own accounts it would seem that the two spies were served with priority, on 16 April a message was received, saying that the amount of 42,08 *Reichsmark* had been withheld from Eppler's salary to pay for outstanding telephone charges[105], in addition to what was already withheld from the salaries of both in March on account of other unpaid bills[106].

100 TNA, London, HW 19/30 ISOS 25357
101 TNA, London, HW 19/30 ISOS 25041
102 TNA, London, HW 19/30 ISOS 25061
103 In Hungarian 'tobacco' in the proper context is slang for money. This strongly implies that Almásy himself must have concieved the code phrases used in Salam W/T communications.
104 TNA, London, HW 19/93, ISK 7395
105 TNA, London, HW 19/30 ISOS 25064
106 TNA, London, HW 19/30, ISOS 25274

Left: Hans Eppler in Front of one of the Ford F8, "Habuba". Note that the condensor is not yet fixed on the vehicle and the rather strange headgear of the three men in the backgroud.
[Dal McGuirk]

Right: Five members of Operation Salam wearing a bizzarre headgear.
[Dal McGuirk]

Hans von Steffens taking inventory of the supplies. The number plates on the vehicles are WH and not WL as it could have been expected for the F8 which were taken over from a WL unit. "Purzel" is the F8 in the centre of the photo.
[Dal McGuirk]

The oasis of Umm er-Rzem where the HQ of PzAA was established in April 1942. When Almásy arrived, Rommel was not there and the other officers they met had serious doubts if the planned mission was feasible at all.
[Rolf Munninger]

Sandstede (l.) and Eppler (r.) standing in front of one of the Ford C11ADF in Tripoli.
[H. Eppler via Archiv Kröpelin]

Tripoli. The Gazelle-fountain near the Grand hotel.

25 April 1942, at the headquarters again[107]

Almásy, together with the two spies Eppler and Sandstede, had left Tripoli again on 24 April to pay another visit to *HQ PzAA*.

However, when they arrived, Rommel was not there and the other officers they met expressed serious doubts about their chosen method of taking the spies to Egypt by motor vehicle. They would have preferred transport by plane or possibly even by submarine. They thought that driving across the desert was a crazy idea, nobody believed it would succeed. The two spies were completely ignored by the officers. It seems that staff officers did not consider Operation Salam to be such an important enterprise as the participants of the mission obviously believed it to be. Although this reception was unexpected by Almásy, he was sure that he had made the right choice.

27 April 1942, the first loss for Almásy's mission[108]

While Almásy was away at the Headquarters of *Panzerarmee Afrika*, von Steffens and the others who remained in Tripoli were busy giving the vehicles a last overhaul, distributing the equipment and the supplies among the vehicles and checking fuel consumption of the loaded trucks. The W/T operators were doing exercises to polish their skills. Only one thing was not to be tested: contrary to von Steffens's opinion, Almásy deemed it unnecessary to test the weapons. He said to von Steffens that the mission did not have a fighting task but just to transport the two spies to the Nile. If they were to encounter an enemy patrol in the desert, then they would see them from afar and try to avoid them. They would be prepared to meet the enemy, while the others most probably would not expect Germans crossing the desert. If they were caught, they had better surrender since their mission would then have failed anyway, and to attempt to fight their way out by force would be pointless. Even on the way back, they would try to drive undetected to avoid the enemy becoming aware of the mission, thus creating a danger for Eppler and Sandstede. To a certain extent von Steffens agreed with Almásy, but once he was off to Headquarters, they tried the weapons anyway. They were back in storage, cleaned and oiled before Almásy returned to Tripoli.

When Almásy arrived at the villa in Tripoli he was confronted with the first loss to the crew of Operation Salam: Hans Entholt was sick and had to be taken to hospital with a severe fever. He was told that the sickness did not seem serious, but

107 Based on Sandstede, unpublished memoirs
108 Based on von Steffens, *Salaam*

that Entholt would definitely not recover for another three to four weeks. It was clear that Entholt could not join the mission and needed to be replaced urgently.

It was von Steffens who proposed to replace the sick Entholt with a doctor. Almásy immediately agreed to this proposal and drove off to obtain the necessary permissions and to find a suitable person. When he came back in the evening, he was happy that permission had been granted and a new man promised to turn up the next morning. This is how it came about that *Unterarzt* Strungmann, seconded from the *Luftwaffe*, joined the mission at short notice. He was looking forward to a big adventure but as yet had no idea of the difficulties he was about to meet.

Tripoli. The horse fountain at the main square.

Tripoli. A lush green park within the old city.

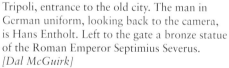

Tripoli, entrance to the old city. The man in German uniform, looking back to the camera, is Hans Entholt. Left to the gate a bronze statue of the Roman Emperor Septimius Severus. *[Dal McGuirk]*

Vehicles & equipment

Since the whole of Operation Salam was to be carried out behind enemy lines, it was preferable to use vehicles captured from the enemy to avoid being recognised from afar. In addition, the permanent lack of means of transport during the desert war was a general problem for both the Italians and the Germans. The supply of vehicles was far less than the demand of the army. A very valuable contribution which kept Axis troops mobile was the vehicles abandoned by Allied forces during their withdrawals. At most times during the Desert Campaign a considerable part of the motorised transport in use with the Axis forces had been captured from the enemy.

Ford "De Luxe" C11ADF

Like many other Allied military vehicles, the Ford C11ADF was manufactured in Canada. Station wagons of this model were commonly used as staff cars with the British and Commonwealth Forces in the North African Campaign. Two versions were built, a 7-seater and a 5-seater, the latter having heavier axles and a bigger luggage compartment. This was therefore better suited for Operation Salam. The station wagon was also called "Woodie", referring to the bodywork which except

The 1941 Ford C11ADF Station Wagon.

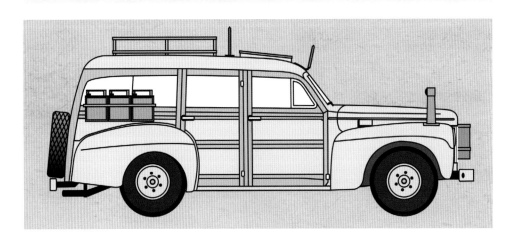

for the engine covers and the mudguards was made of wood instead of metal. The "F" in the C11ADF indicates that the vehicle had right hand drive (as can be seen in the photographs of Operation Salam).

The 96 bhp 3.6 litre V8 petrol engine was made by Ford and gave the vehicle a maximum speed of 70mph (112 km/h). The manufacturer declared fuel consumption as 13 miles per gallon which equals to about 18 litres per 100 kilometres. Of course such a value could not be achieved with a fully loaded vehicle in the heat of the desert and whilst driving in soft sand. Therefore it was necessary to do extensive testing before the beginning of an operation leading deep into the desert.

The C11ADF had a wheelbase of 114" (290cm), an overall length of 194" (493cm), a width of 79" (201cm) and a height of 72" (183cm). The vehicle was two-wheel-drive and was provided with 9.00 x 13 desert tyres. It was fitted out on the production line with blackout equipment (so that no light was emitted at night), rifle carrying stands, map container, map table and a first aid box. Also, for use in the desert, a water condenser was fitted at the front of the vehicle to reduce water consumption when the engine overheated (based upon the same principle as used by the LRDG). The unloaded weight of the vehicle was just less than two tons.

In addition to the standard equipment, for Operation Salam one station wagon, named "Consul", was equipped with a magnetic compass of the type *Askania* "kleiner Emil". When "Consul" had to be abandoned, the compass was changed over to "Präsident". Such compasses were usually installed in German aircraft but could also be used on the ground. The compass was fixed on a pod on the right front mudguard for the driver to be able to simultaneously watch the compass bearing and the road ahead of him. The name of the third station wagon was "Inspektor". It was equipped with the W/T set. Two of the C11ADF, "Consul" and "Präsident", had a roof hatch over the front seats which could be opened in an emergency to fix the MG 15 machine gun on one of the mountings on the front window frame and on the roof behind the hatch. A roof rack was placed at the back of each station wagon's roof; it took the sand ladders carried to unstick the vehicles from soft sand, and for the same purpose each vehicle carried two shovels. Except for some camouflage (which consisted of oil and sand smeared over the vehicles, mainly to divert attention from the black German crosses painted on the side-panels) and windows painted to avoid reflection in the sun, no other special equipment was carried and no further modifications were made to the vehicles. It is worth noting that while the LRDG and the SAS generally used vehicles which were stripped of their roof and doors, Almásy decided to do just the opposite.

The manual for the civillian version of the station wagon, the "De Luxe".

Ford CMP F8 *Flitzer*

The smaller CMP trucks (Canadian Military Pattern) were called *Flitzer* by the Germans. For Operation Salam, in additon to the three Ford C11ADFs, three captured Ford F8s were taken over from the *Fallschirmjäger* of *Kampfgruppe Burckhart* at Maraua in Cirenaica.

The CMP Ford F8 8 cwt.

A logo made of brass as it was mounted on the Ford vehicles.

The rear body of the truck was equipped with a removable tubular superstructure and tarpaulin (it could be used independently as a tent) and was originally designed to take a W/T set. However, W/T equipment was not installed for Operation Salam. The No.12 type cabin took the driver and co-driver while the rear body could accommodate three further soldiers. Operation Salam used this space for equipment and supplies. It was a quite small truck: Overall length 156" (396 cm), body width 75" (190 cm) and height 75" (190 cm). The tyres were 9.00 x 13 as on the C11ADF. The minimum ground clearance under the rear axle was 8.25" (21 cm)[109].

The payload for the F8 was 8 cwt (900 lbs) that is equivalent to about 410 kilograms. The truck had a V8 engine developing 95 hp[110], four forward gears, one reverse and a 6-volt electrical system. The two fuel tanks contained 12 ¼ gallons each (46.3 litres) and the average fuel consumption of the F8 is given as up to 20 miles per gallon. This is equivalent to about 14 litres per 100 kilometres. This value sounds rather optimistic and depending on the load and the terrain to be crossed, the consumption could easily be doubled or more.

The trucks used on this mission were equipped with a water condenser comparable to the one installed on the station wagons. Beside this and the removal of their front bumpers, they did not receive any other special fittings. With one exception: A single F8, "Maria", received a roof hatch and two mounts were fixed on the left side of the cabin-roof, one in front and one at the rear of the hatch, to carry an MG 15 machine gun for use in case of emergency.

The CMP Ford F8 truck was equipped only with two-wheel-drive which may explain at least in part the difficulties the drivers experienced in the soft sand.

---

109 Technical data for the Ford F8 were submitted by Paul Lincoln and Jim Price, both of whom are owners of this type of truck.
110 The CMP trucks had different engines: the ones manufactured by Ford had a 95 BHP engine, the ones by Chevrolet an 85 BHP (same as the British made trucks).

Navigation and communication

Navigation: "Kleiner Emil" (little Emil) was the nickname of the flight compass used by Operation Salam. Askania Werke AG, Berlin-Friedenau, manufactured it. It weighed 380 grams and was equipped with a compensation installation (so the magnetic disturbance caused by the vehicle could be eliminated). Two of these very valuable compasses were with Operation Salam and used to keep to a bearing while driving. They were fixed on the right front mudguard of one C11ADF station wagon and in the middle of the bonnet of one of the F8s.

In addition to this, Almásy had a "Kaufmann Patent" sun compass. It was a Cole Mk.I Universal Sun-Compass which was probably captured from the enemy. Remarkably, Almásy did not mention the use of the sun-compass in his diary for the mission. It is presumed that he did not use it other than at el-Agheila where it was used during the calibration of the magnetic compasses mounted on the vehicles.

He also used a prismatic compass which was either a British Mk III fluid dampened compass or more probably an earlier model of a Barker compass. The type and manufacturer of the prismatic compass cannot be firmly ascertained from the only available photo.

The maps available to Operation Salam were of Italian origin and of little value in the southern regions since they did not show the whole range of the dunes in the western arm of the Calanscio Sand Sea. Due to this unknown dune-belt of immense dimensions, the expedition suffered the loss of two vehicles and much time. Further south, in the Gilf Kebir, the available Italian map was more useful since it contained information provided by the 1933 "Almásy-Penderel

Führer-Kompaß „Kleiner Emil"

im Rundgehäuse nach Abb. 4.

Diese Bauart ist zum Einbau in das Gerätebrett bestimmt. Die Gehäuseflanschabmessungen sind die gleichen wie bei allen übrigen genormten Rundgeräten.

Beide Kompasse können auch mit Rose und Steuerstrich ohne Leuchtmasse geliefert werden.

Prüfungsergebnis

bei einer Horizontalintensität von 0,184 C G S und 18—20° Celsius.

1. Schwingungszeit von 90° Ablenkung bis
   zur Ruhe . . . . 13—16 Sek.
2. Dauer einer Halbschwingung nach 90°
   Ablenkung . . . . 6— 8 Sek.
3. Dämpfung . . . . 78,5 °/₀
4. Neigungswinkel der Rose, in Graden . 25°

Abb. 4. Bauart Lke 6.

Left: The Askania *"kleiner Emil"*. This compass was normally used in aircraft.

Right: Extract of a contemporary brochure.

Left: The SE.99-10 *Agentenfunkgerät* as it was used by Eppler and Sandstede. *[Peter Gierlach and Ragnar Otterstad]*

Right: The Mk.III Prismatic Compass. This example was manufactured by J.H. Steward in London.

Left: The Cole Mk.I Universal Sun Compass as it was used by Almásy during Operation Salam.

Right: Top view of the Cole Mk.I

Expedition" as published in the *Geographical Journal*, as well as the results of the mission of *Capitano* Marchesi to the Jebel Uwenat in 1933. Furthermore, there was a map provided by the German *Luftwaffe* in 1:500'000 which was in fact a copy of the 1935 Survey of Egypt map.

Communication: The W/T (wireless telegraphy) sets used by Eppler and Sandstede were manufactured at *Aussenstelle Stahnsdorf*, a large workshop for such devices[111]. All *Abwehr* W/T sets were made at that workshop which also developed and tested new types. The sets given to Operation Salam were type 100/98 (according to Sandstede) or type 99/10 (according to Eppler)[112]. Almásy received the set with serial number 30, while Eppler and Sandstede got numbers 31 and 32. Set 31 was the one buried later on at Assiut before the spies went down the escarpment to the Nile and set 32 was the one they took with them into Cairo. Both spies had claimed that they had received the first three operational sets of the series so it can be assumed that nos 1 to 29 had been largely experimental sets. The *Agentenfunkgerät* SE.99/10 (Eppler mentioned the type correctly) was manufactured with the objective of utmost miniaturisation. This 10-Watt wireless station used an integrated transmitter, receiver and power supply and was built so as to resemble a cigar-box. It was either to be connected to a wall socket, or if none was available, to a car battery through a transformer. The W/T set could be used on three wavelengths.

111 TNA, London, KV2 / 1467, Eppler, Personal File 1
112 There was never such W/T set as the 98/100, only the SE.98/3. However it was definitely not used by Operation Salam.since it was quite a lot bigger than the SE.99/10 that was available from 1942 and was about the size of cigar-box (Staritz, *Agentenfunk*).

Weapons and equipment

Weapons: Although von Steffens mentions in his book that they were using the MG 42 machine gun, this does not seem very likely. The first time the MG 42 was reportedly used in North Africa was during the battle for Bir Hakeim which started on 26 May 1942. It is not realistic that an enterprise considered an impossible mission by the higher ranks of the *Panzerarmee Afrika* would be provided with a brand new and superior weapon just before a major battle. Sandstede in his unpublished memoirs mentions the MG 15, while in the interrogations by the British Security Service he states that they had two MG 81s with them (the MG 81 was a further development of the MG 15). This sounds more reasonable, particularly since the Luftwaffe supplied the operation and Almásy had good relations with the *Luftwaffe* in North Africa. A further argument for the MG 15 is that it was quite a short weapon compared to the MG 34 commonly used by German infantry – this is a clear benefit, if the weapon was hidden inside the vehicle and mounted only in case of emergency through the open roof hatch. The available photos of Operation Salam indeed only show the MG 15 on the roof of one of the station wagons.

There is no clear evidence of further weapons with Operation Salam. Von Steffens mentions that each member was equipped with a "pistol" and that they had four Mauser 98k rifles with them. Considering that the weapons were thought useful only for self-defence, or in an escape situation if caught by the enemy, for example at a checkpoint, then the pistol makes sense but not the rifle. It was too long to be used quickly from inside the car and we would rather believe Almásy's statement that they were using sub-machine guns. He does not mention a type but we guess that it was the standard MP 40 as it was widely used by German troops.

The Rheinmetall MG 15 was designed specifically as a hand manipulated defensive gun for aircraft.

The Luger P.08 Parabellum. Since this pistol was a standard weapon in the German army, most probably Operation Salam had the same.

75-round double-drum magazine of the type D-T 15.

27mm Walther *Leuchtpistole* as it was used by Operation Salam to signal to the Italian garrison of Gialo.

Sand-ladders: Operation Salam used specially fabricated rope ladders. The dimensions were not noted in any of the available accounts, but can be inferred from a photograph showing them in use. They are estimated to have had an overall length of about 5 to 7 metres, rungs of about 50 centimetres width and a distance of 10 to 15 centimetres between the rungs. From the available photographs we know that each of the station wagons carried four such sand-ladders on its roof rack. Whether the Ford F8 were equipped with them as well is not clear; at least on the photos, no such equipment can be seen on them. This type of sand-ladder was in fact copied from those used by Almásy on his earlier expeditions before the war, a method pioneered by P.A. Clayton in the deserts of Egypt.

Food: Since Operation Salam was attached to the *Luftwaffe* in matters of administration, we can assume that their rations were also of *Luftwaffe* origin. The actual content of their food supplies is not known, with the exception of one item: the chocolate. A discarded *Scho-ka-kola* tin was found at "Two Peak Hill" along the Operation Salam route in Egypt. The label says "Wehrmacht Packung", though this does not preclude it being part of the Luftwaffe rations. Almásy does mention this chocolate to be one his favorites[113].

113 Almásy, **Rommel Seregénél Libiában,** chapter "Night Return". This "energy chocolate" spiked with a generous amount of caffeine is still manufactured in Germany.

Finally: Operation Salam begins!

The preparations for Operation Salam had begun in mid-November 1941 and continued for two and a half months in Germany, until the group had collected all their equipment and travelled to Tripoli. The acquisition of the vehicles and the further preparation in Libya took another two full months, so the mission could only be started after four and a half months of preparation, a considerably greater length of time than the six weeks Bagnold and his colleagues needed to set up the Long Range Desert Group. But finally, Operation Salam was ready.

29 April 1942, start from Tripoli[114]

On 29 April von Griesheim sent a message from Tripoli to Berlin, reporting that after more delays Almásy was now ready to start the mission,.[115] The group finally left Tripoli in the early afternoon, the villa was given back to a *Luftwaffe* unit and no trace remained of their several months' presence.

They drove along the Via Balbia in single file, Almásy in front together with *Unterarzt* Strungmann, followed by the second station wagon with the two spies and then followed by third station wagon and the three Ford F8s. They made good progress at a speed of about 80 kilometres per hour. One team was left behind at some distance from Tripoli to do an exercise in wireless telegraphy, and follow later. It worked fairly well using *Rebecca*. It was agreed that for the first week of each month, the first word on the first page should be used as key. The next week would be page 100 plus 10, 110 and then 220, then 330. The book code was fairly difficult to encode and they had to take care to make no mistake because otherwise the message would become absolutely meaningless.

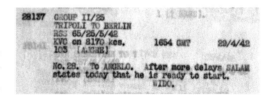

Intercepted Message

The vehicles of Operation Salam lined up in the *Via Cesare Billia*. Note the seventh vehicle at the end of the column which did not belong to the group.
[Dal McGuirk]

114 Based on Sandstede, unpublished memories
115 TNA, London, HW 19/30 ISOS 28137

On the first day, they only managed to drive some 200 kilometres and rested for the night in a *Carabinieri* post at Misurata. As a fortunate occurrence for the German group, an unlucky Italian transport column was surprised and strafed by enemy ground attack planes. The barrels of wine they carried (among many other goods), were perforated by machine gun bullets, and the precious leaking wine was caught in all available containers. There was enough to drink for everybody, including the German group.

Left: *Via Cesare Billia.* In front the three Ford C11ADF and behind them the three CMP Ford F8.
[Dal McGuirk]

Right: "Inspektor" parked on the roadside before the departure to the desert. The Balkenkreuz is visible on the wooden structure of the car.
[Ottokar Seubert]

Left: Two Ford C11ADF and between them one of the CMP Ford F8 at a halt between Tripoli and Misurata along the Via Balbia.
[Dal McGuirk]

Right: Via Balbia. Small repairs on one the F8 standing in the line behind "Inspektor".
[Dal McGuirk]

Whilst the repair on the F8 is conducted, all vehicles are properly lined up on the roadside.
[Dal McGuirk]

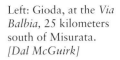

Left: Gioda, at the *Via Balbia*, 25 kilometers south of Misurata.
[Dal McGuirk]

Right: Gioda, the administrative complex of the Italian agricultural settlement.
[Dal McGuirk]

Left: The small convoy takes a rest at Gioda.
[Dal McGuirk]

Right: The C11ADF "Inspektor" at Sirte. The sign of the *Albergo* (hotel) partially visible on the left edge of the photo.
[Dal McGuirk]

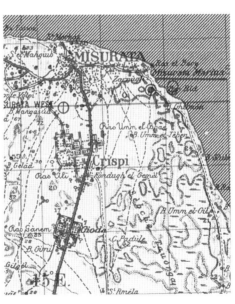

Left: The entrance to Sirte.
[Kuno Gross]

Right: GSGS, Libya 1:500'000, Sheet Misurata, 1942. Gioda, the Italian agricultural settlement is located at the bottom of the map.

The airfield of el-Agheila. The small village and the famous fort are located on the hill visible in the background between the airfield and the Mediterranean.
[Dal McGuirk]

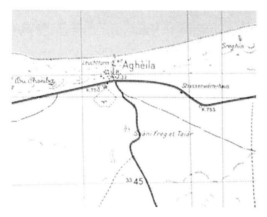

Libyen 1:100'000, Blatt Agheila. Sonderausgabe 1942.

30 April 1942, el-Agheila[116]

On the last day of April, they had a long stage to cover and drove from Misurata to the small village and fortress of el-Agheila. They were not in a hurry, since the last car from Tripoli had still to arrive and Almásy wanted to compensate the magnetic compasses which were fixed to the vehicles. While Almásy was busy with his compasses on 1 May and von Steffens and Beilharz remained with him to assist, the W/T operators carried out a successful test; most of the group then used the opportunity to spend a day at the beach and enjoy the sea. Von Steffens was especially interested in Almásy's work and keen to learn how a magnetic compass was adjusted. It did not take long for somebody to find out where to obtain some alcohol from an Italian *cantina*. Even Almásy, who was rather tolerant in this respect, felt obliged to interfere now and he forbade its consumption.

After the compensation of the compasses was completed, Almásy drove ahead alone and ordered the group to follow to Agedabia the next day. He wanted to gain some time to be able to obtain information about possible minefields, and actual road conditions down to Gialo. Unfortunately, Almásy had given responsibility for driving to Agedabia to *Unteroffizier* Munz and not to von Steffens, who had the higher rank. Von Steffens was annoyed. Not only did he feel bypassed, but worse, the two spies and *Feldwebel* Beilharz were now cracking jokes about him. When they started for Agedabia in the

El-Agheila, calibrating and compensating the compasses. Von Steffens and another member of Operation Salam are standing on the right side of the Ford.
[Dal McGuirk]

116 Based on von Steffens, *Salaam*, and Sandstede, unpublished memoirs

morning of 2 May, they were obliged to drive following *Wehrmacht* rules, staying together but keeping laid-down distances to prevent the whole convoy being an easy target for an enemy ground-attack plane. Due to the lack of driving discipline, the column fell apart quite quickly and Eppler and Sandstede in their fast personal car drove ahead without considering the others. The station wagon was soon out of sight, Munz with one of the F8s tried to follow but the other two trucks drove at the correct speed and soon they lost contact with the others.

Despite the fact that the four vehicles did not drive as a unit, all of them had the same unpleasant experience during the short stage of about 120 kilometres from el-Agheila to Agedabia. Shortly after they had passed the small village of Mersa el-Brega, about 40 kilometres after el-Agheila, they were attacked by enemy planes who strafed them with all the weapons they had. Fortunately none of the vehicles were hit and they came through with nothing worse than shock.

El-Agheila. A piece of the original *Via Balbia* heading to the hill where the old fort is located.

El-Agheila. View from the walls of the old fort towards the Mediterranean. The abandoned old buildings and the mosque can be seen in the background.

Almásy aiming with the prismatic compass. This compass was of British make and was considered as better than German compasses.
[Dal McGuirk]

Almásy aiming at the Askania *kleiner Emil* compass mounted on the right mudguard of "Präsident". The Cole Mk.I Universal Sun-Compass is mounted on the bonnet of the Ford and there is the mounting for the machine gun on the roof. Beilharz is observing Almásy's activities.
[Dal McGuirk]

Almásy adjusting the Askania *kleiner Emil* observed by Hans von Steffens.
[Dal McGuirk]

Von Steffens, with sun-glasses at el-Agheila. Note the "D" (Dolmetscher / Translator) shoulder tiles.
[Dal McGuirk]

When von Steffens arrived at Agedabia later that morning, he was looking for Almásy to complain to him about the behaviour of the two spies. But Almásy got in first and shouted at him, why had he only arrived now, two hours later than the others? Von Steffens replied that he was driving at the prescribed speed and in his opinion it would endanger their whole mission if some of the vehicles were driven at excessive speed. Von Steffens requested that Almásy, as Commanding Officer of the operation, admonish the two spies, and Beilharz and to Munz as well, who were responsible for the group. He insisted this be done in his presence. Almásy promised that he would warn them, however not in the presence of von Steffens.

The third station wagon that had remained in Tripoli for the W/T test had made it to Agedabia as well, arriving late in the evening of 2 May, so the group was now complete[117]. The continuation of the journey was planned for the following day at 06:30 towards Gialo[118].

Hans von Steffens.
[Dal McGuirk]

117 There is no mention of the arrival of the sixth vehicle in the available sources, but it very likely that it too joined the group at Agedabia.
118 TNA, London, HW 19/30 ISOS 28335

Almásy, with cigarette and sidecap, taking some notes assisted by Hans von Steffens. *[Ottokar Seubert]*

Almásy calculating after taking the readings from the compass. Left of him Hans von Steffens and on the right Strungmann and the standing Beilharz with an Italian waist sash. The Cole Mk.I Universal Sun-compass is fixed on the bonnet. *[Ottokar Seubert]*

Agedabia, the old Municipality. This is one of the early buildings of the Italian time and is one of the few historical buildings remaining in that city. A thorough restoration is badly needed.

Agedabia, city and rest station at the *Via Balbia*. Almásy discussing with Beilharz who wears a waist sash, a "fascia coloniale" originally issued to Italian Libyan soldiers in the Italian army
[Dal McGuirk]

3 May 1942, from Agedabia to Gialo[119]

The start from Agedabia was not encouraging. The smouldering conflict between von Steffens and the two spies was not settled. Although Almásy had warned Eppler and Sandstede the previous evening, they obviously did not take it too seriously and had enjoyed their last night in 'civilisation' extensively, and they did not get up in the morning. Eppler's duty that day was to prepare breakfast for the group, but he overslept which caused another complaint to Almásy by von Steffens. While the group supporting von Steffens, Wöhrmann, Körper and von der Marwitz were ready to start as ordered at 06:30 in the early morning, the other group, Munz, Beilharz, Eppler and Sandstede were not. Their argument was that the distance to Gialo, some 250 kilometres, could easily be done that day, even if they started half an hour later. Almásy was already smoking one cigarette after another. The continued tension between the members of the small group did not give him much confidence: it was not good to embark upon such a dangerous mission with the participants already split in two groups.

Finally they left at 08:00 and followed the Italian track due south towards Gialo. After two hours driving, just south of the abandoned old fort of es-Sahabi, they had to face a terrible *ghibli* which blinded the drivers. Although all the windows were closed, fine dust got into the vehicles to the discomfort of the passengers. They had to continue their drive, but their speed dropped substantially. The distance between vehicles had to be reduced so they could still see each other, to avoid losing contact with the lead vehicle.

The drinking water became hot and the drivers tired, but there was no chance of a change, they just had to continue in convoy and hope that it would soon be over. Von Steffens realised that he did not feel well. He considered that this was caused by the workload of recent days and the continuous tension with Eppler and Sandstede, but also the unceasing stress of driving in such conditions. He decided not let the others see his weakness, and carried on.

And all of a sudden the *ghibli* was gone, just a clear and sunny sky again. In front of them a dark line appeared in the yellow sand which had to be an oasis. Almásy in the leading car stopped and the convoy came to a halt. He assembled the men, asked if everything was all right and explained that Gialo was just ahead of them. They had been announced by the W/T station at Agedabia, but to make sure they would not attract friendly fire, Almásy ordered the men to place the big Italian

119 Based on von Steffens, *Salaam*

Istituto Geografico Militare, Carta Dimostrativa della Libya 1:400'000, Foglio 12, Agedabia, 1938.

Almásy and Beilharz standing next to one of the Ford F8. Lined up in the background are "Inspektor", "Maria" and Purzel.
[Dal McGuirk]

Agedabia, rest house. Some tame Dorcas gazelles.
[Dal McGuirk]

On the road from Agedabia to Gialo. Operation Salam stopped next to the wreck of a British Daimler Dingo Scout Car which belonged to the 1st. Armoured Division.
[Ottokar Seubert]

The Italian flag was hoisted on the first vehicle of the column to avoid the Italians shooting at the cars – which were not to be recognized as being in German possession from far. Almásy in dark coat standing with the back towards the camera.
[Dal McGuirk]

flag on one of the cars, in order that the Gialo garrison would recognise them as friends and send out a guide to bring them through the mine fields. They were very lucky that the *ghibli* had ceased at the right moment, otherwise they might have missed Gialo or driven into the minefields.

Wöhrmann fixed the mast on Almásy's Ford and hoisted the flag, then they advanced slowly towards the oasis and soon they saw movement, an Italian officer with five soldiers came up to them and talked with Almásy. Then the officer climbed into Almásy's vehicle and guided them through the mines. The track in the soft sand was worn out and each truck had to try to take the best line for himself. So it happened that Sandstede suddenly changed direction and von Steffens had to react to avoid bumping into him. Von Steffens got stuck with his F8 but Sandstede and Eppler – probably not realising the situation they had caused – continued without stopping to help him. Von Steffens was furious and Wöhrmann, in his truck, realised that the other vehicles were driving on. They had to help themselves and von Steffens had already removed one of the spades and started shovelling like mad. He ordered Wöhrmann to prepare the sand-ladders. All the shovelling did not help much since the very soft sand slipped back into the hole again. He was beside himself with anger. Then the inevitable happened: it became black in front of his eyes …

Von Steffens, who always claimed to have a lot of desert experience, had just behaved like a complete beginner: instead of working steadily and drinking water beforehand, he shovelled like mad and became completely exhausted. No wonder, after the immense heat of the day, with the small quantity of water he had consumed combined with the intense efforts to dig out the truck.

Naturally the others had come back, once they had realised that one of the F8 trucks was missing. Together with the Italians and some natives of the oasis who came by, they got the truck out of the soft patch of sand. Von Steffens was taken to the Italian garrison hospital. After he regained consciousness, the Italian doctor explained to him that he had had a serious circulatory collapse and he was not allowed to leave his bed. The doctor said he would have to stay in hospital for another four to five days..

Von Steffens felt ashamed that he, an old desert hand, had collapsed and not one of the first-timers. Later that day, Wöhrmann visited von Steffens in hospital and complained that Almásy was shouting at him because of the ditched truck although it was in fact Sandstede who had caused the misfortune. What was more worrying for von Steffens was that Almásy now had a good reason to get rid of him. Wöhrmann told

Between Agedabia and Gialo. A Libyan FIAT truck heading towards Gialo on the lifeline supplying the oases in the South.

Remnant of the Desert War. A rusty old "Jerrycan" in the *serir* between Agedabia and Gialo.

Gasr es-Sahabi. The ruins of the old Italian fort 100 kilometres down the way from Agedabia to Gialo.

A.M. – *Amministrazione Militare*. The famous Italian meat tin as it can still be found everywhere where Italian soldiers stayed.

Left: Crossing *serir* on the way to Gialo. Hans von Steffens standing as second from the right. (Original photo blurred). *[Dal McGuirk]*

Right: The same scene. Note that the number plate on the back of the first car had been turned. It shows now the word "Pass" instead of the WH number. *[Dal McGuirk]*

Shortly before Gialo von Steffens got badly stuck in soft sand with "Purzel". This is one of only two photographs where the rolled out sand ladders can be seen. *[Ottokar Seubert]*

him that Almásy had already explained to the group that von Steffens was too sick to continue the journey and that he had to return.

Von Steffens decided to stay in the hospital for the night but the next morning he wanted to be on duty again and to show the others that he was fit for the mission[120]. Von der Marwitz sent a message to the Ic of *Panzerarmee* that SALAM had safely arrived at Gialo[121].

120 In his publication, **Salaam**, von Steffens claims that he had serious problems with his heart and that this was the reason for his collapse. We cannot judge definitely – but the circumstances that caused his collapse do not necessarily indicate a problem with the heart. Most probably he suffered from heatstroke but used the situation to leave the mission in 'honour'. Since the transport of the two spies was the one and only task of the operation, it was evident that von Steffens had no chance in his dispute with them and sooner or later he would have to go.
121 TNA, London, HW 19/30 ISOS 28195

Also "Maria" got stuck. Since the trucks were heavily loaded and had only a two wheel drive, getting stuck in soft sand was not a rare occurence. Note the Italian soldier and the Libyan civillians who indicate that it must have happened just within the range of Gialo oasis.
[Ottokar Seubert]

Arriving at Gialo. The Italian flag is hoisted on one of the Station Wagons to avoid any misunderstanding with the garrison of the oasis. The windows of the cars are painted to avoid reflections in the sun. Visibility for the drivers must have been rather poor.
[Dal McGuirk]

Operation Salam has reached Gialo. "Consul" and Inspektor" are parked in front of the Italian *Presidio*. Four Italian Lancia 3Ro trucks and the entrance gate of the barracks in the background.
[Dal McGuirk]

The same view of the *Presidio* in 2012.

Gialo Oasis

"The oasis group of Gialo includes the actual oasis of Gialo with its main village el-Ergh, the oasis of Augila which is located 30 kilometres west-northwest and the smaller oasis of Gicherra about 27 kilometres north-northeast of Gialo. All three oases of the Gialo group are located in flat sand fields which are embedded into the surrounding serir.

The oasis of Gialo is located above an underground aquifer consisting of limestone and clay strata which carries groundwater at a shallow depth. Access to this slightly brackish water is by total of 466 wells which are used to irrigate approximately 50'000 date palms and 100 gardens where barley, wheat, vegetables and fruits are grown.

The 2,762 inhabitants (census of 1931) live in the three villages of el-Ergh, el-Lebba and esc-Scerruf. El-Ergh is where the administration for the whole of the oasis-group is located. Administrative buildings, a guesthouse, military barracks, an Italian-Arab school, vehicle workshops, fuel depot, airfield and a wireless telegraphy station are located here. The villages are built with low, windowless houses and narrow, curved lanes. The inhabitants are either traders or farmers. As to domestic animals, only goats and donkeys are available.[122]"

Force E under Brigadier Reid captured Gialo as part of with Operation Crusader in November 1941. In early January 1942, Gialo was made the new headquarters of the Long Range Desert Group but was abandoned again on 23 January after Axis forces had started their successful counterattack[123].

After the withdrawal of the Allied Forces, a platoon of German *Fallschirmjäger* of the *Kampfgruppe Burckhardt* along with an Italian army unit occupied Gialo. The parachutists were relieved in March 1941 by the reduced 3rd platoon of *Gebirgsjäger* of *Sonderverband 288* under *Leutnant* Kiefer. Junkers Ju 52 transport planes with the task of strengthening the Italian battalion there flew them to Gialo. It was they who suffered the casualties during the air attack by the two Beaufighters of 272 Squadron mentioned by Almásy[124] on 5 April 1942. When they were ordered to leave the oasis only a short time later, they underwent another strafing by enemy

View from the *Presidio* in direction North. On the left, the Italian school of the oasis and on the right two Lancia 3Ro trucks.
[Dal McGuirk]

View back (South) towards the *Presidio*. The nose of one of the Lancia 3Ro trucks is just visible
[Dal McGuirk]

Munz, unidentified, Sandstede and Eppler (from left to right) walking towards the location of the destroyed old fort of Gialo.
[Dal McGuirk]

122 This contemporary description of the Gialo Oasis group is taken from *Militärgeographische Beschreibung von Libyen* that was published in January 1941.
123 PRO, London, War Histories, *Special Forces in the Desert War 1940–1943* page 126
124 Almásy, *Rommel Seregénél Libiában*, chapter "Easter Sunday"

The centre of Gialo oasis. In the direct centre, the white-washed *Presidio*, behind it the barracks with the high entrance gate and oposite the *Presidio* the Italian school.
[Dal McGuirk]

Left: View from the fort down to the center of Gialo
[Dal McGuirk]

Right: Walking out of the village (from left to right: Munz, unidentified, Sandstede, Eppler
[Dal McGuirk]

The old fort of Gialo which was destroyed in November 1941 when "Force E" under Brigadier Reid attacked and conquered the oasis.
[Dal McGuirk]

Left: Walking towards the airfield (from left to right: Eppler, Sandstede, unidentified, Munz.
[Dal McGuirk]

Right: (From left to right: Unidentified, Strungmann, Eppler, Munz, Sandstede.
[Dal McGuirk]

Visit to the graves of the victims of the British aerial attack on Gialo of 5 april 1942, Easter Sunday. (From left to right) Munz, Eppler, unidentified, Sandstede, Strungmann.
[Dal McGuirk]

The palm gardens of Gialo. Compared to 1942, there are many more palmtrees today. In recent years the plantations have been connected with those of Gicherra which is some 30 kilometres away from Gialo.

Right: The Italian barracks at Gialo. Today they are used to accommodate a number of small shops and a car workshop.

planes. This time they did not suffer any casualties, but the plane sent to transport them, one of the rare Savoia Marchetti S.74s[125], was slightly damaged. The enemy planes withdrew due to concentrated defensive fire and a few days later the Germans were flown out[126]. The German 2cm anti-aircraft guns had just been removed from Gialo a few days before Operation Salam departed from the oasis[127]. From then on the Italian garrison manned the last Italian outpost alone and Caproni *Ghibli* planes patrolled the area. The enemy sat 400 kilometres south of them at Bir Zighen.

125 The Savoia Marchetti S.74 was a four-engined Italian airliner that entered service in 1934. Only three such planes were built and beside a crew of four, it could carry 24 passengers.
126 Based on Kost, *Gebirgsjäger in Libyens Wüste*, page 55 ff
127 TNA, London, KV2.1467, Eppler, Personal File 1

Blenheim Z 7610 was the aircraft that was used by Major De Wet for the last flight to search for Kufra after Z 7513 did not return. *[G.J. Mostert via András Zboray]*

The detachment of 15 Sqn SAAF at Kufra in the happier days before they undertook the disastrous flight. *[G.J. Mostert via András Zboray]*

3 – 9 May 1942, the tragedy of the 15th Squadron SAAF Blenheims[128]

While Almásy and his group stayed at Gialo, experiencing troublesome days until they finally decided to take the detour via the south instead of crossing the dunes of the sand sea, another tragic story unfolded in the area of Kufra which indirectly helped Operation Salam pass unnoticed in the desert.

Following the capture of Kufra from the Italians by Free French forces on 28 February 1941 the garrisoning of Kufra was left to the Sudan Defence Force. For much of 1941 the Oasis remained a sleepy backwater providing occasional headquarters for the Long Range Desert Group, but seeing little other action.

In the spring of 1942, following the rapid gains of the *Panzerarmee* on the Mediterranean coast, and in anticipation of a major counterattack (which was pre-empted by *Operation Theseus*), the British command felt the need to strengthen the Kufra base by the addition of a fighting Air Force unit. The task fell to 15 Squadron of the South African Air Force which had only recently transferred to Egypt after supporting the Ethiopian campaign. 15 Squadron was equipped with Bristol Blenheim Mk. IVs, a multi-purpose twin engined aircraft.[129]

Three Blenheim Fighters (Z7513, Z7610 and T2252) with a full assortment of crew and ground support personnel were selected for the task, forming a detachment of 15 Sqn SAAF at Kufra, to be commanded by Major de Wet. They had a threefold task: To reconnoitre the approach routes to *Kufra*, to warn the garrison of Kufra in case any enemy approach was detected, and to give air cover in case of such an enemy attack.

The ground support crews arrived at Kufra on 24 April with one of the Sudan Defence Force (SDF) supply convoys, and after the base had been set up at the patched-up bombed-

Blenheim Z 7610 under maintenance inside the hangar of Kufra.
[G.J. Mostert via András Zboray]

The Vickers Wellignton of Sqn Ldr Warren who detected the single Blenheim Z 7513 after a search flight of five and a half hours on 9 May.
[G.J. Mostert via András Zboray]

128 Based on: TNA, London, WO 169/7288, Sudan Defence Force, Kufra Garrison War Diaries, 1941 July – 1942 Aug and RAF Proceedings of Court of Inguiry, Kufra, 1st June 1942 (Forced Landing of three Blenheim Aircraft – SAAF No. 15 Squadron – Near Kufra on 4th May 1942).

129 While by 1942 the Blenheim Mk.IV bomber became obsolete for frontline duty, it was still very valuable in areas where the enemy air opposition was not too strong. The Mk. IVF long-range fighter version was armed with four 0.303 in (7.7 mm) machine guns in special gun pack under the fuselage. About 60 Blenheim Mk. IVs were converted into Mk. IVF fighters.

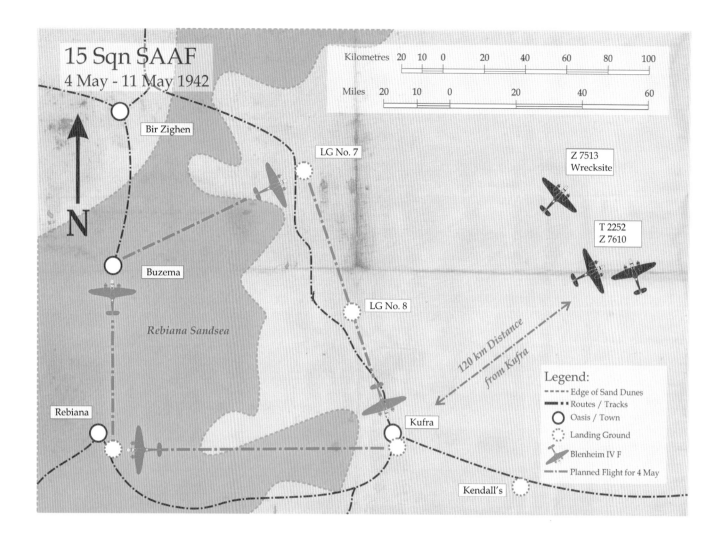

15 Sqn SAAF
4 May - 11 May 1942

Kilometres 20 10 0 20 40 60 80 100

Miles 20 10 0 20 40 60

N

Bir Zighen

LG No. 7

Z 7513
Wrecksite

T 2252
Z 7610

Buzema

Rebiana Sandsea

LG No. 8

120 km Distance
from Kufra

Rebiana

Kufra

Kendall's

Legend:
- - - - - Edge of Sand Dunes
▪▪▪▪▪ Routes / Tracks
○ Oasis / Town
⬤ Landing Ground
✈ Blenheim IV F
— ▪ — Planned Flight for 4 May

The empty flimsy cans of the rescue team are still at the same site as they were left in 1942.

out Italian hangar at Kufra airfield, the three aircraft flew in via Wadi Halfa on 28 May.[130]

On 3 May, the radio sets were tested and the three planes were prepared for their first familiarisation flight, planned for the next day. Each aircraft was equipped with rations for four days and 37 litres of water. In the evening, Major de Wet briefed the crews about the following day's route which looked roughly like a square: From Kufra to Rebiana, 83 miles (133 kilometres) on bearing 269°, then Rebiana to Buzema, 51.5 miles (83 kilometres) on bearing 358°, then *Buzema* to (Landing Ground) LG.7, 64 miles (103 kilometres) on bearing 63° and from LG.7 to *Kufra*, 83,5 miles (134 kilometres) on bearing 162°. At the planned true airspeed of 150 mph (240 km/h) the flying time should be 1 hour and 52 minutes and the estimated time of return to Kufra was therefore at 07:42.

When they took off in the early morning of 4 May, they had three more persons on board who acted as a lookout, the

130 Unpublished Diary of G.J. Mostert, aircraft mechanic, SAAF 15 Sqn. Det.

Air Mechanics N St M Juul, RJ Swanepoel and CF van Breda. Once airborne, Major de Wet in Z7513 checked the radio and found it to be working fine. But after 07:10, none of the machines acknowledged any more signals from Kufra. Although Rebiana, with its black stone hills amidst the bright yellow sand dunes is visible from far away and the post at the oasis kept a sharp outlook for the planes, they were not seen nor heard by anyone. It would appear that the crews were convinced that they had reached Rebiana and changed course for Buzema. Then, only a few minutes before the estimated time of arrival, they sighted a Landing Ground which they thought was LG.7. From there they headed back to Kufra where Major de Wet decided not to land, since there was still some time left, and they flew away again. And then the tragic sequence of error, human failure, bad weather conditions and technical problems began …

At 07:10, the base station at Kufra had picked up a signal from the Blenheims and Z7610 was heard asking for a bearing. When the base responded, there was no reply from the plane. The direction finder station radioed '120-3-0527' which means: "Steer 120° (Zero wind), third-class fix, time 05:27"[131]. The three aircraft never reached Kufra[132]. But when at about 09:00 the starboard engine of T2252 started giving problems, Major De Wet ordered the planes to make a landing in the open desert at 09:15.

It is not clear what went wrong. But considering the location of the landing and the bearings and flying times reported together with the planned speed of the planes, then it becomes clear that they flew not back to Kufra on course 120°, but directly eastward on bearing 88°; the place was about 132 kilometres away from Kufra! Pilots and observers discussed their positions and came to different conclusions, but finally they were convinced that they were only about 30 kilometres away from the oasis. In fact, they were completely lost. They did not know where they were nor did anybody else at the base. At 11:00, Z7610 took off again and flew in a southwesterly direction but returned after half an hour without finding Kufra. Another attempt was made at 14:00 again without success and a third one at 15:35 on a course of 240° for approximately 130 kilometres. This last attempt must have come very close to the Oasis – but they did not see it and returned. At the garrison it was recognised that something had gone terribly wrong and all outposts were contacted. None had seen the three planes, only Tazerbo reported that they had heard an aircraft west of the oasis.

By midday it was considered that the planes were lost and orders were given to organise search parties to *Rebiana, Buzema* and LG.7. Unfortunately no other planes were available at Kufra and only the SDF could assist with its trucks. During the day, several weak signals were received by the direction finder at Kufra. 42°,

131 The actual bearing for their approach should have been about 160°. They obviously came from NW instead of NNW!

132 Juul testified in the court of enquiry that they returned to Kufra and, as they had time left, decided not land and flew on. Francois DeWet, a nephew of Major DeWet who is most familiar with the subject informed that he is convinced that this was not the case. Although the real wind direction and wind speed were different to that what they believed to be from the weather prediction of the previous day, the flight was very bumpy and the inexperienced navigators could not apply wind drift. Applying the real wind drift to their planned flight path and the change of direction on course 305° and the reciprocal course of 125° for the flight duration as per the navigation log found in one of the planes, brings them to the exact spot where they landed.

The temporary graves of the crews of T 7610 and Z 2252. The bodies of the airmen were transferred to the Acroma Knightsbridge cemetery in the 1960ies.

The main spar and a few parts of the undercarriage is all what remains of Z 7513.

48° and 50° and the station at Mersa Matruh got one at 203°. When the doubtful information was plotted on the map, it was calculated that the lost planes must be between 96 and 112 kilometres northeast of Kufra and immediately a patrol of the SDF under *Bimbashi* Stubbs was sent to that area. It was not possible to obtain another plane to fly to *Kufra*. The lost men were obviously confident that they would be found soon and no instructions regulating the use of water were given, so they drank too much of the precious fluid. Had it been rationed to 2.5 litres a day, it would have lasted for at least four days.

On 5 May, Major de Wet ordered all remaining fuel pumped into Z7513 and two further attempts were made to find the oasis without success, but on the return flight the plane ran out of fuel and had to land about 40 kilometres north of where it had started. The group was now split into two parties. The ground search party had been on its way since 07:00 and had received a very strong signal, so *Bimbashi* Stubbs was convinced that he would soon find the stranded aircrews. But then they ran into very difficult, rocky country which slowed their driving. The need for an air search was recognised. De Wet and his men shot Véry lights into the sky by but they were not seen that night as a dust storm came up (the same storm which the *Salam* party had encountered the day before on their approach to Gialo).

On May 6 the last available water was distributed among the men. The air support ordered, three Bristol Bombay[133] planes, also had no luck. One of them had engine trouble and remained at *Wadi Halfa*; the other two could not find Kufra due to the dust storm and had to land at "Kendall's Dump" some 70 kilometres east-southeast of the Oasis. They were kept grounded by the sandstorm for two days, posing a further problem for the garrison commander at *Kufra*. But the situation for the stranded crews in the sandstorm had become desperate; Major De Wet wrote in his diary that from 14:00 men started dying. In the meantime, the ground search party was as close as 10 kilometres to the given fix, but could get no further.

The next day, two more parties were sent out from Kufra by truck. One was to find the two force-landed Bombays – it failed to find them and returned to the base two days later. The other was to take supplies to *Bimbashi* Stubbs and to assist in the search for the Blenheims. The sandstorm continued that day and visibility was sometimes less than 30 metres.

On the fifth day since the Blenheims had been lost, the two motorised parties met at the fix where the planes were supposed to be. Although visibility had improved considerably, they found no trace of the lost planes and their crews. It was discovered later that at one time they had been as close as about 3.5 kilometres from the true location – due to the sandstorm and the terrain they had seen or heard nothing. Finally, a Vickers Wellington two-engine bomber was sent to *Kufra* to start a belated search from the air, and it also experienced difficulties with bearings given by the direction finder. After landing, the crew was briefed about the situation and immediately set off for a search of the designated area. It found no trace. While the search was going on, Major DeWet wrote in his diary that beside him, only Shipman and Juul were still alive.

133 Two-engine transport plane

Remnants of Blenheim
Z 7513.

On 9 May, Sqn Ldr Warren took off in his Wellington for another search early in the morning and after a flight of five and a half hours he detected the single Blenheim Z7513. Unfortunately it was too late for its crew. All of them were found dead. Based on a sketch they found with the navigator of the Blenheim, they continued their search for the other two planes, returned to *Kufra* for refuelling and set out again. After another two hours they returned without success.

The next day, the search party on the ground was instructed to drive to the plane which had been located, but could not manage to find it, while the Squadron Leader made another unsuccessful attempt to find the two planes still missing out in the desert. During the day, the two Bombays, another Wellington and a further Blenheim arrived at Kufra to assist the search. Again no sign of the missing men was found that day.

Warren returned to the single Blenheim he had found before and started the search anew. On 11 May and at a distance of only 40 kilometres he detected the two missing planes close to a low ridge. They found only one survivor: Air Mechanic N St Juul. The bodies of the eight other men were found lying around the aircraft. Some were shot (by themselves, as the subsequent Court of Inquiry revealed) and others had died from thirst and exposure to the heat[134].

A Court of Inquiry was held at Kufra on 1 June which after an extensive hearing of witnesses found the principal cause of the accident to be lack of experience in desert flying by pilots and observers. The crew had received their training in South Africa, Rhodesia and northern Kenya and was totally unprepared for desert conditions. Their plight reads like a full checklist of things not to do in a desert emergency – sadly they paid the ultimate price.

134 The locations were re-established during a search expedition by András Zboray and Francois
    DeWet in 2001 and visited again by Kuno Gross and the DeWet family in 2009.

4 May 1942, first reconnaissance flight[135]

While the SAAF Blenheims were preparing for their ill-fated flight some 400 kilometres to the South, in Gialo, much to the surprise of the other members of the group, von Steffens got up from his bed and reported to Almásy that he was fit for duty. He was not really fit, nor was it a good idea to try to show the others how 'tough' he was; he would have done better to stay in hospital and recover from his collapse. In reality he knew that he was not fit but wanted to prove that he was important for the mission and hoped to recover enough to be able to carry on with the others.

However, he was reasonable enough to tell Almásy, who was quite surprised to see him again so soon, that he would not continue the journey in case he was not up to it. He wanted at least not to remain uselessly bedbound, but attend to the final preparations before the planned departure from Gialo the next day. It was already known that the Italian maps for the region were inaccurate since they did not show the immense western dune belt of the Calanscio Sand Sea. This was the information given to them when they met the German *Fallschirmjäger* officer who had occupied the oasis earlier that year. Almásy found it incredulous that the Italians did not draw a dune belt which has an extent of about 280 by 80 kilometres on their maps, particularly as it was easily visible from very far, even from the *palificata*[136]. It seems that not even the pilots of the *Ghibli* planes thought it necessary to correct the maps accordingly.

Almásy left for a reconnaissance flight with the crew of one of the *Ghiblis* to find out whether the dunes were passable by motor vehicles, and what is their true extent. While Almásy was away with the plane, the group prepared for the following day's departure. Von der Marwitz, who had to remain at Gialo and was later known by his codename OTTER, was setting up his W/T set, Eppler and Sandstede together with Wöhrmann were to fill the canisters with fresh water, and von Steffens together with Munz and Beilharz loaded rations on to the vehicles. Körper was busy with the engines of the vehicles and checked them for one last time. Checking the rations, von Steffens noticed that several days' rations of cigarettes and chocolate were missing, as well as normal food rations. When Beilharz and Munz were asked if they knew about it, they confirmed that in Tripoli, Eppler and Sandstede had made free use of the stocks which were intended for the coming mission …

Gialo, the camp next to the *Presidio*. Whilst the Germans were establishing their camp, they became the attraction of the day for the children of the oasis. [Dal McGuirk]

Unlike the LRDG, Operation Salam was equipped with quite considerable comforts: tents and sleeping bags. A Lancia 3Ro truck standing between the camp and the walls of the *Presidio*. [Dal McGuirk]

---

135 Based on von Steffens, *Salaam*

136 (It) *Pista palificata*. Italian desert track marked with iron poles (*pali*) in distances of about 1 kilometre.

Hans von Steffens is inspecting the ration crates. The soldiers do no longer wear a correct and full uniform but are without shirt and walking in sandals.
[Dal McGuirk]

Left: Two members of Operation Salam are refuelling "Präsident". Note the jerrycans with the white cross: They are designated to carry potable water not fuel.
[Dal McGuirk]

Right: A modern view of the camp site under the Tamarisk-tree from the roof of the *Presidio*.
[Dal McGuirk]

Members of Operation Salam at leisure under the Tamarisk-tree. The purpose made sand ladder is stored behind Munz.
[Dal McGuirk]

They had hardly finished loading the equipment, rations and fuel canisters when the truck came back with the filled water canisters, so all vehicles could be readied.

Back from his flight, Almásy was quite happy. The Italian pilot let him fly the plane – Almásy was a passionate flyer – and they even presented him with an Italian pilot badge which made him visibly very proud. However, the result of the flight was less encouraging: the suspected dune belt was of immense size and blocked the planned route of the expedition from Gialo directly to Dakhla oasis in Egypt. To learn how deep the dune belt was, Almásy wanted to fly over it. But the Italians had strict orders not to cross the 22nd degree of longitude and so they returned without that information.

There was no real option to bypass the obstacle to the south, since it would have brought the group too near to the enemy-occupied oases in the south. It was therefore decided to try to cross the dunes, in the hope that they did not extend too far. Almásy had good experience of driving in sand and he saw no other possibility than just to try it. Too much effort had been put into the preparations. It just had to work out. But it was clear that crossing the dunes meant that more fuel would have to be carried and the original time schedule could no longer be kept.

In the evening a message was sent out saying OTTER was now operational and would contact SCHILDKROETE[137] daily at 09:00, 15:00 and 20:30, starting on Tuesday[138]. A further circumstance was discovered which caused serious difficulties with W/T traffic for the rest of the operation: Two powerful Italian transmitters which were located in Gialo seriously disturbed the reception there.[139]

137 SCHILDKROETE was the codename for the W/T station of Aberle and Weber with HQ Pz AA.
138 TNA, London, HW 19/30 ISOS 28337
139 TNA, London, HW 19/30 ISOS 28336

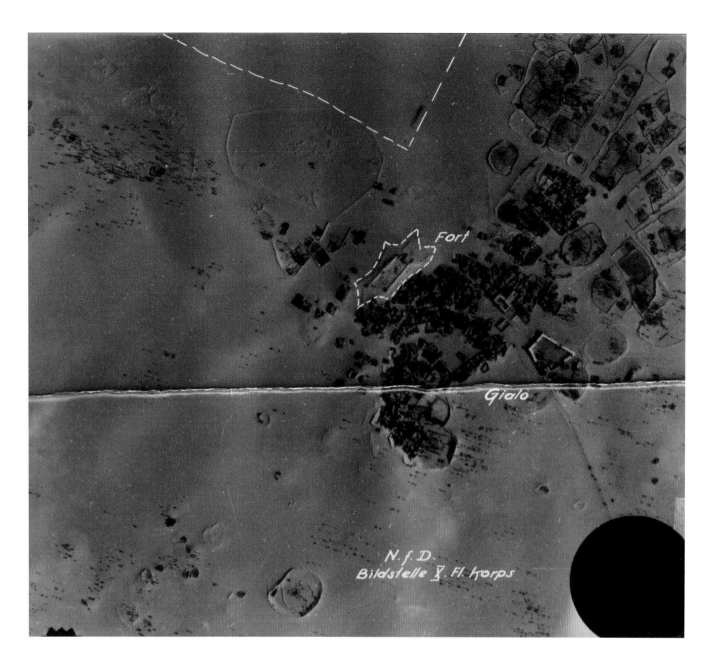

German aerial photograph of Gialo taken in
1942. The white marked area with the description
"Fort" refers to the old fort which was destroyed
in November 1941 when Brigadier Reid's Force E
captured the oasis from the Italians.
[Kuno Gross]

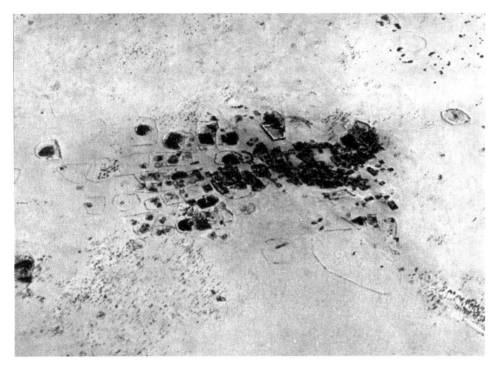

Undated aerial photograph of Gialo. From the air it is visible, how tiny this oasis was amidst the vast expenses of the desert.
[Kuno Gross]

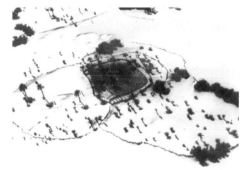

Left: Low altitude aerial view of the populated area of Gialo.
[Kuno Gross]

Right: One of the gardens of Gialo.
[Kuno Gross]

Almásy together with an officer of the *Regia Aeronautica* in the courtyard of the *Presidio* at Gialo. Note the "field made" short trousers and the *Sahariana* 1934 shirt.
[Ottokar Seubert]

View from inside the courtyard of the *Presidio* to the entrance gate.

While the German group was still optimistic, the Commanding Officer of the SDF garrison of Kufra was now seriously worried about the missing Bristol Blenheim bombers of the 15ᵗʰ Detachment of the SAAF. There was hope that they had come down at one of the emergency landing grounds on the air route from *Gialo* to *Kufra* or somewhere in the surrounding oases.

The going over the flat
serir after Gialo was
very good.

5 May 1942, due southeast[140]

No one in the group except Almásy had any experience in driving in dunes, and the
soft sand caused the group trouble from the very beginning. After they had started
in the morning at 08:30[141] and had crossed about 130 kilometres of plain *serir*,
they reached the dunes and tried to enter them. The vehicles were overloaded and
the two-wheel-drive, together with the inexperienced drivers, caused them to get
stuck over and over again. They were fascinated by the sheer size of the sand dunes
but had to recognise that they had met a serious obstacle. Towards evening the men
were completely exhausted from pushing the vehicles and shovelling sand. Water
consumption was much too high and it was already clear that the provisions were
not sufficient for the whole of the planned distance. They had to rest for the night
at the foot of a huge dune, tired and de-motivated. None of them saw any possibility
of carrying on. The dunes were just endless. When one ridge was passed, the next
came in view. And the next … and the next …

The Italians had promised that one of the *Ghibli* planes would come out and drop
water and fuel. But it did not come. Probably it could not find the tracks of the group.
The W/T connection with OTTER or SCHILDKROETE could not be established.
It was frustrating for everyone. Sandstede, who had swapped his ration of cigarettes
for liquor in Tripoli, was happy that he had his strong Italian *Sarti*. He recognised
that von Steffens was still not in good condition and the doctor, Strungmann, did
not give a healthy impression either.

140 Based on Sandstede's unpublished memoirs. This episode is avoided in von Steffens' **Salaam**
     and in Eppler's **Rommel ruft Kairo,** however it is mentioned briefly in the French/English
     version, Operation Kondor..
141 TNA, London, HW 19/30 ISOS 28405

Left: The first dunes, uncharted on the maps, appeared soon on the horizon.

Right: Except Almásy, none of the group had any experience with sand dunes.

Almásy explaining the route to the members of Operation Salam. Note the Askania compass on "Präsident". [Dal McGuirk]

There was no other option for the group, so the next morning they went on in the general direction of east-southeast, deeper into the dunes. Their motivation was already at 'zero' and von Steffens and *Unterarzt* Strungmann distributed *Pervitin*[142] to the men to keep them going. Most of the men were obviously physically unfit for such strain and Almásy realised that he had no choice but to try to keep them moving on. A withdrawal would have brought shame on him and he refused to give up. He thought it would lift the mood of the group to have a good breakfast, so they cooked hot sausages. They dug out the vehicles which had been left as they were the previous evening, and shortly after the start of the day's stage they found an area where they thought they might make better progress towards the east. But this was not the case and soon they were in trouble again. *Unteroffizier* Wöhrmann,

142 One of the earliest uses of methamphetamine was during World War II when the German military dispensed it under the trade name *Pervitin*. It was widely distributed across all ranks and branches, from elite forces to tank crews and aircraft personnel.

considered the strongest of the group, gave up before mid-day. He threw down his shovel and refused to move any further. Almásy tried to get him going again but Wöhrmann was completely stubborn and refused to continue work. Von Steffens and *Unterarzt* Strungmann did not give a much better impression and in the late afternoon they had made not much more than 10 kilometres. As if this was not enough, Almásy's Ford C11ADF "Consul" suffered a damaged rear-axle and had to be taken in tow.

It was clear that under such circumstances the group would never be able to reach their target, nor even to proceed any further. It made no sense to try to go on. With a heavy heart, Almásy gave the order to break off and return to *Gialo*. They camped again at the foot of a dune – it could have been the same one as last night, they all looked the same. An emergency repair was done on Almásy's car during the night and it could drive again the next morning.

The third day they tried to drive back to *Gialo* on the direct route but they could not manage, even though the motivation of the group was fairly high. Von Steffens and *Unterarzt* Strungmann hardly communicated; they seemed to be suffering from *Wüstenkoller*[143]. They did not fully make it out of the sand dunes, although they avoided many of the mistakes they had made when entering the dunes two days before. But when they made camp that evening they had to reckon with the fact that they had already consumed most of their water. It was an uncanny evening. The wind which normally blew all the time had completely ceased. They were just waiting, eating, and drinking more liquor. Then all of a sudden they heard a strange humming. "Listen!" Almásy said, "the dunes are singing. A unique event."

Standard Army leather map case and typical contents including pencils, fountain pen, small ruler, device to measure distances on various scale maps, compass, note pad, map and map holder, and perspex grids to plot map quadrants *(Zielgevierttafel mit Planzeiger).*

[Dal McGuirk]

The overloaded cars of Operation Salam became stuck in the soft sand again and again. The same happens in modern times.

143 Literally translated as "desert rage ".

That evening they were able to send a W/T message to SCHILDKROETE saying that they had found impassable sand dunes south of *Gialo* which were not shown on the Italian maps. Further, Almásy indicated that he intended to do a reconnaissance flight the next day and that he had set up a dump of water.[144]

Further south, the ground search for the lost SAAF Blenheims had been ended for the day and still no sign had been found of the planes.

A little later in the evening von Steffens, who was now really sick, started to cry, while the doctor lay pathetically on the sand. Again Almásy tried to lift their mood but had no better idea than to tell stories about the First World War. He did so until one of the others told him to just shut up. They chain-smoked one cigarette after another and slowly the whole group fell asleep.

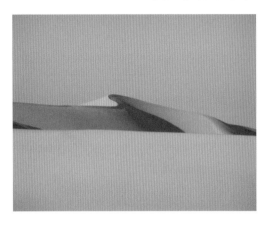

One dune ridge followed the other and the inexperienced drivers had great difficulties to cross them.

8 May 1942, return to Gialo[145]

A nasty surprise awaited the group in the morning: the drinking water which already had a fairly brackish taste when taken at Gialo, was now hardly drinkable. This was unusual for they were sure that the water canisters had been thoroughly cleaned before filling. The taste of the breakfast coffee was awful and everybody feared the moment they would have to drink plain water, only a few hours later. Luckily they were soon out of the dunes and could make good speed again on the firm surface of the *serir* desert. They reached Gialo in the evening.

A reconnaissance flight of two Italian Caproni Ca 311 had only seen seven friendly vehicles 12 kilometres south of Ma'aten Rasceda, near Gialo, in the early morning, but nothing more of interest on a second flight down to *Campo 5* later on[146].

When the vehicles halted, *Unterarzt* Strungmann, who had been motionless in the vehicle the whole day, jumped into the first well he saw with all his clothes and gear. It took the men a considerable effort to get him out again. It appeared he had become quite deranged.

The first casualty of the group, Entholt, had become sick in Tripoli, but now not only his replacement seemed to be lost to the mission, but also von Steffens, who was an important member of the group.

144 TNA, London, HW 19/30 ISOS 28316
145 Based on Sandstede, unpublished memoirs
146 Bundesarchiv Freiburg/Militärarchiv, RH19 VIII – 76; Luftaufklärung 3.5.42

Left: Once a dune was climbed a steep descent followed.

Right: Finally they were out of the dunes and reached Gialo towards the evening.

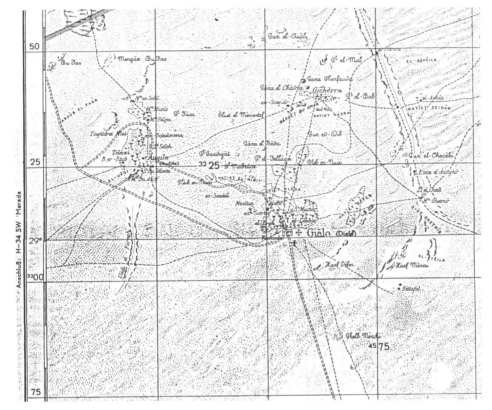

Deutsche Weltkarte 1:500'000, Afrika, 1941. Blatt NH 34 SO Audjila.

The problem of the undrinkable water also had to be solved somehow and soon it was found that it had been taken from the wrong source. There was no good water at *Gialo* at all. Once taken from the well, it remained drinkable for only about three days. This did not disturb the inhabitants of the oasis and the Italian soldiers since they could draw it fresh from the well each day. But no-one who left Gialo for a longer journey would ever have taken this water. It was well known among the natives that good water which remained drinkable for a long time was to be found at Bir Buttafal, some 30 kilometres southeast of Gialo. Almásy had in fact warned his men and instructed them to take it from this slightly remote place. But since he had left for his first flight and nobody really believed that there could be such a difference in the quality of the water, they had just taken it from the next accessible well within the palm gardens of the oasis. It was a mistake which could have had serious consequences for the group.

Since the water from the wells at Gialo could not be kept, the good water had to be obtained from a location out in the desert, called Bir Buttafal. The German flag was hoisted to avoid that the Italians would shoot at the vehicles believing they were the enemy. Note the "bison" insignia on the back of the vehicles.*[Ottokar Seubert]*

Left: Eppler trying to find out the direction to Bir Buttafal from inhabitants of Gialo. Dr. Strungmann standing to the left *[Dal McGuirk]*

Right: Eppler, who was fluent in Arabic, discussing with people from Gialo. *[Dal McGuirk]*

9 May 1942, water from Bir Buttafal and a second reconnaissance flight [147]

While most members of the group badly needed rest the following day, the ever-energetic Almásy left again with a *Ghibli* plane to search for the desperately needed passage through the dune ridges. He was even prepared to find the dunes impassable for his vehicles and had already started to prepare an alternative route[148]. But when he came back, he told his men that he was now confident they could manage it. Together with the day's rest, this message helped to raise the men's spirits again.

Bir Buttafal was not a well as they had imagined it. There was in fact nothing to be seen, apart from a few low tamarisk trees: there was no surface water anywhere.

147 Based on Sandstede, unpublished memoirs
148 TNA, London, HW 19/30 ISOS 28316

Although they doubted there was any water, they took their spades and started to remove the sand, as they had been told by the old man from Gialo who had shown them the place. Soon something nobody thought possible happened: When they had dug out just a shallow hole, the sand was wet, and then they reached water. Beautifully clear water was there less than a metre below the barren surface. They enlarged the hole to a sufficient size so they could easily refill their canisters. Once back at the oasis, they had the water tested by the Italians and it was found to be very good. Their problem was solved.

In the meantime the cars were checked and overhauled and Almásy's "Consul" properly repaired.

It was decided to wait two more days to give the two sick men a chance to recover. They had to drive six vehicles and they were only nine men, not even two per vehicle. To lose two men would mean a serious problem for the whole operation. On 11 May, *Unterarzt* Strungmann felt fit for the journey again but von Steffens started to claim that he still had problems with his heart and the strain was just too great

Left: It just sounds unbeliveable that there should be fresh water out there.
[Dal McGuirk]

Right: The *serir* at Bir Buttafal is absolutely flat and devoid any plants. But fresh water can be found after digging for only about one metre. Eppler watching the two men from Gialo digging.
[Dal McGuirk]

As promised: Fresh water!
[Dal McGuirk]

The water is filled into the various containers. Beside the German Jerrycan, they use British Flimsies and even a wooden barell previously used for Italian red wine.
[Dal McGuirk]

for him. A drastic step had to be taken and a return to Tripoli was arranged for him, since he had not only become useless for the mission but his health was in considerable danger.

While the Salam party was preparing for the next attempt, the air search from Kufra had finally located the three missing South African aircraft with the sole survivor.

In the afternoon of 11 May, Almásy having decided to remain in Gialo for two days for the men to have a rest, Ic informed von Griesheim (WIDO) in Tripoli that following the group returning to Gialo due to the difficulties of the terrain, they intended to start again on 10 May, but he had no confirmation yet of this happening[149]. Obviously von Griesheim did not know the answer since he later asked Almásy (SALAM) if they had started as announced[150].

A Caproni Ca.309 "Ghibli" of the *26ª Squadriglia Aviazione Sahariana*, in pre-war colours.
[Giorgio Apostolo/ Aerofan]

149 TNA, London, HW 19/30 ISOS 28637
150 TNA, London, HW 19/30 ISOS 28512

From Gialo to Assiut

After the first attempt ended in failure in the dunes east of Gialo, the convoy returned to its base to re-supply and start the operation again.

12 May 1942, new start[151]

It had been a long night and Almásy made it clear to his men that this was the last attempt they could make. They would either manage to reach Assiut or have to give up the whole operation.

Left: The second attempt to cross the sand sea. The German column standing in the flat *serir* watching the dune barriers to the east. (Original photo blurred)
[Ottokar Seubert]

Right: The lower dune-ridges of the sand sea. Even these dunes were difficult to cross with the heavy two-wheel-drive vehicles.
[Ottokar Seubert]

When they started in the morning, the vehicles were packed again. The luggage and the equipment were reduced to the essential minimum. Each man had just one set of clothes; only the two spies had their civilian clothes stowed in a metal case. This was so as to carry as much fuel and water as possible. Even weapons were reduced to what they thought was indispensible for their self-defence in an emergency. Almásy explained that if they were detected on the approach, secrecy would be lost, and a fire fight would make no sense; if they ran into an ambush on the return journey, they would hardly be in the position to win the battle. Rations consisted mainly of tinned food, chocolate, cheese and the Italian tinned meat, the so called "*asino morto*" ("dead donkey") after the two letters "A.M." for "*Amministrazione Militare*" (Military Administration) stamped on the tin. In addition to a sack of onions and another filled with lemons, Sandstede managed to 'smuggle' two bottles of liquor.

151 Roughly based on Sandstede's unpublished memoirs and Eppler's publications

The small convoy of six vehicles followed the easily visible tracks of the "Motor- and Air-Route" for 65 kilometres over flat *serir*. Speed was good and soon they reached the Landing Ground No.1, where they turned due east until they reached the edge of the dunes again. But this time they followed them south for another hundred kilometres. Almásy did not want to risk anything and only crossed the first dune ridge at a clear gap where he thought that he could easily enter the difficult zone. Then they drove north again, searching for further easy passages for their heavy vehicles. After 46 kilometres it was found that the 'going' was getting more and more difficult and they had to take one of the possible routes further south. Again they turned and followed their own tracks back for about 10 kilometres, where they thought they might be able to cross the dunes. But the two-wheel-drive vehicles were just too heavy with their full load and the experience of the drivers was still not adequate. They were zigzagging into the immense dune-field and after driving for 25 kilometres, they had penetrated hardly 10 kilometres. Then they stood before an immense dune. It was maybe 40 metres high and obviously there was no possibility of bypassing it. Almásy knew the capabilities of his men and did not want to subject them to additional stress for the moment. It was decided to make an early camp for the night at the foot of the dune. The mood was still good and the following morning they would see how they could get on.

The dune ridges of the Great Sand Sea. With today's vehicles and if not with a heavy load, they are not a major obstacle. For Operation Salam with its two wheel-drive cars and the unexperienced drivers they were almost impossible to cross.

The leading vehicle became stuck in a soft patch of sand and had to be taken out by using the sand-ladders. Von Steffens at the left, Almásy behind the car and Körper holding the end of the sandladder.*[Ottokar Seubert]*

After hitting a patch of very soft sand between two dune ridges this light vehicle got seriously stuck despite being equipped with big low-pressure sand-tires. Extensive use of shovel and sand-channels were needed to free the car.

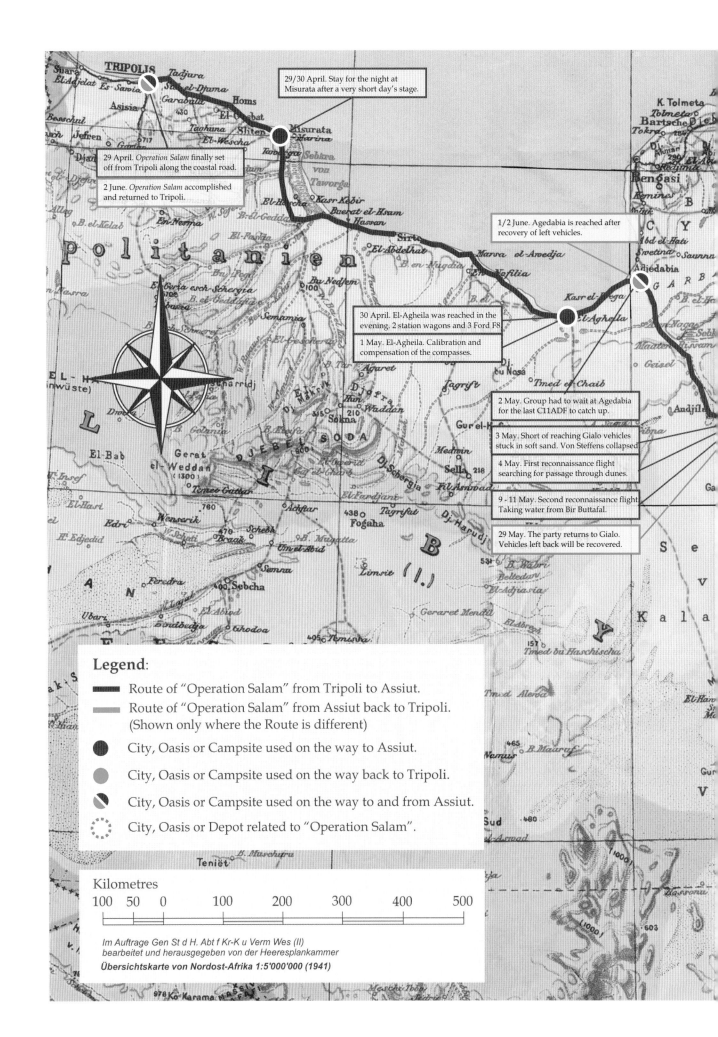

29/30 April. Stay for the night at Misurata after a very short day's stage.

29 April. *Operation Salam* finally set off from Tripoli along the coastal road.

2 June. *Operation Salam* accomplished and returned to Tripoli.

1/2 June. Agedabia is reached after recovery of left vehicles.

30 April. El-Agheila was reached in the evening. 2 station wagons and 3 Ford F8

1 May. El-Agheila. Calibration and compensation of the compasses.

2 May. Group had to wait at Agedabia for the last C11ADF to catch up.

3 May. Short of reaching Gialo vehicles stuck in soft sand. Von Steffens collapsed

4 May. First reconnaissance flight searching for passage through dunes.

9 - 11 May. Second reconnaissance flight Taking water from Bir Buttafal.

29 May. The party returns to Gialo. Vehicles left back will be recovered.

Legend:

━━━ Route of "Operation Salam" from Tripoli to Assiut.

━━━ Route of "Operation Salam" from Assiut back to Tripoli. (Shown only where the Route is different)

⬤ City, Oasis or Campsite used on the way to Assiut.

⬤ City, Oasis or Campsite used on the way back to Tripoli.

◓ City, Oasis or Campsite used on the way to and from Assiut.

◌ City, Oasis or Depot related to "Operation Salam".

Kilometres

100 50 0   100   200   300   400   500

Im Auftrage Gen St d H. Abt f Kr-K u Verm Wes (II)
bearbeitet und herausgegeben von der Heeresplankammer
Übersichtskarte von Nordost-Afrika 1:5'000'000 (1941)

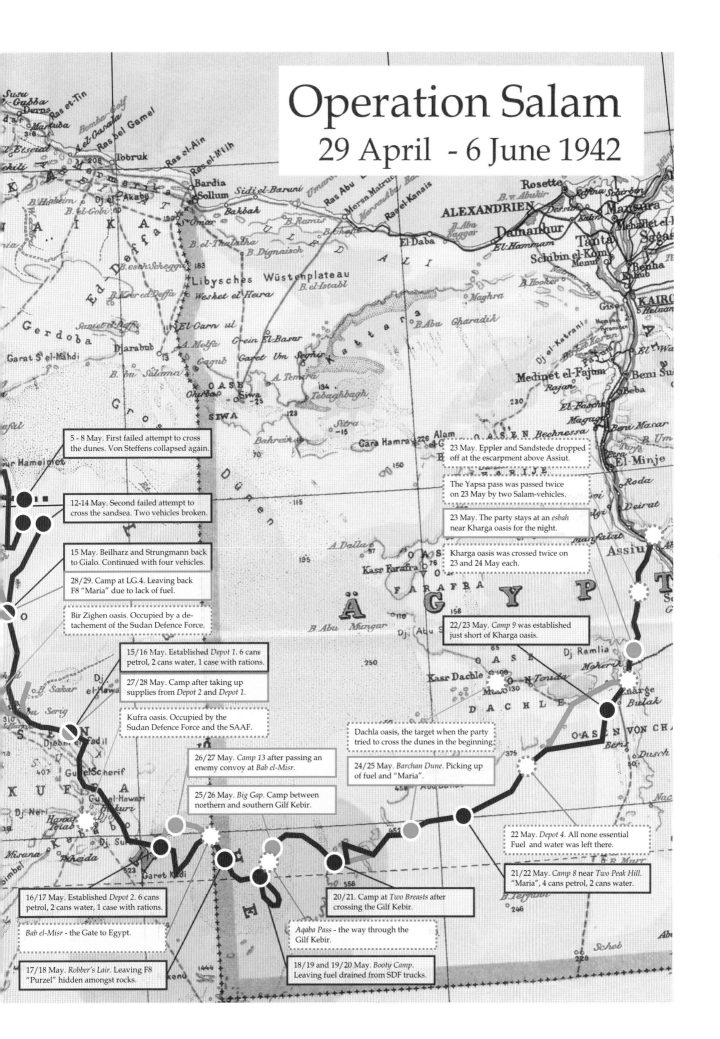

Operation Salam
29 April - 6 June 1942

5 - 8 May. First failed attempt to cross the dunes. Von Steffens collapsed again.

12-14 May. Second failed attempt to cross the sandsea. Two vehicles broken.

15 May. Beilharz and Strungmann back to Gialo. Continued with four vehicles.

28/29. Camp at LG.4. Leaving back F8 "Maria" due to lack of fuel.

Bir Zighen oasis. Occupied by a detachement of the Sudan Defence Force.

15/16 May. Established *Depot 1*. 6 cans petrol, 2 cans water, 1 case with rations.

27/28 May. Camp after taking up supplies from *Depot 2* and *Depot 1*.

Kufra oasis. Occupied by the Sudan Defence Force and the SAAF.

26/27 May. *Camp 13* after passing an enemy convoy at *Bab el-Misr*.

25/26 May. *Big Gap*. Camp between northern and southern Gilf Kebir.

16/17 May. Established *Depot 2*. 6 cans petrol, 2 cans water, 1 case with rations.

Bab el-Misr - the Gate to Egypt.

17/18 May. *Robber's Lair*. Leaving F8 "Purzel" hidden amongst rocks.

Aqaba Pass - the way through the Gilf Kebir.

18/19 and 19/20 May. *Booty Camp*. Leaving fuel drained from SDF trucks.

20/21. Camp at *Two Breasts* after crossing the Gilf Kebir.

24/25 May. *Barchan Dune*. Picking up of fuel and "Maria".

Dachla oasis, the target when the party tried to cross the dunes in the beginning.

22 May. *Depot 4*. All none essential Fuel and water was left there.

21/22 May. *Camp 8* near *Two Peak Hill*. "Maria", 4 cans petrol, 2 cans water.

22/23 May. *Camp 9* was established just short of Kharga oasis.

Kharga oasis was crossed twice on 23 and 24 May each.

23 May. The party stays at an *esbah* near Kharga oasis for the night.

The Yapsa pass was passed twice on 23 May by two Salam-vehicles.

23 May. Eppler and Sandstede dropped off at the escarpment above Assiut.

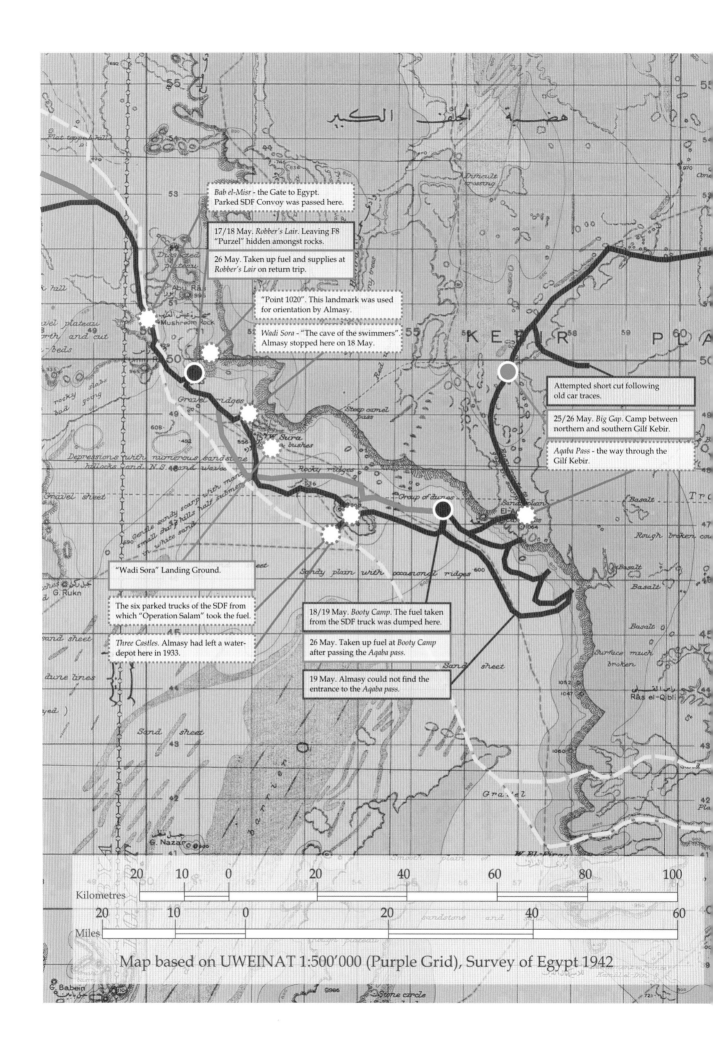

Bab el-Misr - the Gate to Egypt.
Parked SDF Convoy was passed here.

17/18 May. *Robber's Lair*. Leaving F8
"Purzel" hidden amongst rocks.

26 May. Taken up fuel and supplies at
Robber's Lair on return trip.

"Point 1020". This landmark was used
for orientation by Almasy.

Wadi Sora - "The cave of the swimmers".
Almasy stopped here on 18 May.

Attempted short cut following
old car traces.

25/26 May. *Big Gap*. Camp between
northern and southern Gilf Kebir.

Aqaba Pass - the way through the
Gilf Kebir.

"Wadi Sora" Landing Ground.

The six parked trucks of the SDF from
which "Operation Salam" took the fuel.

Three Castles. Almasy had left a water-
depot here in 1933.

18/19 May. *Booty Camp*. The fuel taken
from the SDF truck was dumped here.

26 May. Taken up fuel at *Booty Camp*
after passing the *Aqaba pass*.

19 May. Almasy could not find the
entrance to the *Aqaba pass*.

20   10   0   20   40   60   80   100

Kilometres

20   10   0   20   40   60

Miles

Map based on UWEINAT 1:500'000 (Purple Grid), Survey of Egypt 1942

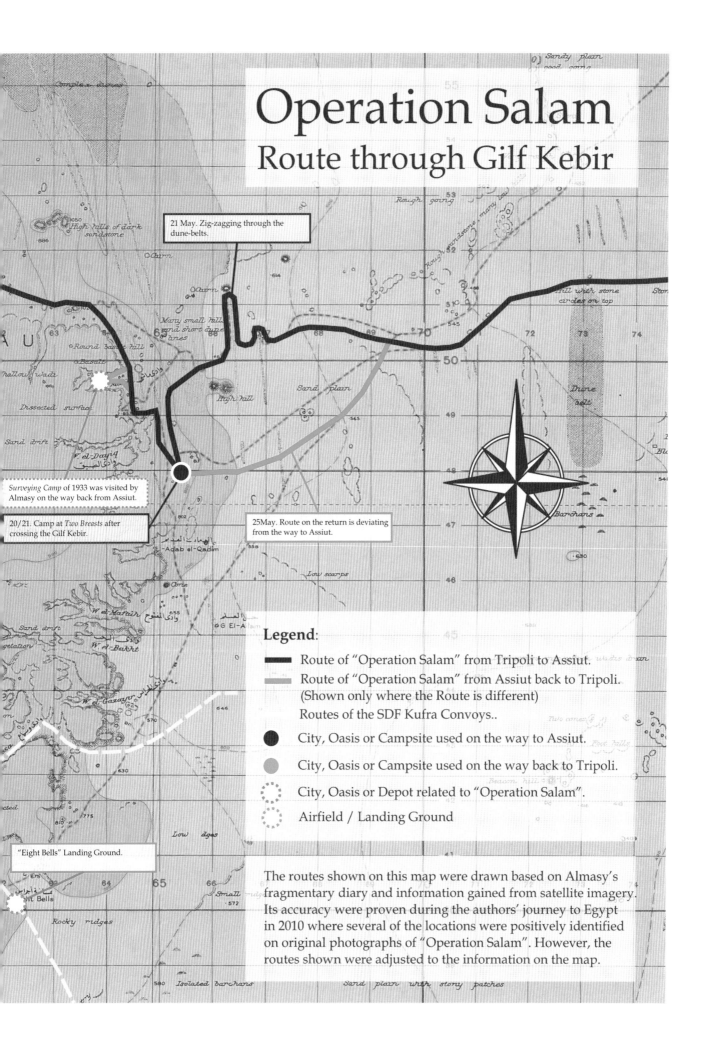

Operation Salam
Route through Gilf Kebir

21 May. Zig-zagging through the dune-belts.

Surveying Camp of 1933 was visited by Almasy on the way back from Assiut.

20/21. Camp at *Two Breasts* after crossing the Gilf Kebir.

25May. Route on the return is deviating from the way to Assiut.

"Eight Bells" Landing Ground.

Legend:

— Route of "Operation Salam" from Tripoli to Assiut.
— Route of "Operation Salam" from Assiut back to Tripoli. (Shown only where the Route is different)
  Routes of the SDF Kufra Convoys..
● City, Oasis or Campsite used on the way to Assiut.
● City, Oasis or Campsite used on the way back to Tripoli.
City, Oasis or Depot related to "Operation Salam".
Airfield / Landing Ground

The routes shown on this map were drawn based on Almasy's fragmentary diary and information gained from satellite imagery. Its accuracy were proven during the authors' journey to Egypt in 2010 where several of the locations were positively identified on original photographs of "Operation Salam". However, the routes shown were adjusted to the information on the map.

Map overview

The route of Operation Salam as it is shown in this map was reconstructed based on Almásy's diary, information taken from intercepted W/T messages, the statements of the captured spies and Hans von Steffens but using also the local experience of Kuno Gross, Rudolph Kuper and András Zboray as well as information provided by contemporary maps. Without doubt, Almásy himself could only have provided the best map, but he never drew it, or it has since been lost.

13 May 1942, impassable dunes, crisis and a decision[152]

An early start in the cool air of the morning brought better conditions to drive in the sand. Two vehicles were sent away, one to the north and one to the south to search for a good passage. They returned without success. It seemed that they were in a trap; there was no way to make an easy crossing. With no other option, they had to cross the huge dune with all their vehicles if they wanted to proceed. Almásy saw no other possibility than to try by brute force and he drove at it with speed in the hope of crossing the soft area and climbing the slope. But he got stuck. They had to do much digging and use their sandladders, but managed to cross the first ridge. Then the other cars, one after the other; everybody had to help to push dig and push again. They no longer knew how many times they had dug out their vehicles; the steering of one of the F8 trucks seemed to have suffered damage when the truck jumped a very small but steep dune, only about a metre high. But then bad luck struck again and Almásy's Ford was damaged. The gearbox of "Consul" was fractured, the vehicle was no longer driveable. Everybody in the group was so completely exhausted that they did not even consider their situation, only lay down in the sand. A plane passed by in the distance. It could not be recognised as Italian or enemy, and they were just too tired to care. The day was gone, hardly any progress had been made and two of the six vehicles were damaged. Luck was not with them and Almásy saw his dream dwindling.

It was clear that the operation was in the most serious crisis since the start. Körper, the mechanic of the group, was desperately trying to fix the damage to the gearbox of the lead car, while Almásy was walking up and down, smoking one cigarette after another. The rest of the group could not do much and just sat around in deep frustration.

When Körper reported to Almásy that there was no possibility of repairing "Consul" the operation seemed to be at an end. But not for the Hungarian desert explorer. Too many times he had been in difficult situations in the desert and very often he could not count on any external assistance. He could simply not accept going back and reporting to his German superiors that he had failed. This was his operation and he knew only too well that he could not beat the desert with this weak group. It was the moment to take a drastic decision. The mechanic was told to fix the steering of the Ford F8 as well as possible, to have the truck driveable again the following day. Two men were instructed to prepare a good meal, Sandstede was instructed to put his W/T set in service and the others were ordered to remove all equipment

152 Based on Sandstede, unpublished memoirs

"Präsident" receiving some repairs during the attempt to cross the dunes. Körper under the vehicle and Munz assissting him. [Dal McGuirk]

and supplies out of "Consul" and distribute them among the other vehicles. Almásy's vehicle had to be abandoned in the sand sea. When Sandstede had his W/T set operational, Almásy had already made his decision. The message he had written on a piece of paper and given to Sandstede to send to the *Panzerarmee* was simple but clear: "Almásy to Ic: Dune region east of track impassable. One car fallen out on account of damage to gears. Am reorganising the undertaking via Zighen and Kufra to the Gilf Kebir Kharga route known to me."

Sandstede was ordered to keep quiet about the message and not to tell the group. While the men were still busy, Almásy only told them that the next day they had to get out of the dunes; then he walked away. In the evening, the message was sent to inform the Ic of the circumstances and that the whole route had to be reorganised[153]. To avoid a confrontation with the enemy on the new route, the Italian command at Gialo was asked to send a *Ghibli* for aerial reconnaissance to the area of Bir Zighen[154]. A second message was sent to OTTER informing him of the damage to one car in the dunes and that they intended to reach *Campo 3*[155] the next day and then to send back two vehicles to Gialo[156]. Another message from OTTER to SALAM said that the German Consul (SEPP) had left Gialo for Tripoli by air, and working with the W/T set was nearly impossible in the evening due to the interference of the Italian transmitters. Von der Marwitz wanted to search for a better location the following day[157].

153 TNA, London, HW 19/30 ISOS 28341
154 TNA, London, HW 19/30 ISOS 28497
155 In fact they did not leave the dunes near *Campo 3* the following day, but came out at *Campo 4*
156 TNA, London, HW 19/30 ISOS 28342
157 TNA, London, HW 19/30 ISOS 28552

While the Salam group was struggling in the dunes, a ground party was assembled in Kufra with the grim task of burying the dead, and recovering the force-landed aircraft. This party probably involved most of the vehicles and men available at Kufra, leaving the Oasis at 09:00 in the morning.[158]

The C11ADF "Inspektor" was equipped with a W/T set. Two members of Operation Salam trying to send a message to the base at Gialo.
[Ottokar Seubert]

14 May 1942, out of the dunes

None of the men had asked much the previous night and most of them were convinced that they would give up and return to Gialo, once they had left the dunes and gone to sleep. Nobody had really recovered from the hard work of the previous day when they got up and started to get out of the sand. The problems were the same, but since the same load now had to be carried by five instead of six trucks, the vehicles were even heavier. At least they did not have to spend time searching for passages since they could more or less follow their own tracks. It was difficult enough, and when they approached the flat *serir* west of the dunes the sun was already low. They took a rest and it was time to inform the group of the new route. While most of the men simply had no idea what it meant to drive via the Gilf Kebir, they were just happy to learn that they would drive around the sand dunes. Only *Unterarzt* Strungmann insisted angrily that they return to Gialo and give up the operation. He knew that Kufra was occupied by the enemy and assumed they would be caught. However in the mean time the rest of the group had accepted Almásy as the leader of the operation and experienced his skills in the desert. They were convinced when he promised them that he would plot the route with care that

158 TNA, London, WO 169/7288, Sudan Defence Force, Kufra Garrison War Diaries, 1941 July – 1942 August. There is no record, but it is quite conceivable that in the days following the loss of the aircraft, all available resources including the vehicles available at the *Bir Zighen* post were diverted to the ground search, leaving a perfect opportunity for Almásy and companions to pass unnoticed.

night, since he knew the area fairly well from his pre-war travels. To make some more distance in the day, and to get farther away from Gialo, he ordered the drivers to follow him to Landing Ground No. 4, another 125 kilometres to the south.

W/T communications were not satisfactory at all. SALAM was only able to call OTTER and OTTER would call WIDO and SCHILDKROETE. But since the Italian transmitters at the same location seriously disturbed OTTER's position, the flow of information was far from satisfactory. It is not clear why SALAM was not given an alternate station to call, should they be unable to contact OTTER. BERLIN complained that they were left wholly uninformed about the goings-on in the desert[159].

159 TNA, London, HW 19/30 ISOS 28194

15 May 1942, a new route

The night was spent at the emergency landing ground named *Campo 4*[160] on the motor- and air route from Gialo to Kufra (Position Km 275 from Gialo on the *palificata*). The situation for the whole operation was critical and Almásy had to work all night to figure out the new route avoiding the impassable dunes of the Calanscio Sand Sea.

That night everything was re-calculated and the whole trip reorganised. He decided they must go via Kufra. This meant a detour of 500 kilometres for both the outward and return journeys; an increase of 1'000 kilometres. Instead of the 2'000 kilometres originally reckoned for the journey in Tripoli, it was now about 3'000 kilometres[161] with no way of getting supplies of water and fuel!

The endless dunes of the Calanscio Sand Sea in the light of the early morning.

At first it seemed impossible for the vehicles to carry sufficient supplies to keep going. However the task had to be carried out, Almásy had invested his whole self in the operation and insisted he was capable of getting the two spies to Egypt through the desert by car. If he was to give up now, he would lose his reputation. To improve the fuel situation, he decided to drive with only two station wagons, "Inspektor" and "Präsident", and the two commercial trucks, "Maria" and "Purzel". The latter two would have to be sacrificed, since there would not be enough fuel to reach the Nile valley with all the vehicles. "Purzel" would travel 800 kilometres, "Maria" a

---

160 In the 1930s the Italians had prepared eight emergency landing grounds along the marked road from Gialo to Kufra.
161 Almásy in his diary writes 4'000 kilometres for the total distance. However, measuring the actual distances on the map, this is clearly in error.

A camp in the flat *serir*. Dr. Strungmann on the left. Note that Operation Salam even carried beds with them. The bed inside "Präsident" might be the one of Almásy. *[Dal McGuirk]*

further 500. The last 200 kilometres to the Nile valley would have to be driven with only one vehicle, there and back; that is 400 kilometres, a considerable risk. What was more, the number of the party had to be reduced again. Only five would accompany Almásy: Munz, Körper, Wöhrmann as signaler, Eppler and Sandstede. Only for those few would supplies and water be adequate.

Almásy decided to send Beilharz and *Unterarzt* Strungmann back to Gialo with only one vehicle, "Habuba". Beilharz had problems with his stomach and Strungmann still suffered from his *Wüstenkoller* from the first dune attempt. Furthermore the F8 "Habuba" had a damaged gearbox and so was no longer reliable. To continue with a damaged vehicle and two crew members with health problems would not only have reduced the quantity of water available for each person but would have led to certain disaster for the whole operation. Almásy signalled to OTTER that if the vehicle did not arrive by the next evening, an Italian aircraft should come the next day to their assistance from Gialo along the *palificata*. A further request was made for all known information about the enemy in the Kufra area[162].

Beilharz was ordered to take fuel and water and establish a dump at *Campo 4* to supply the group on the last stage of the return journey[163]. If the worst came to the worst Almásy thought he would still be able to signal the air operations command

---

162 TNA, London, HW 19/30 ISOS 28343
163 In the diary Almásy states Campo 5 as being that depot, but this is in contradiction with the entry of 28 May where he wrote that the dump should have been made at *Campo 4*. In the same place he wrote that any pursuing enemy patrol would probably not dare to follow them beyond *Campo 5*, clearly *Campo 4* was the site of the intended dump and the entry of the 15th was in error. Furthermore Almásy would hardly have ordered Beilharz to drive farther than *Campo 4*, since this was the last place he knew. It is possible that in the stress of the moment Almásy mistakenly thought the place they were was Campo 5 as the incorrect name appears a day later in their pre-departure radio message.

One member of the group even placed his bed inside the car. Dr. Strungmann sorting out his things and another member of the group preparing breakfast in the back of one of the F8.
[Dal McGuirk]

Preparing breakfast in the back of a Ford F8.
[Dal McGuirk]

to let them have some petrol dropped at the foot of the Gilf Kebir, somewhere around the "Three Castles"[164].

Eppler and Sandstede were not overjoyed at the thought of driving through the Kufra oases[165]. They feared, not unreasonably, an encounter with the enemy. According to aerial reconnaissance, the northernmost British post was supposed to be near *Bir bu Zerreigh* (Km 425 of the *palificata*). The idea was to turn southwards before then to avoid being sighted by the enemy. At any rate, between kilometre 400 and 425 the *palificata* runs on a bearing of 210 degrees, parallel to the dunes.

Almásy had been calculating the new route throughout the night. He slept for only two hours. The food had to be redistributed and vehicle loads changed around again since only four of the original six vehicles remained available for the operation. Departure for the new approach was finally at 08:30. A little earlier, at 07:00 Beilharz and *Unterarzt* Strungmann started out northwards with the damaged F8 truck[166].

Driving on the flat *serir* was easy and as far as kilometre 410 on the *palificata* no traces of the enemy were seen, even the dunes in the south looked somewhat more open than they had expected from the experience of the previous days. They drove on a course of 180 degrees for the next 10 kilometres, then 118 and in between the dunes on a bearing of 75 degrees. After going about 25 kilometres, they suddenly crossed the 4 or 5 day old tracks of three enemy vehicles coming from Bir Bu Zerrigh to Bir Dakkar and back. They continued southeast, out of the dunes. Soon they were out of the danger zone of the enemy post. They purposely drove through it during the early afternoon when they thought that the soldiers manning the post would be asleep. At 15:00 Sandstede became hopelessly stuck in the soft sand. The men had to work for two hours until "Maria" was free again. About 18:00 they reached the *Jebel Gardaba* north of the *Hawaish Hills*[167].

Scarcely were they on firm ground than they had a stroke of luck. Almásy found the traces of the old *Trucchi*[168] track dating back to the years 1932–1935. At that time the *palificata* did not yet exist and the heavy diesel trucks made their way through the hills with their double tyres. It was easy to follow the track. They camped on it

---

164 Conspicuous formation of three hills along the western edge of the Gilf Kebir.

165 While in present day use the term "Kufra Oasis" is restricted to the main oasis centered on the village of El Giof, in the thirties and forties the term included all the outlying minor oases of Tazerbo, Zighen, Buseima and Rebiana.

166 TNA, London, HW 19/30 ISOS 28640. In the message *Campo 5* is mentioned incorrectly as the starting point.

167 In the transcript of Almásy "4 o'clock" is mentioned as the time they reached the hills. Since this is in contradiction with the two hours they were digging from "3 o'clock", the time when they reached the hills was changed to more realistic 18:00 here.

168 *Trucchi* was a private transport company employed by the Italian government to supply the oasis of Kufra.

at the foot of a *gara*[169] at 19:00, having completed 210 kilometres that day. Almásy arranged a petrol cache for the return journey to be carried up the hill and hidden between the crags: 4 cans of petrol, 2 cans of water; "Dump I".

In the mean time Beilharz and Strungmann had arrived safely back at Gialo, as attested by a message signed by Beilharz and sent at 16:13 GMT to the German consulate in Tripoli for Entholt or von Steffens. This requested spare parts for the damaged truck, gears and a battery, to be sent immediately by plane to Gialo[170]. Later in the same evening the news about the new route was forwarded to von Griesheim in Tripoli by von der Marwitz together with the notice that Almásy might not transmit any messages for three days before and after reaching the destination should the situation become critical[171].

The same morning two of the force-landed SAAF Blenheims were flown back to base, while the third which had had its engines over-boosted (Z.7513, the aircraft that landed away from the other two) was abandoned.[172] Presumably the ground parties returned to Kufra in the afternoon. This was a remarkable spell of luck for the *Salam* party. Up till now the diversion helped them pass unnoticed, but their intended bypass of Kufra the following day was taking them almost exactly on course for the forced landing site of the Blenheims …

16 May 1942, bypassing Kufra

The camp on *Trucchi* Track where they had spent the night was noted as "Dump I". On this day they had to bypass the enemy occupied oasis of Kufra on its eastern edge, and to avoid having to camp for the night near the oasis an early start was due.

Entering hilly country. Two vehicles of Operation Salam in front of the big hill. *[Ottokar Seubert]*

Departure was at 06:00. Clearly with the smaller group Almásy had more success in organising a timely morning departure, the greatest challenge on all desert ventures. The old track was easy to follow, but the terrain was difficult and rocky. They tried, after covering 60 kilometres, to change course to a bearing of 142 degrees,

169 Rocky hill rising from an otherwise flat desert.
170 TNA, London, HW 19/30 ISOS 28345
171 TNA, London, HW 19/30 ISOS 28513
172 TNA, London, WO 169/7288, Sudan Defence Force, Kufra Garrison War Diaries, 1941 July-
    1942 Aug

The landscape North and East of Kufra is a fascinating mixture of –sometimes- soft sand and rocky hills.

but were forced to keep to the original track, as everywhere else was impassable rocky ground. After driving another 40 kilometres on the track[173], Almásy noted: "May Allah bless *Trucchi*, for this real 'smugglers road' around the danger zone". The track emerged from the hills and crossed some dunes which lay ahead. In these sandy areas the old traces were of course invisible. Crossing the dunes was extremely difficult for the heavily laden vehicles and their inexperienced drivers: both Commercials became stuck. At last they were south of the dunes at about 80 kilometres north of Kufra. There was a thick *shabura* so any enemy aerial reconnaissance would have been useless (of course, unknown to Almásy, the enemy at that moment had no such capability). Almásy left the track on a bearing of 125 degrees through the more open area of *garas* which was good for driving. Suddenly he recognised that they had crossed the old track to Tedian el-Khadem, the most easterly branch

173 The copy of the IWM version of the diary is a photostat. The original must have been typed on thin duplicate-typing paper. This particular page was wrinkled, obscuring a few letters and most of the kilometre value in question. However enough of the lower parts of the digits are visible that 4 is certain, it is read as 40, as Almásy used round kilometres elsewhere in the diary, probably approximating the travelled distance, but it could equally be 43, 46 or 48 (the rounded top and bottom of the second digit is visible, but not the middle).

of the vegetation zone of Kufra. Now and again fairly old enemy tracks were seen. It was obvious that they patrolled to the north east and east but it seemed they had not found the "Trucchi Track".[174] East of Ain el-Gedid they cut across the track of the patrol undertaken by the Italian *Maggiore* Rolle[175] dating back to March 1934 when he returned to Kufra from a surveying trip to the edge of the Gilf Kebir, linking the Italian and the Egyptian triangulation systems[176]. Almásy even recognised beyond doubt Rolle's *alamat* since it was his custom to stick palm leaves into the stone pyramids.

In the afternoon the group came out of the *gara* region into open *serir* with isolated high hills.

A big surprise: due east of el-Giof, the main village of the Kufra oasis, they found 104 fresh truck tracks! Almásy had no idea that enemy columns were running from the East towards Kufra, coming from the direction of the Gilf Kebir. They altered course and followed the enemy tracks eastwards. There was soft sand with difficult going and the enemy trucks had often got stuck. Finally Almásy was able to ascertain from reading the tracks that half of the big column had driven to Kufra, and the other half from Kufra. The returning tracks were without doubt this morning's, the first ones about two days old.

Close to the evening Sandstede became stuck again. When they freed the vehicle, Almásy left the track of the enemy convoy and turned south to a big double *gara*. Before they reached it they cut across several hundred fairly old tracks parallel to the ones they just had left.

Because of the sharp rocks that can easily damage a tyre, fast driving is not recommended in this area.

Further east of Kufra, towards the border of Egypt, the going gets better again.

Camp was made in the saddle between the two hills at 18:30. The distance covered in the day was 250 kilometres. Upon the *gara* they deposited "Dump II": 6 cans of petrol, 1 can of water, 1 case of rations. Almásy tried to report the finding of enemy lines of communication but Wöhrmann could not hear either OTTER or SCHILD-KROETE. In the evening, OTTER relayed a message to TRIPOLI which by the wording was clearly intended for Almásy, in the hope that von Griesheim might make contact. The message was in response to Almásy's last received message sent on the morning of the 15th, informing him that the truck with Beilharz and Strungmann had arrived safely at Gialo, and no information could be obtained on the Zighen area.[177].

---

174 In fact probably the tracks they saw were those of the ground search parties that in sandstorm conditions become rapidly obliterated.

175 *Maggiore* Ottavio Rolle was the Italian commander of the Kufra Garrison from 1931 to 1934; he did a surveying trip to the Gilf Kebir from Kufra, almost exactly following a west-east axis. He was the one who welcomed Almásy to Kufra in 1932.

176 To determine the borderline between Egypt and Libya.

177 TNA, London, HW 19/30 ISOS 28497

Left: Camels are driven back from the pasture to the village of el-Giof.
[G.J. Mostert via András Zboray]

Right: Whilst the camels were the most important means of transport in the desert for many centuries they had been replaced by trucks during WWII.
[G.J. Mostert via András Zboray]

Left: The ongoing fight between the vegetation of an oasis and the rolling sand of the wind driven dunes
[G.J. Mostert via András Zboray]

Right: The precious water to irrigate the gardens and tiny fields had to be drawn in a burdensome way.
[G.J. Mostert via András Zboray]

The Kufra oases

"The Kufra oases are generally understood as the whole group of oases in the south-west of Libya which stretches for 600 kilometres and covers Tazerbo in the north-west, Bir-Zighen, Buzema, Rebiana and the actual oasis of Kufra until Djebel Archenu and Djebel Auenat in the southeast. There is no natural connection between these oases. The oasis of Tazerbo consists of an oblong basin covering an area of about 165 square kilometres and lies about 30 metres below the surrounding desert. The basin of Bir Zighen is uninhabited but has particular importance since the groundwater level is very high and can be reached after only a little digging. The oasis consists of six main watering places, of which Bir el-Harasc is the most important. The vegetation is very sparse and only small groups of palm-trees can be found. The oasis of Bzema is located 50 kilometres south of Bir Zighen, halfway between Tazerbo and Kufra. A crescent-shaped basin is located west of the Djebel Bzema and contains a salt lake. Sumptuous palm-trees grow here and a small village of stone houses is populated by about 80 inhabitants. Rebiana is the oasis 73 kilometres south of Bzema and 130 kilometres west of Kufra and consists of several small settlements with about 365 inhabitants.

The actual oasis of Kufra consists of three individual basins, el-Hauari in the north, el-Giof in the middle and el-Tallab in the south. The surface of the surrounding desert plateau is about 450m above sea level. Its edges are very much eroded and it falls in several steps down to the basins. The connection from one basin to the other is mostly low and wide, in particular the middle and the southern basin blend into each other to form a long basin, about 20 kilometres wide and 50 kilometres long. It is called the Wadi el-Cafra. The groundwater reaches the surface at several locations and creates small salt lakes. Normally the groundwater can be found at about 4 to 5 metres below the surface.

Left: The salt-water
lake north of Kufra
that was often visited
by the members of the
LRDG and the 15 Sqn
SAAF. It has nearly
disappeared today.
*[G.J. Mostert via
András Zboray]*

Right: Members of 15
Sqn SAAF spending
their free time at the
lake of Kufra.
*[G.J. Mostert via
András Zboray]*

Left: The appearance
of the houses at el-
Giof give an impres-
sion of the arduous
living conditions in
the Kufra oases.
*[G.J. Mostert via
András Zboray]*

Right: The market at
el-Giof where the local
population was selling
the produce of the
oases.
*[G.J. Mostert via
András Zboray]*

*The oasis of Kufra is comparatively densly populated. The census of 1937 re-
corded 4,700 inhabitants in six major settlements: el-Giof, et-Tag, Buma, Buema,
ez-Zurgh, et-Tleilib, and et-Tallab. Palm plantations and gardens surround these
settlements, except et-Tag. In addition to about 100'000 date-palms, about a
hundred oil-trees are found. In the gardens fruit is grown (apples, peaches, apricots,
oranges, lemons, figs) and grain is planted (wheat, millet, barley) and also vegetables
lilke tomato, egg-plant, onions, melons and cucumber are found. Each garden is
surrounded by a wall and has its own well.*

*The main settlements of Kufra are the villages of el-Giof, the commercial centre
with about 2,'500 inhabitants, a market, Italian-Arab school and a hospital, and
et-Tag which is located on top of the sandstone plateau. It was the former main
location of the Senussi with its mosque and other sacred buildings, administrative
installations and living quarters.*"[178]

After the Italian conquest of Kufra in January 1931, et-Tag underwent a major
restructuring. The Senussi installations were demolished and replaced by the new
Italian fort and W/T installation. A landing ground was constructed at Buma between el-Giof and et-Tag. On 28 February 1941, about ten years after the Italians
took Kufra and after a short siege, the garrison had to surrender to the Free French
"Column Leclerc". Since the Free French did not have the means to maintain
Kufra from their remote posts in Chad territory, the Long Range Desert Group
had to take over garrison duty in April 1941. Major Bagnold, the commanding
officer of the LRDG even had to take over the civil administration of the oases.
The new supply route was now from Wadi Halfa through the desert and the first
of the so-called "Kufra Convoys" arrived on 28 April 1941. To maintain Kufra

178 This contemporary description of the Kufra oasis group is taken from ***Militärgeographische
Beschreibung von Libyen*** that was published in January 1941

"Credere – Obbedire – Combattere" (Believe – Obey – Fight). The fascist principle written on one of the buildings of et-Taj, the fortress in the hills above el-Giof. The wrecked Chevrolet WA 30cwt belonged to LRDG G-patrol.
[G.J. Mostert via András Zboray]

The former *Zawiya* of the Senussia was transformed to a hospital by the Italians. As such it was still used by the South Africans in 1942. The trucks in front of the building: (From left to right) A Ford of the 15 Sqn SAAF, Ford 01 V8 patrol car of the SDF, Chevrolet 1311X3 15 cwt of the SDF.
[G.J. Mostert via András Zboray]

as the headquarters of the LRDG was a difficult and costly task and fuel was always short. In January 1942, when Gialo became the new headquarters of the LRDG, Kufra was entirely placed under the responsibility of the Sudan Defence Force which took over garrison duty in July, 1941.[179]

179 *The Kufra Convoys*, Unpublished Manuscript, Bagnold Papers, Churchill Archives, London.

17 May 1942, into Egypt

After an early breakfast at "Dump II", Almásy wrote in his diary: "Start 06:40, course 122 with the intention of getting on to my old Gilf – Kufra route. To the east, a large group of high black *garas*, not shown on the Italian map. No mapping was done here outside the depression and Jebel Kufra. What were they doing from 1931 to 1939 then?"[180] Soon the small convoy of vehicles had to turn southwards on account of the group of hills. Here too, they found hundreds of older tracks running from Kufra towards the Gilf Kebir. Suddenly they came upon two abandoned enemy trucks, four wheel drive Chevrolet 3-tonners, the latest model but with high-pressure tyres. The odometers showed only 433 miles (697 kilometres). This figure solved the puzzle for Almásy: the trucks must have come from Wadi Halfa. The German assumption that Kufra was supplied from the south from French territory was incorrect. Wadi Halfa, the rail-head of the Sudan Railway and of the Nile steamers from Shellal[181], was the supply base. The trucks had the identification markings of the Sudan Defence Force, who were responsible for supplying and maintaining Kufra oasis.

Left: Approaching the Gilf Kebir. *[Ottokar Seubert]*

Right: "Präsident", driven by Almásy, leading the small convoy. *[Dal McGuirk]*

"Präsident" followed by an F8 and "Inspektor" driving in hilly country. Note the "Pass" plate at the back of one of the C11ADF. *[Dal McGuirk]*

180 In fact, the Italian efforts for proper mapping in the southern regions had practically ceased after Kufra was conquered in 1931. There was no economical demand for such maps.
181 Small village on the banks of the Nile upstream from the Aswan barrage, a short distance south of Aswan.

In the absence of Entholt, Almásy had employed Wöhrmann to keep the log-book up to date. But Wöhrman had no initiative and had to be told everything to write. It was frustrating for Almásy to see that the men still could not understand, despite their experience in the Calanscio Sand Sea, that a long range expedition through this realm of death is nothing more than a flight: a flight from the desert itself. It seems that the men were not aware of the extent of the danger. They depended completely on Almásy's knowledge and ability to guide them through the desert. Almásy complains several times in the diary that the men are useless, he must do everything himself on this operation.

It is amusing to read Almásy's honest opinion about his men. In his book on his wartime experiences in Libya[182] he included a chapter on the desert crossing of Operation Salam, titled "Desert Patrol". While places, names and times are changed or omitted, clearly this chapter is based at least in part on the Salam diary, with one striking difference: The German companions are portrayed – clearly to satisfy the requirements of the censors and the publisher – as "blue eyed, blond german lads, who only stepped on the soil of Africa a few months ago, yet they live and behave as if they had never known anything but life as a desert patrolman".

The terrain facing them was horrible for driving. Cut-up plateaux, soft shifting sand, trailing dunes of the *garas*, necessitated constant changes of course and checking bearings after finding each new way through. Since Wöhrmann was incapable of reckoning bearings and distances, Almásy was continually forced to stop and check the courses on the useless Italian map. It is remarkable that neither Eppler, who claimed to have quite some experience in travelling the desert during his later interrogation by the British Security Service, nor any other of the crew members, had even basic navigation skills.

According to the covered kilometre distances, Almásy concluded that they should already be on the *serir* which he was familiar with due to his travel to Kufra in 1932. But dunes were suddenly appearing before them blocking their way. Almásy was sure that on the previous occasion he did not sight them north of his route. They were impassable for the group with their overloaded vehicles, so they were forced to turn north to cut across the main enemy lines of communication again. Another frustrating detour of 100 kilometres. However Almásy still displayed the explorer spirit; already he was curious to see where the route of the British supply trucks reached his old track of 1932 along the western edge of the Gilf Kebir.

At noon the convoy's tracks were found again, on very difficult terrain. The tracks were all old. Clearly the enemy had moved his line of communication further northwards to avoid the bad terrain. However, Almásy did not wish to make any more detours, they did not have one drop of fuel to spare, so they followed the old trail towards the East, up to the Gilf Kebir. They had to pass patches of soft sand and trailing dunes on the leeward side of the *garas*, in which the British had also become badly stuck, but finally they were through. Where Almásy expected to reach the broken foothills of the Gilf Kebir lying beyond the frontier of Italian territory, they encountered a low stony plateau. It was flat as a table with little craggy knolls and a black shale surface. After a few more kilometres on the old trail, they joined the fresh tracks of the 104 trucks they had discovered the day before.

Left Page: "Robber's Lair" on the western side of the Gilf Kebir. The F8 "Purzel" was hidden some hundred meters further inside these hills. Munz working on "Inspektor" and Wöhrmann standing in front of "Maria". "Purzel" is the F8 in between. *[Dal McGuirk]*

On the stony surface the tracks joined together into a veritable road. Several such roads ran, yellow and shining, over the black plain. "Reichsautobahn", said the men jokingly.

In the deep layer of dust they noticed fresh tracks; after some kilometres Almásy realised that they were running in their planned direction towards the Gilf Kebir. Seven vehicles made the fresh tracks, urging caution.

Suddenly a cloud of dust appeared on the horizon. Almásy in the leading vehicle turned off and led the column to cover behind a small group of rocks. From above one of the rocks, he could see through field glasses five plumes of dust. But he also saw something else: along the eastern horizon the majestic escarpment of the Gilf Kebir and – by no means far to the south east – the high rectangular rocky tower of his triangulation point "1020". Now at last he was on familiar territory, and after a few kilometres he expected to be back on his own map. "Allahu Akbar."[183]

They had to drive carefully in order not to inadvertently overtake the enemy column in front. The main line of communication actually did run into Almásy's former track. After a short time they drove through the only possible way which Almásy had found here before, the narrow defile between the two rounded white rock outcrops which he then had named *Bab el-Misr*[184]. They had definitely crossed the frontier.

Almásy now felt secure and noted into his diary: "Now everything is familiar to me, the valleys with the red sand bottom, the mighty wall of rock on the left, the tangle of foothills on the right, only one thing is new: the great road beaten out with many hundred tracks which extend across every valley bottom, right to the edges. In May 1932 I discovered this mighty plateau, I was the first to drive along it here, groping and searching; the war had drawn its traces with gigantic claws even here in this hidden and secret world."

At last the four vehicles arrived on the plain, round the southwest spur of the Gilf Kebir. As soon as possible they left the enemy tracks, keeping close to the indented foothills of the wall of rock. At the exit to the plain they saw another four abandoned enemy vehicles. One of them was an old Fiat probably captured in Kufra and abandoned here for some unknown reason. Nothing more was to be seen of the column in front of them, the dust plume had disappeared. Almásy was sure that some old tracks ran along the foothills here, but he knew that the main enemy route ran further out, across the level *serir* where the driving was easier.

In one of the openings among the rocky foothills not far from "Wadi Anag"[185] he looked for a good hiding place. They found a suitable deep flat-bottomed valley with a single entrance. Even if anyone should drive into the re-entrant they would not see them until they had turned around the last corner of rock. They stopped to camp at 18:00. The place was likened to a "Robber's Lair".[186]

---

183 God is Great!
184 "The Gateway to Egypt"
185 A *wadi* very close to Wadi Sora, where Patrick Clayton first found prehistoric engravings in 1931.
186 Almásy used the term "robbers camp" in his diary entry for the day.

After 12 hours of driving, the day's performance was 240 kilometres, 100 of which were the diversion around the dunes, not contributing to their progress. They intended to park the Ford F8 named "Purzel" here, and continue with only three vehicles to save on fuel. "Dump III" was hidden in a cleft of rock with 6 cans of petrol, 3 cans of water and 1 day's rations for four men. Almásy had the identification markings of the vehicle painted over, removed everything which would give a clue that Germans have used it and left the following note on the inside of the windscreen:

"Cette voiture n'est pas abandonnée. Elle rentrera à Coufra. Défense d'enlever aucune pièce." (This vehicle is not abandoned. It will be returning to Kufra. Do not remove any part.)

Should it be found, the British would be led to believe that the vehicle belonged to their Free French allies[187]. The maps and logbooks hitherto used were hidden, to leave no clues about where they had come from in case of possible capture.

Gilf Kebir & Wadi Sora – the "Cave of Swimmers"

The centre of the Libyan Desert (or Eastern Sahara as it is now called) remained one of the last 'white spots' on maps into the 20ᵗʰ Century. This vast area, roughly equaling India in shape and size, occupies what is now the eastern part of Libya, north-western Sudan, and all of Egypt to the west of the Nile. The lack of any wells or settlements due to the hyper-arid climate meant that the central parts remained inaccessible and unknown even after both poles had been conquered.

It was only with the advent of the motorcar and aircraft that the interior grudgingly opened up to exploration. In 1925 the Egyptian Prince-explorer, Kemal el-Din, mounted a major expedition supported by the same type of Citroen half-tracks which achieved the first motorised north-south crossing of the Sahara just two years earlier. On this journey, the Prince discovered a vast sandstone plateau with imposing vertical cliffs rising 300–400 metres above the generally flat surrounding desert, occupying the central part of what was then the 'white spot'. He named it the Gilf Kebir ('great wall') on account of its wall-like appearance from a distance. This plateau lies centered on the Tropic of Cancer, some 200 kilometres in length and 100 in width, almost completely within the present-day boundaries of Egypt. Its extent and interior remained subject to much speculation up to the early thirties, fuelled by stories of the mythical Zerzura oasis, thought by some to lie within this blank area on the map.

In the early thirties, several expeditions were mounted to explore the unknown western side and the interior of the Gilf Kebir. The most well known is the 1932 Almásy-Clayton expedition, taking along a De Havilland Gipsy Moth aeroplane to aid exploration, which resulted in the discovery from the air of a large fertile

---

187 Almásy was obviously not aware at this point that the Free French who had conquered Kufra in February 1941 no longer took any part in the supply of Kufra. Any search party following the traces of Operation Salam who found the hidden truck would not have believed that the French intended to come back to get their vehicle.

In the main cave of Wadi Sora. (From left to right) Sandstede, Körper, Eppler, Almásy and Munz.The photo was taken by Wöhrmann.
[Dal McGuirk]

The persons on this group photo were indepentendtly identified by Eppler and Sandstede. (From left to right) Munz, Eppler, Almásy, Sandstede and Körper. The photo was taken by Wöhrmann.
[Dal McGuirk]

The rock paintings in the main cave at Wadi Sora.
[Ottokar Seubert]

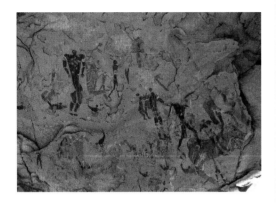

The famous row of "swimmers".

valley. Subsequent expeditions succeeded in reaching this, and another two valleys, on the ground. Almásy was convinced they had found the "three valleys of Zarzura", while others remained skeptical – nevertheless the interior and the extent of the plateau were finally drawn firmly on the maps of the area. In the autumn of 1933 Almásy led another expedition to the Gilf Kebir area, first leading the German ethnographer Leo Frobenius and his archaeologist assistant Hans Rhotert to Jebel Uweinat to see the rock art sites discovered by Almásy earlier that year. Continuing their exploration along the western Gilf Kebir, in a secluded little inlet Almásy came upon a pair of large wind-eroded shelters containing some exceptional prehistoric paintings. Some of the figures appeared to be floating in a swimming-like posture, the name "cave of swimmers" soon stuck to the larger of the shelters. The discovery of these shelters certainly counted among Almásy's greatest achievements.

This shelter soon attracted the attention of archaeologists, as the figures and scenes depicted were unlike any other recorded in the vicinity. Unfortunately the site was much damaged, and the fragmented scenes made little sense, it was only in 2002 that another large shelter containing the same type of paintings ("cave of the beasts") was discovered nearby (ironically, only a short distance from the Salam "Robber's Lair"), enabling a more precise definition of this unique "Wadi Sora culture", appearing only along this short, isolated stretch at the western foot of the Gilf Kebir.

18 May 1942, unexpected supplies

That morning the small group only started on their way at 09:25 because of the need to re-distribute the load to the three remaining vehicles. Almásy chose to drive close to the foot of the hills as far as Wadi Sora, where he showed the men the caves with the prehistoric rock-paintings which he had discovered back in 1933. One of the men picked up an India rubber (pencil rubber) of the German *Reform* brand. It must have been lost by one of Almásy's travel companions, Elisabeth Pauli, when she was copying the rock-paintings in the cave.

They continued towards "Three Castles". Here too they saw many old enemy tracks in the undulating country between the cliffs and these three remote isolated hills, but one could see that the enemy mostly preferred to drive across the *serir* to the south of the *Three Castles*.

Having arrived on top near the three *garas*, Almásy climbed very cautiously over the crest with his vehicle. He was very right to do so. Below on the plain, about four kilometres to the south, where he formerly had his landing ground, a group of enemy vehicles were seen! He observed them for a long time with field glasses, but there was no movement at all. Not a living soul, but only the vehicles. However, the vehicles did not look as if they had been abandoned because of damage.

Almásy recalled that he too had made a petrol dump here at this conspicuous spot. As it is one third of the way between Wadi Halfa and Kufra, could this be an enemy petrol dump?

First they went to a shelter at the eastern "Castle" to check on an old water store which Almásy established in 1932 and re-newed in 1933. Eight soldered Shell canisters containing water from Cairo were still there[188]. Some cans were rusted through and empty, but four were still full. He opened one cautiously in order not to shake up the water. Then they poured it into a cooking pot, and it was found clear and odorless. Each of them took a sample of the 1933 vintage and found the water excellent.

Almásy left one vehicle on the South side of the eastern "Castle" and gave orders for it to be driven immediately to the middle "Castle" in the event of any movement being observed on the plain below. This was to serve as a warning to him while he drove down in ground cover to the group of enemy vehicles. He descended the slope with Munz, then moved out to the plain. They were six of the latest 5 tonners, all loaded with black steel drums. The drums bore the legend: "M.T. Benzine 70 C", with capacity of about 50 litres each, but unfortunately all were empty. The vehicles were not abandoned but obviously only parked. On the front were chalked the words "Refueled for return journey". Almásy took a support of the canvas, opened the right tank of the vehicle and dipped the rod into the filler pipe. It was found to be full, the left tank likewise. The next truck too, and the next, all six, that was 12 full petrol tanks. Measuring the length, width and depth of the tanks, a quick calculation gave 500 litres of petrol. This changed all his plans. He found that he could make the journey to the Nile valley with both station wagons and probably even take one Commercial with him back home. They drove back to their comrades. The F8 truck was immediately unloaded, and with the warning signal still in operation, they hurtled down to the British trucks again. Rapidly they drained the contents of all but one of the full tanks (the draining bolt of which they could not loosen) into the empty drums available on the trucks.

One of the rusted-through cans of Almásy 's 1932/33 water cache with the characteristic soldered seal was at its place in 2010.

"Three Castles" – the conspicious hills on the flat plain at the foot of the Gilf Kebir.

188 One of the rusted-through cans with the characteristic soldered seal was still there in 2010.

The view from "Three Castles" down to the plain where the trucks of the Sudan Defence Force were parked.

Wöhrmann and Almásy draining the fuel from the six parked 1941 Chevrolet C60L Cab 12 of the Sudan Defence Force. *[Ottokar Seubert]*

Some of them now examined the load of drums more thoroughly, and triumphantly found a full drum. Almásy examined the vehicles. The odometers showed the exact distance from Wadi Halfa to here. Gradually he began to understand: the enemy column went from Wadi Halfa to the first third of the distance – about up to the Prince Dune – and left a number of vehicles behind there which supplied petrol for the vehicle column up to that point. Then the journey continued to here, the second third of the distance, and these six trucks stayed behind loaded with the empty petrol drums. When the column returned from Kufra these trucks were collected, their tanks being full. The batteries had all been taken out, probably to be put back on the return trip. The markings were of the Sudan Defence Force, green, red and white with the silhouette of a camel rider.

The twelve drums were loaded on to their truck. With some difficulty it was freed from the soft sand broken by many wheels. While the truck roared back to the "Three Castles", Almásy once more went to the six enemy vehicles one after another. "They shall not fight against us any more", he wrote in his diary. Removing the cap of the oil filler, several handfuls of the finest desert sand was poured in, very carefully and cleanly so that nothing should be noticeable. He took care not to fill the same amount of sand in each, so the trucks would be able to make different distances before the engine seized. "Then they will think it is the evil sandstorm, the *ghibli* which had done this".

Left: "Booty Camp". The barrels full with fuel drained from the parked SDF trucks were dispersed amongst the rocks so that they were not visible from far. *[Dal McGuirk]*

Right: "Booty Camp". Despite searching for it extensively in 2010, the authors could not identify the location. *[Dal McGuirk]*

Now they had the task of getting their loot to safety as soon as possible. Almásy drove with all three vehicles from the "Three Castles" in a north-easterly direction into the hilly terrain in the direction of el-Aqaba. After about 20 kilometres a pointed hill and a ridge cleft by the wind offered good cover. The petrol drums were distributed along the ridge among the black rocks in a way that they could not be recognised even from a short distance from vehicles which might follow their tracks. Then they drove back to the "Three Castles" and fetched the load of their little truck which had been left behind.

Now everything was assembled at the new dump. Their day's performance was small, only 120 kilometres, and about 30 kilometres of that back and forth, but it was well worth it, their return journey was assured now, at least as far as fuel was concerned. They named their camp by the pointed hill and the cache "Booty Camp".[189]

While Almásy and his group were happy about the supplies they had found, the *Ic* of *PzAA* became more and more worried since no message had been received from the group, and asked von der Marwitz at Gialo to provide information urgently[190].

189 This is one of the few locations along the Salam route that could not be positively identified.
    A half-day extensive search in the area by two of the co-authors in 2010 produced no results.
190 TNA, London, HW 19/30 ISOS 28776

Somewhere here… One of the rocky ridges where we thought we would find the remnants of "Booty Camp".

Despite a systematic search with three cars we could not finally locate the place where "Booty Camp" must have been.

On this day Wöhrmann finally succeeded in contacting SCHILDKROETE and passed his report of them reaching the Gilf Kebir in the evening. While the British did not intercept this message, the one forwarded by Weber to von der Marwitz the next day was.[191]

191 TNA, London, HW 19/30 ISOS 28686

19 May 1942, where is the Aqaba Pass?

"Booty Camp. Start at 07:15. A bad day: I did not find the entrance to el-Aqaba", was the laconic first entry in Almásy's diary for that day.

In the morning the three cars drove towards "The Gap"[192] of the Gilf Kebir from which the *wadi* of el-Aqaba emerged. They soon came upon fairly old enemy tracks and were convinced they led out of the pass. Almásy offended against a fundamental rule of desert travel which is valid to this day: never to follow any tracks if unsure exactly where they lead.

They drove along the foot of the Gilf Kebir far beyond el-Aqaba, in an easterly direction, and then back again closer up to the escarpment and into several *wadi* entrances each of which Almásy thought to be the el-Aqaba entrance. Everywhere innumerable British tracks ran criss-cross over the scree slopes as if the enemy had likewise searched for a way up the pass. Once it used to be simple, there was only one East – West track along the escarpment, and Almásy's own tracks emerging from the pass. Now everything was changed by the innumerable tracks and also perhaps by the heavy rains of 1935 which may have destroyed the traces he was looking for.

The terrain did not help. Here the runoff from the cliffs formed a 20 kilometre wide scree slope skirting the main mass of the Gilf which is cut into innumerable ridges and shallow *wadis* running perpendicular to the cliffs. The ridges are strewn with football-sized boulders which grow in size as one gets closer to the cliffs, a terrain almost impassable to any vehicle. The only feasible way is to keep a distance, and drive up in the sandy bed of one of the watercourses. The question is which one?[193] Without any clues to help, it was no use pressing on. They had to return to their starting point in order to take bearings from there on the two foothills and on the "Three Castles", first of all to determine their exact position and second to determine the position of the wadi of el-Aqaba. There would still have been time to set off afresh, but in the scree

192 "The Gap" of the Gilf Kebir was noticed from the plain by Clayton in 1931, but it was Hubert Penderel who recognised its true nature from the air in 1932, being a broad valley separating the North-Western and South-Eastern parts of the Gilf Kebir, and offering a passage through. The 1933 Almásy – Penderel expedition was the first to enter it on the ground, and discovered a pass, the "Aqaba" leading down to the plains below to the south west that was fit for motor vehicles. Almásy calls it the "Great Break" or "Great Rift", but Clayton's earlier name is the one that took hold.

193 Even today, with the benefit of modern navigation, it is very easy to pick the wrong wadi and struggle on for hours, even though the actual entrance of the pass is clearly visible ahead, some 10 kilometres away.

A Goodyear 10.50 x 16 Sand Type. The tyre was left back together with its rim by an SDF convoy.

Another tyre left back in the desert.

"A bad day: I did not find the entrance to el-Aqaba", was the laconic first entry in Almásy's diary for that day.

The entrance of el-Aqaba from a distance. The plain in the foreground is deceptive, it is almost impassable for cars except in the shallow wadis.

Almásy looking at a piece of petrified wood lying in the desert sand. Note the bag of the camera in his hand.
[Dal McGuirk]

Munz observing trough the binoculars.
[Dal McGuirk]

Almásy aiming with the prismatic compass and Eppler observing trough the binoculars.
[Ottokar Seubert]

Munz, Körper and Wöhrmann standing behind "Präsident" searching for tools to do a small repair on one of the vehicles. *[Dal McGuirk]*

Almásy's car had broken a spring and Munz and Körper had to fit a replacement. In contrast to the high spirits of the previous day, these events brought down the mood of the small group again. The last entry of the day was: "Depressed spirits in our camp. The day's performance was only about 80 kilometres."

A W/T message was intercepted that evening from OTTER at Gialo sent in the name of Beilharz, aparently in response to the urgent request for information on Salam by Ic the day before. The message was deciphered in three parts (with a two week delay), and was possibly sent repeatedly due to bad reception at the other end, originally dated the 15 May (since one last communication was received from Almásy on the evening of the 18 May) It stated that no SALAM – OTTER link had existed since the 15th when Strungmann and Beilharz left *Salam* with the damaged vehicle, parts were removed from Beilharz' truck and installed in the leading car, and gave information on the intended new route[194]. It was further said in another message dated 25 May, probably a continuation or repetition of the previous ones that the broken down car was to be brought back to Gialo and upon the return of SALAM, a fuel dump was to be established at *Campo 5*[195]. It was estimated that Almásy would need 16 days to complete the journey there and back, and would ask for air support should it be necessary. Nobody then knew that there would be no further communication from SALAM until the group had returned to Gialo.

The last entry of the day was: "Depressed spirits in our camp. The day's performance was only about 80 kilometres."

194 TNA, London, HW 19/30 ISOS. 28640 and 28687
195 TNA, London, HW 19/30 No. ISOS. Could this be a reason why Almásy found no supplies at *Campo 4* on his return?

20 May 1942, Gilf Kebir

A new approach was to be tried this day. They started at 06:45 and Almásy led the way right up to the scree slope. Driving conditions were frightful and the three cars had literally to be pushed in places. Straight away Almásy found the outlet of the right wadi with the help of the previous day's direction finding. In the riverbed itself they saw only his old tracks. The enemy had evidently looked for el-Aqaba but not found it. For a moment they paused – perhaps the enemy had mined the pass from above or blown it up at its narrowest point. There was talk of that in 1937; Almásy had even been asked for his opinion on whether it was feasible.

Almásy calculating the route. Next to him, with the binoculars is Munz.
[Dal McGuirk]

Almásy, Körper and Munz at rest after calculating a new course.
[Dal McGuirk]

Körper, Munz and Wöhrmann.
[Dal McGuirk]

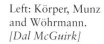

Left: Körper, Munz
and Wöhrmann.
[Dal McGuirk]

Right: Standard Army
issue 6x30 binoculars
with case.
[Dal McGuirk]

"Inspektor" crossing
the dunes after the Gilf
Kebir. Note the "Pass"
plate on the front of
the vehicle and the
front windows covered
with paint to avoid
reflections which could
warn the enemy.
[Ottokar Seubert]

"Maria" crossing the
dunes after the Gilf
Kebir. (The original
photo is blurred).
[Dal McGuirk]

Observing from a
dune. (From left to
right) Körper, Munz,
Wöhrmann, Sandstede
and Eppler.
[Ottokar Seubert]

Almásy drove in front and looked for traces of mines, but on reaching the top he found the solution to the puzzle. A number of enemy vehicles had indeed, about a year ago, driven down the great rift of the Gilf Kebir, but could not find the entrance to the pass even from above, and went down into the plain through "Penderel's Wadi"[196] which was east of el-Aqaba.

They went north through "The Gap" at high speed. Almásy's old tracks were frequently visible. Unfortunately he tried to follow Clayton's track at the point where he found a shortcut across the little eastern plateau. With their overloaded vehicles it could not be done, and they lost valuable time.

At last they drove around the northern point of the plateau, and continued in a south- easterly direction. Seven years ago Almásy had discovered this passage, the secret gateway for breaking into Egypt.

There was concern about crossing the difficult part of this previous entry into the Gilf Kebir, but Almásy's old tracks – which a British patrol had also followed – led them surely. The trailing dune which blocked the way was negotiated with the greatest caution. First Almásy stopped the cars and traversed the only possible driving route on foot. All three vehicles crossed safely, and he took care beforehand to keep a driving channel free for the return journey where the sand must not be churned up. Sandstede drove as usual like a mad man, the result was a bent track rod and a broken shock absorber. Almásy noted here: "Except for Munz the men cannot drive; only Körper shows good driving ability. How different were my Sudanese!"

(From left to right)
Munz, Eppler, Körper.
[Dal McGuirk]

196 The precise location of "Penderel's Wadi" is not known, it is likely to be the wadi immediately
to the east of the Aqaba Pass.

They made camp at "Two Breasts"[197] on the plain on the eastern slope of the Gilf Kebir. The day's performance was 290 kilometres, though of this 60 kilometres was done in the fruitless effort to "shorten" the route. They stored 3 cans of petrol and 2 cans of water. The radio did not work; supposedly the transformer was damaged.

The same evening, an intercepted message was sent from *AST Tripolis* to Seubert in Berlin. It relayed the information received the day before, "Salam reports arrival in Gilf Kebir". While obviously this message was received with a sigh of relief, indicating that the party had successfully bypassed the enemy at Bir Zighen and Kufra, it was in fact this message which provided the first red flag the following day to the message analysts at Bletchley Park that something was going on …[198]

(From left to right) Wöhrmann, Körper, Munz. *[Dal McGuirk]*

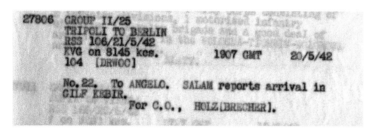

The dune ridges after the Gilf Kebir were bypassed instead of being crossed. *[Dal McGuirk]*

Luftwaffe issue tropical pith helmet, *Tropenhelm.* *[Dal McGuirk]*

197 A conspicuous pair of rounded hills of the same height at the northeastern approaches of the Gilf Kebir.
198 TNA, London, HW 19/30 ISOS 27806

"Präsident", "Maria" and "Inspektor" on the way to Kharga standing in front of "Two Breasts", the distinctive hills on the eastern side of the Gilf Kebir.
[Ottokar Seubert]

21 May 1942, due east

For this day, Almásy was very optimistic and wrote that he "should like today to get as far as south of the Dakhla oasis, and as I have anyhow been suffering from insomnia for a few days, I sound the reveille at 04:00. We actually get away at 06:30. I cannot move eastwards or make good my course of 60 degrees, as there is an endless trailing dune east of *Two Breasts*. The last time coming from Abu Ballas I drove through the mountains north of here, hence we go in a northerly direction. Right behind the first mountain we can drive round the trailing dune and we shall be on our course."

But the good going soon came to an end, to be replaced by low plateaus and small hills with their repeated trailing dunes which were a real nuisance, only occasionally interrupted with broader plains with stretches of smooth gravel and now and again a piece of open *serir*. The vehicles suffered terribly on this kind of ground and probably the drivers as well. Almásy had to constantly stop to mark the changing course on the map. This time he could not draw in the stretch they had done, but only put in tiny points on the map sheet with a sharp pointed pencil to disguise their route in case they would get caught.

Almásy set course to the north of the broad belt of dunes which he last saw out of the aeroplane in 1932. However this time their crossing was much farther south, so he did not know how far the dunes stretched towards the north. By now he recognised that perhaps it would have been wiser to follow his old route towards Abu Ballas, there was no saving in kilometres on this new route because of the constant detours.

However they had been lucky with the dunes. They struck upon the group of hills from which the long trailing dunes started, and they could get around comparatively easily at the foot of the hills. At about 11:00 a larger conspicuous peak loomed up far away on the horizon. The peak was straight in line with the front of the radiator. Almásy could not believe it at first, but he had hit precisely on Two Peak Hill[199] in spite of these fearful detours he was forced to make.

Despite the encouraging sight, the mountain appeared unattainable. For an hour the three vehicles drove towards it and it still remained far away. It was indeed a very good landmark, visible from 50 kilometres away.

The group finally arrived at the base of the hill in the heat of noon. The *Flitzer* was to be left behind here. From now on there were only the two vehicles left, so as to save fuel. The redistribution of the loads went on quickly. Almásy left behind 4 cans of petrol and 3 cans of water. The *Flitzer* also still had one tank full. Without more ado, they pressed on.

Bagnold's mapped route[200] passed not far from the place. After scarcely 20 kilometres the two remaining cars came upon the old tracks in places. The ground became easier. They crossed largish sandy plains, with single isolated hills which afforded fast going and good points of orientation. Almásy was driving as far as possible straight at these hills after taking bearings, as by now his eyes ached terribly from endless compass driving. He was driving in front, navigating and plotting the course at the same time, a heavy burden on only one man.

Difficult to cross country.
[*Ottokar Seubert*]

A small sand-dune trailing the leeward side of a hill.
[*Ottokar Seubert*]

199 This conspicuous peak, the only major landmark within a radius of 50 kilometres, was the farthest point attained by W.J. Harding King on his pioneering camel expedition of 1911.
200 Routes on the Survey of *Egypt maps*.

Two peak hill from a distance.

He decided that they must camp a little earlier today as otherwise the men would go slack on him. At 18:00 they came to a convenient camping ground at the foot of one of the many solitary hills. Distance covered was a very good 230 kilometres. From here on it was also decided not to give any revealing names to the campsites, the place they stayed at was simply named "Camp 8".

Wireless communication had broken down again. Wöhrmann reported that the transformer was not working. Almásy noted that the men messed around with it for an hour, and then came in for supper with the transmitter still out of action. He wrote, clearly irritated: "Three radio operators and a mechanic are not able to find out what is wrong. In this undertaking I have to do everything myself. *Pit* and *Pan*, riding in the radio car, are the most untidy fellows I have ever had with me. The inside of the radio car looks frightful. Equipment, personal effects, weapons and rations all mixed up together. I am merciless in having everything turned out, and find the fault in a few minutes. Some angular object has snipped through the cable leading to the transformer. When I instruct Wöhrmann to install a new cable, he reports that he cannot do it, as he has no technical training. I have to actually fit the cable myself, but in spite of that the transformer does not work."

A new search with the torch revealed that an interconnecting cable was cut as well. Now at least the transformer was running, but there was still no contact. Now the fault was assumed to be in the instrument itself. Almásy was not a radio technician, and could do no more to help. The conclusion was that the next day Sandstede would have to try with his instrument.

While in the desert, Almásy had been fuming quietly about the lack of communications and the incompetence of his men, but he was unaware that all this was in fact aiding their success. The message of *AST Tripolis* to Seubert the day before was decyphered very fast (obviously messages sent to *Abwehr* Headquarters in Berlin had priority over operational messages between local stations), and was spotted by one of the dozens of young women employed in Bletchley Park as Intelligence Analysts.

Jean Alington was in her early twenties at the time, and could thank her position to an uncommon stroke of luck. Having been summoned through an acquaintance to an interview for some exciting but confidential government job in the countryside, she was only told that knowledge of German was a must. With a good but not outstanding mastery of the language gained in school, she boarded a train taking with her the only German book she had found on her shelf to practice. By a strange twist of fate, the interview (which she passed with flying colours) consisted primarily of translating the first chapter of the very book she had been practicing with on the train![201]

In May 1942 Alington was working on the German High Command Enigma decrypts and *Abwehr* decodes. She spotted the phrase "Gilf Kebir" in a message suggesting that some enemy unit was moving behind British lines towards Egypt. She asked for permission to search for more information among the Abwehr de-

201 Alexandra Taylor, daughter of Jean Howard, personal communication with András Zboray

codes, and was told that if she wished to give up her lunch hour or work overtime, she could please herself …[202]

She soon found other traces of this unit among the *Abwehr* hand and machine cipher decrypts, including one Enigma message dated 29 April from AST Athens (ADOLF) decrypted on 5 May, which provided the link between SALAM and Almásy[203].

Fortunately for Almásy and *Salam*, because of the overriding priority given to messages originating from the *Panzerarmee Afrika* on account of the impending attack of which the British were already aware of at this stage, the decodes were processed with several days' delay. While the decyphered message informing ANGELO that SALAM reached the Gilf Kebir must have triggered a flashing warning to Alington, the more revealing messages sent (and intercepted) over the 13 – 15 May period were only decyphered and made available to the analysts on the 25 May. These further messages confirmed the picture: An enemy unit was moving from Gialo through the Gilf Kebir towards Kharga Oasis. However by the time this conclusion was reached, Almásy was already well on his return journey …

22 May 1942, within reach of the objective

The small group left their camp at 07:30 and continued the journey east. The terrain now became somewhat better, long empty stretches with good directional points to follow. Still there were several troublesome rocky plateaus which had to be driven over or gone around. Over and over again they crossed Bagnold's 1932 tracks, still clearly visible[204]. Almásy calculated that he must do a further 80 kilometres from their camp of their previous night before establishing the last dump[205]. He chose a precipitous "wind ridge" between two small *garas* lying about 10 kilometres apart right across their course, despite the lack of any unmistakable landmarks. On the return journey they would have to rely on retracing their own tracks. But there were no other landmarks, and the dump had to be south of Dakhla in order to be able to divert there on the way back if necessary. 4 cans of petrol and 2 cans of water, and the maps of the route covered so far, were left behind in a cleft in the rock.

A few kilometres after leaving the dump, they encountered one of the sad reminders of the plight of the Kufra refugees of 1931.[206] A few camel skeletons, a human skull

202 Letter of Jean Howard to Brigadier Bagnold, 31 March 1978, Bagnold Papers, Churchill Archives, Cambridge

203 TNA, London, HW 19/93 ISK 7165

204 The original text mentions the year 1934, but this is an error since it was Bagnold's 1932 expedition that took this route from Kharga to Uweinat.

205 The diary reads "I must do 80 kms more than yesterday before I can establish the last depot", literally that reads the depot must be 310 kilometres from camp. However Almásy also says a few lines later that the depot must be south of Dakhla, that is more in line with 80 kilometres from camp. Most probably this error was introduced when Almásy's original German text was translated into English.

206 Almásy gives more detail in his diary about the Kufra refugees, who fled the oasis in 1931 before the advancing Italian troops, and tried to make their way to the Egyptian oases over 700 kilometres of waterless desert. Many perished on the way, but some of the luckier ones were saved by the efforts of P.A. Clayton and the *Mamur* of Dakhla. These events are also covered extensively in his book **Unknown Sahara**.

bleached snow-white, and nearby the narrow tracks of the high-pressure tyres of the two Fords of the *Mamur* of Dakhla, who made heroic efforts to try to save as many as he could from certain death.

In the afternoon the terrain turned worse. They kept a sharp lookout for any tracks on the Kharga – Bir Messaha line, but to their astonishment they crossed only a few old tyre tracks, many of them doubtless Almásy's own. Almásy was surprised to note that apparently no enemy lines of communication ran from Egypt to Kufra.

Towards the evening they finally reached the Abu Moharig dunes bordering Kharga oasis on the West. They turned north and drove as fast as the miserable terrain allowed, in order to reach the Kharga – Dakhla road before darkness. They did not succeed, as they must have arrived at the dunes somewhat further south than the intended point; the road lay some distance to the north. It was becoming dark when they camped in an undulating sandy plain offering scarcely any cover, perhaps only a few hundred metres from the road. But Almásy dared not risk driving across and missing the road in the darkness, nor looking for it with the headlights. The most important thing for them now was radio communication. Eppler's set was working perfectly and he transmitted his callsign to the star-speckled sky. They gathered around to watch, holding their breath, listening to the whistle in the headphones. SCHILDKROETE did not answer. Nothing but silence.

Almásy found that they had scarcely enough petrol to get back. He wrote in his diary: "Everything was discussed and planned in detail, I was only to radio and they would drop fuel, water and food for me in any grid square I asked for. Now the set tuned in to our point of departure is broken, and the station at the other end does not answer. Probably they are changing their position right now. I begged them to leave SCHILDKROETE at one fixed point[207]."

He worked out once again their remaining fuel and the average consumption. If they drove through Kharga Oasis by road instead of over the dunes in order to remain unobserved, they should just be able to make it. If the worst came to the worst, Almásy thought that they should have to obtain petrol by cunning or by force. His mind was made up: in order to save petrol they would remain on the road. They had covered 250 kilometres that day over very difficult terrain, and camped in the immediate neighborhood of Kharga Oasis.

Kharga Oasis and Assiut

El-Kharga oasis, "the outer oasis", is the most southern and eastern of Egypt's five "western oases", roughly 200 kilometres to the west of the river Nile. It is also the biggest of these oasis depressions; the Kharga basin has an overall length of about 150 kilometres and a width of 20 to 80 kilometres, although vegetation grows only in a narrow intermittent belt running along the centre of the depression. Kharga had been a major crossroads for desert caravan routes since antiquity, as attested by the Ancient Egyptian temples and the remnants of a chain of Roman fortresses. The infamous Darb el-Arbain (the route of the forty days), starting at el-Fasher in the Sudan, passing through Kharga, and terminating in Assiut, was one of the principal supply routes of the oriental slave trade from medieval times down to the middle of the nineteenth century.

"The easiest approach to Kharga is by the railway which forks from the Cairo – Luxor line at the station "Oasis Junction" and reaches the oasis after 198 kilometres.

The population of Kharga numbers 8,600 of which the main settlement Kharga alone numbers 8'000. Also located in the main settlement are the government buildings, post office and hospital. The village of Beris is located in the south of the depression at about two days' march from Kharga. Dates, fruit and rice are grown in the oasis.

Kharga is an important outpost in the southern Libyan desert, a potential supply base for an advance on the middle Nile valley."[208]

Assiut is located on the banks of the Nile about 375 kilometres south of Cairo. It is, and was for centuries, the largest settlement in the Nile valley south of the capital. A railway line was completed in 1875 and it had a population of 51'431 inhabitants in 1928. After the erection of the irrigation dam in the1920s, industrial scale cotton plantations became possible in the region.

207 Almásy's statement that the Luftwaffe would drop him fuel at any point on the journey he asked is subject to question. The Luftwaffe planes did not have sufficient range to provide fuel to Almásy that far south at all. Maybe he was referring to the route planned at the start; maybe it is just to be taken as a rhetorical statement to express how remote the group was from any sort of supply.
208 This contemporary description of the Kharga oasis group is taken from *Militärgeographische Beschreibung von Nordost Afrika* published in 1940.

Left: El-Kharga oasis, "the outer oasis", is the most southern and eastern of Egypt's five "western oases". Today it is much more a modern Egyptian town than a romantic oasis as the traveller may expect to find.

Right: Despite the modern appearance of the town, the palm gardens remain still as they always were.

After many days in the desert, the lush green of the palm gardens provides a welcome view for the human eye.

Left: Despite that animals were replaced largely by machines – the donkey is still a common view in Egypt.

Right: A fuel station at Kharga. Without sufficient supplies of fuel the modern traveller could not do the long journey through the desert.

The temple of Hibis that was built approximately 500 BC is found about 2 kilometres to the North of the town in a palm grove.

The ancient Christian cemetery at al-Bagawat. The buildings date from between the 3rd and the 7th century AD.

Kharga, the railway tracks.
[Dal McGuirk]

The modern road from Kharga to Assiut. Hardly anybody driving on it has an idea on who drove here in 1942.

Looking from the modern road towards the nearly forgotten old track to the Yabsa pass.

23 May 1942, to Assiut, dropping the spies

After the night at "Camp 9", they were aware that they had a very difficult day ahead. Almásy was determined to reach the objective on the Nile, and to do a large part of the return journey if possible. For the first time since the departure from Gialo, Almásy distributed Pervitin to all members of the operation, for the tiredness of the day before had still not worn off.

The two Fords started north in the first light of dawn and soon reached the Dakhla – Kharga road about 15 kilometres southwest of Kharga. Almásy knew everything here from earlier visits, the *barchans* of the Abu Moharig by the road, the iron tracks of an abandoned railway line to the phosphate mines, and the mighty wall of the Egyptian limestone plateau to the east.

After 5 kilometres Almásy stopped to drum into the men in the second car – Munz, Wöhrmann and Sandstede – that it was vital not to get left behind under any circumstances, to halt when he halted, and to start when he started. The submachine guns were held at the ready, but arms were not be used unless Almásy himself opened fire. It was most important not to get separated, particularly since Almásy was the only one who knew the way through and out of Kharga.

They entered the oasis from the east, and drove past the railway station. Tension was high. As yet, nothing stirred. After a sharp turn they went down a newly laid out avenue towards the *markaz*[209]. This new avenue did not please Almásy, it had not existed when last he visited the oasis. The road branching off to Moharig must have changed as well.

Two Egyptian *ghaffirs*[210] stood in the small round square in front of the way up to the *markaz*. Only one of them carried a pistol, but both stood in the road. Almásy stopped, unruffled. One of Egyptians gave a respectful greeting in Arabic, pointed to his mouth and said "no inglisi". Almásy returned the greeting and told him that he spoke Arabic. The man was pleased and told him that the cars had to go to the *markaz*, as all persons passing through had to report to the *Muhafiz*. Almásy replied that the *Bimbashi* would of course report, but he was only driving the *Bimbashi's* luggage, and so they had to hurry to the railway station.

209 Arabic: Seat of the local government (Egypt)
210 Arabic: Watchmen

"Where is the *Bimbashi*?" asked the Egyptian soldier.

"In the fourth car", replied Almásy, pointing behind him.

The man looked, astonished, in the direction the two cars had come from. Almásy asked him:

"How many cars are there behind me?"

"Only a second one" answered the *ghaffir*.

"Good." Almásy pointed to one of the *ghaffirs*: "You stay here, and wait for the other two cars. The *Bimbashi* is travelling in the fourth car. You will show him the way to the *markaz*." Then he turned to the other:

"And you get on the running board and show me the Moharig turn-off."

"Hadr, Effendi."[211] He gave a military salute and got on to the car. Almásy was only interested in getting these two separated quickly, before they had the time to think about the passage of two cars so early in the morning. After a few hundred metres they reached their goal, the main road which leads to Moharig. Almásy halted, let the man off, thanked him, and drove off at once. He saw the second car directly behind him in the wing mirror.

Eppler standing in front of "Inspektor" near the distinctive rock in the ascent of the Yabsa pass.
[Dal McGuirk]

211 Arabic: "Yes, Sir"

"Präsident" and
"Inspektor" (From left
to right) Munz, Eppler,
Körper, Almásy
[Ottokar Seubert]

Left: Looking down to
the plain in the direc-
tion of Kharga.

Right: Driving up the
small old track to the
top of the escarpment.

They drove through the oasis in the glow of the rising sun, passing on their right the ancient temple of Hibis, then on the left the early Christian necropolis of Bagawat. The road was excellent. It ran along the railway embankment and crossed it where the old road from the *markaz* used to lead to Moharig. Almásy kept looking for an *esbah*[212] bordering immediately on the road, so he could fetch water on the way back without much loss of time. At the 35th kilometre stone there stood an *esbah* with its spring, scarcely a hundred paces to the right.

They continued at a steady speed on the road towards Assiut, finally reaching the last obstacle: the Yabsa Pass, 50 kilometres from the *markaz*. In the cool morning they had no difficulty driving the cars up the steep old Roman road, they even had the time to take a couple of photos of the vehicles making the ascent. On the top they snapped a photo of the road sign warning of the dangerous descent, then continued non-stop towards their final goal.

Almásy was pleased to note that the excellent quality of the road had a very good effect on their petrol consumption. The road seemed little frequented, but unfortunately the roadbed itself was heavily rippled. The next few hours of monotonous driving passed without incident[213]. Finally at kilometre stone 30 before Assiut Almásy started to look for a suitable spot to park the second vehicle out of sight off the road. The ground offered no shelter, but at kilometre stone 29 there stood a small limestone hill to the right. They drove up to it, and Almásy stressed to Körper and Wöhrmann that they must wait in the cover of the hill for three hours, until 17:00 for his return. If he should not be back by then, they were to follow his track cautiously. In any case the two of them had enough petrol, water and food to be able to drive back to the last dump, even alone. They would of course have to follow their outward tracks most carefully from kilometre stone 15 on the Dakhla road -- where they had come in that morning – as otherwise they would never find their way back.

On the top of Yabsa pass. Almásy standing next to the warning sign "Dangerous descent. Drive in bottom gear".*[Ottokar Seubert]*

The same spot in 2010. The sign is gone, but the mound in the background is recognisable.

212 Arabic: Farm
213 Sandstede in his memoirs claims, that they have passed a British truck which noticed them, but Almásy does not mention this. It is rather inconcievalbe that a solitary truck would have travelled that road of over 200 Km without any water or fuel along the way. Given the other inaccuracies in Sandstede's memoirs, Almásy's account of not meeting anyone along the road is more credible.

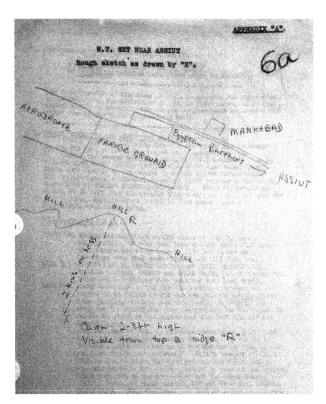

APPENDIX "A".

W.T. SET NEAR ASSIUT
Rough sketch as drawn by "E".

6a

AERODROME

PARADE GROUND

Egyptian
Barracks

MANKEBAD

ASSIUT

HILL

HILL
R

HILL

2 kms or less

HILL

Cairn 2-3ft high
Visible from top of ridge "R"

Eppler's sketch about the situation at Assiut. *[TNA, London, KV 2/1467, Epplers Personal File]*

With the remaining car Almásy cautiously drove east by compass with Munz, Eppler and Sandstede, to find the old caravan track which was somewhere to the east of the motor road. He had lost his way once years ago in this region, and got into the worst possible terrain in the *hirashif* of the limestone plateau. They found the ancient camel trail exactly where it was supposed to be according to their map.

Now everything was comparatively easy. At 14:00 the car reached the edge of the plateau. Scarcely four kilometres below them lay the huge green valley with the glittering Nile, the great white city of Assiut, the countless *esbahs* and country houses. Few words were said, a few handshakes, one last photograph, a short farewell, and then he was driving back on his own tracks with Munz.

Nor did they waste any time on arriving back at the waiting car; just a few minutes later the two vehicles were back on the road again, facing once more the stretch of 2'200 kilometres which they had just completed.

They reached the Yabsa pass after dark. With a quick decision Almásy had the camouflage paint removed from the headlights and they drove down the steep snaking road with all lights blazing. He decided to spend the night at the *esbah* he had selected at kilometre stone 35. From there they could cross the oasis early the next day, before anybody was awake.

In the pale moonlight they crossed the palm gardens to the *esbah*. The yelping of a small dog and the traditional long drawn cry of warning: "Miin?" broke the silence. They exchanged greetings with the owner, whose small son immediately brought them a jar of delicious fresh milk by way of greeting. The men had already prepared camp, and he invited the five people living in the *esbah* to tea. He apologised to the head of the family that they had no sugar, explaining that "our loads were wrongly distributed", and their sugar was on the other vehicles which would be coming later. The owner of the *esbah* immediately had some sugar brought out from the house and Almásy used this opportunity to buy a big sugar loaf from him for 20 piasters.

The good *fellah* told him everything he wanted to know, and filled his canisters with excellent water from the well. He would willingly have gone on talking to these people for hours, but they had to be off tomorrow before daybreak, so as to cross the oasis unmolested if possible.

Almásy arranged with the head of the family for him to milk his cows an hour before sunrise, and to bring them fresh milk for breakfast. They had travelled 420 kilometres this day; the remaining men were very tired.

Return to Gialo

After the party had separated the day before, Eppler and Sandstede were no longer members of Operation Salam but had opened the new chapter of Operation Kondor. For the remaining four men of Operation Salam, the whole long track through the desert had to be made once more – starting with the first obstacle: the second crossing of the Kharga oasis.

24 May 1942, Kharga again

The *fellahin* had kept their word, the fresh milk tasted wonderful, and soon the two cars drove off in the first light of dawn towards Kharga. The lingering question among them was whether they would have the same luck again and cross the oasis unrecognised, or if an alert enemy was lying in wait for them. They entered Kharga the same way they had left it the day before and found that there was one solitary guard on the roundabout at the *Markaz*. Ignoring him, they drove past without stopping, and Almásy saw in the side mirror that the man was running behind the second car in a futile attempt to make them stop.

At the railway station they stopped for a moment to take a photograph of the stacks of grain piled up for loading. A fat railway employee appeared in his nightgown and gave them a friendly greeting. After what Almásy had learnt yesterday from the peasants, it did not seem necessary to disappear too quickly into the desert. They could spare themselves a good bit of the miserable terrain if they just drove on along the Kharga – Dakhla road and turned off south just before Dakhla, to disappear into the great void again.

Their single problem was to find the tracks of their outward journey again. After a comparatively easy trip on a south-westerly course, they tried reconciling the courses on the map and worked out by the odometers where they had to cut their track of two days before[214]. Everybody was surprised that Almásy's calculation was correct to within 500 metres.

---

214 In his diary, Almásy mentions them as yesterday's tracks – that is obviously an error.

Bagawat just north of Kharga. This necropolis
was built by the early Christian population of
the oasis in the 5th century.
[Dal McGuirk]

It was easy to keep to the track to begin with, but the closer they got to "Dump IV" the harder it became. In this horrible terrain there was only wind-blown sand on the upper surface, and it seemed to have shifted overnight. They lost the track several times and had to look for it on foot. Almásy could not risk missing their vital petrol dump. The track finally died out for good during the last kilometre left to the dump. Almásy started to reproach himself on how thoughtless it was not to dump the petrol near an unmistakable landmark, but then he recognised the steep wind ridge over which they slithered the day before and drove instinctively to the group of rocks where the cans had stayed hidden. Almásy's men declared that this was not the dump, but there in the cleft of the rock lay the black cans, so precious to them. A large snake had found its way into a fissure above the hiding place, and stared at them with glowing emerald eyes. Munz wanted to kill it, but Almásy intervened and told him that it was the *djinn* of their hiding place and hence of their return journey too. This visibly impressed the men.

"Barchan camp". After refuelling the three vehicles, the empty jerrycans were burried at the foot of a sand-dune.
[Dal McGuirk]

A number of these 16 jerrycans burried by Körper were found again in 2001.
[HBI Köln / Archiv Kuper]

The jerrycans were stamped with their manufacturing year: 1941.
[HBI Köln / Archiv Kuper]

Reaching open terrain, they continued west at good speed. At midday they drove past the campsite of two days ago without stopping. Late in the afternoon the two station wagons reached Two Peak Hill which was visible for more than 50 kilometres from the east. They put the *Flitzer* they had parked there into running order in only a few minutes, finished a box of *Scho-ka-kola* discarding the empty tin[215], and then drove on as far as the great *barchan* dunes about 60 kilometres to the west, camping on the lee side of the biggest of them.

The day's journey was a full 410 kilometres, a very good achievement in light of having to look for the tracks, the bad terrain, and having to halt at both the dump and the parked *Flitzer*.

Since the Germans had no other expeditions into this southern area and since the location was "Barchan Camp" it is excluded that the canistres were left back by somebody else than "Operation Salam".
[*HBI Köln/Archiv*

The discarded *Scho-ka-kola* tin found at the foot of Two Peak Hill.

215 The tin was found in November 2000 by András Zboray.

25 May 1942, back through the Gilf Kebir

The night was spent next to a *barchan* dune. The men had an extended rest after the exhausting recent stages, and they struck camp only at 09:30. In the morning they fuelled the cars, and buried the empty jerrycans no longer needed in a neat row in the sand along the leading edge of the *barchan*.[216]

On the outward journey they experienced the terrible terrain along the direct route from the "Two Breasts", so Almásy drove first due west to get onto his old Abu Ballas – Gilf Kebir route. Again his navigation was precise. They crossed the 1933 track just where he had calculated. The track was easy to follow; as Almásy drove by compass the last time, they just stayed on the same course if the track was lost. The men were amazed how they hit upon the old track every time, or often just "felt" it beneath their wheels.

Almásy's car, "Inspektor", facing towards the Aqaba pass.
[Dal McGuirk]

216 In the elapsed years the barchan was moved by the wind. The re-exposed jerrycans were found by Samir Lama and Rudolph Kuper in 2001.

"Inspektor" at the bottom of the Aqaba pass during the return journey. Note the Askania compass on the right front-mudguard.
[Dal McGuirk]

View back up the
Aqaba pass. "Maria"
followed by "Präsi-
dent".
[Dal McGuirk]

Körper and Munz draining some fuel from the tank of "Inspektor" into a small bowl, probably to clean some small mechanical parts of one of the vehicles.
[Dal McGuirk]

The last time Almásy had found the way into the Gilf Kebir was with the aid of a reconnaissance flight[217]; this time he had to plot the course to the "Two Breasts" so as to fetch the petrol dumped there. From the dump the small group followed the tracks of the outward journey and again they succeeded in getting past the critical trailing dune without any of the vehicles becoming stuck. It had been a good idea to leave a suitable undisturbed sand slope for their return journey.

Almásy plotted a course to his "Surveying Camp" of 1933, so by taking a bearing on the great cairn they had erected on the plateau at the time, he could check their exact position and the accuracy of the odometers.

The passage through "The Gap" of the Gilf Kebir was without incident. They camped at a scenic spot in "The Gap" with the intention next day of photographing the giant dunes jutting into the Gilf in a favorable light before starting off. Progress for the day, in spite of the mountainous terrain and the late start, was 250 kilometres.

A leftover from Sandstede: A bottle of the Italian Sarti liquor.
[Dal McGuirk]

Standard Army Tropical Rucksack worn on canvas 'Y' straps (not shown).
[Dal McGuirk]

217 That flight was made by Penderel, not Almásy as the diary text would imply.

26 May 1942, enemy convoys!

There was to be no photography in the morning; thick clouds covered the sky, and there was a cold north wind blowing.

The journey to el-Aqaba was another test of patience. On their arrival Almásy left two vehicles at the entrance to the pass, and drove back with Munz onto the great red sand plain, in order to mark out a landing field there. He laid out the airfield precisely by the four points of the compass, drove along the boundaries, exactly 1.5 kilometre along each side of the square, and inscribed a deep circle in each corner, in the middle of which they put a can. Then he drove along the diagonals, and made a big circle in the middle, and "Campo A" was ready. It was to serve for an operation against Wadi Halfa, the starting point of the enemy supply line. They coasted down the pass to the spot where the deep-cut wadi emerged on to the sloping scree. Here the empty British petrol drum, brought with them specifically for this purpose, was placed in the middle of the route, and the wadi was barred from one side to the others with big stones.

On the drum he painted in big letters: "This is NOT el-Aqaba. The pass lies 2.3 miles (3.7 kilometres) further east. Don't try. Most difficult to turn cars further up!"

If a British patrol should come looking for this pass, the men would be most grateful for the "accurate" information.

En route to their dump of captured petrol, they spotted a small cask, and beside it a big tin, placed next to a track used by the enemy The container bore the inscription "Emergency Water" and the tin contained six tins of corned beef and a bag of biscuits. It was a welcome addition to their stores which had grown scanty by that time.

Refilling with petrol took some time. This time Almásy would have liked to empty the tank of one of the six parked enemy vehicles which they could not open on the way out. They drove to the "Three Castles", he took the car carefully over the skyline and – about 2 kilometres east of the parked trucks – saw a camped column of 28 enemy vehicles.

In a fraction of a second Almásy vanished discreetly below the skyline, and now all of them, with field glasses, climbed up to the rocks of the "Castle". About 5 kilometres east of the first column was another of about 30 vehicles. A long way out on the plain there was a third which they could not count exactly in the shimmer of the mirage. On the southern horizon the dust clouds of a fourth column were rising; it was also moving in the direction of "Three Castles". Clearly nothing could be done about the 45 litres of petrol they still wanted to siphon off.

It was imperative that they reach their hide-out in the gorge of the "Wadi Anag" in order – if possible – to get out of the mountains via the "Bab el-Misr" pass before these columns. With machine guns at the ready, Almásy drove by compass towards the "Wadi Anag". Before they reached the protection of the gorge, the first vehicles of the column appeared on the skyline barely 4 kilometres behind them, making them wonder whether they had been spotted.

The entrance of Aqaba pass was blocked by a line of stones to confuse enemy vehicles. (From left to right) Munz, Wöhrmann and Körper.
[Dal McGuirk]

Amazingly, the line of stones erected by Salam was still recognisable in 2010

They could not take along the parked *Flitzer* now, not with four men to four vehicles. At least one machine gun had to be manned. They also lacked the 45 litres of petrol which they hoped to acquire. What was more, they found that the water pump of the parked car needed to be dismantled for maintenance or repair. Almásy gave his orders rapidly – the two best wheels of the parked F8s were to be taken off and their defective tyres left in their place, empty jerrycans were to be hidden in a fissure in the rocks above, and all tracks were to be thoroughly obliterated. They were to go on as soon as the job was done, before the enemy reached the place. They had an opportunity to cut across the foot of the plateau and perhaps to get away from the place unnoticed with a start of a few kilometres.

While the men were working, Almásy went to the entrance of the gorge and watched the enemy columns through his field glasses. The leading vehicle – an open tourer – had stopped exactly opposite their entrance about 2 kilometres away, and was waiting for the other vehicles which were coming up in a single file. He tried to measure the speed of the various vehicles by watching as they passed the binocular graticule – about 20 kilometres per hour.

First there were 15 vehicles, then 20, finally 26 as the last two rolled up. He saw the crews unloading freight and rolling it towards a group of vehicles stopped a little to the side.

The work seemed easy and Almásy soon saw they were handling empty petrol containers. So this column was about to leave six vehicles with the empty barrels in order to pick them up again on the way back from Kufra. Perhaps there still was an opportunity for some loot?

Many of the men knelt in the sand, remained motionless in that position for some minutes, and he realised they were saying their midday prayers – Muslim soldiers of the Sudan Defence Force.

Almásy's men had not yet finished transferring the loads and taking off the wheels. They could still get away from here easily, though not unobserved. Now the men of the enemy column lay in the shade of their trucks, it was difficult to count them through the shimmering air, about 65 men. He returned from his observation post to their hiding place and now at last they were ready to move.

Before driving out of the shelter of the gorge into the open plain, Almásy stopped once more for a last look at the enemy column. The convoy had started in the last five minutes, now the Germans were cut off! As Almásy had foreseen, six vehicles were left behind, but this time under guard. Apparently it had been noticed that petrol had been stolen from the other column.

To confuse the enemy, Almásy placed an inscribed fuel drum at the entrance of the Aqaba pass. It reads: "This is not El Aqqaba. The Pass lies 2.3M further East".
[Dal McGuirk]

Munz, Körper and Wöhrmann inspecting an emergency rations and water depot placed by the enemy. It was a welcome addition to their scanty supplies.
[Dal McGuirk]

"Robber's Lair" on the return journey. (From left to right) "Purzel", "Inspektor", "Maria" and "Präsident". Note the wheel to be changed leaning on the right side of "Maria". *[Ottokar Seubert]*

"Robber's Lair" in 2010. The tires removed from "Purzel" are still lying in the desert sand.

Bab el-Misr. When the German vehicles drove through the parked SDF convoy, Almásy gave the Leica to Wöhrmann: "Take a photo in passing. I will lean back so that you can make the exposure past me."
[Dal McGuirk]

Bab el-Misr. Another photo which provides a dramatic proof that Almásy's diary is true and not an invention. [Dal McGuirk]

On the narrow mountain track between here and "Bab el-Misr" there was no chance of evasion. It was exactly 20 kilometres to there, and now it was 15:00. Those people were sure to drive till 17:00, beyond "Bab el-Misr". Considering their low speed Almásy gave them 45 minutes to get ahead, and then drove cautiously after them. On the other side of "Bab el-Misr" he wanted to disappear towards the south or north.

During the wait they had their meal, and all this time Almásy kept an eye on the plain in the direction of "Three Castles", from where the first of the other three columns was soon likely to appear. After exactly 45 minutes the first car appeared on the horizon. The group was now stuck between two enemy columns at about the only spot along the route where there was no alternate passage through the mountains.

They left "Wadi Anag" and immediately went along a deep rain gully towards the trail. It was unlikely that the guard at the six vehicles left behind had seen their three vehicles. After a few minutes they were driving along the tracks of the column itself. Almásy had the machine gun inside the vehicle so as not give them away.

They went quietly kilometre after kilometre and soon they could see the large circular basin of the valley beyond which is the narrow entrance of the "Bab el-Misr". The enemy column was camped just in front of the entrance.

Almásy stopped for a moment and waved Munz with the other station wagon and Körper with his *Flitzer* alongside: "Close all windows and follow quietly just behind me. No shooting, at most salute!" They both grinned broadly: "Yes Sir!"

He gave the Leica to Wöhrmann: "Take a photo in passing. I will lean back so you may take the shot past me."

The deep cut traces of the innumerable trucks that have passed this way are still visible today.

They were the same Chevrolet trucks. The men were preparing to camp for the night; some were lying in the shade under the vehicles. Some were standing about dispersed, and he drove so as to leave them on his right. The sun was low down on the left so they could hardly recognise the markings on their vehicles. He raised his hand in salute and the Sudanese returned it. They were tall thin black men from the White Nile. The Germans had to proceed quite slowly on account of the stony ground and Wöhrmann was able to take six photographs. Almásy tried to see what was loaded on the trucks and passed quite close to one truck whose cover was turned back. The load was cases, not piled very high; that meant heavy weights, probably ammunition.

This bizarre meeting was over in a few seconds, and they drove through the narrow entrance of "Bab el-Misr", along the worn track on to the low plateau. The tracks of another column were before them, it must have passed here quite recently, probably during the noon hours before the Germans had reached Three Castles. Exactly 12 kilometres from "Bab el-Misr" the left rear tyre of Almásy's car was punctured; lucky that it did not happen near the enemy column. On reaching the plain he counted the tracks of the column preceding them – 22 trucks and five large vehicles with much greater width of wheels. Could they be armoured cars? He measured and made a note of the width of the wheels[218].

Driving straight into the setting sun eventually became unbearable. They drove for half an hour towards the blinding disc, and then Almásy could stand it no longer. There was a small *gara* south of the wheel tracks, they turned off and soon a well-concealed camp was set up. Their most difficult task for the following day was to find their "Dump II" again.

On the outward journey they had come by another route, and now Almásy had to find that *gara* again by precise navigation and dead reckoning. The *gara* – coming from the west – appeared to stand alone, but now seen from the east there were dozens of similar peaks lying between their camp and the western horizon. They had not covered a great distance, approximately 210 kilometres, but the day had been eventful enough.

218 These vehicles were not armoured cars but 10 ton Mack trucks.

Ford 01Y patrol truck
of the Sudan Defence
Force.
[Tim Farnden]

Ford 01A V8 patrol
car of the SDF.
The vehicle had been
heavily modified for
its use in the desert.
*[G.J. Mostert via
András Zboray]*

The Sudan Defence Force
and the Kufra Convoys[219]

It is little known, but the Libyan Desert was the scene of one of the greatest logistical feats of the Desert Campaign of WWII. After the capture of Kufra by Leclerc in February 1941 it became apparent that the Free French had neither the manpower nor the logistical capability to maintain a garrison, and the task fell to the Sudan Defence Force. All supplies for the subsequent two years had to be trucked in from Wadi Halfa on the Nile, across 1'200 kilometres of barren and waterless desert.

There is nothing published on these convoys. While the accomplishments of the LRDG are well known, war historians have completely ignored this unglamorous but immense feat. Not surprisingly Ralph Bagnold fully recognised the importance of the convoys. Among his personal papers deposited at the Churchill Archives, there are draft chapters of an intended book on the history of the LRDG, the fifth of which describes the SDF convoys. Bagnold never published these writings; instead it was W.B.K. Shaw who wrote the "official" LRDG history, undoubtedly using some of Bagnold's compiled material. However, the Kufra Convoys were left out and their history forgotten.

The Sudan Defence Force (SDF) was established in 1925 by the British administration of the Sudan to protect its borders. Later on the SDF was also employed in the Desert Campaign of WWII. The background for the founding of the SDF was that the British did not have enough men to garrison their Empire exclusively with British troops, and almost every territory had a local militia or an indigenous regiment. Prior to 1925, the garrison of the Sudan comprised a British battalion around the capital, and battalions of the Egyptian Army, both Egyptian and Sudanese, in the regional capitals. After the anti-British riots in Egypt in 1922, the British thought it desirable to remove all Egyptian troops from what was nomi-

SDF cap badge.

A somewhat worn out Chevrolet WA 30 cwt patrol truck of the SDF.
[G.J. Mostert via András Zboray]

219 Based on: *SDF Kufra Garrison, War Diaries*, National Archive, Kew and *The Bagnold Papers*, Churchill Archive, Churchill College, Cambridge

Trucks returning from a trip to Kufra are being loaded at Wadi Halfa.
[Archive LRDG Rhodesia via Jonathan Pittaway]

Trucks leaving the ferry on the eastern banks of the Nile.
[Archive LRDG Rhodesia via Jonathan Pittaway]

nally still Anglo-Egyptian Sudan, and set up a native Sudanese force which is directly under British command, with exclusively British officers.

In the mid to late 1930s, the SDF was used to counter the aggressive actions of Italian military forces under Marshal Italo Balbo based in Libya. In December 1933, the Italians probed various positions in the Jebel Uweinat area along the poorly defined border between the Kingdom of Egypt, the Sudan, and Libya. Responding to this, the SDF was ordered to occupy the Merga oasis and then the area around the Karkur Murr spring at Jebel Uweinat[220]. When Italy conquered Ethiopia, the SDF was reorganised and expanded. By June 1940 it comprised twenty-one companies, including five Motor Machine Gun Companies, and a total of 4'500 soldiers.

During the Second World War it was expanded again to as many as 20'000 men to counter the threat from the neighboring Italian territories: Libya to the north-west, and Eritrea and the newly-conquered Abyssinia (Ethiopia) to the east.

The SDF also played an active role during the Desert Campaign along the Sudanese border with Libya in North Africa. Here it was used to supply the Free French and then the LRDG garrisons stationed in the former Italian Fort et-Taj at the Kufra oasis after the Free French had captured the fort from the Italians in March 1941.

In April 1941, shortly after the Free French had captured the oasis of Kufra, it was recognised that the place had to be maintained from the Sudan. The SDF and Bimbashi Lonsdale, an officer who had already explored part of the route in peacetime, met this unexpected demand successfully.

Kufra is located about 1'000 kilometres north-west of Wadi Halfa, and while it offers almost every variety of desert surface and desert landscape, there is nothing green over the whole route, except the miniature oasis of Selima lying almost hidden in a crack in the earth's surface about 320 kilometres from Halfa. Water, not very palatable unless drunk in tea, is available there. It is also available at Bir Misaha on an alternate route to the north, and at Jebel Uweinat about 650 kilometres from Wadi Halfa and to the south of the direct route to Kufra. Convoys were dependent on what they could carry, enough for drinking, but not for washing or shaving.

220 TNA, London, WO 32/3535 Report on the Occupation of Merga and Oweinat 1933-34, General Staff, SDF

A variety of trucks lined up at the start of a convoy to Kufra. This particular convoiy was carrying the equipment of the 15 Sqn SAAF.
[G.J. Mostert via András Zboray]

A Chevrolet C60L GS at Wadi Sora.
[G.J. Mostert via András Zboray]

In soft terrain the trucks had to spread out to avoid becoming stuck in the tracks of another vehicle.
[G.J. Mostert via András Zboray]

The convoy on its way to Kufra.
[G.J. Mostert via András Zboray]

The route maintained without much variation was Wadi Halfa – Selima or Bir Misaha – Sand Dune Gap – Gebel Kamil – Eight Bells – Wadi Sora – "Kendall's Dump" – Kufra. During July, August and September 1942, after there were signs of enemy activity around Kufra[221], attempts were made to find routes avoiding the long wadis – Wadi Firaq and Wadi Wassa – where there was a danger of ambush, but no practicable routes were found owing to the soft sand.

Another difficulty was that the town of Wadi Halfa, with its Railways and Dockyards, lies entirely on the east bank of the Nile. Lorries, personnel and loads for Kufra all had to be ferried across on barges, and when the river was in flood a small tug might pull manfully for two hours before it reached the landing place. The troops' quarters were all on the east bank and the workshops on the west bank, until new buildings on the west bank were ready in September 1942.

60 vehicles were withdrawn from the Kassala area in Sudan to start the convoys, and with more from the Khartoum area, they set off by road from Khartoum for the journey to Wadi Halfa on 17 April 1941[222]. They moved by the desert route. Three Chevrolets were lost through cracked cylinder heads, shades of what was to come.

The first convoy left Halfa on 28 April 1941 with a party of LRDG to act as guides. Seven Chevrolets had been lost by the time Bir Misaha was reached. *Bimbashi* Lonsdale then decided to go to Kufra with the Fords, leaving a native officer to follow to Jebel Kamil, where he was to dump his loads to be picked up and taken on to Kufra by the returning Fords.

The second convoy left Wadi Halfa on 18 May with 20 Chevrolets and reached Kufra eight days later with all its vehicles. Seven or eight days were the normal time for the journey. The fastest time ever made was 36 hours by two 15 cwts required to help in the rescue of the missing crews of 15 Sqn SAAF in May 1942.

The third convoy was less fortunate. 34 Chevrolets had to be left at Selima owing to a shortage of fan-belts, so a party was sent back to Wadi Halfa where it was understood there were plenty, but it only succeeded in obtaining enough to take 18 vehicles on to Kufra. Fan-belts were a constant worry on this route, the extreme heat caused rapid wear, sometimes the pulleys were out of alignment, the quality of the belts was poor and supplies were short.

In July 1941, the first SDF Troops were sent to Kufra to relieve the Free French, some of whom were taken in SDF lorries as far as Tekro, the first oasis in Chad. In June, 19 ten-ton Mack diesel lorries were received. The first convoy of Macks left for Kufra on 14 June. Eleven more Mack lorries were received in August. One of the difficulties with these trucks was tyre pressure. If pressure was high, there was a strain on the engine, and they tended to stick in the sand. If lowered, they ran more freely, but had punctures in the rocky places.

---

221 In fact it was Operation Salam that let the British to conclude that there were "enemy activities" in the area around Kufra.

222 The vehicles consisted of 41 Ford 30cwt, 37 Maple Leaf Chevrolets, 1 wireless van and 1 ambulance van.

Tracks in the endless
sand-plains.
*[G.J. Mostert via
András Zboray]*

In the early stages no workshop, no repair lorry and no recovery section were available. Many Chevrolets which had broken down in the desert were loaded on Mack lorries returning empty from their trip to Kufra. Therefore cannibalisation was of necessity often practised. Towards the end of 1941, breakdowns became more frequent owing to the strain on the vehicles.

During 1941, five convoys per month were sent to Kufra with a total payload of approximately 250 tons, but in 1942 the number of convoys had to be increased. The average convoy consisted of 30 vehicles, 20 for payload and the remainder for domestic petrol and oil. Extra convoys were sent to Selima or Bir Misaha to dump petrol to make as much payload space available as possible, but the ratio of 2:1 was never materially changed.

In July 1942 the route was marked out with poles or empty petrol tins every five miles (eight kilometres) as far as the "Sand Dune Gap"[223]. Bir Misaha came into use instead of Selima owing to its better water supply. After August 1942 every possible vehicle had to be pressed into service to supply Kufra and convoy turn-arounds had to be speeded up. One was off again 23 hours after arriving back at Wadi Halfa. This could only be done by organizing maintenance squads of ten men who took over the vehicles for cleaning, oiling and greasing as soon as they arrived, and gave the drivers a few hours rest. Two platoons of No. 34 Coy and some of the ten-ton Macks carried troops on the raid from Kufra to Gialo in September 1942.

The commitments at this time were 1'000 tons of supplics per month to be brought to Kufra. The main troubles were with big ends and gearboxes. The spares situation was difficult, and vehicle wastage reached 25%. In spite of all this only one lorry load failed to reach Kufra.

At the end of November, due to the developments on the main front at el-Alamein, the pressure to maintain Kufra suddenly ceased, and it became possible to run convoys there from Cirenaica.

223 This is the gap originally found by Clayton during the 1932 expedition, about 5 kilometres south of 22N, roughly 80-100 kilometres from both Missaha and Selima.

27 May 1942, reaching "Dump II"

The group had spent the night at "Camp 13", at the *gara* near the enemy line of communication, and Almásy wanted to start particularly early today since he was expecting to lose much time looking for their "Dump II". It was also essential to disappear as quickly as possible from the enemy convoy route. He nearly overslept, and only rose – startled – from his camp bed at 05:00. The men, who were gradually showing signs of exhaustion, were lying in perfect slumber. He was particularly worried about Körper; he looked miserable, worn to a shadow. Despite this belated reveille they were on the road by 05:45.

The enemy route crossed territory unknown to Almásy. At first it was a sandy plain good for driving with many large *gara* groups north and south, although the Italian map was completely blank. Then there were some low stony plateaus across their direction of travel and one could see how the enemy column tried again and again to bring the trail down to better ground.

The column which preceded them the day before wheeled off south in the face of an especially forbidding plateau. From the manner in which the column was being led, Almásy had already determined that there was a desert expert ahead of him. He followed their fresh tracks in spite of the five conspicuously wide tracks which made him suspect armoured cars. The track passed around the plateau in a masterly manner and on the open *serir* joined an older set of tracks, in which ten unusually wide tracks were also visible. Probably the leader of the column had gone over this route repeatedly and knew the best ground.[224]

The Ford C11ADF "Präsident" with Wöhrmann standing behind the mounted MG 15. Note the additional mounting on the back, the sand-ladders in the roof rack, the *Askania kleiner Emil* and the Cole MK.I Universal Sun-Compass. *[Ottokar Seubert]*

224 From Bagnold's account we know that while the Chevrolets were driven by Sudanese drivers, the White 10 tonners always had British drivers.

The wrecked SDF 1942 Ford pickup truck opposite the entrance of Wadi Bakht, which still has the SDF insignia painted on the roof.

The wreck of a White 6 x 6 truck. It was used by the SDF as well as by the Heavy Section of the LRDG. This particular wreck has wheel-rims of Italian origin.

The wreck of a Maple Leaf Chevrolet 1543X2 truck used by the Kufra Convoys, outside Wadi Sora.

At 08:00 Almásy sighted suspicious dots on the horizon and recognised a column through his field glasses. The trucks were however off the tracks on which the Germans were driving, with their radiators facing them. It was obviously an empty column on the return journey from Kufra to Wadi Halfa. Almásy turned away to the north and passed the halted column just close enough to allow him to count the vehicles – 22 trucks and one car. Probably it was the column whose six parked cars he had doctored with sand a few days ago.

Gradually they emerged from the group of hills and Almásy stopped in order to mark his dead reckoning on the map. The large double *gara* laying only a few degrees north of their course should be their "Dump II". Almásy's men were not convinced, and Wöhrmann was as usual particularly pessimistic. Almásy covered the 12 kilometres to the *gara* which now – seen from the east – seemed quite unfamiliar to him, but as soon as they arrived at the foot of the hill he found their outward tracks, and a few minutes later they halted, laughing, at their dump. He had never imagined it would be so easy, the plot of his dead reckoning course showed an error of barely 600 metres over a distance of 300 kilometres.

Almásy now tried to find the place where on the 16th they had had their first surprise of 104 fresh tracks, along the northern edge of the enemy tracks, but Wöhrmann was unable to calculate the corresponding distances for him, and by the time he stopped – somewhat annoyed – they had passed the place by 11 kilometres. So he left the broad stream of the convoy routes and reverted to a compass course. The next challenge was the passage through the narrow dunes at the foot of the hills before Kufra, but they still had five hours of arduous driving before they could get there.

The drive by compass went without a hitch, and at exactly the spot calculated they crossed the old track of *Maggiore* Rolle and this time Almásy even had the good luck to drive past a triangulation mark set up by Rolle and marked on the map.

Arriving at the dunes, this time Almásy did not take any chances. There were only four of them, much too tired to dig out cars stuck in the sand. He stopped at the foot of the dunes and went ahead on foot to find the best passage and marked it with piled-up stones. They got through these bad dunes without trouble in three such stages, and from a long way off he could already see the road markings of the old *Trucchi* trail.

They spent endless hours ploughing through these wild Hauwaish Mountains along their own trail, along this blessed "smugglers road". He pondered aloud how these mountains had acquired the name "the wild beast". The Bedouins had told the Egyptian explorer Hassanein Bey, first to travel through these mountains with his caravan in the year 1920 that the name "Hauwaish" perhaps meant rather spirits, *djinns* and suchlike, who inhabited the hills in the guise of snakes. Just as he was telling this to Wöhrmann, once more they encountered a very fat snake, bigger than the one in Gilf Kebir. He recalled the prophecy of the three protecting *djinns*, and Munz and Körper also stopped beside him, exclaiming: "Now we will certainly get home!"

They reached their number one camp with the first petrol dump in daylight. Almásy's calculation showed the comfortable fact that – barring accidents – they should easily reach *Campo 4* on the *palificata* with all three cars. They could be content with today's run, 340 kilometres.

Great Sand Sea

The Great Sand Sea is the second largest continuous sand covered area on Earth (after the *Grand Erg Oriental* in Algeria). It is a huge mass of sand which originates from the chain of wind-excavated depressions paralleling the Mediterranean coast from Gialo in Libya to the Qattara Depression in Egypt. It is called the Great Sand Sea in Egypt, but the Calanscio Sand Sea to the west in Libya is a continuous part of it, as is the Rebiana Sand Sea, which is the southern extension of the Calanscio Sand Sea lying to the West of Kufra. The western edge of the Rebiana Sand Sea may be considered the edge of the Libyan Desert.

The prevailing winds sculpt this great mass of sand into huge longitudinal crested dunes (*seif* dunes) stretching uninterrupted for hundreds of kilometres, with smooth sand-filled or even sand-free corridors between the dunes. The structure of these complex interrelated forms was first studied and described by Ralph Bagnold, whose book is still the standard work on the subject[225] .

This peculiar alignment makes north-south travel very easy among the dunes, but any east-west traverse requires crossing the dunes, as was discovered by the Rohlfs expedition of 1873 which was forced to turn north and follow the alignment of the dunes to Siwa, marking their farthest point west by a cairn at *Regenfeld*[226].

The eastern sides are generally steep, while the western sides rise gradually, with pockets of soft sand. A west-to-east crossing is relatively easy, but it can be a challenging task in the opposite direction.

---

225 Ralph A. Bagnold, *The Physics of Blown Sand and Desert Dunes*
226 "Rain field", a location in the Great Sand Sea named by the German explorer Gerhard
    Rohlfs on account of the unexpected rainfall encountered there (Rohlfs, *Drei Monate in
    derlibyschen Wüste*)

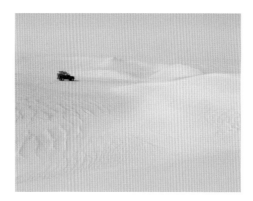

Left: The Land Rover appears lost amidst the endless Sandsea.

Right: View from the top of a dune ridge.

The nature and form of the dune ridges can be quite varied.

Left: View from a dune ridge down to the Gassi, which is often free of any sand.

Right: Sunset somewhere in the Calanscio Sand Sea.

Patrick Clayton accomplished the first east-to-west crossing of the Egyptian part of the Great Sand Sea in December 1932, building" Big Cairn"at the spot he reached on the far western side. However this is not the end of the entire Sand Sea but only a large flat sand-free plain, bordered on the north and west by the Calanscio Sand Sea. During WWII, this route was regularly used by the Long Range Desert Group to get behind enemy lines.[227] While the interior of the area is completely immersed in sand, some outcrops of rock offer a glimpse into the geology of the country below. South of Ain Dalla runs a scarp, first encountered by Rohlfs and Zittel, which contains the all-important K/T (Cretaceous/Tertiary) boundary, and in the lower beds a mass of upper Cretaceous marine fossils, including the ammonite *Libycoceras ismaeli* described by Zittel. Coming from the south, the scarp appears as a chain of low hills, prompting Rohlfs to name it "Ammonite Hill", confusing later travellers like Bagnold, who came from the north looking for a prominent hill on the horizon.

Contrary to expectation, the interior of the Sand Sea is not completely lifeless. Two species of plants, *Cornulaca monacantha* and *Calligonum commosum* manage to survive in the northern areas, up to 100 kilometres south of the oasis depressions, but beyond the sands are indeed lifeless.

28 May 1942, in the dunes again

From the camp on the *Trucchi* trail they started before 05:00, as they secretly harboured the hope of reaching Gialo the same day. Almásy followed the *Trucchi* trail as far as possible up to the Zighen dunes, a good way beyond the spot where they had found the trail on their journey here. Then – as always on this continent – the unforeseen happened. Almásy did not look at the map before entering the dunes, Wöhrmann did not tell him the directions and distances taken on the outward journey, so they suddenly found themselves in rolling dune country on soft drift sand, gliding with ever-increasing speed over ridges and valleys of dunes on an uncertain northerly course. For good measure he corrected this course towards northwest[228] on every dune-back they reached. After an hour they were definitely caught in the dunes. His vehicle was stuck axle-deep, with 50 metres of ploughed-up track, and he only succeeded with much shouting and waving to halt the other two vehicles in time on reasonably firm ground.

The usual digging ensued, then the recovery work with rope ladders, followed by the calculation of the distance covered – according to which they should long ago have reached the *palificata*. There was a gnawing uncertainty that perhaps they had crossed the trail on this crazy dune trip without sighting

Driving north on the *serir*. The first dune ridges of the sand sea are hardly visible on the horizon. *[Dal McGuirk]*

The last hills north of Kufra in the shimmering heat.

227 One of their abandoned Ford F30 CMP trucks still rests in the sand west of Ain Dalla.
228 The diary is in error here, they were East of the correct route, so the correction must have been made towards the northwest, not northeast as stated.

Reaching the flat *serir* north of Kufra.

the poles, and finally they made the decision to double back to where they last saw the road marking of the *Trucchi* trail.

Only then did Almásy see on the map that he should have travelled further southwest and west. It was too late for reproaches, they had travelled more than 100 kilometres, used up their precious petrol and were still stuck in the dunes. He dared not attempt another break out through the dunes, so there was nothing else but to travel back south, towards Kufra, in order to reach the *pista palificata* south of Bir Zighen. That also meant they had to pass the enemy outpost lying at Bir Abu Zereigh.

After a lengthy drive south a *palo* of the great trail appeared at last on the horizon. It was at kilometre 445 from Gialo, just 20 kilometres south of Bir Abu Zereigh and about 39 kilometres from the spot where they had left the *palificata* on the outward journey. Almásy could do nothing but order the men to make ready their weapons for action.

There were relatively few enemy tracks on the *palificata* itself but one could see that the stretch between Kufra and Zighen was travelled every few days. Bir Abu Zereigh was near kilometre 425 and there the *palificata* mades a sharp turn to the north east.

In the shimmering midday heat it can easily happen that one overlooks the next iron pole of the *palificata* where the direction changes. Yet any stop near Bir Abu Zereigh to search the valley or the vicinity by driving around in a criss-cross manner would have exposed them to the enemy. Soon the critical kilometre pole was reached, with a sign pointing left to the well where the enemy outpost was encamped.

Somewhere in the *serir*. Munz leaning agaisnt the mudguard of "Inspektor"
[Dal McGuirk]

Munz sitting in
"Inspektor". Lined up
behind are "Maria"
and "Präsident"
[Dal McGuirk]

Körper sitting behind
the steering wheel of
"Maria". Note the ad-
ditional equipment on
the truck: MG mount-
ing, condenser and the
Askania compass on
the engine bonnet.
[Ottokar Seubert]

Somewhere in the *serir*.
Wöhrmann leaning
against the back of
"Maria".
[Ottokar Seubert]

The endless row of high iron poles which indicated the trail at intervals of one kilometre now started to bend in a big curve towards the northeast. The surface was soft, real dune country; Almásy could not stop to glance at the map and Wöhrmann was useless as a navigator. After a while Almásy noticed that the iron posts did not carry the crossed tin panels with the inscribed kilometre number of the Palificata, but small tin cans which they had only seen here and there on the Trucchi trail. So in spite of everything they had gone astray. The compass showed a few degrees north by east, he got Wöhrmann to hold the map under his nose as he drove, and saw that the *Palificata* should run at about 30 degrees here. At that moment three quite fresh tracks passed from the left on to this mysterious trail. An enemy patrol was somewhere immediately in front of them, and would certainly return sooner or later to Bir Abu Zereigh. It was not possible to evade it by going right, toward the real *palificata*, because everywhere there were high impassable dunes. Almásy quietly cursed the Italian map which did not show one anything. They were now moving on a *Pista Fustificata* marked at kilometre distances which was not the Kufra – Gialo trail marked on the map.

The enemy patrol must have been just in front of them. Almásy crossed its track and tried to evade it by turning a little west, but after only a few hundred metres he found an equally fresh trail of a second patrol, in fact 3 vehicles. They could not consider stopping, they raced up and down the flat backs of the dunes, expecting at every ascent of the steep sand slopes to collide head-on with the returning enemy vehicles. The tracks on their right turned sharply right and Almásy saw at once that this patrol was going toward Bir Dakkar; so he decided to go on along the trail not marked on the map. Gradually it dawned on him that this trail was perhaps marked some time ago by the *Trucchi* men, and led to the *Poste Trucchi*, an old camp with two stone buildings which he had seen recently from the reconnaissance aircraft. He knew the true *palificata* was 12 kilometres east of there, so as soon as they were past the dunes he would travel by compass eastward.

Some movement flickered to their left in the distance, difficult to see clearly among these hills and valleys of glaring sand. That something disappeared and re-appeared according to whether their vehicles descended into the rolling valleys or climbed up the back of the dunes. One … two … three dark spots … vehicles! It was the enemy patrol, driving on a parallel course. They could only hope the enemy had not yet spotted them. Almásy could not yet dodge to the right, there were a few tense minutes before he found the dune valley wide enough to turn east at full speed.

After scarcely 10 kilometres they had made it, the poles of the real *palificata* appeared on the skyline and after a few minutes they laughed as they reached the well-preserved tracks of their outward journey. They had to try to reach the *Campo 4* airfield near kilometre 275 before nightfall. Perhaps the enemy patrol would be confused by their fresh tracks and follow them, but he thought they would not venture beyond *Campo 5* even then.

They arrived at their goal before sunset, and had the last bitter disappointment – the petrol dump had not yet been set up by Beilharz as ordered when he was sent back to Gialo[229]. They had to leave the *Flitzer* behind here, and it even remained questionable whether they would be able to reach Gialo the next day with the two station wagons. The day's journey was 370 kilometres.

29 May 1942, reaching Gialo

The night was spent at *Campo 4*, 270 kilometres from Gialo, at the same place where Almásy had decided two weeks earlier to take the dangerous southern route, unable to pass the dunes of the Calanscio Sand Sea with the small convoy.

He noted in his diary: "We took it easy in the morning, shaved and washed as far as possible. Our store of water lasted out the whole trip. Near the camp on the *Trucchi* trail I was able to leave behind 7 well-concealed filled water-canisters. The average water consumption of my men which I had fixed at 5 litres daily on account of them being desert novices went down from the initial 6 litres to 3 litres per man per day."

A marker of the former "Motor- and Air Route" from Gialo to Kufra. It was well visible from the air as well as from the ground.

229 This statement of Almásy is rather confusing. On 15 May he wrote that Beilharz should establish such a dump at *Campo 5*, but at the return trip Almásy was looking for it at *Campo 4* that was actually the place where they had separated. Since he mentioned *Campo 5* together with the distance from Gialo (316 kilometres) it can hardly be assumed that it is a simple writing error. Also in the report of Beilharz relayed to IC (HW 19/30 No. 28777, WESTERN DESERT AREA, 25 May 1942) *Campo 5* was mentoned very clearly as the intended location of the dump. It is plausible that in the stress of preceding events, Almásy actually gave verbal instructions for *Campo 5.* to Beilharz, but in reality he meant *Campo 4*, and on his return journey he simply passed the established dump at *Campo 5*. However, there is no proof since there are no records whether Beilharz had established this dump at all. The SDF had sent a patrol north from Bir Zighen on 15 June 1942 that reported that they had found a fuel dump of 80 gallons at *Campo 3* (IWM, Message Folio No. 04809, 16/6/42). Since the Italians did not use the emergency landing grounds for normal air traffic, it is possible that Beilharz had mistakenly placed the dump at *Campo 3*.

Approaching Gialo in the last vehicle – "Präsident". The Italian flag is already hoisted on the back of the car and Körper and Munz are preparing the signal pistol.
[Ottokar Seubert]

In sight of Gialo. Munz is firing the pre-arranged three white flares to announce their return after the successful mission.
[Dal McGuirk]

The *Flitzer* was taken to the furthest corner of the landing ground and left there for later recovery. Then they moved along the *palificata* northward, towards the starting point and terminus of their mission. The only new track on this once so busy route was that of their Commercial truck which had gone back to Gialo a fortnight ago with *Unterarzt* Strungmann and Beilharz.[230]

This message was sent on 4 June from Tripoli and mentions the wrong date for the arrival at Gialo.

Almásy was watching the petrol-gauge indicator with growing anxiety; gradually it became certain that they could not reach Gialo with both cars. At *Campo 1*, only about 70 kilometrees before reaching Gialo, as a precautionary measure they had to empty the tank of the "Präsident" in order to make sure to reach Gialo with at least the "Inspektor". They completed the last stage with the four of them in one vehicle. But Almásy did not intend to abandon the vehicles left behind and wrote: "The day after tomorrow I will go back to *Campo 4* with the Commercial at Gialo and one of the cars. From there we will go up the 80 kilometres into the *Sand Sea* to repair the "Consul" left behind there, and after two days all my vehicles will be reunited at Gialo except for the *Commercial* parked at the *Gilf Kebir*.

Exactly at noon they came to the southern perimetres of Gialo aerodrome. Munz fired the pre-arranged three white flares with the Véry pistol, the others hoisted the Italian tricolour flag, under whose aegis they had started their trip, and had now successfully completed it.

A message sent on 4 June 1942 from TRIPOLI to Berlin informed that SALAM had returned after completing the mission to Gialo on 28 May. However, the date mentioned is definitely wrong; it should read 29 May[231].

29 May 1942, bad luck for SCHILDKROETE

While Almásy and his group had spent a quiet night in the desert at *Campo 4*, further to the Northeast, Rommel's all-out attack against the Allied-held Gazala line, *Operation Theseus*, was at a critical stage. The radio transmitter of Operation Salam (call sign SCHILDKROETE), formally attached to the HQ *Panzerarmee Afrika* at Mamelin in the Cirenaica with *Unteroffizier* (NCO) Werner Aberle and *Gefreiter* Waldemar Weber as W/T operator, were ordered to join Rommel's Tactical HQ to make good a shortage of W/T operators.

Rommel's habit of leading from the front might be debatable, but probably it was his direct personal involvement in the course of the battle at this critical moment which saved the day for the Axis offensive. To be so close to the enemy means an

---

230 This observation supports the idea that Beilharz never returned to make a dump at *Campo 5*. However it does not rule out that he did so at *Campo 3*, still ahead of them.
231 TNA, London, HW 19/31 ISOS 29084

A Humber "Box" Heavy Utility 4x4 Staff Car which was used by the British army.

The wrecked vehicle lies south of Gialo along the track to Kufra.

A Ford 01Y of the Sudan Defence Force.

In 2010, the wreck was not at its place any more but brought down to Kufra by Libyan officials to be displayed at a memorial remembering Graziani's 1931 attack on the oasis.

extraordinary risk for an HQ. Exactly this dreaded situation came about. The HQ came under direct attack by a New Zealand battalion – Rommel was lucky and was not captured. Aberle and Weber were not so lucky. Operation Salam's W/T transmitter quickly fell into the hands of the enemy, so fast that Aberle and Weber had no chance to destroy all of their documents.

As if it were not bad luck enough to be captured by the enemy, among the documents found with them was the novel *Rebecca*, the book used for the secret code. While this English version was perfectly suitable for Eppler and Sandstede who were operating behind the lines in Egypt, it was disastrous for Aberle and Weber. The British interrogators soon became suspicious when they found that neither of them could speak English. Investigating the book carefully, they found erased writing on the inner cover of the book which they made out as as "50 escudos". This was the hint they needed to conclude that the book must have been sold in Portugal. During an investigation in Lisbon shortly after, it was found that a member of the German Embassy had bought 6 copies of that particular book at once in a bookshop. The British were now convinced that Aberle and Weber did not have this book for leisure reading, but as the basis to code and encode W/T messages.[232]

30 May 1942, recovery of the vehicles

Almásy's diary ends with the return to Gialo, and we no longer have the writings of Eppler and Stanstede for guidance. The only sources of information from this point onwards are from intercepted W/T messages which allow the remnant of *Salam* to be traced back to Tripoli and the last chapter of Almásy's book "With Rommel's Army in Libya".

At this time *Major* Wittilo von Griesheim was on a special mission in the south of Libya. He sent a message to ANGELO on this date, explaining that he would continue his journey as far as Murzuk to inspect his *Gudrun Stellen*[233]. Further, he intended to participate in a patrol towards the Tibesti Mountains with motor vehicles and camels[234]. On 31 May von Griesheim messaged *Major* Seubert and made him aware of the desperate shortage of vehicles. He proposed to take over Almásy's vehicles once SALAM had returned to Tripoli as the only feasible solution. However, anticipating that the vehicles might not be

232 Sansom, *I spied Spies*
233 *Gegenstellen/G-Stellen*. Translated as "remote stations" for W/T traffic.
234 TNA, London, HW 19/31 ISOS 29025.

completely serviceable, as a fallback option he also asked for approval to purchase two suitable vehicles in Tunisia[235].

As expected, Almásy found Beilharz and the repaired F8 "Habuba" at Gialo. The only vehicle to complete the whole mission, the C11ADF "Inspektor", was refuelled and stripped of all unnecessary loads. Both headed south again to recover the other vehicles. There were the C11ADF "Präsident" at *Campo 1*", the F8 "Maria" at *Campo 4*, and the most difficult one, the C11ADF "Consul" in the dunes of the Sand Sea. The last F8, "Purzel", left behind in the Gilf Kebir, had to be considered lost. In the late afternoon of 31 May they were back at Gialo, and immediately prepared for the journey back to Tripoli, which they reached with no further difficulties.[236]

Little survives on the fate of the *Salam* vehicles. After a lengthy correspondence with Seubert on the desperate need for some vehicles, on 27 June von Griesheim confirmed that two *Salam* vehicles were taken over, with the remainder being under repair.[237] However the rapidly advancing *Panzerarmee* was also in constant need of transport, and apparently Seubert's approval was overridden, for a grateful message by von Griesheim thanking Seubert for his intervention only mentions one vehicle being allocated for his own personal use, all efforts to obtain more rebounding from Rommel's staff.[238] There is one surviving photograph which shows Seubert on the road to Nalut with the ex-*Salam* Ford C11 ADF station wagon in the background, probably taken in September 1942[239]. The fate of the other vehicles remains unknown.

The wreck, lying near Bir Zighen was stripped of all usable parts.

235 TNA, London, HW 19/31 ISOS. 28834.
236 There is no evidence for this date, but given their known arrival to Gialo on the 29 May, and their confirmed arrival to Tripoli on 2 June, it would be very difficult to envision the sequence of events with any other date
237 TNA, London, HW 19/32 ISOS. 31462
238 TNA, London, HW 19/34 ISOS 34072
239 TNA, London, HW 19/34 ISOS 33878

Extensive date palm plantations are on both sides of the asphalted *Via Balbia* between Misurata and Zliten. The photo was taken either shortly before or after Operation Salam.
[Dal McGuirk]

Along the *Via Balbia* between Misurata and Zliten
[Dal McGuirk]

2 June 1942, back to Tripoli and new orders

Almásy with the remainder of his men and vehicles arrived back to Tripoli on 2 June 1942 and stayed in the facilities of the German Consulate[240] awaiting new orders.

After the enemy captured SCHILDKROETE on 29 May, a new receiving station was ordered by Seubert to replace them, at first only to listen for messages from Eppler and Sandstede in Egypt. They were not allowed to reply or to send their own messages to KONDOR. It was feared that after the enemy got hold of *Rebecca*, either it would put the two spies in serious danger if they continued to use the same code, or the British had already captured KONDOR and were now trying to send faked messages, pretending they were Eppler and Sandstede.[241] However, as stated by Seubert after the war[242], despite all the listening, no W/T message was ever received from KONDOR[243].

Apparently after a week of listening to nothing but silence, Seubert changed his mind. On 8 June, 11 days after the capture of SCHILDKROETE, he ordered all stations to establish contact immediately with Almásy via W/T and to make sure that W/T communication was taken up with KONDOR; the same instruction was given to von Griesheim. Furthermore, Almásy was ordered to proceed immediately to the Tactical HQ of the *Panzerarme*e and to set up a W/T station to communicate with KONDOR from there. *Stellenleiter* Niese and Häusgen were instructed to place themselves at the disposal of Almásy in order to get communications with KONDOR working. Seubert requested Almásy and Niese to send the required call-signs and frequencies to *Abwehrstelle Athen*, to enable communication between KONDOR and Athens. A report was to be provided to Seubert on completion of these tasks[244]. Separately *Abwehrstelle Athen* (ADOLF) was instructed to establish communication with KONDOR, drawing on any necessary support needed from Niese.[245]

240 TNA, London, HW 19/31 ISOS 29269.
241 TNA, London, HW 19/32 ISOS. 31320
242 Seubert, *Die Nachhut,* No. 2 (1967), page 16
243 See also TNA, London HW 19/33 ISOS 31977 and 32533
244 TNA, London, HW 19/30 ISOS 29397
245 TNA, London, HW 19/95 ISK 10801, HW 19/33 32062 and 32316

Road inside Zliten.
Note the local people
sitting in the shadow
of the buildings during
the midday heat.
[Dal McGuirk]

Major von Griesheim
was always short of
vehicles and therefore
the handing over of
the cars of Operation
Salam to him was
most welcome. *Major*
Seubert standing on
the left, with one of
the Salam Ford
C11ADF behind him.
[Ottokar Seubert]

PART 3:
THE AFTERMATH

British Countermeasures:
Operation Claptrap

British special forces and in particular the *Long Range Desert Group* dominated the desert and British intelligence was able to intercept and decipher the *Abwehr's* W/T messages. One may wonder why Almásy's party was not intercepted and caught by an enemy patrol at least on the way back from the delivery of the two spies to Assiut.[246]

Intercepted messages

British Intelligence intercepted the messages sent and received by Operation Salam from the beginning of the enterprise. However, the number of messages intercepted every day that had to be deciphered was huge, and priorities had to be set. In regard to the North African theatre, all eyes were focussed on Rommel's *Panzerarmee Afrika* where everybody was anxious to recognise the next attack early enough to be able to alert their own army. Messages related to preparations for Operation Salam did not receive high priority. It was only the message of 19th May from Tripoli to Seubert stating that SALAM has reached the Gilf Kebir which alerted Jean Alington, working in Hut 3 at Bletchley Park. While her superiors appeared uninterested, over the next few days she kept following the flow of decyphered messages for further clues. On 25 May the decodings of a near complete batch of the messages sent by Almásy and OTTER became available, and she immediately realised that an enemy unit was moving across the Libyan Desert towards Egypt. She feared that the enemy might detect a decoy signals station which the British had placed somewhere south of Siwa to deceive the Germans with faked messages simulating troops massing in that area[247].

---

246 Based on the messages filed in WO201.2139, Enemy Intelligence Units, Operation Claptrap
247 Jean Howard (nee Alington) to Brigadier Bagnold, 31 March 1978, Bagnold Papers, Churchill
    Archives, Cambridge.

However despite Jean Alington's best efforts, the ten-day delay in processing the intercepted messages meant that Almásy was already well on his return journey when the information gained from the *Salam* intercepts was passed on to GHQ ME in Cairo. The inability of *Salam* to make contact with OTTER or SCHILDK-ROETE also worked in Almásy's favour, as after 17 May there was no radio traffic which could have given them away to the listening enemy.

25 May 1942; alert and reaction

Once the nature of the operation became clear at Bletchley Park on 25 May, the reaction was immediate. On the very same day (when Almásy had already delivered the two spies to Assiut, had passed Kharga again and was just crossing the Gilf Kebir for the second time), GHQ ME sent a most urgent secret message to *Kaid* Khartoum[248] saying they had information about enemy intelligence activities in the area of the Gilf Kebir, and asking for patrols to be sent out to locate the enemy and if possible capture them. As the SDF were providing the garrison of Kufra and running the Kufra convoys at that time, so they were the closest military unit to intercept the enemy in the region.

On 26 May 1942, a message was sent with the information that GHQ ME had ordered Squadron Leader Smith-Ross to fly to Wadi Halfa to lead the patrols on their search for Almásy. The same message said it was thought the enemy was moving from Gilf Kebir towards Kharga Oasis. However as decoding of the messages was lagging four days behind Almásy's actual position – the search would therefore be conducted in the wrong direction.

By 3 June, the connection between Almásy and SALAM had clearly been made, and Operation Claptrap was launched by GHQ ME to capture him. The operational brief for 3 June gives a summary of what was known up to that time: It was recognised that an enemy intelligence service unit under *Hauptmann* Almásy had returned to the base at Gialo, but the nature of the mission was still not clear. SDF patrols were still in position to the north, west and south of the Gilf Kebir, since further enemy missions were expected. Two days later special liaison officer Smith-Ross reported from his position at Eight Bells just south of the Gilf Kebir that everything had been done to block the passages through the Gilf Kebir, and that a small party was posted to guard the wells at Bir Misaha. He wanted to leave one patrol at Eight Bells while another one would move to Kufra on that day. Since Gialo was considered too far away from Kufra to send a patrol to search the neighbourhood, it was planned to make a reconnaissance flight by one of the planes available at Kufra.

A small reconnaissance patrol of No.5 MMG Company, Eastern Arab Corps under Walter Brown had searched allong the bottom of the escarpment of the Gilf Kebir. Near the Wadi Aqaba they met fresh car tracks and when they found an abandoned

---

248 During the Condominium in the Anglo-Egyptian Sudan, after 1910, the Governor General presided over an executive council, that included the Inspector General, the civil, legal, and financial secretaries, the General Officer Commanding the Troops – The *Kaid* – and two to four other British officials appointed by the Governor General.

The Chevrolet 1533X2 T8 Te Taniwha of T2 Patrol, LRDG parked near the lake of Kufra in late 1942. During the time of Operation Salam, none of the LRDG patrols was available to help to intercept Almásy. *[Brendan O'Carroll]*

rest place and a German water bottle, it was clear to them that these were the traces of Almasy and his men.[249]

Kaid Khartoum complained in a message to GHQ ME that although his ground troops were in position he could not carry out the ordered operations satisfactorily unless the planes requested were available at Kufra. When he wrote this message, the only serviceable plane at Kufra was a Bristol Blenheim of 15 Sqn SAAF – one of the planes involved in the "Kufra Tragedy".

Another summary from GHQ ME reveals that they were not entirely happy with what was going on. The senior RAF officer at Kufra took the only serviceable plane, the Blenheim, to fly to Wadi Halfa to attend a conference. Beside the fact that he arrived late, it was found he had only a vague idea of what was happening – and it was stated that Kufra now had no aircraft. In the meantime, information was received that on 23 May at 08:00, two British Army vehicles had passed Kharga towards Assiut, and on the following day at 07:00 the same two vehicles had passed the oasis once more, again without stopping.

The British were sure that the Germans were maintaining the "Almásy Commando" as an equivalent to the LRDG which was operating over a wide area from its base at Gialo. They assumed this unit to conduct operations to Upper Egypt via Zighen, bypassing Kufra, then through the Gilf Kebir to the Nile Valley. They even assumed that a permanent W/T post had been established at the Gilf Kebir. But the first real sign of Almásy's group was found by a SDF patrol operating from Zighen, when, about 18 kilometres from their post, fresh traces of three vehicles similar to theirs were seen.

249 Sudan Archives, Durham University, SAD.739/12/52/55

After Aberle and Weber were captured on 29 May, a report was received from the Eighth Army on 5 June. It stated that, according to captured documents, the afore-mentioned "Almásy Commando" probably consisted of six sections, each equipped with a W/T transmitter, and that their HQ was at Gialo, from where the units undertook journeys of 16 to 24 days. The misinterpretation of the six codenames of the W/T transmitters related to Operation Salam as independent sections at full strength made the British believe that Almásy had a group of considerable size under his command.

Then, on 10 June 1942, Inter Services Liaison Department (ISLD) reported that they had been informed by London that the German group had returned safely and Almásy had reported the completion of his assignment. It was regretted that they had not been able to capture the German unit, but it was thought nevertheless that valuable information about the setup of the *Abwehr* in North Africa had been obtained.

Traces of car tyres are clearly seen in the undisturbed surface of the sand. Until the wind blows them away.

13 June 1942, traces of the enemy

The British were nervous and probably angry that Almásy had escaped them. On 12 June a message was sent from GHQ ME to *Kaid* Khartoum that they had received information from the RAF that the post at Uweinat had been attacked. Based on this message, a strong patrol from Kufra had been ordered to investigate the matter – it was found that the post was still in place and there had been no enemy attack at all. HQ RAF ME then received an order to investigate the origin of this false report, and to make sure that units remained calm.

The LRDG's Survey Section, stationed at Kufra under Captain Ken Lazarus, together with a patrol of the SDF posted to Bir Zighen, were searching for traces of enemy activity on 13 June, when they discovered the fresh tracks of 12 vehicles just east of LG. 6. Along these tracks they found five empty German fuel containers and empty Italian ration tins.

As it was believed that further missions would be carried out by the "Almásy Commando" the LRDG at Siwa had asked the Egyptian Frontier Force to send a patrol to Ain Dalla on 15 June, and a squadron of the same unit was ordered to move to Kharga and the area of Dakhla on 21 June to establish permanent posts there and to carry out occasional patrols to the Gilf Kebir.

On 15 June the SDF Zighen patrol found 80 gallons of petrol dumped at LG. 3[250] and only one day later a LRDG patrol returned from road watch near Marble Arch and reported many tracks south of Gialo.

250 This fuel dump was possibly the one Beilharz had placed at Almásy's order, but it was not seen by the returning German group.

23 June 1942, more enemy patrols?

The patrol of the Egyptian Frontier Force sent to Ain Dalla reported that they reached the place on 19 June and had investigated the mound and the well, but found no fresh traces of vehicles. It could be concluded that nobody had approached the vicinity of the springs for several months.

Tension mounted again when the Zighen patrol observed approximately four 30 cwt-size vehicles passing LG. 3 rapidly in the night of 22 to 23 June. They followed the tracks to the south, and came to the conclusion that an enemy patrol must be operating south of LG. 6. A warning was given to all convoys on the way to Kufra and they were instructed to stop and wait at "Kendall's Dump" while a patrol from Kufra was sent out to reconnoitre the area between Wadi Firaq and "Kendall's Dump". To prevent the enemy using "The Gap" in the Gilf Kebir once more a LRDG patrol was sent out to mine the two entrances to the Aqaba Pass, but was instructed to leave a clear lane for possible own movements[251]. Since an extensive search, by ground patrols in co-operation with air-reconnaissance, had provided no further evidence of an enemy presence, it was presumed that the patrol had returned north and the search was called off.

On 8 July 1942 a regular reconnaissance patrol sent north from Kufra found 14 fresh enemy vehicle tracks one mile north of LG. 2. The tracks were then followed until LG. 4 where it was observed that some tracks led east, as had already been seen at LG. 3.[252] Since it was not realised that they had found the traces of Operation Salam rather than those of a further German enterprise, the LRDG initiated a fresh search further east. From Siwa a patrol was sent down to Ain Dalla, and searched as far as the area of "Big Cairn" in the Great Sand Sea. Nothing was found – indeed it was doubted that the vehicles reported by the SDF patrol from Zighen on the night of 22 to 23 June were real.

An abandoned CMP truck somewhere between Kufra and Gialo.

The truck is a CMP Chevrolet 12 cab C60L.

The cut out roof hatch was obviously was a field modification. Some faded paint markings are still visible.

251 TNA London, WO 169/7288, SDF Kufra Garrison, War Diaries. 1941 July – 1942 Dec.
252 The tracks of 14 vehicles may be explained thus: initially five vehicles went south; "Consul" was left in the dunes. Then one vehicle with Strungmann and Beilharz returned, then Beilharz went down to establish the fuel depot and returned. After that the three vehicles that had completed the mission returned. Then Almásy came down again with one vehicle to recover "Consul" and "Maria" and returned with all three vehicles.

LRDG cap badge

LRDG – Long Range Desert Group, the sting of the scorpion

The LRDG had its beginnings in July 1940, when Major Ralph A. Bagnold, a Royal Signals officer, geographer and desert explorer, conceived the unit. Following Italy's entry into the war in June 1940, Egypt was considered to be under threat from the Italians in Libya. Consequently, the British Middle East GHQ urgently needed intelligence as to the enemy situation in southern Libya close to the Egyptian border.

Bagnold, together with a small group of fellow explorers, had ventured into the Libyan Desert in the 1920s and 30s gaining considerable knowledge of desert travel, navigation and survival techniques. Armed with these abilities he offered his services to General Sir Archibald Wavell, Commander-in-Chief Middle East, to lead a patrol far behind the lines to try to establish Italian dispositions and intentions. With southern Libya well beyond the range of aerial observation, he immediately authorised Bagnold's plans for an overland reconnaissance unit to be formed, and gave him six weeks to recruit and prepare the force. This was officially designated No.1 Long Range Patrol Unit, also known as the LRP, but later changed to the Long Range Desert Group.

The LRDG comprised individual patrols: W, R, and T were the New Zealand patrols with their vehicles bearing Maori names starting with that letter. The others were the Guards (G), Yeomanry (Y) and the Southern Rhodesians (S). Initially the patrols consisted of 27 to 32 men travelling in 11 especially adapted trucks, either 30 cwt Chevrolets or Fords. They were led by a commander's point vehicle which in the early days was a Ford V8 15 cwt and later a Willys jeep. By 1942, LRDG strength had peaked at about 350 personnel and the patrol sizes were halved, so each now had 18 to 20 men in five or six vehicles. Consequently, their designations changed to R1, R2, T1, T2, G1, G2, etc. and W Patrol had been disbanded. The patrols were overseen by a headquarters unit, and supported by signals, survey, and light repair sections. In addition, there was a heavy section (trucks for logistical support) which was employed to transport supplies to bases and to establish forward hidden dumps which helped to extend the range of the patrols to great distances. The LRDG also operated two WACO light aircraft which were used for liaison work, evacuating the sick or wounded and delivering spare parts.

The principal role of the force was reconnaissance, mapping and intelligence gathering. Each patrol was a completely self-contained independent body capable of travelling hundreds of kilometres deep into enemy territory.

A great part of the information the Eighth Army received about enemy movements came via the radios of the LRDG stationed behind the lines. Their most significant intelligence-gathering role was the road watch which entailed constant observation, day and night, between 2 March and 21 July 1942, of the Tripoli-Bengasi road (Via Balbia) far behind enemy lines. This was undertaken to assess the enemy's strength in Cirenaica where Middle East HQ was planning an offensive. A well-concealed patrol would provide a roster of two men, who in 24-hour shifts lay hidden close to the road and recorded every sighting of enemy armour, artillery, supplies and troops travelling to and from the front line. Though considered a very tedious task by the LRDG, it proved to be one of the group's most valuable activities.

A Ford F30 patrol
truck of T Patrol,
LRDG, approaching
Wadi Sora.
[Brendan O'Carroll]

Two Ford F30 patrol trucks of S Patrol, LRDG, parked in front of the "Cave of the Swimmers" whilst a part of the crews visits the rock paintings. *[Archive LRDG Rhodesia via Jonathan Pittaway]*

Five Ford F30 trucks of an LRDG patrol at rest outside Wadi Sora. Note the smaller Ford F8 pilot truck (second from right).
[Archive LRDG Rhodesia via Jonathan Pittaway]

CMP trucks of the M.E. Commados and a Chevrolet patrol truck of the LRDG outside Wadi Sora. The LRDG served as their guide from Wadi Halfa to the North where the Commandos were to attack Tobruk in September 1942. *[Michael James Duffy via Jonathan Pittaway]*

As experts in desert travel and navigation, the LRDG were often asked to guide others to their objectives. These included units like the Special Air Service (SAS), the Libyan Arab Force, the Free French, the Sudan Defence Force and various commando teams. Furthermore, the LRDG undertook other activities such as inserting, supplying, and collecting British and Arab undercover agents, recovering downed airmen, and rescuing Allied prisoners of war. Between December 1940 and April 1943, there were only 15 days when a patrol was not operating behind or on the flanks of the enemy. The unit had lived up to its unofficial motto, as penned by Dr. F.B. Edmundson, New Zealand Medical Corps and LRDG medical officer, 'Not by strength, by guile'.

The patrols became masters of behind-the-lines desert operations and over time developed a more aggressive role. In the early days they would undertake mine-laying, attack remote Italian forts, and undertake small-scale machine-gunning of road convoys. Their vehicles mounted a variety of heavy and light machine-guns and each patrol had a heavy truck-mounted gun. Initially this was a single-shot 37 mm Bofors anti-tank gun. Later the more versatile Italian automatic 20 mm Breda gun replaced it.

By 1942, they were working alongside the SAS, transporting them to their objectives, mainly Axis airfields, where many aircraft were destroyed using set time bombs. The LRDG would pick up the raiders and take them home again, while at the same time usually trying to avoid enraged pursuers. Eventually the SAS acquired its own transport and from then on operated independently.

The LRDG trucks now carried heavier armament which enabled them to operate more offensively. Using hit-and-run tactics they would ambush Axis convoys, attack supply dumps and targets of opportunity, and then melt into the desert. The LRDG came and went so quickly that the Italians called them *Pattuglia Fantasma* (Ghost Patrol), as they never knew where or when these raiders were going to strike next. This caused the Axis forces so much concern that they were forced to withdraw badly needed troops and aircraft from the front lines to protect their rear areas. Part of their success was due to their being such a small force which could easily conceal themselves behind enemy lines in the shadows of dunes and wadis, or disperse over a wide area to become difficult to find.

Almásy's departure from North Africa

Operation Salam was completed and Almásy was ordered to join the HQ of *Panzerarmee Afrika* to take up communication with KONDOR. But soon he found himself useless and returned to Europe. His further employments during wartime remain vague.

Before 8 June 1942, meeting Hans Rhotert

When Almásy was back in Tripoli, he met Hans Rhotert, his travelling companion of the 1933 Frobenius expedition in Egypt. Rhotert was then involved with *Sonderkommando Dora,* shortly before departing to its base at the oasis of Hon[253]. This meeting was actually the only moment when Almásy came in touch with *Sonderkommando Dora,* another mission conducted by the *Abwehr.*

11 or 12 June 1942, joining HQ *Panzerarmee*

On the evening of 8 June, a message from Seubert was received by Almásy at the German Consulate in Tripoli, ordering him to proceed immediately to the Tactical HQ of the *Panzerarm*ee and to set up a W/T station to communicate with KONDOR[254].

The *Panzerarmee* at the time was in all-out battle against the Allies along the Gazala line, and in particular the Free French and the Foreign Legion at Bir Hakeim. The delivery of supplies was critical, and apparently when information was received that Almásy had been ordered to join *PzAA* HQ, they jumped at the chance to employ Almásy's skills as a desert scout. He was immediately assigned to one of the supply columns, to plan their route across the desert and guide them from the coastal road south to Tactical HQ on the front line.[255]

253 Rhotert talked about this encounter to Rudolph Kuper.
254 TNA, London, HW 19/31 ISOS 29397
255 Almásy, ***Rommel Seregénél Libiában,*** Chapter "Delivering Supplies"

German trucks
advancing against
the "Gazala Line".
Note the 2cm AA gun
mounted on the bed of
the captured CMP.
[Rolf Munninger]

Almásy and one other unidentified member of Operation Salam, Körper, Munz or Wöhrmann, drove east along the coast road with two vehicles[256]. Allowing some time for preparation, it must have taken them at least two, possibly three days to reach the vicinity of the front line. Almásy's narrative starts when they stopped to rest for the night, probably at Derna, and were to join a convoy of 250 trucks at an assembly point on the *Via Balbia*, somewhere between Derna and Gazala. They started at 04:00 on 11 or 12 June, and reached the assembly point on the coast road by early morning. From here they had to guide the convoy 60 kilometres to the south to Rommel's HQ near Bir Hakeim.

During the morning, Almásy and another *Hauptmann* scouted and mapped the route to be taken, including the narrow corridor prepared through the Allied mine-fields of the overrun Gazala line. They were to drive 40 kilometres due south, then curve eastward for another 25 kilometres before reaching the entrance of the corridor. They returned by noon, and the column was ready to start. As they could expect ambush by Allied light armour circling the Axis lines and attacking from the south, the convoy was assigned five *Panzer* for protection. From the coast to the edge of the minefield Italian fighter aircraft provided air cover, after which the *Luftwaffe* took over.

Almásy, leading the convoy, was accompanied by a signals officer who could make flag signals to direct the following trucks. Immediately behind them followed one of the *Panzer*s, then an open truck with an anti-aircraft gun mounted, then the long line of heavily-laden transport trucks. There was a strong northerly wind blowing from behind them and Almásy was concerned on two counts, about the cooling

256 It is not known if these were two of the *Salam* vehicles or if they were assigned other cars
     for this mission, however in light of von Giesheim's difficulties in obtaining vehicles, most
     probably *Salam* cars were used.

of the truck engines, but also the dust blown ahead and obscuring their view. However navigation proved easy, their scouting tracks of the morning were still perfectly visible. Almásy started to zigzag along the plotted route to allow some forward visibility free of the dust. Progress was slow; after the first 20 kilometres he began to realise that they would not make the crossing through the minefield before nightfall.

The large dust cloud of the convoy attracted the attention of Allied artillery located not more than 10 kilometres to the east on the other side of the front line. A little earlier, where the convoy had to make the gradual eastward turn, Almásy had heard a whistling sound. At first he thought the air was escaping from one of the tyres, but the whistling became a loud roar followed by the impact and explosion a mere hundred feet away. Two more shells followed, but all were widely off the mark, clearly fired from a great distance. More worrying was the likelihood that the artillery observers would have alerted the RAF; they could well expect an enemy fighter attack within half an hour.

The convoy left the vegetation zone skirting the Mediterranean coast, and was now driving through barren desert. In the distance Almásy spotted something that did not quite fit into the landscape. He stopped on a rise to steady the field glasses, and could make out two … three … four enemy tanks in the shimmer of the mirage. Three red signals were sent up from the Véry pistol, and the convoy commander immediately caught up, giving his instructions: The convoy should continue on course without halting, while the escorting *Panzer* took on the enemy. Some of the escorting Italian fighters also split off to join the party, but the little skirmish finished before it started – the British tanks thought better of it in light of the superior enemy forces, and hastily retreated towards the south.

Smoke rising from destroyed vehicles gives evidence of the heavy fighting in the desert. *[Rolf Munninger]*

A good part of the vehicles used by the Germans were captured CMP trucks.
[Rolf Munninger]

Despite the hindrances, the column did reach the edge of the minefield by late afternoon. The Gazala line was 4 kilometres wide, and extended 80 kilometres to the south. A few days earlier *Panzerarmee Afrika* led by Rommel circled this barrier in the south, and now held positions opposite the left flank of the enemy at Bir Hakeim. A direct route was cleared to the German positions across the minefield in the last few days to facilitate the delivery of supplies. This corridor was just wide enough to allow the passage of the largest armour, but two trucks could not pass each other.

Immediately on arrival the convoy started the crossing, while Almásy stayed behind and moved to the rear to discuss with the unit commanders where and how to make a desert camp once on the far side. As the sun was setting, one of the anti-aircraft guns suddenly opened up near the front of the convoy. Soon all available machine guns opened fire. What was to follow was described by Almásy as his worst battlefield memory.

The column was attacked by a squadron of Spitfires, on their last sortie of the day. The front of the convoy, crossing the cleared corridor in single file, with no opportunity to break away to the left or right, offered an easy strafing target. Almásy jumped into the shallow depression of an abandoned machine gun position, fully expecting to die at any moment. In reality the attack probably lasted only a few minutes, but it seemed an eternity. When it was quiet again he crawled out of the hole and looked around. There were trucks scattered and moving about the desert everywhere in the twilight. Far up at front there was a truck ablaze, and there was a large fire further ahead, but apparently the attack had caused relatively minor damage and casualties. As the dispersed vehicles re-grouped, it became apparent that a pair of Messerschmitt 109 largely foiled the attack by about twelve enemy aircraft.

In his car Almásy returned to the front of the column. One of the blazing trucks had been hit before the minefield, but the other was inside the cleared lane. One third of the convoy had already passed further into the corridor, but the rest was blocked, there was no way around the burning truck. Camp had to be made there, with a fresh start at dawn the next day.

On awakening next morning, Almásy found everything drenched with thick dew, very unusual for June. It was bitterly cold getting out of the damp sleeping bag. After some hot coffee Almásy and the officers re-assembled the dispersed trucks, then he went ahead to see the situation in the corridor. As the sun rose, everything was covered with a thick blanket of fog. Walking up the corridor to the burnt-out truck, it became evident that the only way to continue would be by clearing a by-pass route in the minefield, as the truck could not be moved. Lacking mine-clearing equipment, the truck crews started to probe the sand with various makeshift poles and tools. Soon they found the first "bedpan", then another. The delay was frustrating, but at least in the fog there was no danger of another air attack. The British had done a thorough job; on the short single-track detour, half a dozen mines had been found.

Finally they were across the minefield. As the convoy was being re-organised into the regular column to continue, they witnessed high above them an aerial battle between Allied fighters and the same two *Messerschmitt* which had come to their rescue the previous evening, resulting in two German victories. Immediately thereafter, the convoy departed and reached HQ with no further difficulty. Soon Almásy and the convoy officers were facing Rommel in front of his caravan, who only said: "Thank you", shaking each of them by the hand.[257]

Almásy met Rommel separately at his Tactical HQ near Bir Hakeim and supposedly reported: "*Herr Generaloberst*, Operation Salam successfully completed, Operation Kondor can begin". It was only then that he learnt what had happened with SCHILDKROETE. Supposedly it was personally Rommel who told him the story, and it was not to be overheard, it was clearly embarrassing for him. It was he who ordered Aberle and Weber to leave Mamelin and to join his mobile Tactical HQ since he was short of W/T operators. Then, in the confusing movements of the battle, Rommel's HQ was overrun by the enemy. While Rommel had barely escaped, Aberle and Weber had been captured with their vehicle. Almásy was perplexed by the occurrence, and stated at the end of his report about Operation Salam that he could have taken a complete Regiment to the Nile. Rommel, however, replied that he hoped he would soon have his whole army on the Nile by a much more direct route. He promoted Almásy from *Hauptmann* to *Major* and decorated him on the spot with the Iron Cross first – and second class[258]. When Almásy had reached HQ *Panzerarmee Afrika* from Operation Salam, everything seemed possible for the advancing Axis forces under Rommel. The Nile and Cairo were expected to be reached soon and the final defeat of the Allies was near. With this imminent success

---

257 Almásy's account ends here, events from here on may only be reconstructed from secondary sources.

258 Carell, **Die Wüstenfüchse**, "Unternehmen Salaam. Carell's book is not a fully accurate report and there is no evidence that Rommel and Almásy are quoted correctly by him. However, there is photographic evidence showing Almásy in his tropical uniform and wearing the Iron Cross, First Class (EK I). There is no proof of the precise statements of Rommel and Almásy on this occasion.

in mind, *Panzerarmee Afrika* was not interested in ordering a further mission from the *Abwehr* to take spies to Egypt. There would not even be time to prepare such a venture before the enemy was defeated.

Nobody could then imagine that the Allied forces, now directly commanded by Claude Auchinleck, were already preparing a new holding line near a small railway station which was no more than a name on the map in mid- June 1942. After the Axis forces had taken Tobruk on 20 June, the following thrust into Egypt came to a halt at el-Alamein. The first battle of el-Alamein went on from 1 to 27 July and brought the Axis advance to a halt only some 100 kilometres short of Alexandria. The second battle, fought between 23 October and 5 November, ended in an Allied victory which crushed all hope of the Axis powers to seize control of the Suez Canal and the Middle Eastern oil fields.

Almásy told a somewhat different version of his last meeting with Rommel to Bagnold, when they met in Cairo in December 1950. Supposedly Rommel discharged him with the words "Almásy, this is not your war. Go home …", even hinting that the Germans are likely to lose the war anyway.[259] Whatever were the exact words, it was certainly a firm farewell rather than any talk of further opportunities for Almásy.

July 1942, return to Europe and meeting with Patrick A. Clayton

At the headquarters of *Panzerarmee Afrika*, Almásy met Hans Entholt again. Entholt, who fell ill just at the beginning of Operation Salam had recovered in the meantime, had been promoted to *Unterleutnant* and was serving on Rommels staff. They would never see each other again, since soon after Almásy had left for Europe, Entholt was hit by a mine during the battle of el-Alamein and died from his injuries soon after.

Promoted to *Major*, decorated with the Iron Cross, but frustrated, Almásy must have recognised that his services were no longer needed. In a message to Seubert on the 27th June, von Griesheim is very blunt, saying that the "presence of *Salam* in Tripoli no longer required".[260] Nevertheless Almásy stayed on for another ten days, and on receiving an 8 week leave, returned to Europe on 7 July[261].

After flying to Italy from Libya, Almásy visited Patrick Clayton[262] in POW *Campo* 79 at Sulmona in July 1942. They talked about Operation Salam and it seems that Almásy even gave him descriptions and showed a photograph of the car he had

---

259 Letter of Bagnold to Jean Howard, 2 April 1978, Churchill Archives, Cambridge, Bagnold Papers. The correspondence only refers to this conversation having taken place, but the surprised reaction to Rommel's thinking even at that early stage confirms that the quote is substantially correct. The exact phrase was repeated by Kubassek, (*A szahara bűvöletében*), referring to an interview with Howard.

260 TNA, London, HW 2/32 ISOS 31461

261 Testimony of Almásy during his War Crimes trial, Kubassek, *A Szahara bűvöletében*.

262 Clayton and Almásy travelled the desert together before the war. Clayton became a prisoner of war after the Italians caught him in January 1941 at the so-called "Incident at Jebel Sherif" near Kufra.

Almásy with the Iron Cross which was awared to him for the successful conduct of Operation Salam. [*Kubassek, A Szahara bűvöletében*]

used[263]. Almásy is said to have gloatingly pointed out to Clayton that he had counted on the British to mine the pass through the Gilf Kebir.

Almásy learnt that Clayton was to be transferred to a new location, the notorious *Campo Cinque*, the Italian high security POW camp equivalent to the German Colditz. Although they were not fighting on the same side, in consideration of his old desert comrade – they were never friends, the writings of both men make this very clear – he managed to arrange for him to be transferred to *Campo 29* at Veano in Northern Italy[264] instead.

From his meeting with Pat Clayton in Italy, Almásy supposedly went on to Germany to report to his superior in the *Abwehr*, *Major* Franz Seubert. He requested to be discharged from active service and placed on the reserve officers list in order to complete his book on his experiences in North Africa. This was granted[265].

Back in Budapest he started to write the short book "With Rommel's Army in Libya" which was published after it had passed the censors in January 1943. One statement in his book had passed unnoticed by the otherwise vigilant censors: "I can somehow comprehend combat in the Russian steppe, but here under the African sky, in the world of the oases – the genuine symbols of peace and mystery -- how can men murder one another?"

There is very little information about the activities of Almásy in 1943, but there are some snippets of evidence that he continued to advise the *Abwehr* on Egyptian and Middle East matters. On 22 November 1943, Security Intelligence Middle East (SIME) reported his arrival in Istanbul from Budapest on 5 November, and also the arrival of Baron Kurt von Plessing two days later[266]. Von Plessing was an odd character. He had been born in Graz, Austria in 1890, and when the Austro-Hungarian monarchy was dissolved in 1919, strangely he applied for Hungarian nationality, despite his Austrian ethnicity. He may have already known Almásy from their school years in Graz, and certainly did after he moved to Szombathely in western Hungary, also home to Almásy. In 1936 he went to England, purportedly to study English, and stayed in the same language school in Eastbourne where Almásy had

263 Information provided by the late Peter Clayton, son of Patrick A. Clayton, to the authors in 2009.

264 Clayton, *Desert Explorer*, page 156 ff and Buchheit, *The German Secret Service*

265 Kelly, *The Hunt for Zerzura*, p. 239 ff. Kelly cites no supporting documents or sources. Almásy did make reference to his request to be discharged, which was granted in August 1942, during his testimony during his War Crimes trial (Kubassek, *A szahara bűvületében*). However from later events it is clear that Almásy retained ties to the *Abwehr* at least till the end of 1943.

266 TNA, London, WO 208/1562, SIME Security Summary, Middle East, No. 157, 22 November 1943

studied before the First World War, hardly a coincidence. During the nineteen thirties he had business dealings in Egypt, and was in constant touch with Almásy during their stay there. He became the manager of the Hungarian hunting estate of Prince Jousef Kemal, an avid hunter and a member of the Egyptian Royalty.[267]

Prince Kemal built himself a hilltop lodge in Szeleste, near Szombathely in western Hungary. The Szeleste Manor and botanical gardens were at the time owned by Baron Baich Mihály, and Prince Youssef had been a regular guest on the Estate since the mid nineteen twenties. Apparently he was so fond of the region that he proceeded to build a smaller mansion for himself on a hill on the outskirts of the village which he visited regularly in the summer months. The ‚small manor' of the Baich Estate was made the living quarters of the Prince's manager, von Plessing. Bishop Mikes of Szombathely, to whom Almásy had been secretary in the early nineteen twenties, was also a regular guest on the Estate, as undoubtedly was Almásy himself, though of this there is no record until later. It is very likely that the young Almásy met his first Egyptian contacts there, on one of the hunts organised by Baron Baich.[268] It is known however that Almásy frequently stayed at Szeleste from 1943 till the end of the War in 1945.

The British Security Service already suspected von Plessing of being a German agent in the thirties, alerted by large sums of money which von Plessing drew from Prince Kemal's London bank account. While these sums appear to have been genuinely earmarked for the Szeleste lodge, these suspicions were not entirely unfounded, as post war interrogaton of captured *Abwehr* agents clearly showed von Plessing's association with the organisation from as early as 1940. In 1941 as a cover von Plessing was sent to the Hungarian Legation at Ankara as Commercial Attache, but his true task was to set up an organisation in Syria and Egypt.[269]

It appears that Almásy and von Plessing had worked together on an *Abwehr* assignment, most likely *Plan el-Masri*, in 1941. An intercepted message from von Plessing to Almásy dated 15 May 1942 leaves no doubt: "For ALMÁSY. Am remitting 2'000 *pengos* to TASSILO as soon as possible. Everything will be arranged. Coming soon. Best wishes, KURT PLESSING."[270]

Sometime before September 1943 *Major* Seubert was transferred from Berlin to become head of *AST Sofia*. On 12 October, a message was addressed to Seubert (at the time using the code-name PASA) informing him of an impending exchange of Germans interned in Egypt for Egyptians interned in Germany, and enquiring whether Almásy woud be available to assist in selecting suitable candidates amongst the Egyptian internees, to be turned into agents.[271] It appears that Seubert was in Budapest at the time or very soon thereafter[272], and action was taken fairly quickly as on 19 October Seubert requested Sofia (from Vienna, probably on his way to Berlin) to arrange overnight train tickets for Almásy and von Plessing from Sofia to Istanbul for the 3/4 November. Almásy and von Plessing were expected to arrive to Sofia on 30 October, and to stay in the Hotel Bulgarie, awaiting Seubert's return

---

267 TNA, London, KV 2/2119 Security Services Personal File, Kurt von Plessing
268 Unpublished memoirs of Gyula Czeglédy, one time schoolmaster of Szeleste
269 TNA, London, KV 2/2119 Security Services Personal File, Kurt von Plessing
270 TNA, London, HW 19/6 ISOS 5297
271 TNA, London, HW 19/142 ISK 68010
272 TNA, London, HW 19/142 ISK 68078

A photo of Almásy taken between 1947–49 in Graz, Austria. His 1937 Ford Deluxe cabriolet has the Egyptian number plate ET 13550.
[*Titan Honner*]

(presumably for discussion and instructions).[273] Their arrival in Istanbul was noted by the British intelligence, however either travel plans changed and the two arrived separately, or more likely their arrival was not immediately reported, they were recognised independently a couple of days later.

Nothing further is known about their activities in Istanbul (or elsewhere), but it appears that apart from attempting to recruit agents among the Egyiptian internees, they may have been involved in a scheme to make contact with high ranking Egyptian officials. According to information later provided by Janos Almásy's niece, Baroness Stoerck, to the writer David Pryce-Jones, Almásy "had a secret assignment in Istanbul as liaison between King Farouk and the Germans. Had he been on the winning side, his exploits would have made him a schoolboy hero"[274]. With the strong contacts von Plessing had with Egyptian Royalty, this is not inconceivable, or at least it could have been one of the assignments. This suggestion is further confirmed by an unrelated message from AST Istanbul indicating on the 8 November the presence of Prince Mansur Daud, member of the Egyptian Royalty and a known German sympathizer, as well as other high ranking Arab personalities[275].

Whatever Almásy's mission was in Istanbul it appears to have produced no results and no follow-up. In February 1944 the *Abwehr* itself was absorbed into the SD of the RSHA. Operation Salam was Almásy's most daring mission, but also his last big journey to the desert he loved so much.

273 TNA, London, HW 19/143 ISK 69089
274 Pryce-Jones, *Unity*, p. 241
275 TNA, London, HW 19/145 ISK 71683

The spy-mission: Operation Kondor

Operation Kondor was the reason for Operation Salam and therefore it will be described in a chapter of its own. Until recently only the publications by Mosley, Eppler and Sansom told the story of Operation Kondor, but we can now refer to the interrogation protocols and the confessions Eppler and Sandstede had given to British interrogators immediately after they were captured. It is not the aim here to compare in detail the earlier publications with the protocols and to re-trace the operation in such detail as was done for Operation Salam, but to provide the reader with a general view.

23 May 1942, Operation Kondor begins

After Eppler and Sandstede had separated from Almásy, they first sat down and considered their situation. They had a small canister of water, some food and some liquor with them. Near an *Alam* standing on the edge of the escarpment, they had buried one of their *SE.99/10 Agentenfunkgeräte* together with about 100 pounds Sterling, and Eppler's pistol about 20 to 25 paces away, in case they might have to escape from Cairo[276]. They changed into civilian clothes that they had carried in one of the suitcases, then divided their money between them, drank a few more shots of liquor and walked down the descent towards Assiut and the Nile valley. Their neutral clothing could have belonged to any European in Egypt. By late afternoon they arrived at the train station without having met anybody suspicious of them. Eppler bought two tickets to Cairo and after the train had arrived on time they spent four quiet hours travelling. Upon arrival at Cairo, they realised that British controls were only concerned with military personnel, and did not care about civilians. They chose to take their first lodgings in one of the brothels of Cairo[277].

New Map of Cairo, 1932.

276 Eppler to Kuper, Uncorrected Notes 1998-04-05/06; HBI Köln / Archive Kuper
277 Sandstede, unpublished memoirs

2 June 1942, *SCHILDKROETE* does not answer

Since this initial accommodation was not suitable for their purpose, they hired a flat from a certain Madame Therese Guillemet at No. 8, Sharia Boursa el-Gehedida, and Sandstede erected his antenna on the roof of the building on the day they moved in. At the agreed time, 18:00, he started to send his messages. Five minutes of sending, then five minutes of pause. He repeated it for half an hour and received many transmissions except the one he was waiting for. SCHILDKROETE did not answer. Sandstede concluded that the mistake either must be with the antenna or with the location since higher buildings surrounded their place. They had to find a better place for their W/T station[278].

The *Dahabeyah* on the river Nile.

June 1942, Rommel's spies in Cairo

The purpose of Operation Kondor was to establish a W/T station in Cairo by means of which Rommel's HQ could be supplied with messages about troop movements, arrival of new equipment and whatever might be of interest to the advancing Axis forces. In order to get the information they needed, they started to frequent the various well known places of amusement and refreshment in Cairo such as "Groppi's", the roof-cabaret of the "Continental", and the famous "Kit Kat". While Sandstede was posing as "Sandy" and had a British passport in the name of Peter Muncaster, Eppler was using his original Egyptian passport and appeared under the name Hussein Gafaar, son of the Judge Gafaar. At the Continental, they made friends with the famous belly dancer Hekmat Fahmy, who took them to spend a night on her *Dahabeah*, a houseboat at the banks of the Nile. They not only found the place most pleasant, but thought it would be a better location for their W/T set, and asked Hekmat Fahmy to help them rent similar accommodation for them. One was found and they moved into a *Dahabeah* close to Fahmy's[279].

In addition to the houseboat which they had rented for the sum of 12 Egyptian Pounds per month, Eppler had kept the previous flat for himself near the "New Star" restaurant[280].

The houseboats moored on the banks of the Nile in the Cairo suburb of Zamalek were at that time most fashionable living places, and many of them were rented by staff officers of Middle East GHQ. The *dahabeah* between that of the spies and the one Hekmat Fahmy lived in was occupied by an officer of the British intellligence corps.[281] When he became somewhat suspicious about the high antenna they had

278 Sandstede, unpublished memoirs and TNA, FO 141/852, Correspondence, British Embassy, Egypt
279 TNA, London, FO 141/852, Correspondence, British Embassy, Egypt
280 TNA, London, KV2/1476, Report on Interrogation of Victor Hauer, Appendix "A"
281 Mosley, *The Cat and the Mice*, p. 78. In *Rommel ruft Kairo*, p. 158 ff, Eppler even claims that their neighbour was Colonel Dunstan, SIME, and that he played golf with him on a regular basis. However, this statement is not confirmed by any of the other sources, in particular not in any of the documents available in the TNA. Further, Eppler makes no further mention this special relation in the later part of his book, when he was under interrogation by the British. Therefore, whilst it seems believable that their neighbour was a member of the Intelligence Corps, there is no further evidence that he was Colonel Dunstan.

erected, he was satisifed with the explanation that "Sandy" liked American dance music very much and needed the antenna to receive it from remote radio-stations.

Very soon, the two spies acquired an entourage of such "useful people" as pimps, moneychangers and so-called friends. In addition, they employed a personal servant and a taxi-driver. On the other hand, they failed to contact important people who could have been really useful for their purpose. Prince Abbas Halim, for example, was not contacted because they found that the British watched him closely. What was worse, they were unable to establish contact with HQ *Panzerarmee Afrika* despite the new location of the W/T set [282].

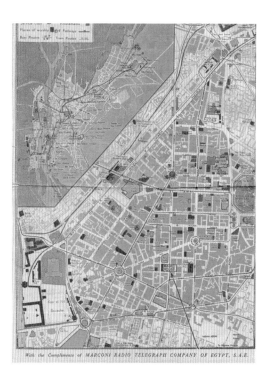

While Sandstede was busy with his W/T set and stayed on the houseboat, Eppler, as Hussein Gafaar, fully entered into his role as the rich young and carefree Egyptian who had nothing else to do than spending his father's money. Nearly every other day, sometimes for several days in a row, they organised merry parties on the deck of their *Dahabeah* attended mainly by young people, sons of rich Egyptians, who arrived with their magnificent cars or motorboats. Most of them were former schoolmates of Eppler and some "nice girls"[283].

The hired driver of the two spies, Mohammed, who was employed for 20 Egyptian Pounds a month, stated under interrogation after his arrest that his duty was to fetch Eppler and Sandstede at 10:00 in the morning from their *Dahabeah* and drive them to the "Hollywood Hairdressers" at Sharia Emad el-Dine, or sometimes to take them to the tailor. Afterwards he normally took them to the "Rivoli", where they usually stayed for 30 minutes to an hour. About midday, he had to drive them back to the *Dahabeah*, where they had their lunch. Later, at about 15:00 in the afternoon he often took them to the cinema and the evenings were usually spent at the "Continental" and at "Groppi's"[284].

In fact, while the two spies had obviously a very good and pleasant life in Cairo, they made no progress in respect of the original purpose of their presence in the city. They could neither obtain valuable information nor were they able to establish communication with the HQ of *Panzerarmee Afrika*.

As Eppler stated later: "We spent our money freely on food, drink and women. When you are in a trade like mine you may as well enjoy yourself while you can.

Coordinating Council for Welfare Work in Egypt, Services Guide to Cairo.

282 TNA, London, FO 141/852, Correspondence, British Embassy, Egypt. Eppler in **Rommel ruft Kairo** claims that he frequently wore the uniform of a British officer to ease his approach to real British in the various bars he visited. As proof, he displays a photograph on page 172 of his book that shows him in British uniform. However; in none of the available documents, neither in the TNA nor elsewhere, does Eppler make a similar statement. It has to be assumed that this is pure fiction and that the photograph was taken much later, when the two spies were already working for the British Intelligence. Furthermore in various documents, Eppler, Sandstede and Hassan Gafaar state that Eppler's English was rather poor.

283 Eppler, **Rommel ruft Kairo**, p. 168

284 TNA, London, KV 2/1467, Eppler, Personal File

You know you are not going to live to enjoy old age, so you play while you work, and try not to think about the firing squad."[285] Though there was no reply from their remote station, the repeated calls from KONDOR had been intercepted by British monitors. They were aware that a new transmitter was active in the Cairo area but since the intercepted messages were very short and never answered, they could not localise it. However, they had been alerted

18 June 1942, the interrogation of Aberle and Weber

Aberle and Weber, KONDOR's remote station with the callsign SCHILDKROETE, were caught on 27 May 1942. The report of their interrogation does not reveal many details. The interrogators only obtained the information that the *Abwehr* had maintained two mobile units with W/T sets and that a third W/T set was at Almásy's HQ in the oasis of Gialo. Eppler's and Sandstede's appearance was described briefly and a short statement was given about the missions under way, but no information could be obtained from either on the method agents in Egypt were using for the transmission of their messages [286].

Daphne du Maurier's novel *Rebecca* was to be used to encode and decode the messages following the *Abwehr's* book code.

One of the interrogators wondered why, among their few belongings, the only book to be found with Aberle and Weber – who did not speak English – was the English version of Daphne de Maurier's novel *Rebecca*. After careful inspection, it was found that the price that had been written on the inside of the dust cover in pencil had been rubbed out. Using the forensic photographer in their laboratories, the British soon deciphered the impression of "50 escudos" and it became clear that the book had been bought in Portugal. Soon after, they received the answer to their query to Lisbon. The wife of one of the German Embassy staff in Lisbon had bought six English copies of *Rebecca* at once in the same bookshop a few months ago. From then on, it was clear to the British that the book had been used to encode and decode W/T messages[287].

21 June 1942, Tobruk taken by the Axis, first difficulties

On 21 June 1942, after Rommel's sudden attack, the Axis forces quickly took Tobruk. This came as a shock to the British. It fell with hardly a fight with the loss of 25'000 Allied prisoners and a vast quantity of supplies. When news reached Cairo that Axis forces had already crossed the border of Egypt, panic was close. General Auchinleck left his HQ to take direct command in the desert and recognised that the next position at Mersa Matruh could not be held. He ordered the withdrawal to el-Alamein, only about 60 miles west of Alexandria. Meanwhile in Cairo, British wives and children were evacuated to Palestine and Sudan and secret documents were burnt. Among the civilian population, the news of the Axis' advance aroused every possible reaction from jubilation to panic. There were chaotic traffic jams

285 Mosley, *The Cat and the Mice*, p. 85
286 TNA, London, KV 2/1467, Special Report on German Intelligence in Egypt & Libya (18 June 1942).
287 Sansom, *I spied Spies*, p. 117

on the road to Khartoum. As a result of this and the fear of damage to property if Cairo were attacked, property prices and exchange rates suddenly dropped dramatically[288].

The problems of the two German spies had already begun. On arrival in Cairo, Eppler decided to pay a visit to his family at 10 Sharia Masr al-Khadim, where he only found his mother, who was not at all happy to see him. His brother, Hassan, was not in Cairo at that time, and his stepfather, the judge Saleh Bey Gafaar, had died on 2 October 1941[289]. Until his stepbrother was back in Cairo, Eppler could not rely on his family. Another problem was that despite all efforts, SCHILD-KROETE remained silent and none of their W/T messages were acknowledged. But the most serious difficulty they had was that they were running short of money. When they arrived in Assiut, they had with them 600 Egyptian pounds and 3'000 pounds sterling[290]. There was not only the problem that their lavish lifestyle cost on average about 20 Pounds a day, but that the pound sterling was not used in Egypt. Due to the Germans distributing forged pound notes everywhere, the pound sterling could no longer be exchanged at banks but only personally at the counter of a British army paymaster. While the official exchange rate was fixed at 0.975 EGP to the pound, exchanging the money on the black market resulted in a much less favourable rate. Exchange was only possible at the rate of two pounds sterling for one EGP which practically halved the value of the two spies' funds[291]. When Tobruk fell, it became practically impossible to exchange British Pounds.

Ramses Station, Cairo.
[Harry Chard]

A peaceful looking festival in Cairo, 1941.
[Harry Chard]

Since the British had a careful eye on the people changing money and since the bars and restaurants were closely watched, it did not take long before Major A.W. Samson, head of the Cairo branch of the British Security Service, was on their track. With his own people and the Egyptian police, he had about 2'000 personnel at his disposal, and the locations of all the places where British Pound notes appeared were marked with pins on a large map of Cairo in his office. To make matters worse for the two Germans, their five-pound notes were soon identified as the same counterfeits as others which had already been found in several places and their origin was clear: Germany. Furthermore, a number of the genuine notes could be traced back to deposits in neutral countries such as Switzerland and Spain which made it highly likely that they had been provided by Germany to a spy[292].

288 Sansom, *I spied Spies*, p. 97 ff
289 TNA, London, KV2/1467, Eppler, Personal File
290 TNA, London, KV 2/1467, 1st. Consolidated Report on Activities of Eppler and Sandstede. The amount of money is claimed much higher, up to GBP 40'000 in various publications about Operation Kondor, however there is no documentary evidence to such claims.
291 EGP 600 plus GBP 3'000 (at an exchange rate of 2:1) equals about EGP 2'100. Considering their average daily expenses as GBP 20, their funds would be sufficient for a maximum of three months, probably less.
292 Sansom, *I spied Spies*, p. 115

Portrait of Hekmat Fahmy.
[H. Eppler via Archive Kröpelin]

Hekmat Fahmy, the famous belly dancer was employed at the roof-cabaret of the "Continental".
[H. Eppler via Archive Kröpelin]

Eppler and Sandstede started to realise that they could not continue like this for long. Not only were they running short of money, but they had not achieved anything since they arrived in Cairo. They started to fear that their superiors would probably not be too happy with them once the Axis had conquered Cairo.

Both of them were writing diaries, and to deceive potential readers, they had started to fill them with descriptions of their achievements of their activities that had no connection with reality. So, they wrote about agents they had hired and travels they had made to obtain valuable information[293].

Hekmat Fahmy, the dancer, their best-known contact in Cairo, could help but only a little. Both of them stated later that she was most ignorant as far as military information was concerned. Only in one case did they have the chance to scan the contents of a briefcase left behind by a British officer on Hekmat's *Dahabeah*, and even this happened without her knowledge[294].

293 TNA, London, KV 2/1467, 2nd Consolidated Interrogation of Eppler and Sandstede. When the two spies were caught, Sandstede managed to throw Eppler's diary into the Nile. But later both of them asserted that its contents were about the same as Sandstede's diary and, that it had also been falsified.
294 TNA, London, KV 2/1467, 2nd Consolidated Interrogation of Eppler and Sandstede. The plan and the documents were found in the suitcase of a British officer, Captain Guy Bellairs, who had relations with Hekmat and had left it back on her houseboat when he went back to the front. After Hekmat's arrest, her *Dahabeah* was searched and the plans were found. Both Eppler and Sandstede confirmed that she could not have known their content since she was only concerned with dancing, drinking etc. and was completely ignorant of military subjects. In particular since she only spoke Arabic , she could not have possibly understood the content of the documents.

The entry in Sandstede's diary for 25 June 1942 reads: "Hekmat has rendered us valuable services. Today I received the plans of the dugouts and fortifications of Tobruk (Mersa Matruh[295]). This pile of material will have to be destroyed – one could cry. I do not dare to keep too much of it – the diary alone is enough of a worry."[296]

The discovery of the plans of the defences of Tobruk might have been very valuable information for Rommel, but unfortunately the plans only fell into the spies' hands four days after Tobruk was taken by Axis forces, and, even worse, it showed the original Italian fortifications and therefore was more than two years out of date[297].

Later, in August 1942, Eppler was heard talking about this subject to Sandstede in the courtyard of their prison at Maadi: "Lord, man; they found plans of Tobruk at Hekmat's *Dahabeah* in a suitcase. I saw the suitcase but never looked inside. That was a bit dangerous[298]. What a coincidence. You wrote Tobruk and (then) Mersa Matruh (in the diary). You bastard, you could never differentiate between Tobruk and Mersa Matruh."[299]

12 July 1942, meeting Victor Hauer and a new W/T set

Returning to Cairo on 11 July 1942, Hassan Gafaar met his half-brother Hans Eppler for the first time after receiving a letter from him. He was told that they had problems with their W/T transmitter and asked for help to find a new one. Hassan arranged a meeting with Victor Hauer of the Swedish legation, whom he knew to be a former employee of the German Embassy since coming to Egypt in 1933 after a childhood spent in Germany. Victor Hauer was brought to Eppler's houseboat and Hauer agreed to help after Eppler explained the difficult situation to him.

To ensure that Hauer would help them, Eppler wanted him to recognise their importance. He told him a made-up story about their importance, the agents they had mustered in Suez and Port Said, the information they gathered from British officers, and it was their function to provide the communication link between Egyptian nationalists, who would soon rise in revolt, and the German Army [300].

295 TNA, London, KV 2/1467, Second Consolidated Interrogation of Eppler and Sandstede. When shown the alteration in the diary (from "Tobruk" to "Mersa Matruh"), Eppler stated that they had no instructions to get plans of Tobruk but that the Ic of *Panzergruppe Afrika*, Major Zolling, had ordered them to obtain plans of Mersa Matruh.

296 TNA, London, KV 2/1467, Second Consolidated Interrogation of Eppler and Sandstede

297 The legend of these plans of Tobruk was the subject of several publications where the plans were even claimed to be for el-Alamein. Of course, such stories lend savour to a spy novel, but in this case the information obtained was without military value.

298 It probably means that it was a bit dangerous for Sandstede to look into the content of the suitcase.

299 TNA, London, WO 208/5520, Interrogation Files, 3rd Report, August 1942. It is not certain whether the Eppler's statement is copied verbatim. It indicates that only Sandstede had seen the plans of Tobruk, not Eppler.

300 The story Eppler told Hauer was not only intended to convince Hauer that he should help these two "most important" spies, but also to make sure that if Hauer conveyed information to any German authority, Eppler and Sandstede would appear in the correct light.

View from al-Gezirah over the Kasr al-Nile bridge to the newly built Intercontinental and Shepheard hotels.

Hauer kept his promise and made a transmitter available which was stored with other German Embassy property kept in the basement of the Swedish Embassy since the German Embassy had closed. On 16 July he informed Hassan Gafaar that the W/T transmitter was ready to be picked up at the Consulate gate[301].

Eppler did not know that on the same day, Hasaan Gafaar asked Hauer was for help, Hauer informed Dr. Radinger, whom he knew to be in contact with British Intelligence that two Germans had contacted him with a request for help[302]. Obviously, Hauer was immediately aware what a precarious situation he was in. As a German national he could hardly refuse to help agents of the German *Abwehr*, especially as the German army was expected to march in to Cairo soon. But on the other hand, he knew that in his official duties he was under observation by the British Intelligence. Therefore, helping the German spies meant immediate and serious danger for him. To inform Dr. Radinger and ask his advice was the only chance he saw to escape this difficult situation, no matter how the war might develop. When Dr. Radinger confirmed that he should "go ahead" provided he was kept informed, the fate of Eppler and Sandstede was sealed.

Unfortunately, the "Hallicrafter" W/T set provided by Hauer still did not enable them to contact their remote station, so they decided they had to search for another method of getting in touch with the HQ of *Panzerarmee Afrika*. It was decided that Sandstede would remain in Cairo, while Eppler would try to reach the German front line to find out what had gone wrong with communications, and then to return with more money[303]. Again, Hassan Gafaar was used to search for a person who might be able to help in this matter.

18 July 1942, seeking escape and a kidnapping[304]

Eppler had spent the early evening with his girlfriend Edith and Sandra, who was Sandstede's girlfriend at "Groppi's" and took them home at about 21:30. Afterwards he went to the "Kit Kat" where he met with Sandstede and some others who were already there. Since Sandstede did not feel well, he left early, but came back to the "Kit Kat" at about 22:30 very excited and addressed Eppler in German: "Come home quickly; perhaps you will really be able to get away now."

---

301 Based on KV 2/1467, Eppler, Personal File, 2nd Consolidated Report on Eppler and Sandstede, Appendix "D" It is rather strange that the two spies appealed to Hauer for a replacement W/T set. First of all, they had to reveal their presence and task to a person unknown to them; second, whatever W/T transmitter he could produce would be quite different from the newly-developed model they had available and were trained on; and third, they already had a second W/T set -- the one they had buried in the sand upon their arrival at Assiut. This second W/T set was only 4 hours by train from Cairo. Whatever their thoughts were, they chose to approach Hauer, and this finally brought disaster to Operation Kondor.

302 TNA, London, KV 2/1467, Eppler, Personal File, Letter by Jenkins to MI5 dated 1 August 1942

303 TNA, London, FO 14/852, Further Report on the Sandy and Eppler Case

304 Based on TNA, London, KV 2/1467, Eppler, Personal File, 2nd Consolidated Report on Eppler and Sandstede. Where information and statements from further documents are included, this is mentioned in individual footnotes. The interrogators mentioned in a note that where discrepancies in the 1st report appear, the 2nd report is more likely to give the true version.

The mosque of Mohammed Ali by night.
[*Harry Chard*]

Heliopolis racecourse.
[*Harry Chard*]

King Farouk's palace in Cairo by night.
[*Harry Chard*]

Eppler was annoyed because Sandstede had spoken to him in German. Nevertheless together they left the '"Kit Kat" to meet Hauer and Hassan Gafaar at the *Dahabeah*. From there – without Sandstede -- they drove to Heliopolis. They arrived at a certain bungalow at midnight. Eppler was very disappointed to find that the Egyptian pilot, who was supposed to take him back to the German lines that very night, was not even at home. They waited for some time, after which Hauer proposed to go to the house of Fatma Amer, a German woman married to an Egyptian, who would be able to help them.

When Eppler arrived at the appointed time and place the next evening, Hauer was not there. He spoke to *Frau* Amer alone, and she assured him that it would be an easy thing to arrange for his return to the German lines. Hauer arrived late and together they left at about 23:00.

What seemed to be an easy task for Eppler started to become more difficult. The pilot was again not home when they next tried to meet him, but on 21 July at the house of Fatma Amer there was another young Egyptian who seemed to know all about Eppler. Together with him Eppler went to a cafe, where they finally met Hasan Ezzat, a fighter pilot with the Egyptian air force[305]. Eppler explained that he had to get to the German lines because they were unable to establish W/T communication and probably their transmitter was defective. However, Hasan Ezzat did not fully trust Eppler, and proposed they should meet el-Masri Pasha together. This was arranged for the evening of Thursday 23 July 1942, 21:00 at Kubbah gardens.

Unknown to the German spies, on the night of 21 July 1942, the case had developed dramatically for Victor Hauer. G.J. Jenkins of the Defence Security Office in Cairo suspected that Hauer knew much more than he had told Dr. Radinger, and if he could only interrogate him, it would certainly put the British on the trail of the German spies. However, there was some question of whether Hauer might enjoy a degree of diplomatic immunity, and it was in any case most undesirable for the British that the Egyptian authorities should know anything about these goings-on. Jenkins therefore took a rather pragmatic decision and ordered Hauer to be kidnapped. When he came out of the cinema in the evening, he was snatched by British agents and then hidden away in a cell of the newly established SIME Interrogation Centre at Maadi. To prevent anyone else becoming aware of this, even other British organisations, Hauer's name was changed to Franz Müller, purportedly

305 The Egyptian air force of 1942 was equipped with mostly obsolete aircraft, such as some dozens of Gloster Gladiator biplane-fighters and Westland Lysander liaison planes. They also had a squadron of outdated Hawker Audax bombers.

an escaped POW, who had been picked up on the streets of Cairo and was to be interned in Palestine. The kidnapped Hauer was thoroughly terrified to be told that escaping a firing-squad depended on him forgetting ever being called Hauer, and on the degree of his co-operation with the British. One week later, Jenkins confirmed to MI5 in London that both his own police under Major Sansom and the Egyptians were still hunting for Hauer, whose disappearance had been reported by the Swedish legation[306].

23 July 1942, meeting with el-Masri Pasha[307]

Eppler together with his half brother Hassan Gafaar went by taxi to the appointed location in the Kubbeh gardens. When Hasan Ezzat arrived, he told them to proceed alone to the petrol station on the main Cairo-Heliopolis road and to wait there.

About half an hour later, a dark-brown four-seater car arrived at the new location: it belonged to el-Masri Pasha, who was at the wheel. With him were Hasan Ezzat, the aviator, and Anwar el-Sadat, who was a signals officer in the Egyptian army. Eppler was told that he had to prove to Hasan Ezzat he was really a German. The only thing Eppler could propose was that they should visit him at home, on the *Dahabeah*. This would also give Anwar el-Sadat the chance to have a look at the defective W/T set and try to repair it.

On their return, after el-Masri Pasha had left them, they went to the 'Kit Kat' to pick up Sandstede. Hassan Ezzat told them that he knew an Egyptian who had lived in Germany before the war and had returned to Egypt with a W/T set. He agreed to contact this man to send an emergency message on behalf of Eppler and Sandstede. Sandstede then prepared the following message for him:

The mosque of Mohammed Ali within the citadel of Cairo.
[Harry Chard]

"To Abwehr 1 H West, ANGELO. Please guarantee our existence. We are in mortal danger. Please use wave-length No. 1 at 09:00 Tripoli time. Max and Moritz"[308].

Both Eppler and Sandstede were sure that this W/T set did not belong to the German army (of which the *Abwehr* was part) but most probably to the *SD* which was separate from the *Abwehr* and dealt with political matters. However, they had no choice but to try it. Hasan Ezzat was sure that it would work and he could provide a response within six days. All four of them reached the houseboat shortly before midnight.

306 TNA, London, KV 2/1467, Eppler, Personal File, Letter by Jenkins to MI5 dated 1 August 1942
307 Based on TNA, London, KV 2/1467, Eppler, Personal File, 2nd Consolidated Report on Eppler and Sandstede. Where information and statements from further documents is included, this is mentioned by individual footnotes. The interrogators mentioned in a note that where discrepancies in the 1st report appear, the 2nd report is more likely to give the true version.
308 TNA, London, V2/1467, Eppler, Personal File, 1st Consolidated Report on activities of Eppler and Sandstede 29 July 1942

The monument of Ibrahim Pasha.
[Harry Chard]

The Sphinx in front of the Pyramids.
[Harry Chard]

Major A.W. Sansom, head of S.I.M.E. in his Cairo
office in 1942.
[H. Eppler via Archive Kröpelin]

Since they assumed that something must be wrong with their W/T sets, Anwar el-Sadat was shown the German W/T set installed under the radiogram and hidden by a lid of carved wood [309]. While el-Sadat was quite impressed by the hiding place for the W/T set, he formed the impression that the two spies concentrated on enjoying their lives rather than on their real reason for being in Cairo. El-Sadat got into the cabinet and found the W/T set a solid piece of work which had been carefully installed. Despite careful examination, he could not find anything which appeared to be faulty[310].

The second supposedly defective W/T set was an American "Hallicrafter", a type known to el-Sadat, but he could do nothing on the spot, and so proposed to come back and fetch it the next day.

Apart from Anwar el-Sadat coming to fetch the unserviceable "Hallicrafter", nothing else happened during Friday the 24 July 1942. But the noose around the two German spies was already set and was ready to be tightened.

25 July 1942, the capture of the German spies[311]

Major Sansom had fixed the raid on the two German spies for 02:00 in the morning on Saturday. At his request, the river police was co-opted for the purpose, and their launches were drawn up beforehand under the nearby Zamalek Bridge. When they approached the houseboat, they found it in darkness.

Eppler had come to the houseboat late that night and found Sandstede already asleep. He first smoked a cigarette and then had fallen asleep for a short time, when he was woken by a noise outside. At once he was aware what this meant: a raid! He went to wake up Sandstede but found him already awake and going to burn the papers. Eppler rushed down to the lower deck to open the sea cocks to scuttle the boat. Then Eppler took out a coin and asked Sandstede: "Heads or Tails?" Sandstede chose "tails" and won – what meant that he should try to escape.

---

309 Mosley, *The Cat and the Mice*, p. 109
310 The W/T set was not faulty at all. El-Sadat was right. The transmitter was in perfect working order. The reason none of the calls was answered was the order of the *Abwehr* after SCHILDKROETE had fallen into enemy hands.
311 Based on Sansom *I spied Spies*, p. 130 and Eppler *Rommel ruft Kairo*, p. 215 and Mosley, *The Cat and the Mice* p. 141

Armed with their Tommy-guns, Sansom and Captain Effat of the Egyptian police stepped onto the boat and Effat shouted: "Police" to observe the niceties before they broke the door down. Thanks to the information they had received from Hauer, they knew exactly where they had to go.

While Eppler stayed to try to hold them, Sandstede followed their plan and left the houseboat through a hatch where the engine had been. Eppler took a pair of socks, rolled them into a tight ball, and threw it at the intruders Major Sansom and Captain Effat. They all ducked, thinking it was a hand-grenade, and Eppler seized his chance to slip through and reach the upper deck. But he did not get far; policemen were everywhere. Eppler was handcuffed immediately. Now Major Sansom realised that Sandstede was missing, but soon the river police brought him ashore, and he was arrested as well. While the police were thoroughly searching the *Dahabeah*, the two arrested spies were first taken to an Egyptian police station for the sake of formality, and were then handed over to the British Interrogation Centre at Maadi. At first they were declared to be 'Prisoners of War' to get them away from the Egyptians and into the hands of the British, and only then they were declared 'spies'.

Two of the guards in the Maadi POW Camp where Eppler and Sandstede were interred.
[H. Eppler via Archive Kröpelin]

Hekmat Fahmy, living two boats further away, was arrested at the same time, as were all the other persons who were suspected of involvement in the spy case. Within a short time Major Sansom's organisation had all their contacts rounded up.

29 July 1942, interrogation of the spies and the other arrestees

Together with the raid on the two spies, many other people suspected of being involved with them were arrested and interrogated on 29, 30 and 31 July. All arrested persons were released immediately afterwards, with the exceptions of Fatma Amer, Hassan Gafaar, Hekmat Fahmy and five others who later turned out to be only insignificant players in the case[312].

A palm tree on the shores of the Nile.

After the war Hans Eppler always claimed that he had not given any information to his British interrogators, despite their using torture and "truth drugs"[313], but in reality the situation was quite different. By 29 July 1942, four days after the arrest of the two spies, the "1st Consolidated Report of

312 TNA, London, KV 2/1467, Eppler, Personal File. Interrogation of
      Persons connected with the Eppler and Sandy Case.
313 Eppler, *Rommel ruft Kairo*

View over the Nile, central Cairo.

Hans Eppler and Hans-Gerd Sandstede in the
Maadi POW Camp.
[H. Eppler via Archive Kröpelin]

Sandstede (sitting) and Eppler (standing behind
Sandstede) in the "VIP Camp" as they called the
Maadi POW Camp.
[H. Eppler via Archive Kröpelin]

the Activities of Eppler Johann [alias Hussein Gafaar] and Heinrich (sic.) Sandstede [alias Peter Muncaster][314] had been typed and distributed by the British Security Service. Hans Eppler quite freely provided most of the information in this report. There are many fewer statements from Hans-Gerd Sandstede. It could be that Sandstede knew less than Eppler, but certainly his attempted suicide, when he cut his wrists just one day after their arrest, played a part. The report included information about Operation Kondor and also about several other *Abwehr* missions in Africa. The report contained eight full pages of information. The "2nd Consolidated Report" dated 31 July 1942, and the "3rd Consolidated Report" on of 2 August 1942 filled seven more pages.

One of the open questions for British Intelligence since the capture of SCHILDKROETE, Aberle and Weber, had been how the code used by the *Abwehr* worked. On 6 August 1942, Eppler and Sandstede answered this question in extensive detail[315].

On 23 August 1942, about one month after the two spies had been snatched; the "Detailed Interrogation Report" containing 60 pages of information was typed

It seems that the two German spies were much more successful in providing information to the enemy than they had been prior to their arrest to their own masters.

8 August 1942, the prisoners meet again

8 August 1942 was the first occasion when Eppler and Sandstede could talk to each other again after the interrogation had started in earnest. The discussion between them took place in front of a tent in the POW camp; it was overheard by the British interrogators, and gives very good evidence about what had motivated the two spies since their arrest[316].

Eppler was convinced that their superiors had been aware beforehand that the two spies had no chance, and it was "all over" with them, despite the fact that they had talked a lot to the Interrogation Officers: "I thought it all over. Since they

314 TNA, London, KV 2/1467, Eppler, Personal File
315 TNA, London, KV2.1468, Eppler, Personal File 2, Consolidated
    Interrogation Report on Eppler and Sandstede, 6 August 1942
316 TNA, London, KV 2/1467, 3rd Report (intercepted discussion
    between Eppler and Sandstede). The discussion is quoted here in its
    relevant parts. It gives excellent evidence about the thoughts and
    intentions of the two spies and clearly shows the difference to the
    later publications, where Eppler was involved in a relevant way.

[the Germans] made no attempt to save us, why should I not tell everything to them [the British] and thus save our lives? "

Sandstede replied: "We must do whatever we can to save our lives. They would do the same."

Eppler was also angry with Almásy about their present situation when he said: "Those bastards; Almásy and the others. All of them have received the Iron Cross 1st Class. To hell with them. That is why I decided to tell everything, to save our lives [...] My dear old Sandy; if they do not hang me, I say, IF they do NOT hang me and if I ever meet Almásy again, God, how shall I beat him up![317]"

Sandstede mentioned: "They have treated me awfully well and I have told them everything. What else also do they want from us?" Eppler replied: "Only two things may happen: either they let us live or they will shoot us."

Sandstede: "I am glad about one thing: We had our fun. 3'600 pounds we ran through just in time."

In the meantime, Victor Hauer, who seemed to have disappeared without a trace at the time of the two spies' arrest, was still in British hands. He is no longer mentioned in the documents with his true identity but under the name of Franz Müller with a "legend" saying that he was a German POW who had escaped but was recaptured.[318]

During an identification parade, all three, Eppler, Sandstede and Hassan Gafaar, identified the officers of the Egyptian Airforce, el-Sadat and Ezzat, and thereby confirmed their guilt. On 17 August 1942 Eppler identified el-Masri Pasha during such a parade, who was arrested on orders of the Egyptian Prime Minister on 14 August 1942.

Maadi POW camp
[H. Eppler via Archive Kröpelin]

Both, Sandstede and Eppler make a very relaxed impression on this photograph.
[H. Eppler via Archive Kröpelin]

Eppler and Sandstede in well fitted civilian clothes.
[H. Eppler via Archive Kröpelin]

317 TNA, London, WO 208/5520, Consolidated Interrogations Report of two POW. CSDIC/Middle East. The reason Eppler was angry with Almásy and disappointed that they were not rescued could be that Eppler explained to his interrogators, that whilst still in Tripoli, Almásy had promised them that, should they have the misfortune to be captured, they would be exchanged for Major P.A. Clayton, of the LRDG, who had been caught on 31 January 1941 during the "Incident at Jebel Sherif". There is no way that Eppler could have learned that Almásy had really received the Iron Cross at that time – but he guessed right.

318 TNA, London, KV2/1467, Eppler, Personal File, Letter to Defence Security Office, Egypt, dated 1942-08-26

12 August 1942, measures in Egypt

The two Egyptian Army Officers, Hasan Ezzat and Anwar el-Sadat, were arrested on 12 August 1942 and found guilty by the Egyptian Court of Enquiry, discharged from the Army and interned for the duration of the war, but not tried before an Egyptian court martial. The former Chief of Staff of the Egyptian Army, el-Masri Pasha, was also interned for the duration of the war, but considered as a civilian internee[319].

Left: Modern Cairo with its always dense traffic.

Right: Downtown Cairo.

On 25 August 1942 the case was discussed of the civilians arrested in connection with the case, and it was decided that Hekmat Fahmy should be released with a severe warning. Pere P. Dimitriou (the Hungarian priest in the Church of whom the transmitter was hiden during *Plan el Masri*) was to be deported to Palestine by the military authorities. Fatma Amer and Hassan Salik Gafar were to be interned for the duration of the war[320].

December 1942, a new agreement for the two spies

In December 1942, Eppler and Sandstede signed an agreement with the SIME office in Cairo represented by Major E. Tilly. It was agreed that the two German spies should start to work for SIME (then still attached to CSDIC Cairo) with the main task of counter-espionage against German and Italian suspects. They accepted the new job under the condition that they were not to be sent back to Germany after the war since they feared they could be recognised by other members of the German *Abwehr* or, even worse, by former POW they had interrogated in Egypt. The British accepted this condition and it was agreed that the British would help them to settle down in Northern Rhodesia. From then on they worked without interruption for the "Maadi Interrogation Center", could move freely in British uniform, and even

319 TNA, London, KV2/1467, Eppler, Personal File, Letter from Defence Security Office, Egypt, 19 October 1942
320 TNA, London, FO 141/852, Espionage, 25 August 1942. Hekmat Fahmy claimed that she was imprisoned due to her connection with the spy case. However, the available documentation neither provides evidence that she was conveying military information to the spies nor that she was kept in prison long after being arrested.

received British Army pay-books under the names of P. Richards and P.B. Anderson[321], although they were still officially registered in the POW camp.

February 1946, return to Germany

The rather bizarre story of Eppler and Sandstede continued after they had changed sides and were now working for the British Intelligence. In 1946, when the British intended to close the POW camp and to transfer the POWs, the idea of taking them to Northern Rhodesia was changed and the decision was taken to send them back to Germany under the new names of H.G. Strauch [Sandstede] and Hans. W. Esser [Eppler]. It was agreed that they should be released immediately upon arrival in Germany, but they were told that the Cairo office was not entitled to provide them with the required release papers. This could only be done in Germany. To make sure that everything would work smoothly, they were given a letter of recommendation[322]. The RAF had scheduled a flight from Cairo to Lydda, Athens, Bari, Udine, Vienna and then on to Frankfurt at the end of the third week of April 1946 to transfer ten German and Italian security internees back to Europe[323]. Among the intended passengers for this flight were Eppler and Sandstede.

Before they were transferred to the airport, Major Tilly asked a promise of them: That they would stay calm and not start a fight when a "particular person" entered the plane at the first stop. The promise was given and within a few hours they were on their way to freedom.

Another person in a British POW camp in Palestine, a certain Franz Müller, was also in the final process of being released after the decision to close down the camp. He was the "particular person" who would be passenger number eleven on the same flight as Eppler and Sandstede. Eppler and Sandstede kept their word and remained calm, and Franz Müller, alias Victor Hauer, left the plane at Vienna. Eppler and Sandstede continued to Hamburg, where the final destination on their journey was the former KZ Neuengamme, now called the 6th Civilian Internment Camp. Upon arrival at the administrative

Eppler in his book claimed that when this photo of him in British uniform was taken, he was still working as an Agent for the German *Abwehr*. In fact he was already on the payroll of the British, working in the Maadi Interrogation Centre in Cairo. *[H. Eppler via Archive Kröpelin]*

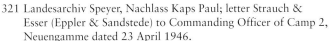

"From then on they worked without interruption for the "Maadi Interrogation Centre", could move freely in British uniform, and even received British Army pay-books under the names of P. Richards and P.B. Anderson".
[H. Eppler via Archive Kröpelin]

---

321 Landesarchiv Speyer, Nachlass Kaps Paul; letter Strauch & Esser (Eppler & Sandstede) to Commanding Officer of Camp 2, Neuengamme dated 23 April 1946.
322 Landesarchiv Speyer, Nachlass Kaps Paul; letter Strauch & Esser (Eppler & Sandstede) to Commanding Officer of Camp 2, Neuengamme dated 23 April 1946
323 TNA, London, KV2/1467, Eppler, Personal Files, C in C ME, telegramme dated 18 April 1946

block office, during the registration procedure, their papers were taken from them, and among these papers were the recommendation letters they had received in Cairo.

Bad luck for the two former spies, as they were previously enlisted in a POW camp for enemy agents and political prisoners. Consequently they were transferred to a camp with a similar purpose, and soon realised that they were not only among thousands of political prisoners, Nazis, former KZ-guards and members of the SS, but also that nobody here had the slightest intention of releasing them to their promised freedom. They took the earliest opportunity to address a letter to the commander of "Camp 2" where they explained their desperate situation.

However; it took until 17 July 1946 for the necessary confirmation to be received in Neuengamme, and they were finally released to freedom in Germany[324].

---

324 Landesarchiv Speyer, Nachlass Kaps Paul; Letter Strauch & Esser (Eppler & Sandstede) to
Commander Camp 2, Neuengamme dated 23 April 1946

Further *Abwehr* missions in Libya

The missions under Ritter and Almásy were not the only ones conducted in North Africa by the *Abwehr* but formed part of a wider range of activities. It is not the task of this book to provide an exhaustive description of all the missions, and therefore only those that might have had something to do with Almásy are explained here.

Operations of Regiment z.bV. 800 Brandenburg in North Africa[325]

The missions of the *Brandenburger* in North Africa are still shrouded in mystery. Operation Salam was only one of the missions they took part in. There is not much evidence about the activities of the *Brandenburger* during the desert campaign and the following is a summary.[326]

Both Gerd Sandstede and Hans Eppler informed the British Security Service during their interrogations that they had been transferred from the Interpreter Company at Meissen to the 15th Company of the *Lehrregiment Brandenburg* in early 1941. 15th Company consisted largely of Germans who had formerly lived in South West Africa (today's Namibia). They both stated that in January 1942 half of the 15th Company was sent to North Africa and assigned to the command of Leutnant von Koenen while the other half remained at Brandenburg[327]. When asked for more specifics, Eppler explained that he had not heard that the other half came to Africa subsequently nor had he heard about the 13th Company.

Why that question to Eppler? At the time of Eppler's interrogation the 13th Company under Oberst Hecker was active in Libya as well. It conducted trials for an amphibious landing in May 1942 along with the Italian *Battaglione San Marco* and used one of the rare *Land Wasser Schlepper*[328] amphibians.

325 TNA, London, WO 208/5520; Third detailed Interrogation Report of Eppler Johann
326 Text based on: TNA, London, WO 208/5520; Third detailed Interrogation Report of Eppler Johann and Trojca, *Küstenjäger-Abteilung "Brandenburg"*
327 The second half of 15th Company was in fact sent to Finland and never to North Africa.
328 The *Land Wasser Schlepper (LWS)* was developed as a light river cargo carrier with amphibious capability and entered regular service in 1942. It was produced in very small numbers and one of these rare unarmoured vehicles was sent to North Africa for testing and eventual operational use.

Eppler mentioned to his interrogator that he had met Leutnant von Koenen and others of the 15ᵗʰ Company at HQ *Panzerarmee Afrika* at Umm er-Rzem near Derna early in April 1942, when they paid a visit to *Major* Zolling who was the Ic [329] of the Panzerarmee Afrika.

Eppler explained that he had been told that the half company took part in an abortive amphibious attack against Tobruk in March 1942 and had suffered losses[330]. It had subsequently been used for guard duties under *Major* Zolling. Eppler said that he had also met *Wachtmeister* Wilscher with *Leutnant* von Koenen. Wilscher was the one who first recommended the transfer of Eppler to the *Lehrregiment Brandenburg* and he was then the "right hand" of von Koenen. Eppler further informed his interrogators that it had been planned that Almásy should resume command over this half of 15ᵗʰ Company after he had accomplished his mission from Gialo to Assiut (Operation Salam) and returned to Libya. The idea was to train the unit and to form a *Wüstenpatrouille* (Desert Patrol) similar to the LRDG. The unit was planned to be equipped with captured British Bren Carriers, Ford V8 Lorries, machine guns, mortars etc. It was planned to operate chiefly in the area of Kufra and to harass enemy supply lines as well as to carry out reconnaissance.[331]

This would have been a challenging task for Almásy. It can only be surmised that it was probably just a rumour among the *Brandenburger* not based on a genuine request from Rommel and his unit commanders. Thinking about the LRDG, one would probably doubt that the employment of tracked vehicles such as the Bren Carrier would have been a good choice. Most probably the Germans were inspired by the use of that small vehicle in the Jock Columns and the reconnaissance columns of the Free French during the battle of Bir Hakeim. However, when Almásy returned from Operation Salam in early June 1942 it was just before the fall of Tobruk. Rommel and his *Panzerarmee Afrika* were in high spirits and everything seemed to be possible, even the conquest of Egypt. Nobody was interested any more in forming such an equivalent of the LRDG – what for?

---

329 Eppler's statement that he had met with *Major* Zolling as the Ic of *Panzerarmee Afrika* in April 1942 is not correct – at that time this function was still occupied by von Mellenthin. Hans-Otto Behrendt became acting Ic after von Mellenthin had to take over the function of Ia (Chief of Staff) when both Westphal and Gause were wounded during the battle of Got el-Ualeb on 31 May 1942. Zolling became Ic after Westphal resumed his duties as Ia on 31 August 1942. However, Zolling was most likely a member of the staff of the Ic and the meeting could easily have taken place despite the misinterpretation of Zolling's function.

330 *Operation Hai* was an amphibious mission to cut the railway line between Mersa Matruh and the front line. The commando under *Leutnant* Kiefer was put ashore from a submarine on 18 November 1941 but nobody returned (from Lahousen, Kriegstagebuch). Note: The date does not correspond with the one given by Eppler. There might have been further missions but Lahousen does not mention any.

331 There is actually an *Afrikakorps* veteran who claims that this operation has taken place, that they were driving south to Kufra to protect Almásy's flank during Operation Salam. He even says that they had refuelled at Kufra and drove back then – obviously this person got some parts of Operation Salam and made it into his own story…

Germans in the Sahara – *Sonderkommando Dora*

"Germans in the Sahara": The title of a message sent by GHQ MEF to HQ Tps Sudan and OC LRDG does not refer to *Salam*, but to another operation of the German *Abwehr*: *Sonderkommando Dora*.

The red scorpion used as the unit insignia of *Sonderkommando Dora*.

The German Abwehr, Abteilung *1*, had created a special unit consisting of cartographers, geographers, astronomers and geologists, all in all 13 scientists, with a support crew of about 60 soldiers, people who had pre-war experience in Africa together with a small protective detachment. The unit was sent to Libya in May of 1942 and its tasks were various. The scientists were employed to collect information and to do mapping of the middle and southern parts of Libya, to conduct terrain survey, to find possible locations for future military airfields, to investigate water sources and to find out possible ways of enemy attacks and to carry out many further military and scientific tasks, such as testing vehicles and equipment under the harsh desert conditions. From October 1942 they had the special task of finding out about an assumed concentration of Free French troops in the Tibesti area of Chad. The reports transmitted to Berlin gave clear evidence of French intentions but did not lead to any German countermeasures.

Although not a fighting unit and relatively small, *Sonderkommando Dora* had the full range of light military equipment available to conduct its tasks. Several aircraft and gliders were permanently at their disposal, as were Mercedes and Opel trucks, Horch Kfz. 15s, Kfz. 17s (radio) and VW Kübelwagen. The only six Steyr 1500 ever to see service in Libya were to be found in their motor pool. They were better equipped than many of the front-line units which lacked all sorts of transport and fuel for most of the time. To obtain their data, *Sonderkommando Dora* was equipped for aerial photography and terrestrial surveying with a number of special equipment that a Zeiss engineer had brought with himself. The scientists were able to draw their sketch-maps in the shortest time while en route during their expeditions. The results of their missions were 23 sketch-maps in scales between 1:50'000 and 1:200'000. Their base was at the oasis of Hon, but they undertook expeditions as far west as Ghat, to Waw en Namus and as far south as the Tibesti Mountains (the Dohone Region at Bir Sarfaya), the Tümmö Mountains south of Bir Mushuru and along the Gebel ben Ghnema.

Following the withdrawal of Axis forces from Libya in January 1943, the important scientists of *Sonderkommando Dora* were urgently evacuated back to Germany by aircraft, and finally the remainder of the unit followed in their vehicles from Hon to Tripoli.

In consequence of World War II, the results of the research of *Sonderkommando Dora*, their reports, maps and photographs ended up in various archives in Freiburg, London and Paris. The unique route-maps of *Sonderkommando Dora* were published for the first time in 2003.

SUBJECT:- Germans in SAHARA.

GSI/200/41/Ia.

L.R.D.G.
  G(Ops).

Information from usual sources indicates that a party of Germans left a place which is believed to be UAU EL KEBIR at 0630 hours on 18 July for UAU EN NAMUS. The column was back at UAU EL KEBIR on 21st July.

There have been other reports over the last few months from the same source, of a few Germans in 2 or 3 vehicles at various Saharan stations, mainly passing between HON, SEBHA and MURZUK, where it is believed there is a German wireless station.

Sgd. D.A.F.Home, Lt-Col.
  for D.M.I.

GSIa.
23 July 42.

A detachment of *Sonderkommando Dora* at the western edge of the Harouj el-Aswad in Libya in December 1942. *[Bayer via Archive Michael Rolke]*

The security detachment of *Sonderkommando Dora* on the parade ground at Hon. *[Haeckel via Archive Michael Rolke]*

Their precision is such that even today a traveller can follow their tracks and sometimes they provide more detail than modern maps of the area.

The mysterious *Unternehmen Dora*

Abwehr, Abteilung I was responsible for *Sonderkommando Dora* and photographs, maps, documents and even plenty physical evidence is available on their work, but there is no hard evidence for the existence of the legendary *Unternehmen Dora* which is said to have been an operation conducted by the *Brandenburger* under the responsibility of *Abteilung II*.

The operation is mentioned in several books dealing with the activities of the Brandenburger, but the first doubts assailed the authors of this book when it became clear that the period covered and routes supposedly driven by *Unternehmen Dora* were practically identical to those of *Sonderkommando Dora*. It is very hard to believe that two Abwehr missions were carried out at the very same time in the same region with such similar names. The main sources for *Unternehmen Dora* are the German authors Helmuth Spaeter and Franz Kurowski[332]. It is most unfortunate that neither of them reveals his sources to the reader. Other accounts regarding the same mission are obviously based on Spaether's and Kurowski's accounts with some added statements and again without mentioning the sources.

The German *Bundesarchiv* in Freiburg has some notes about *Unternehmen Dora*. Surprisingly, these are obviously the notes made by either Spaether or Kurowski and not contemporary original documents. The interrogation protocols and reports in regard to Operation Salam and Operation Kondor mention several *Abwehr* missions in North Africa, some planned and some executed; but nothing at all about *Unternehmen Dora*. Further, the diary of *Oberst* Erwin Lahousen, who was in command of *Abteilung II* (and therefore the *Brandenburger* missions), does not mention *Unternehmen Dora* at all.

An interesting hint was received from Mr. Dines-Jones, a Fellow of the Royal Geographical Society in London who stated that the expedition to Gatroun in the south of Libya by "Gruppe Schwerin" in March 1941 was known to the British as *Unternehmen Dora* and had caused some confusion at HQ in Cairo since it was presumed that they would advance into Chad territory. However, this operation had nothing to do with neither the *Brandenburger* nor the *Abwehr* but was conducted by members of the 5th. Light Division in March 1941 and was a reconnaissance mission for the *Deutsches Afrikakorps*[333] to find out about possible Free French activities in the aftermath of the LRDG raid on Murzuk earlier that year.

Till now not the slightest shred of evidence has been found to indicate that *Unternehmen Dora* really took place. We are convinced that it is pure fiction based on rumours and muddled coincidences.

---

332 Kurowski, *Deutsche Kommandotrupps 1939-45* and Später, *Die Brandenburger – eine deutsche Kommandotruppe – z.b.V.*
333 Detailed account in Gross, Chiarvetto, O'Carroll, *Incident at Jebel Sherif.*

Epilogue – summary and conclusions

Total success for Operation Salam and total failure for the subsequent Operation Kondor. All the planning, effort and suffering of the members of Operation Salam were nullified by subsequent events.

Operation Salam – a useless success

After the previous *Abwehr* missions of *Sonderkommando Ritter* which all ended in failure, Almásy's long drive through the enemy-controlled desert was an outstanding achievement. It may be said that the *Long Range Desert Group* did similar raids through the very same hostile desert, and as regular missions rather than something exceptional. That is true, as far as the route, distance and driving are concerned. But while the LRDG, with a few exceptions, only had to fear enemy counter-action while penetrating the northern areas of Libya, Almásy's small group was constantly within reach of enemy patrols as soon as they had left the Italian held oasis of *Gialo*. A comparably daring mission would be the famous *Murzuk Raid* by the LRDG's G and T Patrols at the end of 1940. The distance covered through the Libyan Desert was about twice what Almásy drove. However, even then the Italians were hardly able to control the vast area and so it remains difficult to compare such missions. We subscribe to the opinion of Saul Kelly in *The Hunt for Zerzura* that Almásy's mission shook the LRDG and the British intelligence authorities in Cairo. The thought of an *Abwehr* commando operating at will in the Libyan Desert, completing its mission and return to base before the British could do anything about it, gave serious cause for concern. For Rommel in the meantime had smashed the Gazala line, taken Bir Hacheim and Tobruk, crossed the Libyan-Egyptian border and was advancing on Alexandria, Cairo and the Suez Canal, the jugular of the British Empire. The British could not know at this time that the subsequent Operation Kondor would fail, Rommel would not be able to advance further than el-Alamein and the *Abwehr*'s one and only man capable of carrying out such deep-desert missions would never do it again.

Operation Salam was a success, no doubt, but it was a useless success since the Germans could not use the experience gained for any other comparable missions. The follow-on Operation Kondor, the very reason for Operation Salam, was completely ruined by circumstances and by the two German spies. Operation Salam was, at its most, a personal success – Almásy's own.

Operation Kondor – a complete failure

Reaching a conclusion about Operation Kondor is not too difficult. It was a complete failure from the moment the two spies reached Cairo until the British caught them. It is obvious from the available interrogation protocols that they were neither able to obtain any kind of valuable information in the two months of their "activities" in Cairo, nor could they get in touch with their counterparts allocated to *HQ Panzerarmee Afrika* nor any other W/T station of the *Abwehr*. Eppler was obviously not able to re-connect to old contacts of his pre-war times in Cairo. It is questionable why the *Abwehr* supplied them with British instead of Egyptian pounds and did not provide them with a second W/T station to call if the first should be unavailable for any reason. Although it is known and proven that many members of the *Abwehr*, including *Admiral* Canaris, were unsympathetic to the Nazi cause, it was still an organisation of the *Wehrmacht* and it would not seem reasonable to assume that its planners outright intended the failure of Operation Kondor.

Moreover, it was not only the two spies and the *Abwehr* who caused the failure. A good part of the responsibility remains with *HQ Panzerarmee Afrika*, ultimately even *Generalfeldmarschall* Rommel, who decided that the W/T station SCHILDKROETE was to be employed near the front line due to the lack of W/T operators.

All this together with the efficiency of British intelligence sealed the fate of Operation Kondor. No further attempts to place German spies into Egypt was ever made. At first the Germans were enthusiastic and believed to break through the opposing forces and reach Cairo in a short time. Later, after their defeat at el-Alamein, there was no longer any need for *Panzerarmee Afrika* to have personnel in Cairo – the Axis forces were in full retreat, out of Egypt, then out of Libya to capitulate at Cap Bon in Tunisia in May 1943.

An interesting question remains: Why were the two captured German spies not sentenced to death and executed? This question cannot be answered with a simple statement. While it is "common knowledge" that spies were always executed, the actual truth is quite different. For example, the British intelligence service MI5 successfully turned most of the German spies in the United Kingdom to work against Germany[334]. Captured spies were simply confronted with the decision either to be sentenced to death or to live and work for the British. Since both Eppler and Sandstede fully cooperated with their interrogators, the same applied to them[335].

Another important aspect is clearly shown in the correspondence of the British Embassy in Egypt.[336] To avoid anti-British riots in Egypt, the British Authorities were very keen to keep the whole case at a low profile. The Egyptians involved, like Captain Anwar el-Sadat and Aziz el-Masri Pasha, were not to be sentenced to prison, but either moved to a remote location and put under house arrest, or interned for the duration of the war. Other Egyptians involved, among them the belly dancer Hekmat Fahmy, were to be released with a warning. Considering the fact that Eppler's stepfather had been an Egyptian judge of high reputation, his family connections may also have helped him to survive.

334 Waller, *The Unseen War in Europe* and Crowdy, *Deceiving Hitler*
335 TNA, London, KV2.1467 & KV2.1468, Eppler, Personal File
336 TNA, London, FO.141.852

APPENDIX 1:
PERSONS, NOTES
& EXPLANATIONS

Detailed biographies

The biographies of Almásy, Ritter, the two spies and Hans von Steffens are worth covering in more detail since they are the main actors in this story. For Almásy, much information is available – but still there are blank spots, in particular regarding his later years after Operation Salam. For Eppler and Sandstede we have to rely mainly on their statements given under threat of death when the British Security Service interrogated them after the war in Cairo and their own publications. The information about Hans von Steffens was extracted from his own book and from the same sources as for the two spies. The account for Nikolaus Ritter was taken from his personal interrogation file and from information provided by his son-in-law.

László Ede Almásy

Of all the early explorers of the Libyan Desert, László Almásy (1895–1951) was perhaps the most colourful and least understood character. His supporters praise him as a great scientist-explorer. Others dismiss him as nothing but a Nazi spy with ulterior motives from the beginning. Yet neither could be farther from the truth. He belonged to a rapidly disappearing breed, the romantic gentleman-adventurer, driven by a deep passion for the desert and the unknown.

László Ede Almásy was born on the 22 August, 1895 in Borostyánkő (presently Bernstein, Austria) as the second son of György Almásy, a Hungarian nobleman and noted orientalist, and Ilona Pittoni, of Italian descent. Contrary to popular belief (often fuelled by him to gain higher status) he was not a Count. He received his education in Hungary, Austria and England and was fluent in at least five languages. His family background and upbringing in the cosmopolitan atmosphere of the Austro-Hungarian monarchy probably gave him an outlook that was uncommon in times of universally strengthening nationalist sentiment. At an early age he took a deep interest to mechanics and aviation which largely determined the rest of his life.

Following World War I, during which he served as a pilot in the Austro-Hungarian Air Force, and the collapse of the monarchy, Almásy found himself without a purpose and clear identity. His elder brother inherited the considerable family property, with László only receiving a modest allowance. The lack of funds to fulfill his ambitions followed him throughout his life. For a short time he returned to England to continue his engineering studies, but there is no trace of him ever receiving a degree. Returning to Hungary he took a minor part in the abortive Habsburg restoration attempt, being the driver of Charles IV during his second attempt to reach the Hungarian capital, Budapest. Eventually, through his outstanding mechanical abilities and his contacts in upper circles, he managed to land a job in sales for Steyr, the Austrian car maker which proved to be the turning point in his life.

In 1926 a wealthy friend, Prince Antal Eszterházy, was planning a hunting trip to southern Sudan, and Almásy persuaded his friend to drive a Steyr from Alexandria to the Dinder River in the Sudan on a test run, something never before accomplished by an ordinary automobile. This adventure was Almásy's first experience with Africa and the desert, soon to be followed by several others as Steyr moved him to Cairo as their local representative. On another Steyr-sponsored expedition, Almásy drove all the way from Mombasa to Cairo with Prince Ferdinand Liechtenstein, this time driving for the first time along the unexplored stretch of the Darb el- Arbain[337] from Selima to Kharga.

While his early desert trips may be dismissed as simply thrill-seeking and adventure, Almásy took a deep interest in two desert mysteries that greatly excited the scientific community of the time: the myths of the lost oasis of Zerzura and the lost army of Cambyses. In the brief period 1932–1935 he organised six expeditions to the inner parts of the Libyan Desert, but his goals proved elusive. While three wadis with vegetation were found in the Gilf Kebir, their association with Zerzura is rather circumstantial, and no trace was ever found of the lost army. However the expeditions did traverse vast areas of unexplored country, filling much of the large blank area on contemporary maps. More significantly, on several expeditions spectacular new rock paintings were found, bringing attention to the prehistoric rock art of the region.

Unfortunately for Almásy, his finances never permitted him to go on his own, as he would have wished. Others, who also expected to take some or all of the credit, financed all the expeditions. Given this state of affairs, Almásy was willing to go with anybody who offered to finance a trip, and his choice of companions made him suspicious to both Italian and British authorities that at the time were engaged in a bitter border dispute centering on the Libyan Desert. By 1935 he was considered *persona non grata* on Italian territory, and kept on tight reins by the British authorities in Egypt. His attention returned to his other passion, aviation, and he made no more deep-desert ventures till the outbreak of the War.

World War II provided yet another opportunity for Almásy to go back to the desert at someone else's expense. This time the backer was the *Abwehr*, and he took full advantage of the opportunity. His feat of transporting Eppler and Sandstede from Gialo across the Gilf Kebir to Egypt in the 'back yard' of the Long Range Desert Group, the subject of this book is counted among his greatest achievements. Yet from his surviving diary it is clear that it was just another desert adventure for him, and certainly not something done in the service of a higher cause.

---

337 Literally translated as "road of the forty days".

Following the war he was arrested in Hungary by the new Soviet-installed regime, and tried for war crimes based on his detachment to the German army. After some arm-twisting and possible bribery by some of his influential friends in Hungary and Egypt he was acquitted, but it was clear that he could not remain for long in Hungary or the Soviet occupation zone of Austria. Perhaps with the help of British intelligence (it is rumored but not proven that he may have been working for British Intelligence in the later years of the war) he made his way back to Cairo, making a living from odd jobs including leading hunting parties in other parts of Africa. Ill health and meagre finances prevented him from pursuing his old dream of continuing his quest for the lost army of Cambyses. His brief moment of glory came in 1950 when King Farouk appointed him the director of the newly-formed Desert Institute. However he was unable to take office, having fallen seriously ill the year before. He died a few months later on 22 March 1951 while undergoing treatment in Salzburg from complications arising from amoebic dysentery.

His contemporaries universally acknowledged his immense knowledge and experience of the desert, yet there is also a clear tone of dislike towards him. This may partially be due to his sexual orientation, however he was also a loner, sometimes taking unnecessary risks (something which even shows through in his own writings), and vehemently defending his own opinions on any subject. Among all the slightly negative bias there is one voice that clearly stands out, always speaking about Almásy in a tone of respect and acknowledgement: Ralph Bagnold. Probably the greatest of the small band of explorers roaming the Libyan Desert in the nineteen thirties, he maintained contact with Almásy both before and after the war, and their surviving correspondence speaks of a deep understanding between the two. While their approaches and attitudes may have been different, both men had a common binding trait – the compelling desire to seek out what is behind the next dune or that far rise on the horizon, and the immense joy and satisfaction derived from being able to do so.

Nikolaus Ritter[338]

Nikolaus Fritz Adolf Ritter, later on also known under his cover names Dr. Rantzau, Dr. Renken and Dr. Jansen was born 8 January 1899 in Rheyth as the son of Nikolaus Josef Ritter and Käthe Ritter. He spent his school years near Bremerhaven and at Flensburg and Verden. From 1917 to 1920 he was on military service with the 162. *Infanterie Regiment Lübeck* and was wounded twice during the First World War. After being demobilised from the *Reichswehr* in 1920 he started an apprenticeship in the textile industry.

Due to the bad economic situation in Germany, on 1 January 1924 Ritter emigrated to New York in the United States. There he worked first as an office clerk and later as a foreman. In 1926 he married Mary Aurora Evans. In the following years he developed his professional career and in 1935 he was the general manager of the company *JJ Süsmuth* in New York. In 1926 and 1930 respectively, their two children, Klaus Haveland and Katherina Francis, were born.

338 Information taken from *Preliminary Interrogation Report on Ritter*; TNA / KV 2.86 and
    Manfred Blume, Ritter's son in law

He returned to Germany in 1936 where he joined the *Wehrmacht* and was divorced in 1937. In the same year he was promoted to the rank of *Hauptmann*.

From 1937 on Ritter was working for German military intelligence and after several journeys in Europe to meet agents he travelled to New York to meet several *V-Leute*. He established intelligence networks in the UK and in the USA. His most important success was when he received the drawings of the secret new bombsight by the US company Norden. The Germans copied it and they had it in service before the British received it from their allies. In 1939 he married Irmgard Klitzing and the couple spent their honeymoon in Italy and Yugoslavia.

In his intelligence work he was responsible mainly for the United Kingdom, particularly the air industry in that country. Then, in September 1940, when he was in Budapest, he first met Almásy. One month later he was promoted from *Hauptmann* to *Major*.

On 20 January 1941 he was transferred to *X Fliegerkorps* and made commanding officer of *Aufklärungskommando Nord-Ost-Afrika*. Injured after an aircraft crash on 17 July 1941 he was sent to a hospital in Berlin and after his recovery appointed as Air Attaché at Rio de Janeiro in Brazil. However, this appointment was cancelled and *Major* Ritter left military intelligence and joined the *Flak Art Schule 1*[339] at Rerik in Mecklenburg. He remained with the Luftwaffe, was promoted to *Oberstleutnant* in November 1942 and became the commanding officer of *Nachschub Regiment Hermann Göring*[340] in Sicily and Italy one month later. In March 1944 he became the commanding officer of *Flak Regiment* 63 at Oldenburg and after various other postings he saw the end of the war as *Korps Flakführer IX Korps z.b V.* in the Harz Mountains.

Only a short time after the war's end he was arrested by the British and interrogated by specialists at Bad Nenndorf. He spent more than one year under arrest in Neuengamme near Hamburg. After his release he worked in several occupations and became General Manager of the *Deutsche Hilfsgesellschaft*[341] in 1955. After his retirement in 1964 he undertook several journeys to Africa, the Near East and Middle East. His last journey took him as far as Persia and Afghanistan. Ritter published his memoirs in 1972 under the title *Deckname Dr. Rantzau*.

Oberst a.D. Nikolaus Ritter died in 1974 in Hamburg.

Hans-Willi Eppler

Hans-Willi Eppler was born 7 April 1914 in Alexandria, Egypt, as the son of *Fräulein* Eppler and an unknown father[342]. In 1915 Eppler and his mother returned to her home town of Backnang near Stuttgart in Germany and some time later *Fräu-*

---

339 Anti Aircraft Artillery School No. 1
340 Supply Regiment "Hermann Göring"
341 The *Deutsche Hilfsgemeinschaft* was a social institution of the City of Hamburg to help children of refugees from the eastern areas of Germany and to organize and finance assistance to victims of the allied bombing attacks on Hamburg.
342 Information from Eppler's interrogation filed under TNA, KV2.1467, Eppler, Personal File 1

lein Eppler married a high-ranking Egyptian judge named Saleh Bey Gafaar. Hans-Willi then went to elementary school, later to the *Realgymnasium* at Backnang, and later he lived with his stepfather in Cairo. In 1931 he attended the *Lycée Française* and a school of the *Frères* at Korafich, and from 1933 to 1934 he took an apprenticeship at Bosch in Cairo.

On 19 November 1937, he married a Danish woman named Sonja Wallinin. Then in 1938, he spent six months in Berlin with *Deutsches Kalisyndikat* at *Bernburgstrasse* in charge of advertising and propaganda. Later he worked for *Wintershall*. On account of a disagreement with *D.A.F.* (*Deutsche Arbeitsfront*, the German Labour Front), he left Germany for Copenhagen, the hometown of his wife. Until the end of 1939 he worked at the fur farm belonging to his father-in-law. He returned to Germany and on 1 September 1940, he was conscripted into the *Wehrmacht*. On 9 February 1941 Eppler, who was fluent in Arabic and French, was posted to the Signals Depot Unit, Leipzig, and later to the Interpreters Depot Unit at Meissen. Then in May or June 1941 he was posted to the *Heeresplankammer* (Topographical Department) of *OKH*, then to 15th Company of *Regiment z.b.V. 800 Brandenburg*[343] and subsequently to *Abwehr l H West*.

In February 1942 he went with the Almásy expedition to Tripoli, then to Gialo and in May to Gilf Kebir, Assiut, Cairo. He was one of the two spies taken to Egypt who failed to carry out Operation Kondor.

After capture he became a POW and was interned in Maadi, Cairo, until after the war when he was transferred to Hamburg, Germany, and kept in the former KZ Neuengamme until he was released on 17 July 1946.[344] In Hamburg he made a new start as a black-market dealer in cigarettes. His Danish wife, who had considered him dead, had married another man in the meantime. In 1956, the author Leonard Mosley found Eppler living in Neuforweiler, Saarland, Germany, and interviewed him for the book *The Cat and the Mice* which was published in 1958.

Later on, Eppler settled in France, where he re- married three more times. In 1972, Eppler was living the life of a wealthy man in the 16th *Arrondissement* of Paris, married to a millionaire's daughter named Denise. In this year he claimed 300'000 *Deutsche Mark* back pay from the German Federal Republic since his contract as an agent for the *Abwehr* had never been cancelled[345].

Hans-Willi Eppler's last residence was in Hoevelhof before he died in Paderborn on 18 August 1999.

Eppler published several books about his activities in the German Secret Service. However, his accounts were always doubted, and after comparison with his interrogation reports they can be considered as fiction for a large part.

---

343 TNA, London, WO 508/5520 3rd detailed interrogation report, where Eppler insists that 15 Coy had been sent to Libya – which was actually not true (they went to Finland). It can be guessed that he was only attached to them administratively and only for a short time.

344 Eppler, **Rommel ruft Kairo**

345 This contract exists but has to be considered as a fake, probably produced by Eppler himself. See chapter "Eppler's Agentenvertrag with the *Abwehr*"

Hans-Gerd Sandstede[346]

Hans-Gerd Sandstede[347] was born in Oldenburg, Germany, on 26 October 1913. After his father, Gerhard Sandstede, a professor in chemistry, was killed at the beginning of World War 1, his mother married again in 1920. Sandstede's stepfather, Professor Dr. Osterloh was by 1942 a director of the Teachers' College at Saarbrücken.

Sandstede went to the *Gymnasium* at Oldenburg and after his education he did odd jobs here and there in Germany until the beginning of 1930, when he emigrated to South West Africa (today's Namibia) where he lived with a relative of his late father. Regarded as the 'black sheep' of his family because of his lack of profession, he was obviously possessed of a wanderlust that took him all over the continent of Africa.

From South West Africa he went to South Africa to work at a farm in Kimberley and then on to Durban. Via several stages he finally reached Moçambique, where he worked on a farm for a short time. He moved to a sisal farm in the same country, and later became the partner of a Portuguese who ran a workshop and a small brandy distillery. After seven months Sandstede had to leave Moçambique, since he could not afford the deposit required from foreigners. In November 1931 he moved to Tanganiyka, where the guarantee sum had already been paid in Germany. In 1933 he became a partner in a local business again but in March of that year, after he had received some money from Germany, he went out to a gold seeking expedition to Lupa. While he found only little gold, he was lucky enough to become employed in a gold mine of an Irishman. By early 1934 he went to Dar es-Salam as a salesman for mining equipment where he obtained a post as office manager for the Texas Oil Company.

He was in charge of their shipping interests and stayed there for a longer period, and in 1937 he married a German woman from Dar es-Salam. The beginning of 1938 saw him moving again; first to Kampala, then Nairobi, Mombasa and again Tanganiyka.

After living a roving and adventurous life for many years, , when war broke out in 1939 he was interned at Dar es-Salam as a German national. In early 1940 he was repatriated to Germany as part of an exchange of internees. Thanks to the knowledge and experience gained during his extensive travelling in south and central Africa, Sandstede was employed with the Topographical Department of the *OKW* with the tasks of correcting and translating maps of the region .

Sandstede was then employed with the *Dolmetscher Ersatzabteilung*[348]at Meissen. The members of this unit were normally attached to other signals or intercept units as interpreters. The personnel was 'attached' but not 'transferred' and still remained with their original unit. Sandstede for example was with the 8th Signals Regiment

---

346 Information from "Hamburger Abendblatt" and consolidated interrogation reports of 2 POW is filed under TNA, London, WO/2008 5520.
347 The reports give his name as Heinrich-Gerd but in a personal letter to one of the authors of this book he named himself Hans-Gerd Sandstede.
348 Interpreters Depot Unit

in France when he was recalled to take part in a *Swahili* course. In exceptional cases, transfers took place – as for example in the case of Sandstede and Eppler who were transferred to the *Lehrregiment Brandenburg* to join the *Abwehr*.

After Operation Salam, the subsequent capture of the two spies and their stay as prisoners of war in Egypt and Germany, little more was heard Sandstede. Together with his wife Hilde he lived in Hamburg, Elbvorort, running his business and spending the winters in the United Arab Emirates.

Only several decades later did the German media have him in the headlines again. He was still active in his business as a merchant and travelled to Iraq to sign a contract when international relations with the country turned sour and 76-year-old Sandstede became one of several hundred hostages of Saddam Hussein. After 10 weeks "Rommel's Spy" – as he was called in the German media – was released for "humanitarian reasons"along with seven other Germans on 21 October 1990 .

Hans-Gerd Sandstede died on 10 December 2002 and he is buried at the cemetery of Hamburg Blankenese.

Hans von Steffens[349]

Hans Adolf Kolomann Freiherr von Steffens-Frauweiler was born in on 4 June 1901 in Berlin[350], was about 184 cm tall, had several dueling scars on his face and limped due to a leg wound. He was a cousin of Franz von Papen. After the war of 1914–18, von Steffens took part in several nationalist struggles, in the *Kapp-Putsch*[351] and in the Baltic States, Silesia and the Ruhr. In 1925 he took part in Hitler's Munich putsch and, as a result, to escape the police of the Weimar Republic, he had to leave Germany and joined the French Foreign Legion where he served for 5 years. At the end of his service he remained in North Africa and worked in Casablanca and Tunis as a newspaper reporter.

---

349 The information concerning Hans von Steffens' life and military career has largely been taken from Eppler's interrogation that is filed under TNA, London, KV2.1467, Eppler, Personal File 1 and from von Steffen's *Salaam* as well as from Gert Buchheit's publications. Further information was taken from a post-war letter of *Major* Seubert to Gert Buchheit and from information received by the authors from the "Brandenburger Rundbrief". Von Steffens himself in his book says that he did not think well of Eppler and therefore it can be expected that Eppler wanted to give the worst possible picture of his "colleague" to the British interrogators. Some further information about Hans von Steffens can be taken from Gert Buchheit's contributions in his book *Spionage in zwei Weltkriegen*, where he has a chapter about Operation Salam and Operation Kondor. According to Buchheit, Hans von Steffens had been in North Africa for about 10 years before the war and after the war he is mentioned as "author and freelance journalist". In his own publication (*Salaam*), von Steffens wrote that "Stetten", his alter ego, was a journalist before the war but banned from his profession by the Nazis for his political thinking. He wrote that "Stetten" had volunteered for the Wehrmacht at the beginning of the war but that the SS held him in suspicion. Unless the personal file, if one exists, of Hans von Steffens becomes available in the British Archives, Eppler's account remains the main source.
350 *Stadtarchiv* Karlsruhe
351 The *Kapp Putsch* — or more accurately the Kapp-Lüttwitz Putsch — was a 1920 coup attempt during the German revolution aimed at overthrowing the Weimar Republic.

In 1936 or 1937 von Steffens returned to Germany and was employed at one of the ministries. He is said to have made many trips to Paris on business. At the outbreak of war he was an agent publisher who dealt in books about National Socialism. He volunteered for the army but was turned down on account of his service with the French Foreign Legion. He was eventually accepted by the *Lehrregiment z.b.V. 800 Brandenburg*.

Later he was transferred to *Abwehr, Abteilung III* and worked in Paris in civilian clothes. He spoke good French, some English and some Italian. Then, when the Germans started sending troops to Libya, von Steffens was transferred to *Abwehr, Abteilung II*. He claims in his book "Salaam" that he was travelling on the steamer "Preussen" when the vessel was sunk by air attack. He was one of only 83 survivors. However there is contradicting evidence suggesting that he arrived to Libya by air. In any case he must have arrived in Libya for the first time in late July 1941[352]. He joined at least one journey with von Griesheim to the South, to the area of Murzuk in August 1941. Von Steffens wrote that he was attached to an Italian *Meharist* unit. He maintained W/T communication with *Major* Wido von Griesheim (CO *Abwehrstelle Tripolis*) and *Unteroffizier* Holzbrecher at Nalut and was a fairly good W/T operator himself.

Von Steffens subsequently returned to Germany and was transferred to *Abwehr, Abteilung I H West* before being sent back to Africa with Operation Salam under the command of Almásy. Based on his career, and not least due to his time in the French Foreign Legion, he maintained a very tough military discipline both for himself and others. *Major* Seubert who employed him for Operation Salam knew this and it was thought that his manner would be helpful to keep control over the other members of the enterprise. In fact, von Steffens' behaviour proved to be one of the reasons for the problems which arose among the members of the group.

Reading von Steffens' book where he writes only very negatively about Eppler and Sandstede, the biography given by Eppler after his capture in Cairo is obviously based on information given by von Steffens to Eppler when they were still on good terms. It is worth noting that Eppler does not make any statement about von Steffens' performance and behaviour during Operation Salam at all.

In Eppler's account von Steffens is without any doubt at least sympathetic to the Nazis, while von Steffens in his own book writes that he had to suffer them. It does not need much imagination to understand that a German author, just after the war, would hardly have written a book where he declared himself to have been pro-Nazi. On the other hand, the account provided by Eppler contains several small details which could only have been received by him from von Steffens; for example that von Steffens had received the *Baltenkreuz*[353].

352 A German-Italian convoy of steamers MADDALENA ODERO, NICOLO ODERO, CAFFARO, and PREUSSEN departed Napoli for Tripoli escorted by four Italian destroyers. On the 22nd July the German steamer PREUSSEN was sunk by Swordfish of 830 Squadron 30 miles (48 kilometres) SE of Pantelleria. However there are significant doubt about Steffens' claim to have been on board, since Seubert wrote in a message to von Griesheim on 24 July that von Steffens will be flown from Rome to Tripoli by aircraft around 27 or 28 of July 1941. (TNA, London, HW 19/10 ISOS 8146).
353 The *Baltenkreuz* was a military reward during the Republic of Weimar

After his early departure from the operation and his subsequent return to Germany, no information is available about any further employment with the *Abwehr* or the *Brandenburger*.

Under interrogation, Eppler gave the opinion that von Steffens then returned to the area of Murzuk, this time as CSM[354] with *Sonderkommando Dora* under *Leutnant* Otto Schulz –Kampfhenkel. Von Steffens himself stated that he was intended to join *Sonderkommando Dora*, but it obviously did not happen as he was never enlisted with this special command. On 27 March 1944, he married Hildegard Boenack in Sofia and they had one child. After the war they lived in Karlsruhe. Hans von Steffens died on 13 October 1978 in the *Städtisches Klinikum* in Karlsruhe[355].

354 Company Sergeant Major
355 Stadtarchiv Karlsruhe

Other persons of interest

These biographical notes have been compiled from available books, documents and public sources. They are by no means complete, but are provided as general background information for the convenience of the reader.

Franz Seubert

Major **Seubert, Franz** (1895–1990). Volunteer in World War One, awarded the Iron Cross 1st Class and the *Verwundetenabzeichen*. He left military service in 1918. From 1933 on Seubert was employed as tourism director in Füssen/Allgäu and in 1938 he was reactivated for military service. From 1939, Seubert was with the *OKW/Abwehr* in Berlin and then as *Leutnant* at the *AST* München. Subsequently as *Major* at *Amt Ausl./Abw I H-West 3* in Berlin was the overall leader of Operation Salam. His codename was ANGELO. In von Steffens's book he is named "Grundig". From November 1942 until May 1943 he was *Leiter I* of the *Abwehr Kommando Tunesien*, later in 1943 head of *AST Sofia*. He was Prisoner of War from May 1945 to August 1948 then employed with an academic publisher as historian in regard of inter-European intelligence activities. He was General Manager of the *AGEA (Arbeitsgemeinschaft ehemaliger Abwehrangehöriger)* and publisher of the magazine **Die Nachhut**. He died at the age of 95 years in Munich.

Other members of Operation Salam

This is based mainly on *Salaam – Geheimkommando zum Nil 1942*. Hans von Steffens uses pseudonyms which may be confusing if one reads his book and compares it with the other publications. The military ranks of the participants of Operation Salam are not always given correctly and the function of many of those mentioned is not very clear. Hans von Steffens made clear statements in his book of whom he liked and whom he did not. Since the frictions between the members of the group had a certain impact on the preparation and the execution of the operation it is mentioned here.

The following list provides the most accurate – though still incomplete – information available:

Unteroffizier (NCO) **Aberle, Werner.** Responsible for the W/T truck for SCHILD-KROETE. Captured with Weber Waldemar during *Operation Theseus* in the area of Bir Hakeim on 29 May 1942 by a New Zealand unit.

Feldwebel **Beilharz** (first name unknown). Taken on from *Rittmeister* Hoesch's group. Driver. Before joining Operation Salam, he was temporarily assigned to the *13./Lehrregiment z.b.V 800* together with Munz. He had to return to Gialo with *Unterarzt* Strungmann at the beginning of the operation for medical reasons. Hans von Steffens did not like him.

Fähnrich (Warrant Officer 1ˢᵗ. Class) **Entholt, Hans.** Joined early after a request from Almásy. Did not leave Tripoli with the group but stayed behind due to health problems. Based on recently uncovered personal correspondence, it is now clear that there was a close personal relationship between him and Almásy. Entholt was killed in action near el-Alamein shortly after the end of Operation Salam.

Obergefreiter (Senior Lance Corporal) **Körper** (first name unknown). Recruited in North Africa as a mechanic to the group. He was on good terms with Hans von Steffens and completed Operation Salam.

Unteroffizier (NCO) **Munz** (first name unknown). Taken on from *Rittmeister* Hoesch's group. Driver. Before joining Operation Salam, he was temporarily assigned to the *13./Lehrregiment z.b.V 800* together with Beilharz. He was not a friend of Hans von Steffens and completed Operation Salam.

Unterarzt (equivalent to 1ˢᵗ Lieutenant) **Strungmann** (first name unknown). Medical officer with the group. He was only recruited after Hans Entholt fell ill in Tripoli but was also not fit for the desert. He had to leave the group together with *Feldwebel* Beilharz shortly after Gialo.

Gefreiter (Lance Corporal) **von der Marwitz** (first name unknown). Manned the W/T station at Gialo and remained there during Operation Kondor with the codename OTTER.

Major **von Griesheim, Wittilo.** Commanding officer of *Abwehrstelle Tripolis* (*Ast. Tripolis*) with the codename WIDO.

von Walther, Gebhardt. The German Consul at Tripoli was not an official member of Operation Salam but a personal acquaintance of Almásy who supported the mission. His codename in the W/T traffic was SEPP (maybe related to his nickname "Seppel"). Von Walther (1902–982) joined the foreign office in 1929 and was present in Tripoli in the post of Consul from 27 October 1941 to 19 January 1943 when the consulate was closed due to advancing Allied forces. He served then from 29 April 1943 until 2 August 1944 in Ankara, Turkey.

Gefreiter (Lance Corporal) **Weber, Waldemar.** W/T Operator with *Panzerarmee Afrika* before Operation Salam, codename SCHILDKROETE. He was captured together with Werner Aberle during *Operation Theseus* in the area of Bir Hakeim on 29 May 1942 by a New Zealand unit.

Unteroffizier (Corporal) **Wöhrman** (first name not known). Driver, was recruited in Germany and completed Operation Salam. He was on good terms with von Steffens and was named "Wörner" in the latter's book.

Persons related to Operation Kondor

The key personalities in Operation Kondor, in addition to those listed above under Operation Salam, were the following:

Amer, Fatma. Wife of Dr. Aly Amer; born in Vienna, the daughter of parents born in Moravia and therefore since 1919 a Czech subject until her marriage with an Egyptian in 1931. She assisted Egyptian nationalists and was brought in contact with Eppler by Victor Hauer.

Colonel Dunstan, E. SIME. Principal interrogator of Eppler and Sandstede.

Eppler, Johanna. Mother of Hans Eppler, married to Saleh Bey Gafaar.

Captain Ezzat, Hasan. Fighter pilot in the Egyptian airforce. Was asked to fly Eppler back to German lines.

Fahmy, Hekmat (1902–1970). Famous belly dancer. Toured Europe between 1937 and 1939. Employed at the roof-cabaret of the "Continental" (not in the 'Kit Kat' as it is often stated). Lived on a houseboat on the Nile and helped Eppler and Sandstede to rent their own *Dahabeah*. While the "legend" says that she was in prison for two years and only released after she went on hunger strike in 1944, all available documents show that she neither provided valuable information to the spies nor was she imprisoned.

Gafaar, Hassan. Half-brother of Hans Eppler. Born 1916 in Germany and lived there for 17 years before coming to Egypt. Assisted Eppler and Sandstede and brought them into contact with Victor Hauer.

Bey Gafaar, Saleh (died 2 October 1941). Egyptian former judge. Married to Johanna Eppler, father of Hassan Gafaar and step-father of Hussein Gafaar (Hans Eppler).

Hauer, Victor. Born in Austria 7 October 1907, employed first at the Austrian, then German legation in Cairo. At the outbreak of war taken on by the Swedish legation, Section B, in Cairo with the consent of the British. His agreed task was to look after the interests of German internees and their families in Egypt. Provided a new W/T set to the two German spies and informed the British Secret Intelligence Service of their presence via one of his contacts.

Jenkins, G.J. Defence Security Office Cairo.

Müller, Franz. Alias Victor Hauer.

Doctor Radinger. A gynaecologist in Cairo who was mainly occupied with illegal abortions. Agent for the British Security Service. He was informed by Hauer about the spy case.

Lt. Commander Rodd. GGR, CIC, CSDIC, Interrogation Officer at Maadi.

Major Sansom, Alfred William. Head of the Cairo Branch of the British Security Service. He arrested Eppler and Sandstede.

Major Tilly, E. SIME Cairo. Interrogation officer for Eppler and Sandstede.

Other persons of interest

Many other persons played a role before, during and after Operation Salam or are mentioned in relation to it. The following list is by no means complete.

Alington, Jean. [See: Howard, Jean]

Bagnold, Ralph Alger (1896–1990). Founder and first commander of the Long Range Desert Group during World War II. He was a pioneer of motorised desert exploration during the 1930s. His expeditions included the first east-west crossing of the Libyan Desert (1932). He laid the foundations for research on how sand is transported by wind in his influential book "*The Physics of Blown Sand and Desert Dunes*" (*1941*) which is still a standard reference in the field. He was a Fellow of the Royal Geographical Society from 1944 (FRGS).

Hauptmann **Behrendt, Hans-Otto.** From February 1941 with *Erkundungsstab Rommel* in North Africa. Served temporarily as acting Intelligence Officer (Ic) when von Mellenthin became Chief of Staff (Ia) after Westphal was wounded until Zolling became Ic. Continued work on staff of *Panzerarmee Afrika* until 1943.

Hauptmann **Blaich, Theo** (1900–1975). After the First World War, at the age of 18, Theo Blaich travelled to central America by ship where he worked on banana plantations in several countries. In the 1920s he moved to Africa, to the Cameroons and obtained a Messerschmitt Bf.108 "Taifun". With this private plane and on his own volition he flew north and joined *X. Fliegerkorps* in the rank of *Hauptmann*. Beside his involvement in *Sonderkommando Ritter*, he later became famous with *Sonderkommando Blaich* and the spectacular bombing raid on Fort Lamy in Chad. Blaich was later transferred to Croatia and ended his military career as a *Major* and *Gruppenkommandeur* of NSGr. 7. He died in 1975.

Admiral **Canaris, Willhelm** (1887–1945). After a colourful career in the German Imperial Navy during World War I, Canaris became involved in activities of the far right and was attracted by the ideas of Adolf Hitler. When he was nominated the chief of the *Abwehr* in 1935 he was already a rival to Reinhardt Heydrich who ran the notorious *GeStaPo* in the SS. It seems that Canaris started to distance himself from the Nazis in 1937 after visiting a concentration camp. From then on he began to use his secret connections to support the resistance against the régime but he remained in his position because he was aware that Heydrich and the SS would immediately take over the *Abwehr* once the occasion arose. He collected as much material as possible which could be used against the Nazis but his position weakened when the achievements of the *Abwehr* became of less and less value. It is still not clear whether this development was at least partly caused by Canaris actively working against the régime. In February 1944, Canaris was dismissed from his position and then arrested following the assassination attempt on Hitler of 20 July 1944. When Canaris' secret diaries were discovered in April 1945, Hitler ordered the "*immediate destruction of the conspirators*". He was hanged in KZ Flossenburg on 9 April 1945. Right up to the present day, it remains very difficult to understand the role Canaris played during the Third Reich, because hardly any of the relevant documents survived the war.

Major **Clayton, Patrick Andrew** (1896–1962). Soldier and surveyor, worked for the Desert Survey in Egypt in the 1920s and 1930s, during which time he mapped much of the unknown parts of the Libyan Desert. Member of the Zerzura Club, made a desert expedition with Almásy on one occasion in 1932. Unlike Almásy, Bagnold and the other Zerzura Club members, Clayton was the only one to go to the desert as a profession. During the Second World War he joined the LRDG, and led the famous Murzuk raid. The Italian Compagnia Autosahariana di Cufra at the "Incident at Jebel Sherif" captured him on 31 January 1941.

Leutnant **Häusgen** (first name unknown). Worked with *Major* Zolling, *Ic* of *Panzerarmee Afrika*.

Rittmeister **von Hoesch.** Attached to the Ic of the *Panzergruppe Afrika* as NBO (*Nachrichtenbeschaffungsoffizier*) and assigned to establish *Sonderkommando Hoesch* with the task of taking spies to Egypt. Von Hoesch was killed during a bombing raid on the Gazala line on the night of 7/8 October 1941 before he could begin his mission.

Howard (nee Alington), Jean (1917–2007). Worked as an Intelligence Analyst at Bletchley Park, where intercepted enemy W/T messages were processed, decoded and analyzed. She recognised the term "Gilf Kebir" in the Salam reports having read Bagnold's **Libyan Sands**, and correctly concluded that an enemy unit was moving across the Libyan Desert. However the processing delay meant that by the time relevant information was passed to Middle East Intelligence in Cairo, it was too late to capture Almásy who was already nearing completion of the return journey. In later life she collected much information on Almásy's life. Howard was obviously working on an overall publication about Almásy but did not complete it before her death in 2007.

Al-Husseini, Mohammad Amin (*circa* 1895–1974). A member of the al-Husseini clan of Jerusalem, Palestinian Arab nationalist and Muslim leader in the British Mandate of Palestine. From 1921 to 1948, he was the Grand Mufti of Jerusalem. As early as 1920, he was active in opposing the British in order to secure the independence of Palestine as an Arab state and led violent riots against Jews which peaked during the 1936-1939 Arab revolt in Palestine. In 1937, he fled Palestine and took refuge in various countries and finally in Germany.

Al-Gailani, Rashid Ali (1892–1965). Prime Minister of Iraq 1933, 1936–38, 1940–41. His nationalist sentiments made him strongly hostile to the Anglo-Iraqi Treaty of 1930 negotiated by Faisal I, as he resented Britain's strong residual influence. A group of increasingly powerful anti-British and pro-German colonels made him premier. His subsequent denial of help to the British army, and his expulsion of the Hashemite dynasty, led to intervention by British forces, who deposed him and reinstated Faisal I. He fled to Germany.

Oberst **Maurer, Carl** (?–1964). Commanding Officer of *Amt./Ausl. Abwehr I H West*, superior of *Major* Seubert. Other than that he was a pianist by profession, nothing else is known about Maurer. It seems that he had the codename AMTMANN in the intercepted W/T messages.

el-Masri, Abdul Aziz Ali (1880–1965). Egyptian military officer and politician. Graduated from military staff college in 1904. Participated in a military coup and was sentenced to death twice by the Ottoman authorities in 1915 and 1916. El-Masri was an active fighter for Arab autonomy and the spiritual head of the "Society of the Free Officers" under Gamal Abd el-Nasser in Egypt. In 1941 he was dismissed from his position as Chief of the General Staff of the Egyptian army due to British pressure because of his anti-British activities. He attempted to leave Egypt for Germany during the war and after the failure of Operation Kondor he was interned for the duration of the war.

Major **von Mellenthin, Friedrich Willhelm** Born in Breslau on 30 August 1904. Intelligence officer (Ic) on the staff of *Panzerarmee Afrika* from June 1941 to 15 September 1942. He was promoted to chief of operations (Ia) after both Gause and Westphal had been wounded. When Westphal resumed his duties, von Mellenthin became a supernumerary officer since the position of Ic has been taken over by *Major* Zolling in the meantime. Since in addition he had already been suffering from amoebic dysentery for months, he was recommended to leave to Europe for medical treatment.

Generalfeldmarschall **Rommel, Erwin** (15 November 1891–14 October 1944), A highly decorated officer in World War I, awarded the Pour le Mérite for his exploits on the Italian Front. In World War II he further distinguished himself as the commander of the "Ghost Division" during the 1940 invasion of France. However, it was his leadership of German and Italian forces in the North African campaign which established the legend of the "Desert Fox". Late in the war, Rommel joined – or at least sympathised with – the conspiracy against Adolf Hitler, but he opposed the failed 20 July plot of 1944 to kill the dictator. Because of his great prestige, he was given the option to commit suicide rather than be tried and executed.

Oberst **von Piekenbrook, Hans** (1893–1959). Commanding Officer of *Abwehr 1 H West*.

Baron von Plessing, Kurt (13 September 1890 – after 1952). Born in Graz, Austria. Served in the armed forces of the Austro-Hungarian Monarchy during 1914–18. In 1919 after the disintegration of the Monarchy he became a citizen of Hungary by naturalisaton, and moved to Szombathely. In 1939 (and possibly earlier) he was in Egypt on various business dealings. In 1940 he joined the *Abwehr*, and as a cover was sent in 1941 to the Hungarian Legation in Ankara as commercial attache. He was actively involved in Plan el-Masri (originally it was he who was supposed to smuggle the W/T set that was deposited in the Shoubra church of Father Demeterius into Cairo) in close association with Almásy. In 1943 they have traveled together on a further *Abwehr* mission to Istanbul after meeting Major Seubert in Sofia. In 1948 he became an Austrian citizen and changed his name to Conrad von Plessing. Circumstantial evidence suggests that Prince Youssef Kemal stayed with him in Graz when he was forced to leave Egypt after the 1952 revolution.

Hauptmann **Pretzl, Otto** (1893–1941). German orientalist. He was working with the *Abwehr* under *Major* Seubert. After the fall of France, he recruited V-men from POWs of Tunisian, Moroccan and Algerian nationality. Was killed during a plane crash on 28 October 1941.

Es-Sadat, Anwar (1918–1981). Third President of Egypt serving from 15 October 1970 until his assassination on 6 October 1981. He was a senior member of the Free Officers group which overthrew the Muhammad Ali Dynasty in the Egyptian Revolution of 1952, and a close confidant of Gamal Abdel Nasser, whom he succeeded as President in 1970. During the Second World War the British imprisoned him for his efforts to obtain help from the Axis Powers in expelling the occupying British forces and for his assistance to Operation Kondor.

Valderano, Ronald (Ronnie). The 18ᵗʰ Duke of Valderano (1918–2007) has published several books about his activities on secret service, among them *The Owl and the Pussycat* where he tells how he helped Almásy to escape from Rome to Egypt in 1947. Most probably Valderano was not a real noble but in fact born Ronald Waring, son of a British officer.

Unteroffizier **Wölfel, Max** (died 2006). Claimed to have participated the first ten days of Operation Salam driving a Fiat staff car. His account in Hans R. Meyer's book *Nachts wenn der Sand singt* proved not to be correct in this respect and he is not mentioned in a single one of the documents in relation to Operation Salam. Most probably he met Almásy when both of them were at the HQ of *Panzerarmee Afrika* near Derna before the start of Operation Salam, and constructed his own story later based on hearsay. His account is partially copied from Hans Eppler's book.

Major **Zolling, Ernst.** Succeeded Major von Mellenthin as Intelligence Officer (Ic) on the staff of *Panzerarmee Afrika*.

Notes & explanations

Identification of persons and vehicles on Photographs

Unfortunately, the photos of Operation Salam were not captioned and the identification of persons and vehicles is therefore a difficult task which seemed to be impossible in the beginning.

The only people who could initially be identified besides Almásy were Eppler and Sandstede, since other properly captioned photographs of them existed. The faces of all the other members of the mission were unknown until Eppler and Sandstede revealed the people in the group photo in front of the cave of Wadi Sora in the Gilf Kebir in two individual letters to Rudolph Kuper. From then on the faces of Munz and Körper were known and Wöhrman, who took the photograph, was clear as well. Half of the group was thus identified, but for the others some guesses still had to be made. The identification of the vehicles was a similarly difficult task and was done based on the description of the particular equipment (radio, machine gun) and the identified occupants.

W/T callsigns

The codenames used by Operation Salam have caused some confusion from the beginning of the operation. The interpreters of the intercepted messages at Bletchley Park misinterpreted the six W/T stations used for the operation as six independent units comparable to a patrol of the LRDG – although except for SALAM all of them were static.

Major Wittilo von Griesheim, the Commanding Officer of *Abwehrstelle Tripolis* was using his own nickname as his code: WIDO. The British intelligence considered it a motorised unit driving deep behind the enemy lines.

The codenames for Operation Salam were as follows:

ANGELO	*Major* Franz Seubert, Berlin
KONDOR (CONDOR)	Eppler and Sandstede in Egypt
OTTER	*Gefreiter* von der Marwitz at Gialo
SALAM	Almásy, and the whole group en route
SCHILDKROETE	HQ *Panzerarmee Afrika*, *Unteroffizier* (NCO) Aberle and *Gefreiter* Weber
WIDO / WODI / DIWO	*Major* Wittilo von Griesheim, *Abwehrstelle Tripolis*

Other German codenames which appear in the intercepted W/T messages:

ADOLF	*Abwehrstelle (Ast.) Athen*
GHAS	Ghadames
GUDRUN STELLE	G-Stelle / Gegenstelle (remote station)
HGS	Hans-Gerd Sandstede (KONDOR)
HOLZ	*Unteroffizier* Holzbrecher, *Abwehrstelle Tripolis*
MAR	Callsign for von der Marwitz (OTTER)
MUK	Murzuk
NUT	Nalut
Dr. Rantzau	*Major* Nikolaus Ritter (Berlin)
SEPP	Gebhardt von Walther, the German Consul at Tripoli
"Sprit"	This was misinterpreted by Bletchley Park. It is not a code but in this context is simply the German word for fuel for vehicles
TROLI	Tripoli
WEB (or WEW)	Callsign for Waldemar Weber (SCHILDKROETE)

Only people are mentioned in the above German W/T message codes, for locations did not have such "camouflage". Since British intelligence was able to decipher the German messages, the British had a very clear picture about the actual movement of Operation Salam.

It was suggested in several publications that "Salam" could be an anagram for "Almásy" without the "y". This could be true, but there is no evidence to support it.

Distance units, place names and German military ranks

Two problems arise whenever reading old accounts of the desert war: the spelling of the place names and the different distance units. In this book the kilometre unit has been used, sometimes converting miles (mi) where they are stated in the old reports, with the standard equivalence of 1 mile to 1'609 kilometres.

Dealing with Arabic names, spelling cannot be easily determined due to the characteristics of the language. Historically, the first to transcribe names in Libya were the Italians who conquered the country in 1911 and used mainly a phonetic transliteration for the Italian spelling (with some variations, for example using both "Murzuch" and "Murzuk" or "Kufra" in the early 1930s and "Cufra" thereafter). The British had a similar approach in Egypt, which was under their control. However sometimes the Italian spelling was also used on British maps of Libya, while other times transliterations may be seen which do not originate from the Arabic word, but from a mispronounced Italian spelling.

This book uses the generally accepted Italian names for Libya and the English names for Egypt (i.e. the spelling most frequently used in the English reference works) except for some cases, where the original spelling of the old account has been retained or where no equivalent can be found in contemporary Italian or English texts or maps.

The authors also considered using "Operation Salaam" rather than "Operation Salam". In Arabic the emphasis is on the second syllable of the word "Salaam" (peace) and in speech it sounds rather like "the roaring of a camel". Actually the Arabs call it the "camel sound". European languages cannot describe the real sound of this strange "a" and it could probably best be transliterated by writing "aa" (double "a") in the second syllable. However, in this particular case we are no longer speaking of the transcription of an Arabic word, but of a German military operation with the code name "Operation Salam". The Bletchley Park transcripts were correct letter for letter and it is clear that the code used by the *Abwehr* for the operation was SALAM, irrespective of how linguistically correct it may be.

For authenticity the military ranks of the German army and other particular expressions have been kept in German. These ranks are explained in the glossary.

General setup of the Abwehr

The *Abwehr* under *Admiral* Wilhelm Canaris was an organisation dealing with all kinds of espionage and counterespionage in several sub-organisations. This book uses the German expressions in general, but the organisation chart provides the English expressions as well. The sub-organisations of the Abwehr and its functions were as follows:

Amtsgruppe Ausland under *Vizeadmiral* Leopold Bürkner with the tasks of interpretation of foreign military and political information, liaison with *Wehrmachtsführungssstab*, the various branches of the *Wehrmacht* (Army, Airforce, Navy), the foreign countries Military Attachees in Berlin and with the German Foreign Ministry.

Abteilung Z, from 1938–1943 under *Generalmajor* Hans Oster and from 1943–1944 under *Oberst* Jakobsen, was in charge of the internal organisation and administration of the *Abwehr*.

Abteilung l, from 1937–1943 under *Oberst* H. Piekenbrock and from 1943–1944 under *Oberst* Georg Hansen was responsible for intelligence gathering in foreign countries as is commonly understood to be the job of a secret service. Tasks were to obtain all kind of information relevant to Germany, to maintain spy networks, and to install wireless telegraphy stations. It was organised in eleven departments. Operation Salam was organised and executed by *l H West* (*Abwehr, Abteilung l, Fremde Heere West* – Abwehr, Department l, Enemy Forces West). Abteilung l dealt with Britain, France, Belgium, Holland, Spain, Portugal, Italy, America, Africa, Palestine and Syria.

Abteilung ll, from 1938–1939 under *Major* Helmuth Grosscurth, from 1939–1943 under *Oberst* Erwin Lahousen and from 1943–1944 under *Oberst* Wessel Freiherr von Freytag-Loringhoven and had the task of sabotage and destruction – the most violent role in the Abwehr. Beside the execution of sabotage tasks, the same department also had the duty to prevent enemy sabotage in Germany and in occupied countries and was responsible for preparing commando raids. The Brandenburger mainly carried out the actual "dirty work".

Regiment Brandenburg. A special formation for sabotage and commando operations under *Generalmajor* Alexander von Pfuhlstein.

Abteilung lll, from 1933–1939 under *Major* Rudolf Bamler and from 1939–1944 under *Oberst* Egbert Bentivegni. This department was responsible for defence against enemy espionage and counter-espionage. It also dealt with treason against Germany and the infiltration of enemy spy networks.

The table showing the structure of the Abwehr is based on Müller, Norbert; Kaden, Helma; Grahn, Gerlinde; Meyer, Brün; Koops, Tilman: *Das Amt Ausland/Abwehr im Oberkommando der Wehrmacht*. Since this book uses German expressions for functions and ranks, an English translation is provided.

Aufbau des Amtes Ausland / Abwehr

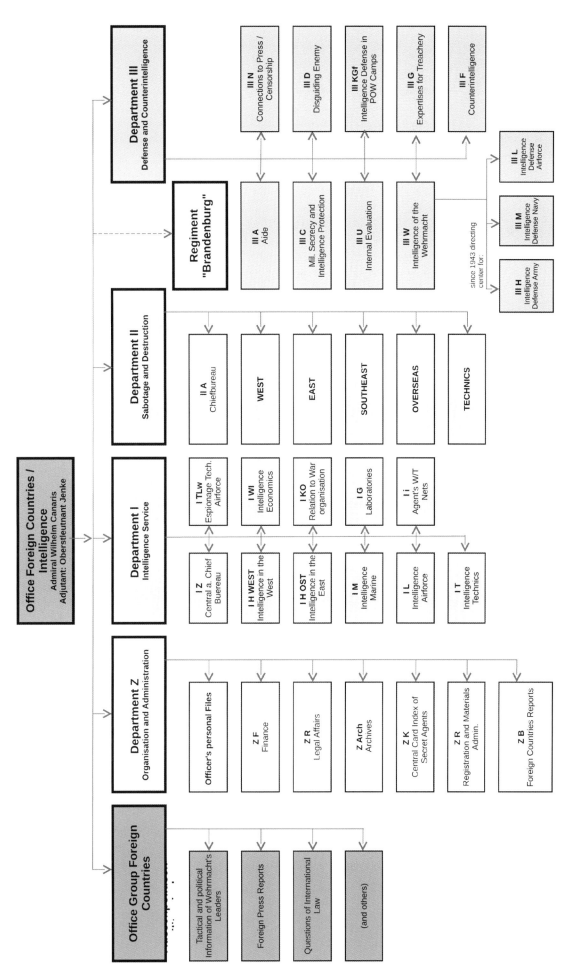

Abwehr, Organisation (English)

Regiment z.b.V.800 Brandenburg

The members of the Regiment z.b.V.800, the so-called *Brandenburger* have a legendary reputation and are widely believed to be some kind of an equivalent to the British Special Forces. But there are considerable differences; one of these is the documentation of *Brandenburger* activities – there is hardly anything reliable about them. In this chapter only the period covering Operation Salam is covered.

Documents relating to operations and missions of British Special Forces are mostly available for research in the British Archives, and a wide range of books have been published about their activities. That is absolutely not the case for the *Brandenburger*. The few existing books provide rather confusing and incomplete information to the reader, usually based on obscure "eye-witness" information. Legend and myth are mixed with hearsay about planned operations and operations which were actually carried out.

Abteilung II of the *Abwehr* had the most aggressive role and attached to it were three *Battalions* of specialised troops – the *Brandenburger*. Their speciality was to conduct independent missions in small units in enemy territory or as advance parties. Later in the war, they were more and more employed in anti-partisan warfare.

The founder of the *Brandenburger* was *Hauptmann* Theodor-Gottlieb von Hippel who had experience of irregular warfare in *Deutsch Ostafrika* (German East Africa) during the First World War under Lettow-Vorbeck. Hippel developed this idea, encouraged by Wilhelm Canaris, who was aware that conventional-thinking German officers would oppose it. Canaris arranged that this new unit should be directly subordinated under *OKW (Oberkommando der Wehrmacht)* to the *Abwehr* and not to the *Wehrmacht*.

The task of recruiting was executed by *Hauptmann* von Hippel under the command of *Oberst* Erwin Lahousen, the head of *Abteilung II*. The unit developed rapidly after the outbreak of the war. Preferred candidates were those who had excellent language skills, hardiness and self-reliance – 'racial origin' was of no consideration the *Abwehr*, since it was more important that soldiers would fit in the environment of their future missions.

There was no shortage of volunteers, mainly *Volksdeutsche*[356] from the Sudetenland, Poland, Czechoslovakia and other countries – not forgetting the former German colonies in Africa, and in particular German South-West Africa (*Deutsch Südwestafrika*). Since their home country had come under South African or British control during World War I, most of them spoke not only German but also fluent English, and were therefore very useful for the *Abwehr*.

Next to the three Battalions of fighting units, the *Brandenburger* had several companies attached directly to HQ serving as a personnel pool for *Abteilung I* and *Abteilung II*[357]. These were interpreters, signallers, *V-Leute* etc. Understanding this, it becomes clear that not all members of the regiment were trained in sabotage and behind the line operations; many were just included in this regiment because they

356 Ethnic Germans
357 In fact, the *Brandenburger* were subordinated to *Abteilung II*

had one or more abilities that the *Abwehr* thought could be useful for their operations. In the case of Operation Salam, none of the *Brandenburger* attached to this mission was of a 'fighting unit' or had any particular 'behind the lines experience'; they were mostly signallers. This explains the many problems they had with military discipline and the complete lack of any desert skills.

Heeresplankammer – topographical section of the army

The *Heeresplankammer* (Topographical Section of the *OKW*) in Berlin under *Oberstleutnant* Douglas was divided into four departments[358]:

- Pl.A I   Osten und Norden (East and North)
- Pl.A II   Westen und Süden (West and South)
- Pl.A III Afrika (Africa)
- Pl. A IV Südosten (Orient)

Eppler and Sandstede were both employed in Pla III under *Kriegsverwaltungsrat* (*Major*) Dr. Eggers. Their task was to correct and translate maps of those parts of Africa that they knew well. In the case of Eppler that meant Egypt, and for Sandstede, East Africa, mainly Kenya, Uganda and Tanganyika.

The Topographical Department received all original maps sent from all over the world, during wartime mainly captured maps. The maps were reviewed and where necessary revised before they were copied and distributed to the *Wehrmacht* units concerned.

In August 1941 maps of Egypt at the scale of 1:200'000 were published. They had been produced from existing maps on the scale of 1:500'000 and 1:100'000. The Germans were not able to produce an overall set of maps for Egypt until that date since parts of the western desert were missing. A special department, attached to the *Abwehr*, was responsible for dealing with incoming information from the many sources the *Abwehr* had. As for Libya, existing Italian maps were found not to be reliable except for the coastal regions, and revision was badly needed. The *Heeresplankammer* had started to issue a completely new series of maps, compiled partly from captured British maps and partly from French maps of Africa in 1:5'000'000 and other scales. In addition to the maps, the *Heeresplankammer* issued a German-Arabic dictionary to explain the various terms used on the maps. Eppler, thanks to his knowledge of Arabic, assisted in the preparation of this dictionary during his assignment to Pla III.

Eppler, during his interrogation, felt sure that Almásy, as soon as he had returned from his mission, had provided a complete report to the *Heeresplankammer* to allow them to add new information to their maps of the area concerned[359]. The British interrogators were convinced that, due to Eppler's activities with the *Heeresplankammer*, his sketches, drawings and geographical statements were reliable.

---

358 Information from Dr. Willy Eggers

359 TNA, London, KV2/1467, 5th Consolidated Report on Eppler and Sandstede. The information is solely based on the statements of Hans Eppler.

The Italian maps – were they really wrong?

Almásy's diary of 17 May 1942 states: "*To the east a large group of high black garas, not shown on the Italian map. No mapping was done here outside the depression and Jebel Kufra. What were they doing from 1931 to 1939 then?*"

Most of the information on the Italian maps in the southern zones was based on surveys carried out in a very short time, during the August-December 1930 reconnaissance missions preparing the attack on Kufra. The goal was to obtain information about the approaches to that remote oasis, not just from the north, from Agedabia via Gialo and Bir Zighen, but also from the west via Waw el-Kebir to Tazerbo, down to the spurs of the Tibesti mountains, looking for a passage to the east among the dunes of the Rebiana Sand Sea, and from the northwest, from Zella. For many areas, the graphical information on these maps was either non-existent or could only be taken as indicative, though the important points had been located by astrofix and were completely accurate, comparable to British maps of later years. In most cases the maps were the result of itinerary cartography (i.e. the cartographic description of a route) of the unexplored desert areas – though based on surveys – instead of real topographic cartography[360]. The northern part of the colony which contained most of the settlements, the big towns and the harbours, was the only area subject to systematic and accurate topographic work. After the Senussia were finally defeated at Kufra, the Italians turned their attention to the region south of the oasis, concentrating their topographic surveys in that area, where the actual boundaries with the other colonial powers were still to be defined: from the Uweinat massif and the border with the Anglo-Egyptian Sudan to the Tibesti mountains and the Aozu strip with the French, up to the western side and the Ghat oasis. These borders were systematically and accurately mapped during the official 1933 and 1934 missions of the *Istituto Geografico Militare*.

Many of the central expanses of the Libyan Desert, especially in very recently occupied Cirenaica, were instead simply mapped in terms of routes between the main oasis groups and the coastal areas, disregarding true topographical mapping. The Gialo oasis and the Libyan side of the Great Sand Sea are an example, as they were actually covered only with quick expeditionary surveys, simple information acquired from *Meharisti* (the Camel Corps) Officers and even old, outdated and low-quality Italian and British maps[361]. The fact that the Italians concentrated their meagre resources to the south-eastern corner of Libya meant that, as a consequence, the zone along the *palificata* and the "Trucchi track"[362] between Gialo and Kufra hardly received any attention, and not much surveying was done there. While the

360 See Andrea Masturzo, *Carte per non perdersi: il deserto libico nel periodo coloniale italiano*, in *Le sfide cartografiche*, a cura E. Casti, J. Levy, Ancona, Il lavoro editoriale università, 2010, pages 116 – 130.

361 See *Carta dimostrativa della Libia Scala 1:400'000 Foglio 21 Gialo*; *Carta dimostrativa della Libia Scala 1:400'000 Foglio 41 Grara El Blata*; *Carta dimostrativa della Libia Scala 1:40'.000 Foglio 32 Gur Et Tibbu*; *Mappa OASI DI GIALO Comando Superiore FF.AA.A.S. scala 1:40'000 – 1942*

362 The original track between Gialo and Kufra, sometimes called "Trucchi" as it was the track used by the civilian transport company Trucchi for their monthly connections to the oasis, was abandoned in the late thirties when the *palificata* was set up, connecting all the new emergency landing strips *Campo 1, Campo 2, ..., Campo 7* between Gialo and Kufra. The new route, surveyed by Marchesi's 1933 expedition, was marked with *pali* (poles), whence its name.

area of the Gialo oasis is shown full of details and fairly accurate on the Italian map, about 70 kilometres further south all details of the land-scape are missing. Nothing is shown other than the "Trucchi Track"[363]. Details on the map start to appear again about 300 kilometres further south, at Bir Zighen[364]; the only features shown in be-tween are the locations where the "Trucchi track" crosses the Wadi el-Faregh or one of the indivi-dual dune ranges.

The Libyan colony saw only very occasional use of the aerial photographic survey techniques avail-able at the time, limited to the northern and coastal areas from 1935–1937 onwards (in that the Italians where well versed, having also created and perfected several instruments like the Santoni camera). These instruments were instead employed in Italian East Africa, where most efforts from 1935 on were directed. Most expert topographers were sent there, and the expeditions in Libya were stopped, delayed or postponed. Only a few coastal areas in Cirenaica were surveyed further, to complete the massive work undertaken in 1911, in some cases with the help of photographs taken in 1941 by German aircraft with the Aschenbrenner camera.

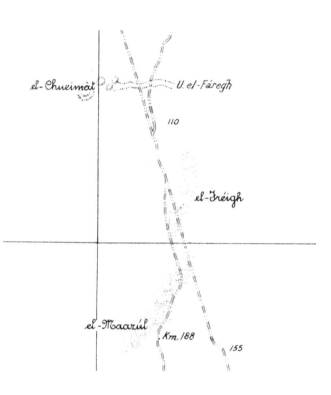

The only details of the landscape shown were those that crossed the two maped routes.

German maps (for example the *Deutsche Weltkarte, 1:500'000, H34-SO, Audjila, Sonderausgabe 1941*) which were in fact only copies of the Italian ones in this region, ended up misinterpreting the "white spaces" on the Italian maps as a flat area of *serir* desert, while the map actually meant that these areas were unmapped, "empty" or simply they were generally not to be driven across. The Germans could not know about the unmapped dunes in this area – they did not even suspect that there could be dunes, since the Italian map showed all the dunes on the Egyptian side of the Great Sand Sea. In fact, the Italians had copied the Egyptian part from the available British and Egyptian maps, and had left empty the dune area on their side of the Great Sand Sea.

While for the Italians this was not an issue – they just followed the *palificata* and had no practical interest in its surroundings – for the planning and execution of Operation Salam it proved to be disastrous, as Almásy expected a huge area of "good going" where in fact there were endless ranges of dunes. The Italian maps were actually not wrong east of the Gialo-Kufra line they were simply empty. If the Italians had instead chosen to mark those areas as "uncharted" on their maps, the Germans would not have misinterpreted them and Almásy could have done better planning of the route from the outset.

363 See *Carta Dimostrativa della Libia, 1:1'000'000, Foglio VI Gialo – Giarabub.*
364 See *Carta Dimostrativa della Libia, 1:1'000'000, Foglio IX Cufra*

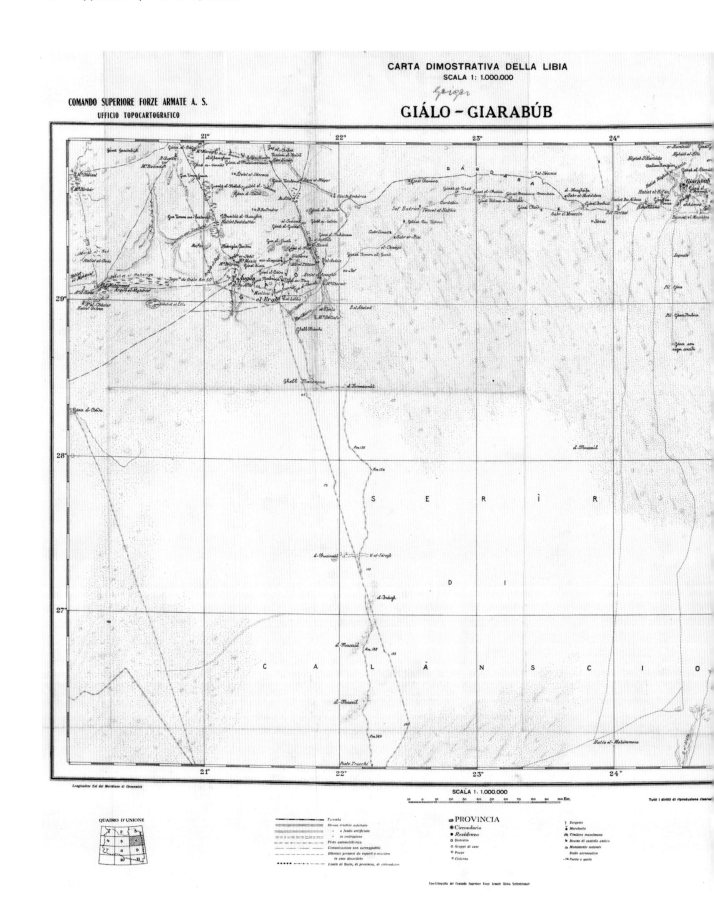

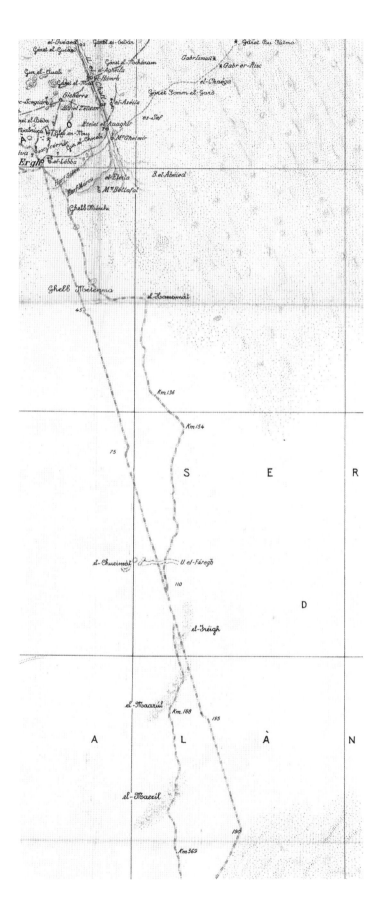

Left: *Carta Dimostrativa della Libia*, *1:1'000'000, Foglio VI, Gialo Giarabub*, 1938. It is clearly visible that the dunes of the western leg of the Sandsea, between Lat 26°30' and Lat 28°30' are not mapped.

Right: The old Trucchi track and the new "Motor- and Air Route" were precisely mapped.

The forged British pounds

Eppler stated that the *Abwehr* provided them with forged British pounds and this was recognised by British intelligence in Cairo, and was the reason why they were caught.

It is true that the Germans tried to destabilise the British economy by producing and distributing counterfeit British pounds on a huge scale. However, it was not the *Abwehr* who was behind this project, called *Unternehmen Bernhard*, but the *Sicherheitsdienst (SD)* as a department of the *Reichssicherheitshauptamt* (RSHA) under Walter Schellenberg. The counterfeit banknotes were prepared and printed by the forced labour of Jewish inmates of Sachsenhausen concentration camp. They also produced other currencies, but concentrated on British pounds and in 1943 alone had a monthly output of 650'000 notes in various currencies and denominations. It was calculated that between 1942 and 1943, The Germans counterfeited about 100 million in British Pounds. The quality of the notes was excellent but still divided into four classes: "A" were used to exchange for other hard currency at banks, "B" to pay German spies in foreign countries, "C" for the desert campaign in North Africa and "D" was to be airdropped over Great Britain[365].

It is probable that Eppler and Sandstede had "B" class notes with them. Whether the *Abwehr* was actually informed about the forged notes is not clear. However, it seems that it was a normal practice for the Germans to pay their spies with counterfeit money. The question remains whether British intelligence became aware of Eppler and Sandstede because they were changing forged British pounds to Egyptian pounds or simply because they changed unusually large amounts of money.

It can be assumed that the British were very vigilant just because they knew that the Germans tried to distribute forged pounds everywhere. The two German spies may have come under suspicion just through the fact that they were changing money.

Eppler's *Agentenvertrag* with the *Abwehr*

In 1972, while Eppler was settled in France, living the life of a wealthy man married to the daughter of a millionaire, he claimed 300'000 *Deutsche Mark* back pay from the German Federal Republic since his contract as an agent for the Abwehr had never been cancelled.

It may sound unbelievable that the *Abwehr* drew up such contracts with its V-men, especially as most of them were not in Germany but in enemy territory where the possession of such a document was hardly advisable. However, Eppler was able to present his contract, dated 18 February 1942 which included all details he claimed.

Seeing a copy of that contract, it looks forged at first glance. It is not typed on any kind of official paper, nor does it show any stamp of the *Abwehr*. Only the representative of the Abwehr, *Oberstleutnant* Maurer, signs it but not by Eppler, which is rather strange. In 1972, when Mr. Kaps, who researched the Eppler-case for the

---

365 Hagen; *Das Unternehmen Bernhard.*

German newspaper *Die Rheinpfalz* asked Dr. Gert Buchheit for his statement, he was informed that the contract seemed to be a blank form into which the name of Eppler was inserted later on (this probably provides evidence that they were using a standard form) and to his knowledge, the *Abwehr* did not use such contracts at all. He further stated that the term "*Amt Aussenabwehr im OKW*" was wrong and it should read "*OKW, Amt Ausland-Abwehr*". It is hard to understand why the *Abwehr* would write its own name incorrectly. A further indication to the document being a forgery is the fact that *Oberstleutnant* Maurer had already been promoted to the rank of *Oberst* in 1938. It may safely be dismissed that he would sign a document in 1942 under his old rank of four years earlier.

The final proof was given when *Oberst* Maurers' signature was compared with one he had given in 1942 on another document[366] – it was completely different. This may not have disturbed Eppler in 1972 since *Oberst* Maurer had already died and the original documents were not yet accessible in Germany, but still held closed in Allied archives.

„Maurer's signature" dated 18 February 1942 on the paper that Eppler presented as his contract with the Abwehr.

Maurer's real signature from a real document dated 28 October 1942.

Where is "Purzel"?

The hiding place of *"Purzel"* was unwittingly discovered in August 1985, when the Italian desert traveler Giancarlo Negro found four tyres, a tarpaulin and a Ford battery by accident in the Gilf Kebir area. At that time, neither Almásy's diary nor the original photographs of *Operation Salam* were publicly known[367]. For this reason, Negro was not aware of the significance of his find until 2010 when, looking in his archive of slides from old trips, he stumbled upon some pictures which showed the same landscape and parts found a few months before, in 2009, by a team of the Austrian Television (ORF). The ORF was in the area to produce a TV documentary with the author Raoul Schrott, and found and correctly identified the location as Almásy's "Robber's Lair"[368].

366 Archive Michael Rolke, message to OKW in regard of maps etc. of *Sonderkommando Dora* dated 10 October 1942 and signed by *Oberst* Maurer.
367 Giancarlo Negro and Roberto Chiarvetto gave a presentation on this topic to the audience of the annual meeting of the new "Zerzura Club" in 2010.
368 Matzek, Tom; *Gipfelstürmer und Wüstenfüchse.*

For decades nobody paid much attention to the fate of the Ford F8 abandoned by Almásy in the Gilf Kebir, but some curious people started to look for it after the publication of *Schwimmer in der Wüste* in 1997 which contained Almásy's mission diary, making it accessible to a wider audience. The discussion went on until the location where the truck was left back in 1942 was finally identified in 2009.

Some even speculated that Almásy went back to the Gilf Kebir on a further, undocumented and unknown expedition and recovered the truck; and others presumed that the Egyptian army could have taken it to one of their barracks for display purposes – as a WWII relic, most likely not knowing its actual origin. Rumours were numerous and varied, and opinions sometimes heavily disputed, but the most realistic scenario was that the truck was found shortly after it was left there, by one of the Allied parties searching for traces of the secret German mission. In fact, since the truck was hidden very close to the main route of the Kufra Convoys, and since the SDF was always short of vehicles to maintain its convoys, it was realistic to assume that *"Purzel"* had been pressed into service with the SDF.

However, after the location was confirmed, it became clear that the little truck could not have been found shortly after it was hidden among the rocks. The tyres had hardened in a deflated state but still fixed to the vehicle (the "weight effect" is clearly visible as a bulge where the tyre touched the ground), and the tarpaulin was torn to shreds by the desert wind. *"Purzel"* must have rested there for many years, possibly even decades, before being discovered by unknown people and driven away – or towed – after a change of tyres.

Unfortunately, who did it and when is completely unknown. A first possible scenario could be that *"Purzel"* was found and taken by people from Kufra, who then used it for transport duties in the oasis; it is well known that after the war many abandoned vehicles were repaired and kept in use for decades. For a Ford F8 though, the first problem would have been how to obtain spare tyres, since their size was not a very common one among Allied trucks (it was limited to a few 8-cwt truck types, while the vast majority were 15-, 30- and 60-cwt with bigger wheel and tyre sizes). Consequently, it would be reasonable to assume that those who found the truck loaded it onto a bigger truck, but in any case the doubts relating to the remaining tyres persist: whoever found *"Purzel"* removed them and left them there. An alternate explanation is that an oil exploration party found it in the late fifties – early sixties, the height of the oil exploration boom in Libya. This period saw the discovery of many remote abandoned aircraft and vehicle wrecks, including the famous "Lady Be Good" B-24 and the abandoned SAAF Blenheim near Kufra. Such a party would have had the necessary spares – most of the oil companies in fact used war surplus equipment at the time – so a set of new tyres and a battery would have been at hand.

Only a short while ago, everybody would have assumed that finding the "Robber's Lair" also meant finding *"Purzel"*. Now the location is known and parts of *"Purzel"* have even been found, but there is still no trace of the truck. Speculations will continue, maybe until some new find will shed some light on this mystery of the desert.

Left: A Ford truck battery at "Robber's Lair".

Right: A piece of a rope as it was used to fix the tarpaulin on the truck.

Left: Remnants of the tarpaulin.

Right: A meat tin „made in Brasil".

Left: A punched jerrycan.

Right: A broken bottle of Sarti liquor.

Left: A German pea-tin *(Erbsen)*.

Right: View out of the cache at "Robber's Lair".

View from "Robber's Lair" towards the plains where the convoys passed.

Three of the tires of "Purzel". Apparently they hardened flat before they were removed from their rims.

The Allies of World War II

The Allies of World War II were the countries that opposed the Axis powers. At the beginning of World War II, they were the United Kingdom, Australia, France and Poland. Canada and New Zealand followed a few days later by their declaration of war.

After the Japanese attack on the USA at Pearl Harbor and the German invasion of the Soviet Union in 1941 those two major powers joined the Allies. Other members included many countries who were either strongly related to one of the big powers or countries who were threatened or even invaded by one of the Axis powers. In regard to the Desert Campaign of the World War II, the term "British" was widely used for those forces which fought against the Italian-German units (and the latter are often called the *"Deutsches Afrikakorps"* even though the term does not apply to all German units in Libya). While the term "British" can easily be accepted in German contemporary records and while Great Britain was a main opponent of Germany, it is definitely not correct to use it as a description for all the forces that were present in North Africa on the Allied side. "British" disregards all those important units sent by the Dominions of Australia, New Zealand and South Africa and it excludes the many Indians who fought for the cause as well as much smaller but no less committed units such as the Free French, the Greeks, the Czechs and the Poles. Therefore, unless a particular unit is named, the term "British" is not used but "Allies" or "Allied forces" which fits much better and includes all nations who fought.

"Robber's Lair".

APPENDIX 2
PRIMARY ORIGINAL SOURCES

I once more go to the enemy vehicles one after the other. They shan't
fight against us any more. Off with the oil filler pipe, and several handfuls
of finest desert dand put in. Very carefully and cleanly so that nothing
should be noticeable. Nor must they have the same amount of sand. One must
do 10 kms, and another 35kms before the engine seizes. Then they will think
it is the evil sandstorm, the Gebli which has done this.

Now we must take our loot to safety as soon as possible. I drive with all
those vehicles from the Drei Burgen in a NE direction into the hilly terrain
in the direction of El Aqqaba. After 20 km a pointed hill and a ridge cleft
by the wind offer good cover. The petrol drums are distributed artistically
amongst the black rocks so that none could be seen by vehicles which might
follow our tracks, then I drive back to Drei Burgen and fetch the load of our
little truck, which we had left behind there.
Meantime evening has arrived, our day's performance is small only 120 kms,
and about 30 of them backwards and forwards, but it was worth it since we
have assured our return journey.

Today Wöhrmann finally succeeded in contacting Schildkroete, and passing

his report on _____ *Taken at B.P.*

19th May 1942 Booty Camp

Start 0715 A bad day. I did not find the entrance to El Aqqaba
In the morning I drove towards the great re-entrant of the Gilf Kebir from
which the Wadi of El Aqqaba emerges. I soon came on fairly old enemy tracks
and was convinced that they led out of the pass. I offended against a
fundamental rule of desert travel: never follow enemy tracks when you don't
know where they come from!

We drove at the foot of Gilf Kebir, far beyond Aqqaba in an easterly direction,
and then back again closer up to the escarpment and into several wadi entrances
each of which I thought to be the El Aqqaba entrance. Everywhere innumerable
British tracks ran criss cross over the scree slopes as if the enemy had
searched for a way up the pass. At one time the thing used to be simple, there
was only one east west track along the escarpment and my track emerging from
the pass. Now everything seemed changed by the innumerable tracks
and also perhaps by the heavy rains of 1935

It was no use. I had to return to our starting point, in order to take bearings
from there on the two foothills and on the Drei Burgen first of all to determine
my exact position and secondly to determine the position of the wadi of Aqqaba,
There would still have been time to set off afresh, but my car had broken a
spring in the scree, and Munz and Koerper had to fit a replacement.
Depressed spirits in the camp. Days performance about 80 kms.

20th May Booty camp.

Start 0645 Frightful driving conditions, the cars had to be pushed over
heavy scree. Straightaway I find the outlet of the wadi with the help of the
direction finding of yesterday. In the river bed lie only my own tracks !
The enemy evidently looked for Aqqaba but did not find it. For a moment
I am beset by fear: perhaps they have mined the pass from above downwards,
or blown it up at its narrowest point. There was talk of that in 1937.
I even had to give an opinion as to whether it was feasible.

I drive in front and look for traces of mines. But at the top I find the
answer to the puzzle. A number of enemy vehicles did indeed, about a year ago
drive down the great rift in the Gilf Kebir, but did not find the entrance
to the pass even up above and went down into the plain via Penderel's wadi,
which is East of El Aqabba. Penderel's Wadi is impassable from below, it is
a steep ravine with many twists and soft drifting sand

I learnt later from Clayton that he mined this pass out of consideration for me!

Page from Jean Howard's transcript of the Salam Diary with her hand written comments and
underlinings.

Almásy, László Ede:
Operation Salam – diary 15 to 29 May 1942

Almásy's partial diary of Operation Salam starts on 15th of May 1942, from the moment of the second start following the fiasco in the Calanascio Sand Sea, and ends on the 29th when Almásy returned to Gialo. The history of this diary is almost as much an adventure as the operation itself.

The existence of the diary was revealed by Michael Rolke, who in 1997 was at the Imperial War Museum in London searching the LRDG papers for traces of *Sonderkommando Dora*. He accidentally found the fragment of Almásy's mission diary among the papers of David Lloyd-Owen without any context or additional information. At first he was not even aware of the importance of this document. The diary was in English, and it was translated back into German to be included in the re-publication of Almásy's writings, *Schwimmer in der Wüste*.

Subsequent information provided to András Zboray by Jean Howard revealed that this apparent extract from the diary of Almásy surfaced in Austria in 1949 or 1950, found by Lt. Col. Count Peter de Salis, who at the time was working for the Intelligence Organization, Allied Commission for Austria. Seeing the name of Bagnold mentioned several times in the document, de Salis forwarded the diary to Brigadier Ralph A. Bagnold through intelligence channels.

All evidence indicates that Bagnold only received an English translation, with the original diary in German probably retained in Almásy's yet unreleased Personnel File with the British Secret Service (MI 5). A copy of this translation was passed on by Bagnold to David Lloyd Owen and after the latter's death was deposited together with other Lloyd Owen papers in the Imperial War Museum (the copy Michael Rolke found).

Another version was prepared by Jean Howard, who was loaned a copy of the same English translation from Bagnold in 1978, together with the cover note of Count de Salis and other forwarders. This is the source of the uncertainty regarding the date it was found, as de Salis' note (as re-typed by Jean Howard) is dated 28 January 1950, while the obviously later forwarding note is dated 2 February 1949, one or other was copied in error[369].

---

369 In a letter to Bagnold (Bagnold Papers, Churchill Archives, Cambridge) Howard qoutes the 1949 date for the forwarding note of Walter Scott (MI8), so probably this one is correct.

The two versions are almost identical with only minor differences. Jean Howard copied the Bagnold version, but made some corrections based on her better understanding of some of the German terminology, but at the same time also making some abbreviations to reduce the task of re-typing.

There is no question as to the authenticity of the document. As it surfaced during Almásy's lifetime, it could even have been with his knowledge that it was passed to Count de Salis. A multitude of other sources confirm the story (including the intercepted W/T messages translated by Jean Howard at Bletchley Park), and the style is clearly that of Almásy, containing many details and references to past expeditions which were not published elsewhere, and only he could have known about. The whole style and format is so similar to Almásy's other writings that it could have been intended as a piece for later publication, rather than a formal diary of a military operation.

The transcript which follows is based mainly on the fuller Bagnold version, but using Jean Howard's more precise text where the two differ materially. There are also some adjustments to place names to match those in Almásy's other writings, and obvious copying and translation errors are corrected. However inconsistencies and other mistakes in the diary – for example some erroneous distances – were left as they were transcribed. These are corrected in the main dialogue of events in this book, with the respective footnotes added.

15th May 1942

Airfield Campo 4. (at km mark 275 of the Palificata Gialo – Kufra)

During the night everything re-calculated and the trip reorganised. We must go via Kufra! A detour of 500 km both on the outward and return journeys, an increased load for 1000 km. Instead of the 2000 km originally reckoned, it is now about 4200 km!

It seemed at first that it would be impossible for the cars to carry sufficient supplies to be kept going. However the task must be carried out. I shall drive with only two station wagons ("Inspektor" and "Präsident") and two commercials ("Maria" and "Purzel"). The two latter must be sacrificed. "Purzel" will travel 800 km, "Maria" a further 500. I must do the last 200 km to the objective with only one vehicle. There and back that's 400 km, can that be managed?

The number of the party must be reduced. Those going with me are Corporal Munz, Lieutenant Corporal Körper, Corporal Wöhrmann as signaller and Pit and Pan. Only thus will supplies of fuel and water be adequate.

I can take the responsibility for sending Corporal Beilharz and Junior Medical Officer Dr. Strungmann back to Gialo with only one vehicle ("Habuba"). I have signalled to "Otter", if the vehicle does not arrive tomorrow evening, the Italian aircraft should go to their assistance the day after tomorrow along the Palificata.

Beilharz must take fuel and water for me to Campo 5 (316 km from Gialo) for the return journey. If the worst comes to worst I will signal the air operations command to let me have some petrol dropped at the foot of the Gilf Kebir, somewhere about the "Three Castles".

Pit and Pan are not overjoyed at driving through Kufra. They fear an encounter with the enemy. According to aerial recconnaissance the British post is supposed to be near Bir Bu Zerreigh (km mark 425 of the Palificata). I shall attempt to turn southwards before then. At any rate, just between km. 400 and km. 425, the Palificata runs on a bearing of 210 degrees i.e. parallel to the dunes.

I have been calculating throughout the night and made the appropriate entries. Only slept two hours. The food had to be distributed afresh and vehicle loads changed around. Departure finally at 08:30. At the same time Beilharz drove back northwards with the doctor.

As far as km 410 on the Palificata no traces of the enemy, but the sea of dunes in the south looks somewhat more open. Course 180 degrees for the next 10 km, then 118 and in between the dunes on a bearing of 75 degrees. After going about 25 km I cross the 4 or 5 day old tracks of three enemy vehicles from Bir Bu Zerrigh to Bir Dakkar, going and coming. Then south-eastwards out of the dunes. We are out of the danger zone, I drove through it purposely during the early afternoon when Tommy is asleep. At 3 o'clock Pan gets hopelessly stuck. The men work for two hours until "Maria" is free. About 4 o'clock we reached the hill of Jebel Gardaba in the Hawaish Hills.

Scarcely are we on firm ground when we are lucky. I find the traces of the old Trucchi Track from the years 1932–1935. At that time the Palificata did not yet exist and the heavy Diesel trucks made a way through the hills with their double tyres.

It is easy to keep to the Track. We camped on it at the foot of a "gara" (rocky hill) at 19:00 hours. Day's performance 210 km. I arrange for the petrol store for the return journey to be carried up the hill and hidden between the crags: 4 cans of petrol, 2 cans of water, Store No I.

16th May 1942

Camp at Store No I on Trucchi Track

Depart at 06:00 hours. Track easy to follow, but the terrain difficult and rocky. I try after covering 60 km to change course to a bearing of 142. Forced to return from the impassable moonscape back onto the track. Another 40 km on the track. May Allah bless Trucchi, the real "smugglers' road" round the danger zone. The Track emerges from the hills and crosses the dunes lying ahead. Tracks of course invisible. Crossing the dunes is extremely difficult, both Commercials get stuck. At last south of the dunes, 80 km north of Kufra. There is a thick "shabura" (sand-cloud) so enemy aerial reconnaissance impossible. I leave the track on a bearing of 125 through the more open sea of "garas". Good for driving. I cut across and recognise the old track to Tedian el-Khadem, the most easterly branch of the vegetation zone of Kufra. Now and again fairly old Tommy tracks. They reconnoitred with patrols to the north east and east but did not find the Trucchi Track! East of Ain el-Gedid I cut across the track of the patrol of the Italian Major Rolle of March 1934 when he returned to Kufra from our meeting point of the Italo-Egyptian triangulation systems. I recognise beyond doubt Rolle's alamat (road signs) since he has stuck palm stems in the stone pyramids as it was his custom to do so.

In the afternoon we are out of the "gara" region into open "serir" (sandy plain) with isolated high "garas".

The big surprise: due east of Giof (main village of Kufra) 104 fresh truck tracks! I had no idea that enemy columns were running from the East towards Kufra. They must come directly from the Gilf Kebir, then? So we alter course and follow the tracks eastwards. Sand dunes, difficult going, Tommy has also ploughed in deeply and often became stuck. Finally I am able to ascertain from a reversing track that half of the big column had driven to Kufra and the other half from Kufra. The returning tracks are without doubt this morning's, the first ones about two days old.

About evening Pan gets stuck again. When we free the vehicle, I leave the track and turn south to a big double gara". But before we reach it we cut across several hundred fairly old tracks parallel with the ones we just left.

We make camp in the saddle between the two hills at 18:30 hours. Day's run: 250 km. Upon the "gara" we deposit Store No II: 6 cans of petrol, 1 can of water, 1 case of rations. I try to report the finding of enemy lines of communication but Wöhrmann cannot hear either "Otter" or "Schildkröte".

17th May 1942

Camp at Store No II.

Start 06:40 hours, course 122 with the intention of getting on to my old Gilf – Kufra route. To the east a large group of high black "garas", not shown on the Italian map. No mapping was done here outside the Depression and Jebel Kufra. What were they doing from 1931 to 1939, then? I soon have to turn southwards on account of the group of hills. Here too hundreds of older tracks in the direction of the Gilf – Kufra! Two abandoned enemy trucks, Chevrolet 4 wheel drive, 3 tonners, latest type, but with high pressure tyres. Odometer shows 433 miles. The puzzle is solved: the trucks have come from Wadi Halfa. Thus the assumption that Kufra is supplied from the south from French territory is not correct. Wadi Halfa, the rail-head of the Sudan Railway and at the same time of the Nile steamers from Shellal is the reinforcement base. The trucks bear identification markings of the Sudan Defence Force.

Through the absence of Entholt I have to see that Wöhrmann keeps the log-book up to date. He has no initiative and has to be told everything. The men still cannot understand, despite the experience in the Sand Sea that a long range expedition through this realm of death is nothing more than a flight. Flight from the desert itself.

The terrain is horrible. Dissected plateaux, soft shifting sand, trailing dunes of the "garas", constantly having to change course and check the bearings for finding new ways through. Since Wöhrmann is not capable of reckoning bearings and distances for me I am continually forced to stop and check the courses on the useless Italian map.

According to the distances in kilometres we should already be on the serir (plain) with which I am familiar, but dunes suddenly appear before us. On the previous occasion I did not sight them North of my route. Impassable with the overloaded vehicles, so we turned North to cut across the big enemy lines of communication again. A detour of 100 km. Frightful! However I am curious to see where the Tommy comes out on to my old track along the western edge of the Gilf.

At noon the Tommy track at last. Very difficult terrain, the tracks are all old, visibly he has moved his line of communication northwards. However, I do not intend to make any further detours, so we go along the old trail, course East, up to the Gilf Kebir. Some difficult places, soft sand and trailing dunes, in which the Tommy also stuck heavily, and finally we arrived. There, where I suspected cleft foot-hills of the Gilf Kebir beyond the frontier on Italian territory, lies a low stony plateau. Flat as a table with little craggy knolls. Surface black shale. A few more kilometres on Tommy's old trail, and then it joins the fresh tracks of the 104 trucks discovered yesterday.

On the stony surface the tracks join together into a veritable road. Indeed even several such roads run, yellow and shining, over the black plain. "Reichsautobahn" say the men.

In the deep layer of dust quite fresh tracks; after some kilometres I realise that they are running in our direction towards the Gilf. There are seven vehicles, caution is imperative.

Clouds of dust in front. I turn off and lead the column behind a small group of rocks. From above I see through the field glasses five plumes of dust. But I also see something else: Along the eastern horizon the majestic rocky escarpment of the Gilf Kebir, and – by no means very far in the south east – the high rectangular rocky tower of my trigonometric point 1020. At last I am on familiar territory, and after a few kms I shall be back on my own map. Allahu akbar!

We must drive carefully in order not to overtake the Tommy column inadvertently. The great enemy line of communication actually does run into my former track. After a short time we drive through the only possible way that I found here before, the narrow defile between the two round white juts of rock that I then named "El Bab el-Masr" (The gateway to Egypt). The frontier is crossed.

Now everything is familiar to me, the valleys with the red sand bottom, the mighty wall of rock on the left, the tangle of foothills on the right, only one thing is new: the great road beaten out with many hundred tracks, which extend across every valley bottom, right to the edges. In May 1932 I discovered this mighty plateau, I was the first to drive along it here, groping and searching; the war had drawn its traces with gigantic claws even in this hidden and secret world.

At last in the plain, round the south west spur of the Gilf. As soon as pracical I left the mighty stream of enemy tracks, hugging the indented foothills of the wall of rock. In the exit to the plain another four abandoned enemy vehicles. One of them an old Fiat, probably captured in Kufra. Nothing more is to be seen of the column in front of us. Some old tracks do run here along the indented foothills, but I know that the enemy line of communication runs outside, across the level "serir".

In a deep re-entrant not far from Wadi Anag I look for our hiding place. A real robber's cache. Even if anyone drives into the re-entrant he will not see us until he has turned round the last corner of rock. Camped at 18:30 hours. Day's performance: 240 km, 100 of them for nothing. "Purzel" is parked here and Store No III is hidden in a cleft of rock with 6 cans of petrol, 3 cans of water and 1 days ration for four men. I have the identification markings of the vehicle painted over, remove everything which would give a clue that we had used it, drive it as deeply as possible into the rock cleft and stick the following legend on the inside of the windscreen:

"Cette voiture n'est pas abandonée. Elle rentrera a Coufra. Defense d'enlever aucune piece." (This vehicle is not abandoned. It will be returning to Kufra. Do not remove any part.)

The Tommies are to think the vehicle belongs to their de Gaullist allies. The maps and log-books hitherto used are hidden. If they catch us they can rack their brains as to where we have come from.

18th May 1942

"Robbers' Camp", Store No III.

We get away at 09:25 hours, because of re-loading, now with only 3 vehicles. I drive close to the foot of the hill as far as Wadi Sora, and there I show the men the caves with the prehistoric rock-pictures which I discovered in 1933. One of the men picks up an indiarubber of German make "Reform". My companion Miss Pauli lost it here at the time when she was copying the cave paintings.

Further on to the "Three Castles". Here too there are many old enemy tracks in the undulating country between the cliffs and these three knolls standing well away, but you can see that the enemy mostly preferred to drive across the "serir" south of the "Three Castles".

Having arrived on top near the three "garas" I let my car climb cautiously over the crest. Rightly so. Below in the plain four km southwards, where I formerly had my airfield, a group of enemy vehicles. I observe them for a long time with the field glasses. No movement. However, the vehicles do not look as if they had been abandoned because of damage. I too had a petrol depot here at one time, it is one third of the way between Wadi Halfa and Kufra. Could this be an enemy petrol store?

First of all I go to the cave in the eastern "Castle" to check on my old water store. I had established it in 1932 and renewed it in 1933. Eight soldered "Shell" cans containing water from Cairo. This store saved the lives of Major Bagnold and his companion in 1935[370] when they had an axle break only 24 km from here, with only one vehicle, and were only to meet their comrades eight days later at el-Aqaba. Some cans are rusted through and empty, but four are full and I open one cautiously in order not to shake up the water. We pour it into a cooking pot, it is clear and odourless. Each of us takes a sample of the 1933 vintage, and find the water excellent!

I leave one vehicle on the South side of the eastern "Castle" and give orders for it to be driven immediately to the middle "Castle" in the event of any movement being observed on the plain below. This was to serve as a warning to me whilst I drove down in ground cover to the group of enemy vehicles. I drove down the slope with Munz and out to the plain. They are six of the latest 5 tonners, all laden with black iron drums. The drums bear the legend: "M.T. Benzine 70 C", thus of French

---

370 An error, the event happened in 1938 when Bagnold and Peel explored the top of the Gilf Kebir plateau.

origin. Contents about 50 litres, but unfortunately all empty! The vehicles are not abandoned but parked. On the front one are chalked the words "Refuelled for return journey". I take the support of the roof canvas, open the right tank of the vehicle and dip the rod into the filler pipe. Full! The left tank is likewise. The next truck too, and the next, all six, that is 12 full petrol tanks! With the tape measure I measure the length, width and depth of the tanks, a quick calculation gives 500 litres of petrol! That changes all my plans. I can carry out the journey to the objective with both cars and probably even take one Commercial with me back home. Munz observe, with his binoculars, the car stationed up on the "Three Castles" as a warning signal. It has not changed its position, the air is clear. Back to our comrades. The truck is immediately unloaded, and keeping the warning signal in operation, we hurtle down to the Tommy trucks. In a twinkling there is an empty drum under each tank and the drain plugs are unscrewed. From eleven tanks the valuable booty flows into the drums. It was annoying that we cannot get the plug loose on the twelfth tank, because that will betray to the enemy that the petrol did not evaporate.

Some of us now examine the load of drums more thoroughly, and in triumph we find one more full drum. I examine the vehicles. The speedometers show the exact distance from Wadi Halfa to here. Gradually I understand what is happening: The enemy column goes from Wadi Halfa the first third of the distance – about up to the Prince Dune – and leaves a number of vehicles behind there, which have supplied petrol for the whole column up to that point. Then the journey continues to here, the second third of the distance, and here these six trucks stay behind loaded with the empty petrol drums. When the column returns from Kufra these trucks are collected, therefore their tanks are full. The batteries have all been taken out, probably being put back on the return trip. The markings are of the Sudan Defence Force, green, red and white with the silhouette of a camel rider.

The petrol has drained out, the twelve drums are loaded on to our truck. We free it from the soft sand broken by the many wheels with some difficulty. Whilst the truck roars back to the "Three Castles" where our third car is still patiently on guard, I once more go to the six enemy vehicles one after the other. They shall not fight against us any more. Off with the cap of the oil filler pipe and several handfuls of the finest desert sand put in. Very carefully and cleanly so that nothing should be noticeable. Nor must they all have the same amount of sand, one must do a further 10–15 km, another 30–35 before the engine seizes. Then they will think it is the evil sandstorm, the "Ghibli" which has done this.

Now we must take our loot to safety as quickly as possible. I drive with all three vehicles from the "Three Castles" in a north easterly direction into the hilly terrain in the direction of El Aqaba. After about 20 km a pointed hill and a ridge cleft by the wind offer good cover. The petrol drums are distributed artistically amongst the black rocks so that none could be seen even from vehicles which might follow our tracks. Then I drive back to the "Three Castles" and fetch the load of our little truck that we had left behind there.

In the meantime evening has arrived. Our day's performance is small, only 120 km, and about 30 km of them back and forth but it was worth it, our return journey is assured.

Today Wöhrmann finally succeeds in contacting "Schildkröte" and passing his report on.

19th May 1942

"Booty Camp"

Start at 07:15 hours. A bad day: I did not find the entrance to el-Aqaba.

In the morning I drove towards the great re-entrant of the Gilf Kebir from which the "wadi" of El Aqaba emerges. I soon came upon fairly old enemy tracks and was convinced they led out of the pass. I offended against a fundamental rule of desert travel: never follow enemy tracks when you don't know exactly where they come from!

We drove at the foot of the Gilf Kebir, far beyond Aqaba, in an easterly direction, and then back again closer up to the escarpment and into several wadi entrances each of which I thought to be the El Aqaba entrance. Everywhere innumerable British tracks run criss-cross over the scree slopes as if the enemy had searched for a way up the pass. At one time it used to be simple, there was only one East – West track along the escarpment, and my track emerging from the pass. Now everything seemed changed by the innumerable tracks and also perhaps by the heavy rains of 1935.

It was no use. I had to return to our starting point in order to take bearings from there on the two foothills and on the "Three Castles" first of all to determine my exact position and secondly to determine the position of the wadi of El Aqaba. There would still have been time to set off afresh but in the scree my car had a spring broken and Munz and Körper had to fit a replacement. Depressed spirits in our camp. Day's performance: about 80 km.

20th May 1942

"Booty Camp"

Start at 06:45 hours. I lead the way right up to the hill slope. Frightful driving conditions over heavy scree. The cars have literally to be pushed. Straightaway I find the outlet of the wadi with the help of the direction finding of yesterday. In the river bed itself lie only my old tracks! The enemy evidently looked for Aqaba but did not find it. For a moment I am beset by fear: Perhaps they have mined the pass from above downwards or blown it up at its narrowest point. There was talk of that in 1937, I even had to give an opinion as to whether it was feasible.

I drive in front and look for traces of mines, but on reaching the top I find the solution to the puzzle. A number of enemy vehicles did indeed, about a year ago, drive down the great rift of the Gilf Kebir, but did not find the entrance to the pass even up above, and went down into the plain through "Penderel's Wadi" which is East of El Aqaba. Penderel's Wadi is impassable from below, it is a steep ravine with many twists and soft drifting sand. The English must have done some fine swearing! (I learnt later from Clayton that he mined this pass "out of consideration for me".)[371]

We go North through the Great Rift at high speed. My old tracks are frequently visible. Unfortunately I try to follow Clayton's track at the point where he found a shortcut across the little eastern plateau. With our overloaded vehicles, however, it cannot be done, and we lose valuable time.

At last over the North point of the plateau, in a south easterly direction. Seven years ago I discovered this passage, the secret gateway for breaking into Egypt, truly the "forbidden path".

I am rather worried as to how shall we get over the difficult part of my former entry into the Gilf, but my old tracks – which the British patrol also followed – lead us surely. The trailing dune which blocks the way is negotiated with the greatest caution. First I get the men to stop and traverse the only possible driving route on foot. All three vehicles get over it smoothly and I take care beforehand to keep a driving channel free for the return journey where the sand must not be churned up. Pit drives as usual like a wild man, and instead of following my tracks drives the "Präsident" head over heels down over the steep part of the dune. A miracle that the vehicle does not turn over at the bottom. The result: broken track-rod of the shock absorber. Except for Munz the men cannot drive, only Körper shows good driving ability. How different were my Sudanese!

We make camp near "Two Breasts" in the plain on the Eastern slope of the Gilf Kebir. Day's performance: 290 km, though 60 km of this in the superfluous effort to "shorten" the route. We store 3 cans of petrol and 2 cans of water. The radio won't work, allegedly the transformer is damaged!

---

371 This comment was added to the diary in red ink after it was originally written. Almásy met Clayton in a POW camp in Italy shortly after the completion of Operation Salaam. This entry strongly supports that the diary was written in the field, or immediately afterwards.

21st May 1942

"Two Breasts" Camp

I should like today to get as far as south of the Dakhla oasis, and as I have anyhow been suffering from insomnia for a few days, I am sounding the reveille at 4 am. We actually get away at 6:30. I cannot move eastwards or go on my course of 60 degrees, as there is an endless trailing dune east of "Two Breasts". The last time coming from Abu Ballas I drove through the mountains north of here, hence we go in a northerly direction. Right behind the first mountain we can drive round the trailing dune and we shall be on our course.

The hardest day so far in terms of terrain. Low plateaus, and over and over again small hills with their trailing dunes that are such a nuisance, broad plains with stretches of shingle and only now and again a piece of open serir. The vehicles suffer terribly on this kind of ground, probably the drivers as well behind me. I have to keep stopping to mark the course on the map. This time I can't draw in the stretch we have done, but only put in tiny points on the map sheet with a sharp pointed pencil. If we get caught, no surveyor in the world will be able to follow our route.

I have set my course north of the broad belt of dunes that I saw last time out of the aeroplane. But I don't know how far the dunes stretch towards the north. It would have been wiser to follow my old route towards Abu Ballas, there will be no save in km on this route either, because of the constant detours.

We've been lucky with the dune, we have actually struck upon the mountain group from which they start, and we can get through comparatively easily at the foot of the hills. At about 11 a.m. a big mountain peak looms up far away on the horizon. Straight in line with the front of the radiator. I would not believe it at first, that I had hit precisely on "Two Peak Hill" in spite of these fearful detours. The check with the navigator's compass showed that we have deviated by only 9 degrees to the south.

The mountain is absolutely unattainable. For an hour I have been driving towards it and it is still far away. A good landmark, visible from 50 km away.

We arrived in the heat of midday. The "Flitzer" is being left behind here. From now on there are only the two cars. The re-distribution of the loads goes on quickly. I am leaving behind 4 cans of petrol and 3 cans of water. The "Flitzer" also still has one tank full.

Bagnold's mapped route lies not far from here. After scarcely 20 km we come upon the old tracks in places. The ground becomes easier. Largish sandy plains, with single isolated hills which afford good points of orientation. I am driving, as far as possible, straight at these orientation points after taking bearings of the hills, as my eyes ache terribly from eternal compass driving.

I must camp a little earlier today as otherwise the men will go slack on me. At 6 o'clock we come to a convenient camping ground at the foot of one of the many solitary cliffs. Day's mileage 230 km.

Wireless communication has broken down again. Wöhrmann reports that the transformer is not working. The men mess around with it for an hour, and then come in to our one-pot supper with the transmitter still out of action. Three radio operators and a mechanic are not able to find out what is wrong! In this undertaking I always have to do absolutely everything myself.

Pit and Pan, riding in the radio car, are the most untidy fellows I have ever had with me. The inside of the radio car looks frightful. Loads, personal effects, weapons and food all mixed up together. I am merciless in having everything turned out, and find the fault in a few minutes. The cable leading to the transformer has been snipped through by some angular object. When I instruct Wöhrmann to lay a new cable, he reports that he cannot do it, as he has no technical training! I have to actually lay out the cable myself, but in spite of that the transformer does not work. A new search with the torch, the compound lead is cut as well! Now at least the transformer is running, but there is still no contact. Now the fault is supposed to be in the instrument itself! I am not a radio technician, and can do no more to help. Tomorrow Pit must try with his instrument.

22nd May 1942

Camp 8.

From now on the camps in the log-book no longer have any names, to be impossible for anyone to find out where we have come from. Left camp at 7:30.

The terrain is now somewhat better, long stretches with good directional points to follow. Still several troublesome rocky plateaux, which have to be driven over or gone around. Over and over again we cross the Bagnold tracks of 1934[372]. I must do 80 km more than yesterday before I can establish the last depot. A precipitous "wind ridge" between two small garas lying about 10 km apart right across the line of course seems suitable. True, it seems somewhat thoughtless to establish a depot in a place where there is no unmistakable landmark that can be seen from afar, and where one is reduced on the return journey to retracing one's own tracks. But there are no proper landmarks here, and I have to lay the depot south of Dakhla in order to be able to deviate there on the way back if necessary. 4 cans of petrol and 2 cans of water, and also the maps of the route covered so far are left behind in a cleft in the rock.

I told my men how in 1931 rather more to the east of here, the Kufra refugees had trod their path in terrible suffering towards Dakhla, and how the heroic Mamur of Dakhla, Abd er Rachman Zoher pushed out up to 300 km into the desert with his two old Fords, after the arrival of the first refugees, in order to save anyone he could. He brought water to 340 men, women and children who had given themselves up to death, and brought the sick and dying into Dakhla in his primitive vehicles. For six days this unsung hero of the desert went out again and again with his Askaris into the unknown realm of death, seeking the scattered groups of refugees. He found more than a hundred dead and of those whom he brought back to Dakhla, more than 40 women and children died there. A year later I crossed further north the tracks of this greatest tragedy of the Libyan Desert, and interred in accordance with the customs of Islam the bodies of a girl and a little boy that had been dried into mummies.

Just a few km after leaving the depot, my story met with sad confirmation. A few camel's skeletons, a human skull bleached snow-white, and … touchingly the narrow tracks of the high pressure tyres of the Mamur's two Fords.

In the afternoon the terrain becomes worse and worse. I keep a sharp look-out for any tracks on the Kharga – Bir Messaha line, but to my astonishment we cross only a few old tyre tracks, many of them doubtless my own.

I would be glad if I could succeed in finding the World War grave of the two aviators which is on our course, and which I drove past in 1932. I find instead on the former Bir Messaha stretch a large road sign with wooden signboards on a post, but not the grave, nor – as I expected – a freshly beaten trail to the Messaha well. So the enemy line of communication does not run via Egypt.

Towards the evening, finally at the Abu Moharig dune I turn north and drive as fast as the miserable terrain allows, so as to reach the Kharga – Dakhla road before darkness. Of course I did not succeed, but I must have arrived at the dune somewhat further south than I wanted, and now the road lies to the north. It is getting dark and we camp in an undulating sandy plain offering scarcely any cover, perhaps only a few hundred metres from the road? But I dare not risk driving across the road in the darkness, or to look for it with the headlights. The most important thing for us now is radio communication. Pit's instrument is working perfectly and he is transmitting his call sign out towards the star speckled heavens. We gather around to watch, holding our breath, listening to the whistle in the headphones. "Schildkröte" does not answer.

I have scarcely enough petrol to get back. Everything was discussed and planned in detail, I was only to radio and they would drop fuel, water and food for me in any grid square I asked for. Now the instrument that is tuned in to our point of departure has fallen out, and the called station on the other does not answer! Probably they are doing another position shift there. I begged them to leave "Schildkröte" at one fixed point. I go aside from the worried, tense group, and think involuntary of

372 An error, the 1932 Bagnold expedition took that route from Kharga to Uweinat.

the men of the Nobile expedition. They may well have gazed with equal dumbness and tension at the mysterious instrument which signifies contact with the outside world of one's fellows, assistance and help.

I work out once again our fuel and the average consumption. If I drive through Kharga Oasis tomorrow by road instead of over the dunes in order to remain unobserved, I shall just be able to make it. If the worst comes to worst, I shall have to get petrol by cunning or force. My mind is made up: in order to save petrol we shall remain on the road. We have covered 250 km today over the most difficult terrain, and are camping in the immediate neighbourhood of Kharga Oasis.

23th May 1942

Camp 9.

We have a heavy day before us today. I am determined to reach the goal and if possible to do a large part of the return journey. For the first time since our departure I am distributing Pervitin to all, for yesterday's tiredness still has not worn off.

We drive in the first light of dawn towards the north and soon reach the Dakhla – Kharga road about 15 km before Kharga. Then no halts on the good road to the oasis. I know everything here, the scattered barchans of the Abu Moharig dunes through which the road snakes in a masterly fashion, the iron tracks of the abandoned railway line, which was once to have led to Dakhla, on the left hand Jebel Ter and on the eastern horizon in the soft red of the breaking day the mighty wall of the Egyptian limestone plateau.

At 5 km I halt and once again drum into the men in the back car, – they are Munz, Wöhrmann and Pan – not to get left behind under any circumstances, to halt when I halt and to start off when I start off. The sub-machine guns are held at the ready, but arms should not be used unless I myself have started it.

We drive past the railway station. There is nothing stirring there yet, after a sharp left turn we go down a newly laid out avenue towards the Markaz (seat of government). This new avenue does not please me, it was not in existence in my time, and now the road branching off to Moharig must be changed as well.

On the small round square in front of the way up to the Markaz there stand two Egyptian ghaffirs (night-watchmen), only one of them carries a pistol. Both of them stand in the road and I stop, unruffled. One of them gives a respectful greeting in Arabic, points to his mouth and says "no inglisi". I return the greeting and tell him that I speak Arabic. The man is pleased and tells me that the cars have to go to the Markaz, as all persons passing through have to report to the Muhafiz (officer in command). I reply that the Bimbashi (Major) will of course report, but that I'm only driving the Bimbashi's luggage, and so we have to drive in a hurry to the station.

"Where is the Bimbashi?"

"In the fourth car."

The man looked astonished in the direction from which we came. I ask him:

"How many cars are there behind me?"

"Only a second one."

"Good." I point to one of the ghaffirs: "You stay here, and wait for the other two cars. The Bimbashi is travelling in the fourth car. You will show him the way to the Markaz." Then I turn to the other:

"And you get on the running board and show me the Moharig turn-off."

"Hadr Effendi." He gave a military salute and got on to the car. I am only interested in getting these two separated quickly, before they have time to think about the passage of two cars so early in the morning. After a few hundred metres we reached the main road that leads to Moharig, hence to our objective. I halt, let the man off, thank him and drive off at once. I see the second car directly behind me in the mirror.

In the glow of the rising sun we drive through the most beautiful of all oases. On our right the temple of Hibis, then on the left the early Christian necropolis, the Roman citadel and the small watch towers, and in between the most wonderful spots of oasis with its bright green fields, the great shady lebah trees and the countless palms. The road is excellent. It runs along the railway embankment and crosses it where the old road from the Markaz used to lead to Moharig. I keep watch for an esbah (farm) bordering immediately on the road, so that I can fetch water on the way back without much loss of time. At km stone 35 there stands an esbah with its spring, scarcely a hundred steps to the right.

The abandoned former prisoners' camps of Moharig lies there unchanged with its half destroyed buildings. I take a few pictures and we continue at uniform speed.

Finally at the Yabsa Pass, 50 km from the Markaz. In the cool morning wind the cars drive uncomplaining up the incredibly steep Roman road. On top we snap a photo of the warning board, and then continue without stops towards our goal.

I notice with pleasure that the excellent quality of the road is having an enormously good effect on our petrol consumption. The road itself seems little frequented. Only where the newly laid Dakhla road enters it are the tracks more frequent and fresher, but unfortunately the road itself is worn into corrugated iron. The following hours pass with monotonous driving, without incident. I wanted to park the second car off the side of the road at km stone 30 before our goal, but the ground does not offer any shelter. At km stone 29 there stands a small limestone hill to the right and I drive up to that, and drum into Körper and Wöhrmann that they must wait in the cover of the hill for 3 hours, until 5 p.m. for my return. If I should not be back by then, they are to follow my track cautiously. In any case the two of them have enough petrol, water and food to be able to drive back to the last depot, even alone. They would of course have to follow our outward tracks most carefully from km stone 15 on the Dakhla road – where we entered this morning – as otherwise they would never find their way back.

I am driving with Munz, Pit and Pan by compass to the east, to find the old caravan track which lies east of the motor road. I lost my way once years ago in this region and got into the worst possible terrain in the "hirashif" (fissured, eroded ground) of the limestone plateau. I steer with extreme caution and the greatest precision by the excellent map. As a reward, I find the ancient camel path exactly where it should be according to the map.

Now everything is comparatively easy. At 2 p.m. we reach the edge of the plateau. Scarcely four km below us lies the huge green valley with the silvery glittering river, the large white city, the countless esbahs and country houses. Not many words are said, a few handshakes, one last photograph, a short farewell, and then I am driving back on our own tracks with Munz.

On arriving at the waiting car we waste no time either, just a few minutes later the two good old vehicles are back on the road again, facing the stretch of 2,200 km that they have just done.

We reach the Yabsa pass only after dark. With a quick decision I have the camouflage paint removed from the headlights and we drive down the steep snaking road with all lights fully on. I decide to spend the night at the esbah I selected at km stone 35. From there I can cross the oasis early enough tomorrow.

In the pale moonlight I cross the palm hedge to the esbah. The yelping of a small dog and the traditional long drawn cry of warning: "Miin?" We exchange greetings with the owner, whose small son immediately brings us a jar of delicious fresh milk as a "Diafa" (present for a guest). My men have prepared camp, and I invite the five people living in the esbah to tea. I apologise that we have no sugar, I offer my excuses to the head of the family, explaining that "our loads were wrongly distributed", so that our sugar is on the other vehicles that will be coming later. He immediately has some sugar brought out from the house and I take this opportunity to buy a big sugar loaf from him for 20 piastres.

The good fellahin tell me everything I want to know, and fill my water cans with delicious sweet drinking water. I would willingly have gone on talking to the people for hours, but we must be off tomorrow before daybreak, so as to cross the oasis unmolested if possible.

I arrange with the head of the family for him to milk his cows an hour before sunrise, and to bring us fresh milk for breakfast. I have travelled 420 km today, and my men are very tired.

24th May 1942

Kharga

The fellah has kept his word, the fresh milk tasted wonderful, and we drove off in the first light of dawn. There is one solitary guard on the round square at the Markaz. We drive past without stopping and I see in the mirror the man running behind the car.

At the railway station I stop for a moment and take a photograph of the stacks of grain piled up for loading. A fat railway employee appears in his nightgown and gives us a friendly greeting. After what I learnt yesterday from the peasants it does not seem to me necessary to disappear too quickly into the desert. I can spare myself a good bit of miserable terrain if I just drive on along the Kharga – Dakhla road and turn off just before Dakhla to the south, to disappear into the great void.

The single problem of the day – whether I shall find the tracks of our outward journey? After a comparatively easy trip on a south westerly course, I try joining the courses on the map and work out by the odometer where we have to cut our yesterday's track[373]. I am correct to within 500 metres.

It is easy to keep to the track to begin with, but the closer we get to the depot, the harder it becomes. In this horrible terrain there is windswept sand only on the immediate surface, and it seems to have shifted during the night. We lose the track several times and have to look for it on foot, as I cannot risk missing our vital petrol depot. The track finally dies out for good during the last kilometers before the depot, and only now do I realise, with bitter self reproaches, how thoughtless it was not to dump the petrol near an unmistakeable landmark, but just simply "somewhere in the area". But then I recognise the steep wind ridge over which we slithered yesterday and drive instinctively to the group of rocks – one of thousands – in the cracks of that the cans have remained hidden. My men declare that this is not the depot, but there lie the black cans, so precious to us, in the cleft of the rock. A large snake has found its way into a crack above the hiding place, and looks at us with glowing emerald eyes. Munz wants to kill it, but I tell him it is the djinn of our hiding place and hence of our return journey too, which visibly impresses the men.

On arriving on the freer terrain we race irresistibly westward. At midday we are already driving past the camping place of the day before yesterday. Late in the afternoon we are at Two Peak Hill, which is visible for more than 50 km from the east as well. We have put the Flitzer we have parked there into running order again in a few minutes, and afterwards we drove on as far as the great barchan dunes, camping on the leeside of one of the biggest.

Day's mileage: 410 kms. Not bad in view of the fact that we had to look for the tracks, had bad terrain and halted at the depot and the parked Flitzer.

25th May 1942

Camp on the Barchan Dune

I have given the men a bit of rest today, and we struck camp only at 9:30. As I had seen on the onward journey that here the direct course from the "Two Breasts" goes through terribly bad terrain, I drive first of all due west so as to get onto my former Abu Ballas – Gilf Kebir route. This time too my navigation is precise, for I crossed my 1933 track just where I had calculated. The track is incredibly easy to follow, and as I drove by the compass last time too, I shall stay on the same course this time,

373 Actually the tracks of two days before.

if the track dies out. The men are amazed how we hit upon the old track all the time, or often just "feel" it beneath our wheels.

Last time I found the way into the Gilf Kebir with the aid of a reconnaissance flight, this time I have to plot the course to the "Two Breasts" so as to fetch the petrol dumped there. From the depot we get on the tracks of the outward journey and this time too we succeed in getting past the critical trailing dune without a vehicle getting stuck. It's a good thing that I left a suitable fairway free on our outward journey.

I plot a course to my surveying camp of 1933, so that by taking a bearing on the great triangular pyramid that we erected on the plateau at the time, I can check our exact position and so check the accuracy of the odometers.

The passage through the "Gap" of the Gilf Kebir was without incident. We cross the tracks of an enormous snake, as thick as an arm, which has slithered across the valley. Munz wanted to drive after it straight away to kill it, but I say that this time it is the djinn on the Gilf Kebir, and according to what caravan leaders believe we have to meet yet a third in order to get home safely. We camp at a scenic spot in the "Gap" with the intention of photographing tomorrow the giant dune that juts into the Gilf in a favourable light, before starting off. Distance covered, in spite of the mountainous terrain, 250 km.

26th May 1942

Camp in the "Gap"

There was no photography, the sky is covered in thick clouds, and there is a cold north wind blowing.

The journey to Aqaba is only a test of patience. On our arrival there I leave two cars at the entrance to the pass, and drive with Munz back into the great red sand plain, in order to plot out a landing field there. I lay out the airfield exactly according to the four points of the compass, drive along the boundaries for one mile, along each side of the square, and inscribe a deep circle in each corner, in the middle of which we put a can. Then I drive along the diagonals and make a big circle in the middle, and "Campo A" is ready. It is to serve for an operation against the starting point of the enemy supply line. We coast down the pass to the spot where the deep-cut wadi emerges on to the sloping scree. Here the British petrol drums, brought with us specifically for this purpose, are piled up in the middle of the fairway and the wadi blocked on either side as the caravan leaders do with big blocks of stone.

On the drums I paint with big letters: "This is NOT El Aqaba. The pass lies 2.3 miles further east. Don't try! Most difficult to turn cars further up!"

If another Tommy patrol should come looking for this pass the men will be most grateful for this "accurate" information.

En route to our depot with the booty petrol I saw along an enemy patrol track a small cask and beside it a big tin. The container bore the inscription "Emergency Water" and the tin contained six tins of corned beef and a bag of biscuits. A welcome addition to our stores which were very scanty by that time.

Putting the petrol into tanks and refilling took some time. This time I would have liked to empty the tank of one of the six parked enemy vehicles which we could not open on the way out. We drove to the "Three Castles", I took the car carefully over the skyline and – about 2 km east of the parked trucks an enemy column of 28 vehicles was camping!

In a fraction of a second I vanished discretely below the skyline, and now all of us with field glasses climbed up to the rocks of the "Castle". About 5 km east of the first enemy column is another of about 30 vehicles. A long way out on the plain, always on my old trail, is a third that we cannot count exactly in the flicker of the Fata Morgana, and on the southern horizon the dust clouds of a fourth column are rising, this is also moving in the direction of "Three Castles". This means nothing may be done about the 45 litres of petrol I still wanted to siphon off!

We have to see to it that we reach our hide-out in the gorge of the Wadi Anag in order – if possible – to get out of the mountains via the Bab el-Masr pass before these columns. In a state of alert with machine guns ready to open up, I drove by compass towards the Wadi Anag. Before we enter the protection of the gorge the first vehicles of the column appear barely four km behind us on the sky-line. Had they seen us?

I could not take along the parked "Flitzer" now. We cannot possibly go on now with only four men to four vehicles. At least one machine gun must have a man. Then we also lacked the 45 litres of petrol that I wanted to "fetch", and we also found that the water pump of the parked car needed to be dismounted. I gave my orders rapidly – the two best wheels of the car to be taken off and our defective tyres left in their place, empty canisters to be hidden in a crack in the rocks up above and tracks to be carefully obliterated. We shall go on as soon as the job was done before the enemy columns get here. We have an opportunity to cut off some of the way at the foot of the mountain and perhaps we'll manage to get away from here with a few km start.

Whilst the men are working I went to the entrance of our gorge and watched the enemy columns through my glasses. The leading vehicle – an open tourer – has stopped exactly opposite our entrance about 2 km away, and is waiting for the other vehicles that are coming up in a single file. I try to measure the speed of the various vehicles with my watch as they pass the grating of the cross-hairs – about 20 km per hour.

Now there are 15 vehicles, now 20, finally 26 as the last two roll up. I see the crews unloading freight and rolling it towards a group of vehicles stopped a little to the side.

The work seemed easy and I soon saw that they were handling empty petrol containers. So this column is also leaving 6 vehicles with the empty barrels in order to pick them up again on the way back from Kufra! Perhaps I can still loot some more petrol?

Many of the men kneel in the sand, remain motionless in that position for some minutes, I realised that it was midday and they were saying prayers, natives of the Sudan Defence Force.

My men had not yet finished transferring the loads and dismounting the wheels. We could easily get away from here, though not unobserved. Now the men of the enemy column have fallen in, it is difficult for me to count them through the flickering air, about 65 men. I returned from my observation post to our hiding place and now at last we are ready to move off.

Before driving out of the shelter of the gorge into the open plain I stop once more for a last look at the enemy column, they have started during the last five minutes. We are cut off! As I had foreseen six vehicles were left behind but this time under guard. Perhaps it had been noticed after all that petrol had been stolen from the other column?

What shall I do now? On the narrow mountain track between here and Bab el-Masr there is no chance of evasion. The distance to there is exactly 20 km and now it is 3 p.m. Those people are sure to drive at least till 5 o'clock, which would be beyond Bab el-Masr. In consideration of their low speed I gave them 45 minutes to get ahead, and then drive cautiously after them. On the other side of Bab el-Masr I shall disappear towards the south or north.

During the wait we had our meal, all this time I kept an eye on the plain in the direction of "Three castles" from which the first of the other three columns was likely to soon appear. Exactly at the 45th minute the first car appeared on the horizon. We have thus come exactly between the enemy columns, and this just at the only spot where there is only one passage through the mountains.

We left Wadi Anag and immediately went along a deep rain gully towards the trail. I do not think that the guard at the six left behind vehicles has seen our three vehicles. After a few minutes we are driving along the tracks of the column itself. I had the machine gun inside the vehicle so that it should not give us away. We went quietly km after km and I could already see the large circular basin of the valley on the far side of which is the narrow entrance of the Bab al Masr. The enemy column is camped just in front of the entrance!

I stopped only for a moment and waved up Munz with the car and Körper with his "Flitzer" alongside: "Close all windows and follow quietly and just behind me. No shooting, at most salute!" They both grin broadly: "Yes Sir!"

I gave the Leica to Wöhrmann: "Take a photo in passing. I will lean back so that you can make the exposure past me."

They were the same beautiful Chevrolet trucks. The men are preparing the bivouac for the night, some are lying in the shade under the vehicles. These are standing about dispersed, and I drove so as to leave them on my right, the sun was deep down on the left so they could hardly recognise the markings on our vehicles. I saluted with the hand raised and the Sudanese rise to return the salute. They are tall thin Negroes from the White Nile. We had to proceed quite slowly on account of the stony ground and Wöhrmann took six exposures. I tried to spot what was loaded on the trucks and passed quite close to one truck whose cover was turned back. The load was cases, not piled very high, that means heavy weights, probably ammunition.

This quaint meeting was over in a few seconds, we drove through the narrow entrance of Bab el-Masr, along the rather worn track on to the low plateau. The tracks of another column are before us, it must have passed along here quite recently, probably during the noon hours before we had reached the Three Castles. Exactly 12 km from Bab el-Masr the left back tyre was punctured, good job that it did not happen as we passed the enemy column! On reaching the plain I counted the tracks of the column preceding us – 22 trucks and 5 large vehicles with much greater width of wheels. Can they be armoured reconnaissance cars? I measured and made a note of the width of the wheels.

Driving straight into the setting sun gradually became unbearable. I drove for half an hour into the blinding disc, then I could stand it no longer. There is a small "gara" south of the wheel tracks, I turned off and soon set up a well concealed camp. Our most difficult task for tomorrow is to find our No 2 depot.

On the way out we came by another route, and now I have to find by precise navigation and dead reckoning that gara again, which – coming from the west – appeared to be standing alone, but which now seen from the east must be one of those numerous peaks lying between our camp and the western horizon. We have not covered a great distance today, approximately 210 km, but the day was eventful enough!

27th May 1942

Camp 13, Gara of enemy Line of Communication

I wanted to start particularly early today since I had to expect to lose much time looking for our No 2 depot, and also it was essential to disappear as quickly as possible from the enemy Line of Communication. I nearly overslept, and only rose – startled – from my camp bed at 5 a.m. The men, who were gradually showing signs of exhaustion, were lying in profound slumber. I am particularly anxious about Körper, he looks miserable and is like his own shadow. Despite the belated reveille we are on the road by 5:45 a.m.

The enemy Line of Communication went across territory that is unknown to me. At first it was a sandy plain good for driving with many large "gara" groups north and south. The Italian map is blank. It would have been a profitable task to triangulate these mountain groups. Then there are some low stony plateaux across the direction of our movement and one can see how the enemy column tried again and again to bring the trail down to better ground.

The column that preceded us yesterday wheeled off south in the face of an especially repellent plateau. I could see yesterday from the manner in that the column was being led that an expert desert traveller was at the head. So I followed his quite fresh track in spite of the five conspicuously wide tracks that made one suspect of armoured reconnaissance cars. As I expected the track passed around the plateau in a masterly manner, and on the open serir joined an older set of tracks, in which ten unusually wide tracks were also visible. Probably the leader of the column has gone over this route repeatedly and knows the best ground.

At 8 a.m. I sighted suspicious dots on the horizon and recognised a column through my field glasses. It was however standing away from the tracks on which we were driving and the cars were facing us with their radiators. An empty column on the return journey from Kufra to Wadi Halfa. I turned away to the north and passed the halted column just close enough to allow me to count the vehicles – 22 trucks and one car. Probably it was the column the six parked cars of which I doctored with sand a few days ago.

Gradually we emerged from the group of hills and I stopped in order to mark the dead reckoning on the map. According to that the large double "gara" lying only a few degrees north of our course should be our Depot No 2. My men are not very convinced, and Wöhrmann particularly is pessimistic as usual. I covered the 12 km to the gara that now – seen from the east – seems quite unfamiliar to me, but as soon as we arrived to the foot of the hill I found our outward tracks, and a few minutes later we halted laughing at our depot. I had not imagined it would be so easy, the drawing of my dead reckoning course shows a deviation of barely 600 metres over a distance of 300 km.

I now tried along the northern edge of the enemy tracks to find the place where on the 16th we had our first surprise of 104 fresh tracks, but Wöhrmann was unable to calculate the corresponding distances for me and by the time I stopped – somewhat annoyed – we had passed the place by 11 km. So I left the broad stream of the great Line of Communication and reverted to a compass course. The next challenge was the passage through the thin dunes at the foot of the Kufra mountains, but first five hours of arduous driving to be done before we can get there.

The drive by compass went without a hitch and exactly at the spot calculated, we crossed the old track of Major Rolle and this time I even had the good luck to drive past a triangulation mark set up by him, and marked on the map.

Arriving at the dunes I did not gamble this time. There are only four of us and much too tired to dig out cars stuck in the sand. I stopped at the foot of the dunes and went ahead on foot to find the best passage and mark it with piled-up stones. We got through these bad dunes without bother in three such stages. From a long way off I can already see the road markings of the old Trucchi trail.

Endless hours through these wild Hauwaish Mountains along our own trail, along this blessed "smugglers road". I keep on thinking at to why these mountains had acquired the name of "wild beast". At the time the Bedouins told the Egyptian explorer Hassanein Bey, who was the first to travel through these mountains with his caravan (1920) that the name "Hauwaish" meant perhaps more spirits, djinns and affari, they live in the hills in the shape of snakes. Just as I was telling this to Wöhrmann, we crossed again the track of a very fat snake, thicker than that above in the Gilf Kebir. I recalled the prophecy of the three protecting djinns, and Munz and Körper also pulled up beside me to shout: "Now we will certainly get home!"

We reached our No 1 Depot with the first petrol store in daylight. My calculation showed the comfortable fact that – barring unforeseen accidents – we should easily reach Campo 4 on the Palificata with all three cars. We could be content with today's run, 340 km.

28th May 1942

Camp on the Trucchi Trail

We started before 5 a.m. as we secretly harboured the hope of reaching Gialo that same day. I followed the Trucchi road as far as possible up to the Zighen dunes, a good distance beyond the spot where we found the trail on our journey here. Then – as always on this continent – the unforeseen happened. I did not look at the map before entering the dunes, Wöhrmann did not tell me about the counter courses of the outward journey, so we suddenly found ourselves in rolling dune country on soft drift sand, gliding with continually increasing speed over ridges and valleys of dunes on an uncertain northerly course. For good measure I corrected this course on every dune back which we reached towards the north east. After an hour we were definitely caught in the dunes. My car was stuck, up to the running boards, with a 50 metre ploughed up track, and I only succeeded with much shouting and waving in halting the other two vehicles on tolerably firm ground. It will not be easy to get out of the desert!

The usual digging and work with rope ladders, calculating the distance covered according to which we should long ago have reached the Palificata, the gnawing uncertainty whether perhaps we crossed the trail on this crazy dune trip without sighting the Pali, and finally the embittered decision to return on our own tracks to where we last saw the road marking of the Trucchi road.

Only there I noticed on the map that I should have travelled south west and west, now repentance was too late, we had travelled more than 100 km, used our precious petrol and are still stuck in the dunes. I dare not attempt another break out through the dunes, so there is nothing left but to travel south, towards Kufra in order to reach the Pista Palificata south of Bir Zighen. That also means that we have to pass the enemy outpost lying at Bir Abu Zereigh.

After a lengthy drive south a "Palo" of the great trail appeared at last on the horizon, it is km 445 from Gialo, that is 20 km south of Bir Abu Zereigh and about 39 km from the spot where I left the Palificata on the outward journey. I could do nothing but order the alert, and ready our weapons for action.

There were relatively few enemy tracks on the Palificata itself but one could see that the stretch between Kufra and Zighen is travelled over every few days. Bir Abu Zereigh is near kilometre 425 and there the Palificata makes a sharp turn to the north east.

In the shimmering midday heat it can easily happen that one overlooks the next iron pole of the Palificata at the place where the direction changes, yet we may not stop near Bir Abu Zereigh nor search the vicinity by driving around in a criss-cross manner. Now the critical kilometre pole has been reached, a sign points left to the well at which the enemy outpost is encamped.

The endless row of high iron poles that indicate the trail at a distance of one km from each other now bends in a big curve to the north east. The surface is soft, real dune country, I cannot stop to glance at the map and Wöhrmann is useless as a navigator. After a while I notice that the iron posts do not carry the crossed tin tablets with the inscribed km number of the Palificata, but small tin casks that we have only seen here and there on the Trucchi trail. So in spite of everything we have gone astray. The compass shows barely a few degrees north by east, I get Wöhrmann to hold the map under my nose as I drive, and see that the Palificata should run about 30 degrees here. At that moment three quite fresh tracks pass from the left on to this mysterious trail. An enemy patrol which is somewhere immediately preceding us, and will unfailingly return sooner or later to Bir Abu Zereigh. It is not possible to evade it by going to the right, toward the real Palificata because everywhere there are high impassable dunes. Really, this cursed map does not show one anything! We are moving on a "Pista Fustificata" marked at km distances, which however is not the Kufra – Gialo trail marked on the map.

The enemy patrol must be just in front of us, I crossed its track and tried to evade it by turning a little west but after only a few hundred metres I found an equally fresh trail of a second patrol, also 3 cars. Stopping is something that cannot be thought of, we race across the flat backs of the dunes up and down, expecting every moment when going up the steep sandy banks to collide head-on with the returning enemy vehicles. There! ... The tracks on our right turn sharply right and I saw at once that this patrol is going toward Bir Dakkar; so let us go on along the false trail not marked on the map. Gradually it dawns on me that this trail was perhaps some time ago marked by the Trucchi men and leads to the "Poste Trucchi", that old camp with the two stone buildings that I saw recently from the reconnaissance aeroplane. I know that the true Palificata is 12 km east from there, as soon as we are past the dunes I will travel by compass eastward.

Something is flickering on my left side, some movement in this difficult visibility among hills and dales, made up of blinding sand. It goes up and down according to whether our vehicles climb up the back of the dunes or down into the rolling valleys, one, two, three dots, dark spots ... vehicles – the enemy patrol! I cannot dodge to the right yet, it lasts a few minutes of maximum nervous tension, then I find the dune valley wide enough and we go east at full speed.

After scarcely 10 km it is done, the "Pali" of the real Palificata appear on the skyline and after a few minutes we laugh as we reach the well preserved tracks of our outward journey. We must try to reach the Campo 4 airfield near km 275 before nightfall. Perhaps the enemy patrol will be confused by our fresh tracks and follow us, but I think they will not venture beyond Campo 5 even then.

We arrived at our goal before sunset, and then had the last bitter disappointment – the petrol store had not yet been set up. I have to leave the "Flitzer" behind here, and Allah only knows whether we shall reach Gialo tomorrow with the two station wagons? Day's journey 370 km.

29th May 1942

Campo 4, 270 km from Gialo

We took it easy in the morning, shaved and washed as far as it was possible. Our store of water lasted out the whole trip. Near the camp on the Trucchi trail I was able to leave behind 7 full canisters well concealed, and the average water consumption of my men, which I had fixed at 5 litres daily on account of them being novices in the desert, went down from the initial daily 6 litres to 3 litres per man per day.

The "Flitzer" was taken to the furthest corner of the airfield, then we moved along the Palificata north-ward, toward the starting point and terminus of our trip. The only new track on this once so busy route is that of our "Flitzer", which went back a fortnight ago with the assistant medical officer and Beilharz to Gialo.

I was watching the petrol gauge indicator with growing anxiety, gradually it became certain that we cannot reach Gialo with both cars. At Campo 1 as a precautionary measure I had to empty the tank of the "Präsident" in order to make sure to reach Gialo with at least my "Inspektor". We did the last 75 km with the four of us in one car. The day after tomorrow I will go back to Campo 4 with the "Flitzer" at Gialo and one of the cars. From there we will go up the 80 km into the "Sand Sea" to repair the "Consul" left behind there, and after two days all my vehicles will be united at Gialo except the "Flitzer" parked at the Gilf Kebir.

Exactly at noon we came to the first kilometre at the southern edge of the Gialo aerodrome. Whilst Munz fired the pre-arranged 3 white flares we hoisted the tricolor on the aerial mast of the car, under the aegis of which we had started our trip and have successfully completed it.

9.3.1942

Wir sind an diesem Tage ca dreihundert Kilometer gefahren und haben
in den Garas die erste Nech kampiert.Immer fast in sichweite von den
Kufra Oasen.Licht wurde keins gemacht,Feuer fuer Kgsenkochen nicht
moeglich da die Nacht klar war und der Schein uns verraten haette.
Die Stimmung war erstklassig und wir waren nur selten in den
Duenen mit dem Wagen versackt.Wir hatten nun auch Routine bekommen
Almasy mit dem Fuehrungswagen fuhr einige hundert Meter voraus und
testete die Piste und wir hinterher 20 Centimeter neben der Spur.
Wenn halt,langsam halt.Nur keine Bewegung mit dem Steuer,denn
die leiseste Bewegung im Sande konnte die erhuertete Sanddecke
zum Einbrechen bringen.Wenn Almasy immSand stockenblieb,dann hielten
wir schon um ihn wider auszubuddeln und er konnte eine bessere Piste
suchen.Auch hatten wir ueberall die Luft aus den Reifen gelassen dass
diese nur zur Haelfte gefuellt waren damit breitere Auflagen auf
dem Sand mehr Halt boten.

10.3.1942

Wir sind in Richtung Djebel Arkenu in ein Gebirge gekommen.Steinhaufe
ueberall,voellige Gleichheit mit ca zehn Meter hohen Felsbloecken
ueberall eine Mondlandschaft wie im Kino.Wir mussten viel Zickzack
fahren und sind vielleicht hundert Kilometer gefahren in Richtung
Sueden.Die Stimmung ist immer noch gut.Es gab keine Pannen und
wir hatten nur dreimal als festgesessen.Diesmal hatten es sich
gelohnt,dass wir lange Schleppseile mitgenommen hatten.Wir hatten
eine Stelle mit Quicksand zu ueberwinden.Das sind Senken zwischen
relativ festem Sand oder felsigen Stellen in denen sich feinster
Sand angeweht hat.Da mussten wir das erste Fahrzeug fast hinuebertra
die anderen konnten mit eigener Kraft im Schlepp des ersten Fahrzeuge
diese Klippen ueberwinden ohne grosse Buddelei.

11.3.1942

Wir sitzen fest.Aus der Wueste heraus hebt sich das Gebirge hunderte
von Metern steil in die luft.Wir haben uns ca 300 Kilometer entlang
dieser Gebirgswad gequaelt.Teils durch Sand,fast hundert Kilometer
auf einem Serir das ist eine flache Wuestengegend mit fester Oberlae
che auf der ununterbrochen der Wind eine Tennisplatz artige flache
leicht gewellte Landschaft gemacht hat auf der man einen Wagen ausfah
kann und dse Steuer nicht zu gebrauchen hat,alles geht geradeaus.
Der ewige Wind nimmt das Papie mit,mit de man sich den Arsch
gewischt hat in die Ewigkeit. Wir trafen auf Spuren die aussahen als
ob wir Tank auf einer Kette gefahren sei.Es stellte sich spaeter
heraus,dass das ein leerer englischer Benzinkanister gewesen war,der
weggeworfen,vom Winde erfasst hunderte von Kilometern duerch die Wue
getrieben wurden und diese sänderbaren Spuren hinterlassen hatte.

Sandstede, Hans-Gerd:

Unpublished Memoirs

The parts of Hans-Gerd Sandstede's unpublished memoirs concerning operations *Salam* and *Kondor* were sent to Michael Rolke by him during his lifetime. It is noticeable that while Eppler tried to portray himself as holding a very important position, Sandstede is much more realistic in his self-assessment. He openly explains that it was only due to their pre-war experience in North and East Africa and their language skills that they had the chance to avoid army service on the Eastern Front.

After several planned operations had already failed in their early stages, Sandstede realised the danger that he still could be sent to the front, and therefore was more than happy to join Eppler for the planned Operation Kondor. He describes the easy months they spent in Berlin with plenty of money, alcohol and women as "very agreeable".

The account of the actual Operation Salam provides some very valuable additional information not found in any of the other available publications, particularly for the preparation stages of Operation Salam. However, the dates given by Sandstede in his memoirs are mixed up, and do not match the real sequence of the operation. Particularly the part describing their journey across the Gilf Kebir is very inaccurate, some parts e.g. the description of the excursion into the "Wadi Zerzura" appear to be outright fiction. It is assumed that these discrepancies are based on the fact that he noted down his memories only many years after the event, and that they were never reviewed. This, at least, has the benefit that his statements were probably not biased by other publications of the same story.

One thing becomes very clear: Sandstede and Hans von Steffens did not like each other at all. While the latter describes Sandstede as a quite useless person without any discipline and permanently drinking alcohol, Sandstede sees von Steffens as somebody who is absolutely unsuited to the desert, who "got sick as soon as the operation reached the desert".

10.12.1940

Am drafted by the army interpreter's school in Halle upon Saale to Strausberg. This is a partially state-owned enterprise under the direction of high-ranking officers. Here one is instructed for missions in Africa. I volunteered because I am able to speak good Swahili, and my English is like that of a native Englishman. The training went on for three months. It was quite interesting to learn about the ideas of people who never were in Africa and how these gentlemen imagine the administration there should be carried out. All colonization failed because exactly such kind of colonizers did not want to deal with the local cultures and wanted to govern the native people with German thoroughness.

28.3.1941

Commandeered to Berlin to *Abwehr 1 Fremde Heere West* for the purpose of a deployment to Africa. The German Air Force had tried in vain to prepare an invasion of West Africa, and now something should apparently be done in East Africa. The powers that were did not yet become completely clear about what should happen now. A lot of time was wasted and I managed to move to other tasks and was transferred to the *Heeresplankammer*, where I plotted ways and routes in East Africa and Egypt.

31.6.1941

My position is becoming difficult. Either I must rejoin the army and go to the eastern front, or to *z.bV. 800* for special assignments. I choose to join the *z.b.V.* I get a terrible fright when I arrive and see a gang of soldiers coming out of the barracks marching in *Stechschritt* (Goose-step). This is just what I wanted to avoid. About a month ago I had met Johannes W. Eppler who also had contacts with the *Abwehr*. We discussed a lot and concluded that Eppler would go to Berlin and suggest that we both go to Egypt, following up on the failed attempt to set down an agent there by aircraft. We were engaged immediately and got a permanent transfer to the *Abwehr 1* on the spot.

23.7.1941

Everything went perfectly and one *Oberst* Maurer briefed us on the methods of the *Abwehr*. We learn how to consume a lot of paper with the application of ink, false ink, rice ink and the use of codes of all kinds. We remain in contact with this gentleman until our transfer to Tripoli.

6.8.1941

Major Hösch takes over. He intends to bring us to Cairo by aircraft. While preparing for the mission we try to dissuade the *Major* from his idea to drop us from an aircraft, since this would be too dangerous. But he cannot be dissuaded. On 9/2/1941 he flies to Tripoli where he is met by a bullet while arriving at the airfield. This saves us from a big failure since he was killed immediately and we are alone again.

10.9.1941

Prof. Prete is now in charge of our employment, we are further trained in wireless messaging and other technical things. Prof. Pretl is a *Schmalspuroffizier*; his rank never became clear to us. Pretl wants to bring us to Alexandria with a speedboat, from where he wants us to take a rubber dinghy to get to the beach. We consider this unsuitable and wait what will happen further. The lessons go on and we make good progress. Then, when we stand almost ready at the end of our training, Pretl goes once more to Vienna to say goodbye to his family and is killed when his aircraft crashes. After we have spent a nice time in Munich, we return to Berlin to wait for other things. Now we get a proper salary, every month 3'600 *Reichsmark*, and get as many food tickets as we want. We can manage perfectly for the moment and we live like Kings. Most of the money is wasted by the end of the month then we have to live on collected dry peas and beans etc. The bars in Berlin are expensive and the girls are even more expensive.

2.10.1941

Hauptmann Weiss takes over our command. In the meantime, we have become swaggering, as if nothing anymore could happen to us and we ignore *Hauptmann* Weiss. He too is swaggering, knows everything better, however, he is not so sure on how he should bring us to Cairo. He assures us that our life is guaranteed by that of a major of the Long Range Desert Patrol, who was captured in Africa by the German army.

5.10.1941

Go to Paris to collect some money I'm still owed from the timber sales.

5.11.1941

We are sent to the village of Stahnsdorf to undertake a major trial with the radio. The assignment went very well. We arrived in civilian clothes and at first nobody knows what to do with us exactly. It helped us to greatly improve our wireless messaging knowledge. We have completed all tasks very well. We received general praise and went back proudly to Berlin.

10.11.1941

Count Almásy takes over the mission. Count Almásy is a splendid guy, quiet and considerate, and knows all about the desert. He wants to bring us to Cairo by car, this rejoices us immensely. Almásy is also a small-time officer in the rank of a *Hauptmann*. We talk long and in detail about our task and understand each other immediately. There are no terms, like "*Jawohl, Herr Hauptmann*", and so on, and from now on it is "Yes and amen".

We got assigned an additional man, a *Wachtmeister* Entholt. A quiet, but snobbish type, who runs around with under strapped saber and so on. However, he remains alone and does not disturb our circles.

Now we start preparing for the mission in earnest, procuring the necessary materials for the mission to Cairo. It is bitterly cold in Berlin. We drive around in an old truck to collect ladders and other materials for the journey through the desert.

13.11.1941

We seriously begin to prepare for the mission. Almásy considers a three-week journey from Tripoli to Assiut, where he wants to drop us off. Long negotiations are necessary with the *Abwehr*, where Almásy apparently meets complications. *Admiral* Canaris apparently does not stand well with the Nazi party leadership, but it goes on. We build rope ladders for the cars, if we get stuck in the sand, these will be used to support the wheels. The food has to be procured, also lodging in Tripoli. Then the transport to Tripoli is a problem.

17.12.1941

Travel with Eppler to Copenhagen to buy Christmas presents. Eppler visits his wife who apparently has thrown him out for good. He was, in any case, in a quite happy mood. We declare our suitcases as a courier's luggage and start our return to Berlin but get into difficulties with the German customs who want to see the content of the suitcases. However, we cannot open them because of the "presents" inside. So back to Copenhagen, where we repack everything and send it with courier's post to Berlin. On the new return journey we are bothered by customs several times, but they find nothing and thus we come back to Berlin intact.

22.12.1941

Am going home for Christmas to Sandskrug but the everlasting disputes with Herta spoil the holidays entirely.

7.2.1942

We are in Berlin again. It is awfully cold and we ride in our truck through Berlin from department to department, as if the town belonged to us.

10.4.1942

Extensive W/T in Strigau which run well. We are again in civilian clothes and are treated first-class. Plenty of Schnapps and women.

12.4.1942

Next to Entholt also Mr. Beilharz joined us. Supposedly an officer, one does not know exactly where the *Abwehr* acquires all these people.

17.4.1942

We have loaded our entire luggage into a carriage and are appended to an express train to Italy.

20.4.1942

In Rome, where we have to stay for two days, Almásy negotiates with the *Oberkommando der Wehrmacht* about the transport to Tripoli.

21.4.1942

Arrival at Napoli. There are problems with the flight to Tripoli. Apparently there is no direct flight to Tripoli and we have to fly via Trapani in Sicily. Since extensive air operations of the British are reported over the Mediterranean Sea no German flight movements are possible. We climb Mount Vesuvius and cast a one-mark coin into the lava.

27.4.1942

Arrival in Trapani. Heavy rain and the aircraft gets stuck in the mud. The undercarriage of the Ju 52 is cracked a little bit and we change into another aircraft.

28.4.192

We fly at an altitude of only a few meters over the water to Tripoli where we arrive about noontime. We are sent to the *Via Caesare Billias*. This is a comfortable villa towards the governor's palace, and we are very happy with it. Catering is provided on a regular basis from the officer's mess and otherwise we feed ourselves. Now and again Almásy cooks his rice *goulash* for us. First he puts on water with rice and cooks the meat. Then the meat has to be added and everything has to be continuously stirred, so that it does not boil over, until all the water has evaporated. Sometimes this lasts for one hour. I suggest cooking the rice at first and then adding the *goulash*, but he wants to know nothing of it. His mother made it that way, so he makes it the same way. It does not matter, leave him with his fun.

Now we are 9 persons:

> Almásy
> *Wachtmeister* von Steffens
> Dr. Strungmann
> *Leutnant* Beilharz
> Wörmann
> Munz
> Aberle
> Eppler
> Sandstede

We were briefed once more by the *Oberkommando* at that time. The main front line was near the border with Egypt, and the gentlemen of the *Oberkommando* actually wanted to know nothing about us. They believed they would reach Cairo without our help. Rommel could not be seen at all, and the staff officer von Mellentin just behaved like a general towards a recruit. They told us on the whole what they expected from us if we would reach Cairo, but they rejected the idea how we wanted to get to Cairo. They would have preferred a quick delivery by an aircraft. Perhaps they could also bring us there by submarine but they considered the incredible journey through the desert as being completely insane, we would never arrive. Eppler and me were hanging around like an oaf and were allowed to leave later, while the staff officers played cards at a round table and apparently had forgotten about us completely. Finally we got a few more well-meant advices for the way, would remain in radio contact, but we would only get further orders if we have arrived at Cairo. It was all simple, no pre-laurels, no schnapps-party, Almásy had to admit that these men leading the desert-campaign never believed in the success of our venture. We went back to Tripoli. The last preparations for the mission were concluded. The five cars ran well.

16.4.1942

Today we have started. Our house was taken over by a front unit as we departed without anyone taking notice. Almásy was ahead in his station wagon, the other station wagon was behind, followed by the three troop carriers, one and a half ton Ford "*Flitzer*" in the rear. We drove at a comfortable pace of 80 kilometres per hour, and spent the first night with the *Carabinieri* in *Misurata*. There was high life all night. During the day an Italian transport column was strafed by English fighter planes. The wine casks were punctured by the bullets, and the wine had to be caught in all kind of vessels available. Thus plenty of drink was available. Food was available as well and we made a small W/T exercise. We left a radio operator in Tripoli, and I had the opportunity to test my radio apparatus, it worked quite well. We have agreed to use the book of Daphne du Maurier, "REBECCA" as a basis for the code. In the first week of every month the first page and the first word would serve as a call sign, then on the following page the next word should be the beginning of the code. In the second week it would be the same with page 100 plus ten, the second week page 220, the third week page 330, and so on. As a cypher code a pawning code was arranged in the way a knight moves on a chess board. The missing letters should run in each case with "Z" beginning backward and all ten lines it should be renewed, that means, with the before last letter again backward filled in the code Carree complement. Besides, only 35 letters were planned, so five high and five broadly. Such a code should never be cracked, because always quite different letters seemed several times completely irritated.

The missing letters should work in this way: Begin with the Z and run backwards. Every tenth line it must be renewed, that means with the second left letter again backwards and filled up in the code carree complimented. Besides that only 25 letters horizontal and 5 letters vertical were planned. This code could never be cracked because all the time other letters occurred in multiple way.

The decoding similarly difficult, one could make a single error and nothing could be understood then. Already during training we made serious errors to the annoyance of the instructors, who nevertheless also made mistakes and produced some nonsense.

We already found out now with the first real trial that we would better have several radio counterparts rather than only one. The operators were the same like all soldiers, ready for transmitting only if they were supervised. In other practices and in our later attempts to get in contact with our counterpart we never made contact, probably because the "brothers" did not sit in front of the apparatus, but went elsewhere enjoying a good afternoon. Also I never received their radio messages they should have sent every two hours, so that we could know how to set our quartzes for the best reception etc. This never worked well; on the whole one-month trip to Cairo, we only had radio communication three times. Already a huge flop.

17.4.1942

We spend this day at El Agheila, a small village in the southernmost part of [the bay of] Sirte. We had a bath, it was spring, and we were in the best mood. Also we made contact with our counterpart W/T station.

18.4.1942

We have made only one hundred kilometers progress and added a day for rest at Agedabia. The cars had to be checked in general, because from now on we were to push forward through the desert till the oasis of Gialo. This Agedabia also had a small military garrison, which, however, did not care about us. We had a splendid raid of British aircraft, which shot at us with everything they had. Fortunately nothing happened at all, thanks God. Deep inside us we were in a constant tension, always wondering if something could cause a failure at the last minute.

Already in Tripoli we were lucky. Our house in the *via Cesare Billias* was near the palace of the Governor of Libya and was inhabited now by the general Badoglio. Every night a courier aircraft passed on its way from Cairo to Morocco, which also dropped a few bombs into the harbor and some other places. During one of these small raids, which were observed and expected every evening at the same time by many soldiers, a bomb fell in the Tripoli harbor on a transport ship that had just arrived, and was loaded up to the rim with ammunition. With a gruesome bang it exploded into the air, it demolished the harbor, but it did not harm us, because the house was well protected and we sat in a shelter. Such a surprise attack in the desert displayed spectacular fireworks. The anti-aircraft defense fired back with tracer bullets and the British dropped flares on parachutes, so everything was illuminated like during fireworks on New Year's Eve in Hamburg, only more intensive bangs disturbed the fantastic sight.

20.4.1942

We arrived at the oasis of Gialo. This oasis had been recaptured several times from the British by the Germans, after the Italians had begun several attacks without success. Because we drove British cars which were still carrying the original unit and company badges, the Italians first mistook us for a British patrol and started shooting at us. However, we hoisted the flag, and bigger damage was prevented. However we had to deviate from the approach track, because the Italians had mined many areas, and we needed a guide to take us through the minefields, which were once laid by the Germans and Italians, but not removed by the British, who however also laid their own mines during the occupation. We were within a hair's breadth from disaster, because after I became stuck several times in the sand, I saw something in black color lying on a dune slope in the distance, which I took to be undergrowth, and drove towards it with the car at high speed. However I became stuck again a few meters before this barrier, and had to find out that what I thought to be undergrowth and support planks for heavy trucks was a row of British anti-tank mines which were uncovered from the sand by the strong wind, and which would have surely blasted me to hell. We saw some war graves in the desert. To be buried there was probably the last thing we wanted.

The oasis of Gialo was a war outpost of a special kind. Here "old warriors" of the Italians and the Germans had given themselves a rendezvous. There were no toilets. In a quite practical way the former house of the command destroyed by bombs was used instead. It was demolished till two meters above the ground, and covered with planks to make a latrine of approx. 25 times 25 meters, which was progressively filled with shit by the soldiers. One only had to pay attention that one did not slip through the openings into the shit. However one could not fall, because at most one leg fitted into the opening, and this was already revolting enough. Here and there railings were made for those, who were not steady on their feet. Almost everybody suffered from diarrhea, because with every thud millions of flies lifted off the pile and spread about the camp, before returning to the shit pool. Everything was overlain by a huge blanket of stench. The soldiers always took care to approach from the windward side to avoid the stench. In addition, the prolific mining of the area was exceptionally obstructive, one had to keep strictly to the limits. A step on a *Tellermine* was definitely the last thing one would do in his life. Otherwise the soldiers have made themselves comfortable. The Italians have brought a few whores into this loneliness, but they were so worn that one had to be a soldier in Africa for a very long time to contract gonorrhea there. On the day following our arrival I passed a group of soldiers, patiently waiting in a row, approximately a hundred Germans and Italians playing cards in the sand or otherwise enjoying themselves. On my questioning what was to be got there, one simply said: "Whores". I looked around and asked, on account of the small house: "How many?" One lifted the thumb: "One." Congratulations!

We did not pitch up our tents for the night, because we wanted to leave on the next day and therefore slept under the cars. It became intensely cold at night. We dug a hole of our size and put ourselves into a blanket, then our companions pushed the car over us. Like this, one was protected against the cold of the night and it was pleasantly warm. From our stores of water we hardly used anything, the next morning we could drive off at daybreak.

25.4.1942

The oases of Tazerbo, consisting of several small properties and the obligatory date palms, lay before the oases of Kufra. These were neither occupied by the British, nor by the Italians. They were merely controlled by the British every now and then. We wanted to drive towards these oases until within sight, and then try to go to the East into the desert, bypassing the oases of Kufra. In the north, there was the Qattara Depression, a salt marsh which was invincible with no way across. This was often tried previously, always without success. How far the Qattara Depression reached to the south was not known, as it was impossible to tell from the Italian maps and charts we had with us where the *serir*, the sandy desert, started. The contours of the Arkenu Mountains[374] were marked vaguely, We had to count on our luck.

If one expects the sand dunes to be only a few meters high as they are in Germany along the coast of the North Sea, one is mistaken. Here the dunes can get to a hundred meters high, stretching for many kilometers far and long through the desert. Crossing the ridges was dreadfully laborious. Over and over again we had to dig ourselves out of the sand, we used water madly and excessively. By the evening of this 25th of April we ended up completely exhausted in a big dune. No way through was to be seen. We also had no more desire to go on. An aircraft had been promised to us to drop petrol and water, but did not arrive. Radio communication with our people at the front did not work either. I had no desire left to do anything. Fortunately I have exchanged all my cigarettes already in Tripoli for schnapps, strong Italian SARTI schnapps, and thus I was well off and had also not caught diarrhea in Gialo from which the others suffered. While diarrhea is not to be feared in principle, it drains the strength out of one in a matter of minutes through the arse. We established a temporary camp. Steffens and the doctor already had a hard time, and the others too started to get into a mad rage.

374 Editors note: The Arkenu mountains are mistaken for the Gilf Kebir here.

26.4.1942

We went further east. The mood had already dropped to zero level. Steffens and the doctor distributed Pervitin to maintain the strength. The three others had their own opinion. None of us has ever experienced such a strain. I smoked a cigarette with Almásy and asked how he imagined this to go on, if the crew is already at its end. "I also do not know", he stated. "We have to try everything to keep the people in mood. We cannot surrender yet. A return at this moment would question the whole enterprise and embarrass me immensely", Almásy said.

26.4.1942

Almásy had spread some good mood. For breakfast we prepared some small sausages. We consumed too much water again, have shaved and drunk a lot. I had sacrificed from my schnapps. We have dug out the cars, and found a depression where we could go on further to the east. On this day we progressed for less than 10 kilometers, from one hole filled with liquid sand into another. About midday the sergeant did not want to go on anymore. He was actually the strongest of our unit. He just threw away his shovel and did not want to do anything any more. Almásy tried his best to persuade him, but he was stubborn like an armored vehicle to do nothing. Also Steffens and the doctor were falling apart. It could not go on like this. Under these circumstances we could not even do another hundred kilometers. Then a part of an axle broke in Almásy's car, which we had to tow from now on, and Almásy with a heavy heart gave the order to turn around.

27.4.1942

On this day we had tried to return to Gialo by the direct route, but did not succeed. Howver, the perspective to meet friends and other people at Gialo kept Steffens and the doctor upright. With these two, it was not possible to talk any more. The mad desert rage had got them. We stopped again beside a big sand dune, it could have been the same one where we were two days ago, and spent the night consuming nearly all our water, which should have lasted for the whole journey to Assiut. Even though Almásy and Eppler warned against using all of it, there was no purpose and reasoning left anymore. The thought to be in Gialo tomorrow made the people mad.

It was a haunting evening. The desert, usually restless, was so quiet today as never before. No wind blew. We lay around and fooled with each other. I brought my schnapps again to the table. We ate canned sausage without cooking anything, and Eppler made tea which we diluted with rum. Suddenly we heard a singing sound which expanded into a loud whistle. "Listen", Almásy said, "the singing dunes, a unique event."

"The wind blows together destinies, but no ass cheeks", a wise Arab said and probably heard and saw these dunes. An everlasting wind blows in the desert, which pauses very rarely. If then by chance a small grain of sand at the foot of a dune slips away, all the surrounding grains follow, and the resulting friction generates the singing sound, which can fade and then grow up to a big volume. A sinister matter, particularly if the mood in the camp is depressed and everybody dwells on his own thoughts. One is nothing in this eternity.

Steffens began to weep, the doctor lay in the sand in apathy and Almásy tried to raise the mood. He tried to tell stories about his time in the First World War, until someone told him to shut up, so he too fell silent finally, and smoked one cigarette after another. We finally crawled away to our sleeping bags. Thank God that one can sleep.

28.4.1942

We are in Gialo again; Almásy tries to find a better way using an aircraft. He comes back in the evening and is in a better mood. The Italians let him fly the aircraft by himself, and have even given him an Italian airman's badge. Probably he has met one of the generals who had it on hand ready to give to him. In any case, he was wearing it quite proudly on his breast, and badly wanted to find a way through the dunes. The next day he tried it again, and after we have filled water into our cans, we got on our way again.

2.5.1942

Again we left in the direction for Kufra, this time driving closer towards the satellite oases. We also found a reasonable ground which supported the cars, and we made a good distance. We have come on this day about 200 kilometers through the eastern Libyan Desert, halting in front of a giant sand dune which blocked our way some kilometers ahead. We sent a car northward and southward to find a passage, but the dune seemed infinite. Finally we tried to force a breakthrough at a place where the dune was maybe 40 meters high. It did not work. We have already dug out the leading car many times, and have practically carried it by hand across the dune, when its rear axle broke, and the steering of a *Flitzer* failed. We were so exhausted that nothing made any difference to us. This time we also saw an aircraft in the distance. Whether it was one of our supply planes, or one of the British, we could not find out, the distance was too big.

The next day we had to drag back the leading car over the dune, turn around and return to Gialo. We have gone one day forward till here, and two days backwards. Again a time delay. We have caught a radio message of the headquarters, asking what was wrong with us and why we were not yet in Cairo. I had the opportunity to send a message back, telling that we had vehicle breakdowns and would have to go back to Gialo to do the necessary repairs.

8.5.1942

We have arrived at Gialo around the evening. The doctor suddenly went mad. He jumped into a well with all his clothes on, and refused to come out again. The wells provided drinking water and had to be kept clean. It took quite some effort to get the man out again. He went completely crazy. Also Steffens complained about heart trouble. The strain was too big for him. Almásy decided to send both back to Tripoli. We also noticed to our great dismay that the water of Gialo was not long lasting, it was foul and unpalatable after four days in the cans. What now? We still had to complete a journey of at least three weeks. A journey where water was the main thing.

Eppler asked some Arabs for good water, and found an old caravan guide who claimed to know a small oasis some kilometers to the west at which one could dig up a well with few spade strokes, and there good water would be available in quantity. We drove off and the old Arab who never rode in a car before could not find the place again, until we brought him back once more near to Gialo, and then he recognized a track. Suddenly he called "Stop!", and then he said, "there you must dig!" We were astonished. No shrubs, grass or other clue to be seen anywhere. Only shimmering desert and dunes. However we tried, and after few spadefuls, something came which we would never have imagined. The nicest and purest water seeped from the ground. We dug a square hole about 1 meter deep and two meters in square, so that the water could settle down and the sand had to have space to settle. Then the cans could be filled with the nicest undisturbed water. We had the water tested in Gialo by a medical orderly and he was convinced after the test that the water would remain fresh for weeks.

Now we had water. The cars were repaired and tested. We left Steffens and the doctor behind us and were now only seven people. The five cars were loaded afresh with petrol, and spare parts based on the experience that we gained during the last days. We have sat together for a long evening and Almásy made it clear that this would be the last attempt which must either bring us to the Nile, or it would have to mean giving up. We reduced our luggage to a minimum. Our private clothes as well as the 40,000 pounds sterling and the few thousand Egyptian pounds we had with us were stowed away in a metal suitcase. We only had our uniform and set of clothes to change, everything else was removed out of the cars to get room for more petrol and water to take with us. We calculated for a three-week journey and the same time back. It was amazing what appeared. We found that still now we were sitting on a dozen English grenades which Manis[375] had stowed away under his seat. Pistols of all kind. I had three boxes of schnapps; two were taken off from me. We might keep two machine

---

375 Editors note: It was not found out during the research, who of the group had the nickname "Manis".

guns, model 42, four rifles, for every one only one pistol, and for each man two grenades. Water was rationed from now on 1 liter per man per day. For each car a big car jack, a so-called *Drumkraft*. Two rope ladders, 50 meters long, to be placed under the wheels if one sank in the sand. Different small jacks. The rations consisted of canned junk, chocolate and cheese and *Alter Mann*, This is the equivalent to the German canned meat, the so-called *Pressindianer*. We also had with us a bag full of onions and another one full of lemons. The rest was water and petrol. I have tied another two bottles of schnapps to the batteries in the engine compartment for all eventualities. In our metal box with the money and the civilian clothes we had a big bottle of petrol and a grenade, which only had to be primed to blow everything up into the air, burning all this stuff in case the British surprised us and we had to surrender.

Now we were very much aware that this third attempt would have to bring us to the Nile and we were prepared for the strain which was awaiting us.

We pushed forward on this day further to the south than before, so that we had a view of the oases of Kufra, from where we have turned to the west[376] and further southwest after the crossing the route which led from Kufra towards the East to the oases of Dakhla. Here we had to be careful, because this route was an old caravan track and was surely used by many cars which brought the supplies for the British garrison in Kufra.

9.5.1942

We drove for approximately 300 kilometers on this day and have camped among the Garas on the first night, always within close view of the Kufra oases. No light was made, fire for cooking food was not possible, because the night was clear and the light would have betrayed us. The spirits were high and we rarely got stuck in the dunes with the cars. By now we gained experience and built up routine. Almásy drove some hundred meters ahead in the leading car and tested the route and we drove behind 20 centimeters outside of his track. If needing to stop, a gradual halt. No movement with the steering wheel, because the slightest movement could disturb the firm surface and make the car breaking into the soft sand below. If Almásy got stuck in the sand, we helped to dig him out again, and he could search for a better way then. We also deflated the tires so that they were only half filled, so their broader surfaces offered more hold on the sand.

10.5.1942

We have reached mountains in the direction of Djebel Arkenu. Stone heaps everywhere, all the same with approximately ten meters high boulders, everywhere a lunar landscape as in the cinema. We had to drive a lot in zigzag and have maybe driven a hundred kilometers in the Southern direction. The mood is still good. There were no breakdowns and we have got stuck altogether only three times. This time it had been worthwhile to take the long towropes with us. We had to overcome a place with quicksand. These are depressions between relatively firm sand or rocky places, in which the finest sand had accumulated. In such places we almost have to carry the first vehicle over, but the others could cross on their own strength supplemented with a tow from the first vehicle without big digging.

11.5.1942

We are trapped. Out of the desert the mountains grow steep into the air for hundreds of metres. We have tormented ourselves for approx. 300 kilometers along this mountain wall. Partly on sand, then nearly a hundred kilometers on *serir*. This is a flat desert area with a firm surface on which the unceasing wind has prepared a tennis court, well-behaved, flat, slightly corrugated terrain on which one can drive a car without having to use steering, everything goes straight ahead. The eternal wind carries the paper with which one has wiped one's bottom to infinity. We hit on tracks which appear as if a tracked vehicle passed. It turned out later that this was an empty British petrol can which, thrown away, was grasped by the wind, and was driven for hundreds of kilometers through the desert, leaving these odd tracks.

376 Editors note: The direction "west" is definitely wrong. It should read "east".

13.5.1942

Almásy has found Bab el-Misr, as he called it, the ascent route to the mountains. A nearly obliterated track was leading him. A caravan must have passed here maybe months or years earlier. It was a narrow way through, northeast of the Djebel Arkenu and to the north of the Djebel Uweinat. Both were to be seen well and I estimate that we were approximately 100 kilometers away from both in a triangle[377]. Maybe a little bit more to the north. More to the north, approximately 50 kilometers away the terrain became mountainous, not pointed peaks any more, rather hilly, but still some hundred meters high. There were here no tracks of any kind, so we had to suppose that no caravan had ever passed here.

The rise was approximately 50 meters wide at the foot of the mountains, then narrowed fast and bent to the south along a distance of approximately 100 meters. Then the valley turned again to the east in steady gradient of approx. 45 degrees on a distance of 300 meters. Then the way confined into a gorge, approx. 20 meters wide, with sidewalls of roughly hundred to 200 meters high. Here water had flown in large quantities. The rocks were washed out but the ground was covered with sand. The sand was dry and without tracks. Blown to a firm surface by the cold wind and drivable for our both cars, which had the lead, the three others had to be pulled. We drove for approximately ten kilometers and have spent the night at half of the height. We have left the first *Flitzer* behind here, after we have reloaded everything which was still needed onto the others[378].

14.5.1942

We made another 10 kilometres at this day. The ascent became more difficult. We had tire punctures and Eppler got the angry and did not want to make any more tea, however he calmed down and we spent a quiet night. Today we doubled our water rations and have used an extra ration of schnapps. The mood improved. The night was very cold, a strong wind blew and we left another car back. We have used a lot of petrol and discussing the situation with Almásy I found out that we had to ration petrol, otherwise we would run out of luck.

15.5.1942

The valley made a strong twist to the north and we have hardly gained any height, so Almásy feared we would be again on the way down from the mountains. We progressed maybe 30 kilometers this day, but always on the same height. On the left and on the right there were high mountains. Broken through by the rugged valleys in which obviously rain had flowed. When? It could not be ascertained.

We camped down on a big open place. "Ideal airfield", Almásy noted, "I have to remember it, and here one can land." It was a firm ground. Salty but not marshy. Everything had completely dried up. Almásy was on the move for the whole day to find another way through to the east and he came back in the evening to the camp completely excited. He had found his Wadi Zarzur.

This Wadi Zarzur was a legendary valley which was apparently used till the turn of the century by nomadic Arabs as a pasture ground. Then it had fallen into oblivion and had never again appeared in the evening talks around the campfires. When Almásy was employed with the Egyptian government to survey the country from 1934 to 1938 in the southwestern regions of Egypt, he was also instructed to find this wadi Zarzur. He even had at his disposal in the last year a small one-engine aircraft, but did not found this Wadi Zarzur[379].

It was too late to look at this valley this day, but tomorrow he wanted to show us the place. The next day only our mechanic and I felt like looking at this valley. We have driven down approximately three kilometers in this open plateau. There were many small, incised valleys. The mountains beside were still high, from roughly hundred to 200 meters. After these three kilometers we turned to the west, for

377 Editors note: None of the mentioned mountains is visible from the location of el-Bab el-Misr.
378 Editors note: It seems that Sandstede is mixing el-Bab el-misr with the Aqaba pass.
379 Editors note: Here Sandstede is in error; Almásy was never employed with the Government of Egypt.

approximately 500 meters then another incised valley appeared to the north. This valley led quite precipitously upwards for approximately 500 meters. There came a peak and on the other side the valley fell to the north into a serir area, again mountainous, but very sloping. Obviously the Libyan Desert is a long way off. Approximately 100 meters before this peak on the left side, to the west, a small side valley opened which was filled up with rock lumps. We had to climb these, and behind there was another valley, about 500 meters long and 100 meters wide. We climbed up the rock lumps into the entrance of this valley. There we saw on the right side two big caves in the cliff face in the form of a big grotto, both were painted with blue and yellowish colors. People in the old Egyptian style were to be seen, also pictures of bulls, gazelles and other animals including birds, many in a brown colour. In the valley we saw stone quadrangles, outlines of houses with sand covering all the stones. Covered by the trickling sand that settles down onto the relics. Big stone slabs lay around. Maybe graves. Other stones were stratified, looking like tombs.

Also hewn stones which were chiseled from the rock were to be seen at the side walls. We could still ascertain this. Some appeared like chambers in which maybe people have lived. Everything was also buried with little fallen rocks as well as fallen down rocks buried the entrance. From above everything looked like a uniform desert, hence, Almásy said he would never have seen it from above, because the contours are blurred. From above everything looked like a uniform sandy surface, and the sun never shines from the side, because in the morning and in the afternoon the high cliffs block the sun from shining into the valley. We camped down here for our resting place, and the next day we went on.

16.5.1942

The way through was 1 kilometer further along the eastern side of this plateau and here we have found a valley similar to the Wadi Zarzur, however substantially smaller and not so impressive. Here a way through was possible for a caravan. Since the slope was about 35 degree steep our *Flitzers* could not ascend without help. However we could clearly see a depression which merged into a *serir*. A large plain opened before us and we could also observe caravan routes. Apparently a route existed here, or perhaps was still in use. We could no longer see the nearly 2000 meter high mountain of Uweinat. We were here, however, in Egypt and not in Sudan as we assumed before, because we had moved too far to the north. Even though we ascended some mountain points and kept a lookout, we had the impression that we have arrived at the eastern side of the mountains of Arkenu.

17.5.1942

We have passed the Akaba pass and found no trace of enemy action. We had found here a petrol dump of the Englishmen and with it the supply route to the oases of Kufra. Here we had to take care and observations not to collide with a British patrol. We have fired our machine guns and checked our other weapons and moved on carefully.

18.5.1942

We have passed by another mountain complex which we called the Gilf el Kebir. No tracks were to be seen, but we have discovered a water depot that Almásy had placed there three years ago. Of the 9 canisters three were rusted and drained empty, the rest was still useable.

We could renew the cooling water for the cars too. We had to leave here the other cars, because the petrol did not last any further, and everything was loaded on to the leading car. In rock niches we have hidden the cars with the weapons and the ammunition and everything else that what was not absolutely necessarily. We have also hidden a lot of food, and have rationed ourselves to a minimum.

19.5.1942

Now we were driving on an almost direct track towards the oases of Dakhla. Unfortunately, we had no possibilities to ascertain our exact position; however, we must have been on the Tropic of Cancer. The mountains drop noticeably towards the east. They are not jagged any more as in the mountains we had passed previously, but hilly with signs of the open desert becoming apparent. Everything is dreadfully dry and bleached. Sand, rock, stones, no living being had been here for a long time. Also we find no tracks of any vehicle or a caravan. Such tracks often remain for many years, because though they are constantly shifted by the sand moving in the wind direction, the contours remain visible for a long time.

21.5.1942

At two adjacent mountains which we called "Two breasts" we have looked upon a favorable resting place. A small cleft looked inviting for a longer break. We checked the vehicle and allowed ourselves one day of rest. We have eaten too much and also have raised the water ration to 1.5 liters.

22.5.1942

We have spent this night near the Abu Moharig dune, after we have crossed some car tracks. Now we have reached inhabited areas, that is where nomads have passed, also the English Desert Patrols have probably driven every now and then along this dune.

23.5.1942

The last day together with the companions. After we had to cross the Japsa Pass, there was no more sense in keeping to secret ways. We had to get to the Nile as fast as possible and we had big luck. Once we saw an English truck on the road which noticed us as it drove past close by but it paid no further attention to us. Then we were stopped by a mixed Arab patrol which asked where from and where to. We were not prepared for it. However no one needed to show papers, Eppler had invented a story of a few words and we could go on. By the evening we came about to the slopes which descend precipitously into the Nile valley and are approximately 50 meters high.

It was a quick good-bye: A short greeting to everybody, a handshake and Eppler and myself were alone. We have made ourselves comfortable for the moment in a small depression. We had a canister of water, the last schnapps and some food. We have taken out and smoothed our civilian clothes. However, they had survived the trip well.

Then we have divided the money. These 100 and 50-pound notes we piled up in a heap. Then it went: one for me, one for you, and thus we have distributed all the notes one by one. We did not exactly know how much money it was. It was not necessary to know. Spirits were high and we drank a few more schnapps.

On the morning of 23rd May we have descended the slopes and have seen nobody on the way who could have stopped us. Then, however, we were already closer to the city of Assiut and did not attract any attention. We had neutral tropical clothes which could have belonged to any Englishman. I have packed our radio in a bag with my pistol and 100 shots of ammunition. Eppler did not like to have the other radio with himself, also he renounced his "cannon" and we have buried both with 100 pounds sterling in a plastic bag and have put a small stone pyramid above it to find again the place if it should be needed.

We came to the railway station at about 11 o'clock and Eppler bought two tickets to Cairo. The train left on time and we had a quiet four-hour journey to Cairo in a first class compartment without any annoyance. At the railway station in Cairo there were some British controls, but they only checked military personnel and left civilians alone. Thus we came unnoticed to the town, where we spent the first night in a brothel.

2.6.1942

We had rented a flat with Therese Germain in the Shara Bursa el-Gedida no. 8 and I mounted an antenna on the roof of the multistoried house at the same day. I sent off my first radio messages at 6 o'clock in the evening: 5 minutes send, 5 minutes of break for half an hour. Everything was as it was rehearsed on the other side. I heard thousands of radios, but not the one I needed.

2.6.1942

There were no answers to my attempts to make contact with our radio station in the desert. It must have been due to faults in the antenna, thus we have rented a houseboat on the side branch of the Nile with two high masts.

Transcripts of intercepted W/T messages

The message transcripts reproduced here in full are excerpts from the ISOS and ISK reports produced in Bletchley Park, identifiable from the date and the indicated message range. As message volume increased, sometimes several reports per day were produced by ISOS, and from 1942 onwards ISK. The translation and analysis of both sources was done by the same persons in Hut 3, and the message headers are identical for both. Unfortunately there is no surviving documentation available to explain the elements of the header, but much may be inferred by the information content.

The source of the reproduced messages are The National Archives, London, HW 19 series, Government Code and Cypher School: ISOS Section and ISK Section: Decrypts of German Secret Service (Abwehr and Sicherheitsdienst) Messages (ISOS, ISK and other series). Individual messages may be found in the following files:

HW 19/6	ISOS 4701-5522	1941 May 01-1941 May 24
HW 19/7	ISOS 5523-6269	1941 May 24-1941 Jun 10
HW 19/8	ISOS 6270-7003	1941 Jun 10-1941 Jun 30
HW 19/9	ISOS 7004-7657	1941 Jun 30-1941 Jul 15
HW 19/10	ISOS 7658-8375	1941 Jul 16-1941 Jul 31
HW 19/11	ISOS 8376-9062	1941 Aug 01-1941 Aug 15
HW 19/12	ISOS 9063-9873	1941 Aug 16-1941 Aug 31
HW 19/15	ISOS 11516-12372	1941 Oct 01-1941 Oct 15
HW 19/27	ISOS 23883-24988	1942 Apr 01-1942 Apr 15
HW 19/28	ISOS 24989-26079	1942 Apr 16-1942 Apr 30
HW 19/29	ISOS 26080-27441	1942 May 01-1942 May 16

HW 19/30	ISOS 27442-28652	1942 May 17-1942 May 31
HW 19/31	ISOS 28653-30019	1942 Jun 01-1942 Jun 16
HW 19/32	ISOS 30020-31527	1942 Jun 17-1942 Jun 30
HW 19/33	ISOS 32528-32767	1942 Jul 01-1942 Jul 16
HW 19/34	ISOS 32768-34090	1942 Jul 17-1942 Jul 31
HW 19/88	ISK 2045-2818	1942 Feb 15-1942 Feb 28
HW 19/93	ISK 6883-8270	1942 May 01-1942 May 15
HW 19/94	ISK 8271-9871	1942 May 16-1942 May 31
HW 19/95	ISK 9872-11030	1942 Jun 01-1942 Jun 15
HW 19/142	ISK 67001-68601	1943 Oct 04-1943 Oct 17
HW 19/143	ISK 68602-69700	1943 Oct 17-1943 Oct 25
HW 19/145	ISK 70851-72400	1943 Nov 04-1943 Nov 14

Message headers contain the following information:

ISOS / ISK unique message number

Line 1: Group identifier – evidently related messages were organized into groups – eg. the communication between von Griesheim (WIDO) and Major Seubert (ANGELO) is always GROUP II/25

Line 2: Source and Destination sations – in some cases this was exactly known (eg. TRIPOLI to BERLIN), however in some cases it was very vague (eg. SALAM messages were only identified as "WESTERN DESERT AREA")

Line 3: Decrypt identifier, consisting of source identifier, message number and decryption date – for all ISOS / ISK messages in 1941-42 the source is RSS (Radio Security Service).

Line 4: Original message information: Sending (and receiving) callsign and frequency, transmission time (GMT) and date

Line 5: Encryption code information (this was omitted in the transcripts below to save space, as it conveys no information on message content and context)

ISOS Transscripts

4992   GROUP I/40

LIBYA to HAMBURG

RSS 350/10/5

EBN on 7830 kcs. to REV on 6850 kcs. 0545 GMT 9/5/41

No preamble

Translation of Hungarian text. Please realize that I have tried everything humanly possible, but have not however, found a suitable person to operate the machine. As desired am leaving the portable set, provided with English instructions for use, and cipher material [Verschluesselung], with agent [Vertrauensmann] here, who will deliver it on [being given the] password [Kennwort]. I shall give RITTER the address and password. Good-bye. G.

5039   I/42

RSS 649/11/5/41

LLA 6824 kcs at 1715 GMT/ 11/5/41

Please provide several Greek pay-books [Soldbucher] for us to pass to Major RITTER.

5040   I/44 HAMBURG to BUDAPEST

RSS 655/12/5/41

To? on 7805 kcs from ARD on 6970 kcs at 0723 GMT/ 12/5/41

For Hauptmann von BARNA. When did KAMARAS and PLESSING leave? Standing by. Expecting anwer at 11hrs. Central European Time. Best wishes

Hauptmann WENZLAU

5041   I/44 HAMBURG to BUDAPEST

RSS 701/12/5/41

ARD on 6970 kcs to FLE on 7800 kcs at 1014 GMT/ 12/5/41
For Hauptmann von POGANY. Can you ascertain from the Aussenamt when MARTIN left CAIRO and [when] his arrival in BUDAPEST is to be expected. Best wishes,

Hauptmann WENZLAU

Dr. KRAEMER

5043   I/40 LIBYA to HAMBURG

RSS 748-9/6/5/41

NEH on 7820 kcs on 30/4/41

From MARTIN. On 27ᵗʰ and 28ᵗʰ from GREECE 300,000 Greeks and English troops alleged to have arrived in ALEXANDRIA. Going to Western Front. King of the Greeks said to be in ALEXANDRIA. Tanks rescued from GREECE are being transported to PALESTINE. Free [? FRYUE] zone reinforced. Malayan troops arrived in CAIRO pyramid camp. 22 English regiments entrained in CAIRO for Western Front. Weather:- temp.20 Celsius, baro.767 rising, cloudless, stronger North-West wind. Flieger korps X informed. BERLIN informed.

5044   I/40 HAMBURG to LIBYA

RSS 44/1/5/41

No call on 6870 kcs at 0505 GMT/1/5/41

ALMAZY is returning to TAORMINA at the beginning of next week. For Major RITTER from Frau RITTER. Thank you for all [your] letters. I write every day. Affectionately.

13/5/41 ISOS 5051 - 5056

5051   GROUP I/40

HAMBURG to LIBYA

RSS 592/11/5

NLE on 11,990 kcs. 1230 GMT. 11/5/41

Report the name of the operator who sent messages Nos. 130 and 140. He must learn to transmit before he sends any considerable traffic again. If necessary apply for him to be relieved by another man.

PRODEHL.

[no date, 14/5/41 ?] ISOS 5095 – 5103

5095   I/40 LIBYA to HAMBURG

RSS 854/13/5/41

RED on 7770 kcs at 0506 GMT/10/5/41

MARTIN's trunk with instructions in English as to use and how to encipher made secure* at the Hungarian Priest DOEMOETOER's Church of ST THERESE, CAIRO, SCHUBRA. Pass word ALMA MATER. Hptm. Von ALMASY arrived here yesterday evening.

RITTER

*Sichergestellt, may also mean "secured".

15/5/41 ISOS 5131 – 5141

5135   GROUP I/40

LIBYA to HAMBURG

RSS 938/14/5/41

NLE on 7830 kcs. 0513 GMT. 11/5/41

[No 139] Major TRAUTMANN. SCORPION. Major RITTER in AFRICA for I Luft. Very much interested in Turkish reports. Please if possible acquire several pay-books of Greek soldiers through S-Kommando [? SKDO] OBLADEN and send them here for II [roman one IDA]. Listening for MARTIN's apparatus lapses for the time being, since nobody near enough to service it yet.

RITTER.

16/5/41 ISOS 5165 – 5168

5165   GROUP I/40

HAMBURG to LIBYA

RSS 106/15/5/41 & 970/14/5/41

Part I [EBN] on 6840 kcs. 0520 GMT. 13/5/41

Part II EBN on 7830 kcs. to GUZ on 6840 kcs. 0520 13/5/41

Ref. your message. Will in future communicate LEOPOLD reports to you as a special unit [Sonderkommando] of AST X to keep you up-to-date. Leave it to you to pass these to Fliegerkorps X according to your own judgment. OBLADEN has taken steps to procure Greek pay-books by way of Sonderkommando.

19/5/41 ISOS 5277 – 5282

5279   GROUP I/44

BUDAPEST to HAMBURG

RSS 592/18/5/41

ECN on 7800 kcs at 0724 GMT on 15/5/41

For ALMASY. Am remitting 2000 pengos to TASSILO as soon as possible. Everything will be arranged. Coming soon.

Best wishes, KURT PLESSING

5797   GROUP I/40

LIBYA to HAMBURG

RSS 81/29/5/41

REB on 11985 kcs.to PAK on 12500 kcs. 1247 GMT. 27/5/41

For direct traffic SKORPION HBG [HAMBURG] [we] suggest the following times and frequencies:- 0800 and 1800 hours, we on 11,500 kcs, you on 12,750 kcs. Code book DER GRAUE FREUND. Basic number [Grundzahl] 17. Beginning 28/5. Please confirm.

RITTER.

5798   GROUP I/40

LIBYA to HAMBURG

RSS 82/29/5/41

REB on 12000 kcs. 1256 GMT. 27/5/41

For Kptn. WICHMANN. Personal. Many thanks for your letter of 8/5. Please appoint a suitable officer if possible and one [unestablished] Civil Servant [Angestellter] Sonderfuehrer. Everything in order here. Imminent success in sight. Letter to follow.

RITTER.

5798a   GROUP I/40

LIBYA to HAMBURG

RSS 82/29/5/41

REB on 12000 kcs. 1303 GMT. 27/5/41

Is Kptlt. OBLADEN's W/T section [Funktrupp] still in ATHENS? If so, [I] would suggest that BRINKMANN be attached to them.

RITTER.

5862   GROUP I/40

HAMBURG to LIBYA

RSS 245, 246, 247/30/5/41

Part   I 0508 GMT

Part II 0513 GMT

Part III 0525 GMT

For Major RITTER. Reference message No. 149.

1) Unfortunately your reply to my letter of 8/5 is not quite clear to me. You say "according to possibility [a] suitable officer". This would fill the place [or position]. To appoint, in addition, an employee [ANGESTELLTEN] to [the position of] Sonderfuehrer is out of the question. [I] repeat [my] enquiry [on] page 3, as to whether you want to place M in this position or, alternatively [whether you have] already made him such suggestions.

2) Do you or the Fliegerkorps happen to be in possession of the personal documents of Lt. Raydt. If so, please send them along so that the documents can be forwarded from here to the new Command [KOMMANDO].

signed: WICHMANN

5954 GROUP I/44

HAMBURG to BUDAPEST

RSS 416/31/5/41, 415/31/5/41

LIF on 7000 kcs 31/5/41

Part   I 0717 GMT

Part II 0727 GMT

[Nos. 013-014] Ask MARTIN or JOSKA whether ALMASY and RITTER's [cipher-] code was deposited in CAIRO with the set or the Hungarian [cipher-] code for the traffic CAIRO-BUDAPEST. In addition, ask whether the Japanese are to carry on W/T traffic with ALMASY or BUDAPEST. There seems to be some confusion. We are hoping for direct traffic CAIRO/ALMASY. Best wishes.

KRAEMER.

6081 GROUP I/44

HAMBURG to BUDAPEST

RSS 33-41/5/6/41

ION on 7000 kcs. to DNA on 7820 kcs. 4/6/41

Part   I 0831 GM.T [No. 24]

Part II 0850 GMT. [No. 25]

Part III 0853 GMT. [No. 26]

[Nos. 24-26] Contin.

4) Which training camps are there in EGYPT?

5) In which localities and buildings are the Army Command Stations [Wehrmachtsbefehlstellen] housed?

6) What fortifications are there on the Western edge of the NILE DELTA or West of the NILE VALLEY?

7) Where is the NEW ZEALAND division, which is being formed, quartered? What is its number?

8) What is happening to the several thousands of Australians, billeted in camps to the North-west of CAIRO and who are reported to be without arms, equipment and vehicles?

6082 GROUP I/44

HAMBURG to BUDAPEST

RSS 36-38/5/6/41

ION on 7000 kcs. 4/6/41

Part   I 0904 GM.T [No. 27]

Part II 0912 GMT. [No. 28]

Part III 0917 GMT. [No. 29]

[Nos. 27-29] Ask JOZKA via EGYPT:

1) Are there difficulties regarding trained [illegible] New Zealand and Indian units?

2) Details concerning South African troops.

3) Are there Indian divisions?

4) Are there Indians organized into regimental works units [Bauabteilungen]?

5) Have reinforcements or reliefs [Abloesungen] from ALEXANDRIA or MARSA MATRUH been observed lately (month of April) en route for the oases?

6083   GROUP I/42

HAMBURG to BUDAPEST

RSS 39 and 41/4/6/41

ION on 7000 kcs. 4/6/41

Part I 0934 GM.T [No. 30]

Part II 0948 GMT. [No. 31]

[Nos. 30, 31] For BOROSS. Many thanks for enquiry. With whom are the Japanese in BUDAPEST to have communication? With the Japanese legation or with you [euch: fam. plural] ? By whom has everything been arranged and who is at the head of the whole affair? KAMARAS will have to leave immediately after the money question has been finally settled. Best wishes.

Dr. KRAEMER.

6084   GROUP I/44

BUDAPEST to HAMBURG

RSS 5/6/41

To ION on 7010 kcs. from DNA on 7820 kcs. 0712 GMT 4/6/41

[No. 9] For Dr. KRAEMER. JOSKA has deposited the set in CAIRO with the code ALMASY. The Japanese will be in communication from CAIRO with BUDAPEST. Best wishes.

BOROSS

11/6/41 ISOS 6295 - 6301

6299   GROUP II/29

CYRENAICA to BERLIN

RSS 793/10/6/41

NEL on 9275 kcs. 1839 GMT 2/6/41

No. 5. For L. Am arriving BERLIN probably 5th June, as operation [Einsatz] had to be postponed till 12th June.

RITTER.

6300   GROUP II/29

CYRENAICA to BERLIN

RSS 787/10/6/41

No call on 9310 kcs at 1841 GMT 7/6/41

No. 7. Did Major RITTER arrive safely? Everything OK here.

ALMASY.

6301   GROUP II/29

CYRENAICA to BERLIN

RSS 785/10/6/41

NEL on 9320 kcs at 1840 GMT 8/6/41

No. 8. For Maj. RITTER. As from 12/6 two HEINKEL 111 are ready for special undertaking, among them crew Oblt. LEICHT, Xth Fliegerkorps.

Ic. SKORPION

Dept.Note. Ic. = Intelligence Officer

6447   GROUP I/40

LIBYA to HAMBURG

RSS 926/14/5/41

RED on 7700 kcs at 0518 GMT. 10/5/41

For HAMBURG I M. Your message 114 of 9/5. I regret that [I was] not previously advised concerning TUNISIA. The unpleasant thing is not loss of [my] own time but the exclusion [Wiederausschaltung] of the Italians once more after the enlistment [Einschaltung] had proved especially difficult. Shall now try ALGIERS.

RITTER.

6449   GROUP I/40

LIBYA to HAMBURG

RSS 105/15/5/41

EBN on 7830 kcs. 0506 GMT. 13/5/41

For Kptn. WICHMANN. I know nothing of being placed directly under ABW. BERLIN once ordered closest connection with ROMMEL, which had already been anticipated by me. In addition BERLIN has inquired whether I m willing to take on more agents [V.-Leute], to which I naturally replied yes. Hope the matter will be settled without friction. Flg. Korps regards me as subordinate to HAMBURG for questions of discipline as well.

RITER.

6458   GROUP II/29

BERLIN to LIBYA [?]

RSS 448/14/6/41

NMO on 8450 kcs. 1451 GMT. 11/6/41

No. 2. Return postponed. From 13ᵗʰ to 15ᵗʰ [I] can be contacted in ATHENS through KNAPPE. Advise Ic AFRICA CORPS that I am bringing several intelligence officers [Nachrichtenoffiziere] and have also requisitioned directly for you V D ESCH in the OKW.

RITTER No. 96.

6861A   GROUP II/29

CYRENAICA to BERLIN

RSS 200/25/6/41

NEL on 9300 kcs. 1916 GMT. 20/6/41

[No 9.] For LUDWIG. On return flight from operation [Einsatz] both a/c failed to receive radio-beacons DERNA and BENINA on account of bad weather. In the night of the 17th and 18th the leading a/c made a forced landing on the sea, the accompanying a/c made a perfect landing in BENINA. After 9 hours in a rubber-dinghy in a heavy sea reached coast off BARCE. Bought to safety by th Sea Rescue Service [Seenot] and the coastal squadron [Kuestenstaffel]. Major RITTER has a heavy break in the right upper arm, Obltn. LEICHT broken ribs, rest of the crew uninjured. The two casualties are leaving to-day by red-cross a/c for ATHENS.

ALMASY, Message No.9.

6862   GROUP II/29

CYRENAICA to BERLIN

RSS 203/25/6/41

NEL on 9300 kcs. 2000 GMT. 20/6/41

No.10. To LUDWIG. Doctors unfortunately ordered transport home. Continuation of work in DERNA is assured. Start and destination [Endziel] still unknown, and will be passed on when received. Detailed report to follow.

RITTER.

6863   GROUP II/29

CYRENAICA to BERLIN

RSS 201/25/6/41

NEL on 9300 kcs. 2047 GMT. 20/6/41

No.11. To LUDWIG for *I G BREDA or Major THORAN. Please break the news gently to my wife that I shall be returning in the next few days to GERMANY in slightly wounded condition.

RITTER.

Note. * rank omitted. I G = in Generalstab.

1/7/41 ISOS 7091 – 7109

7096   GROUP II/29

BERLIN to LIBYA

RSS 976/30/6/41

NMO on 8435 kcs. 1833 GMT. 26/6/41

No.7. Major RITTER arrived in hospital BERLIN on 24/6/41. Hptm. ALMASZY and Oberltn. BLAICH are waiting another few days before departure by air. New date will be announced. ABW I LUFT.

BREDE Hptm. I Gen[eral]st[ab] D

LUFT W. No. 385.

7097   GROUP II/29

BERLIN to LIBYA

RSS 823/29/6/41

NMO on 8420 kcs. 1932 GMT. 28/6/41

No.9. Please report probable time of arrival of Hauptmann ALMASY to Oberltn. BLAICH. Arrange through Hptm. HUMMEL for 2 further neighbouring houses to be turned over to Aufklaerungskommando OKW [Reconnaissance Detachment] [for] 20ᵗʰ July.

RITTER, 449.

4/7/41 ISOS 7171 – 7191

7181   GROUP II/29

LIBYA to BERLIN

RSS 824/29/6/41; 103/1/7/41

NEL on 9310 kcs. 1910 GMT. 28/6/41

120. For KLAPPER. Please send auto-transformer [Autotr[an]sfo[rmator]] by courier to Sonderkommando Major RITTER with Fliegerfuehrer AFRICA. As anode batteries only PIGGI or similar size. Please enclose aerial flex [Antennenlitze].

DEPPERMANN.

7182   GROUP II/29

LIBYA to BERLIN

RSS 633/3/7/41; 103/1/7/41

NEL on 9310 kcs. 1843 GMT. 30/6/41

No.14. For Major RITTER. Hptm. VON ALMASZY left by air this afternoon. [I] have sent in to the new Town Major's office [Ortskommandantur] a report regarding occupation of houses. Houses [are] difficult to obtain. Town Major's office asks for statement of the strength of the new detachment [Kommando].

DEPPERMANN.

7324   GROUP II/29
BERLIN to CYRENAICA or
CYRENAICA to BERLIN
RSS 365/6/7/41
NMO on 8450 kcs. 1855 GMT. 3/7/41

No.3. Watch immediately for MARTIN immediately under former conditions at the same times and frequencies and resume traffic with him. [He] received a gramophone a few days ago.
Major RITTER NO.562.

7353   GROUP II/29
LIBYA to BERLIN
RSS 366/6/7/41
NEL on 9330 kcs. 1932 GMT. 3/7/41

No.16. For Major RITTER. Received report on crash-landing of FIESELER STORCH. Report was made to Adjutant [to] Fliegerfuehrer. Salvage has been begun with Stabsingenieur MUELER.
DEPPERMANN.

7464   GROUP II/29
CYRENAICA to BERLIN
RSS 64/10/7/41
PCK on 11,480 kcs. 1848 GMT 8/7/41

No.18. For Maj. RITTER. Ltn. MUETZE requests W/T training by us as [he is] in DERNA 3 times a week on duty. Please send appropriate orders.
DEPPERMANN.

7624   GROUP II/25
BERLIN to ?
RSS 505/13/7/41
WPA on 8450 kcs. 1922 GMT. 8/7/41

No.4. On the 8th July Wachtmeister VON [Text: VOR] STEFRENS [or: STIFFENS] was dispatched to TR[IP] OLI with people's car [Volkswagen] and 3 W/T sets, engine-driven power unit [Maschinenaggregat] with accessories [Zugehoer], 2 machine pistols, 5 sporting rifles [Jagdgewehre] with ammunition and office supplies [Bueromaterial]. His instructions to cross from NAPLES by steamer. In conformity with your instructions has been ordered not to leave car. Departure of the steamer will be announced by way of ROME. Report arrival in TR[IP] OLI by W/T.
ANGELO No. 661.

7665   GROUP II/29
BERLIN to CYRENAICA
RSS 541/13/7/41
NMO on 9420 kcs. 1000 GMT. 12/7/41

6. Exchange DEPPERMANN and WICHMANN for BRINKMANN and another W/T operator for a fortnight.
ABW I Luft.
Major RITTER. 731.

17/7/41 ISOS 7709 – 7731

7713 GROUP II/29

CYRENAICA to BERLIN

RSS 878/15/7/41

NEL on 9335 kcs. 1830 GMT. 12/7/41

No.23. For Major RITTER. Have advised BRINKMANN concerning exchange. Will take place as quickly as possible. Am leaving here by air, with the next courier machine, probably Monday. Am taking only he most necessary luggage.

DEPPERMANN.

[Note: last 6 groups in message lost]

7714 GROUP II/29

CYRENAICA to BERLIN

RSS 171/16/7/41

NEL on 9220 kcs. 1907 GMT. 14/7/41

No.25. For Major RITTER. Uffz. BRINKMANN arrived at this end with one W/T operator. [We] are leaving by air tomorrow for ATHENS with courier machine. W/T operator EPPLER is still with Interpreter Company [Dolmetscher Kompagnie] in BERLIN, was to be dispatched to this end for W/T training. [We] send best wishes to Herrn Major, too, and wish [him] a speedy recovery.

DEPPERMANN.

18/7/41 ISOS 7764 – 7770

7764 GROUP II/29

CYRENAICA to BERLIN

RSS 436/17/7/41

NEL on 9345 kcs. 1939 GMT. 16/7/41

No 26. For Major RITER. When can we reckon with transfer of Ltn. MUETZE to here since better use can be made of [his] time.

BRINKMANN.

[on or after 21/7/41] ISOS

7908 GROUP II/29

CYRENAICA to BERLIN

RSS 958/21/7/41

NEL on 9360 kcs. 1852 GMT. 18/7/41

No. 27. For Maj. RITTER. Station hit by fire-bombs. Fire extinguished immediately. The water-filter-Apparatus was damaged but can still be used. No further damage caused. Everything O.K.

BRINKMANN.

7909 GROUP II/29

CYRENAICA to BERLIN

RSS 957/21/7/41

NEL on 9400 kcs. 1830 GMT. 19/7/41

No. 28. For Major RITTER. FISELERSTORCH damage about 35 per cent. Repairs at field-repair-station BENGHAZI delayed through lack of spare parts. Report on interruption still not on hand.

BRINKMANN.

8146   GROUP II/25

BERLIN to TRIPOLI

RSS 517/25/7/41

WPA ? on 8420 kcs. 1907 GMT. 24/7/41

No.11. People's car is being shipped from NAPLES on 24/7, as far as can be seen, escorted by a soldier. Wachtm[eister] VON STEFFENS will set out with set by aircraft for TRIPOLI in 3 or 4 days.

ANGELO 1001.

8314   GROUP II/29

BERLIN to CYRENAICA

RSS 950/30/7/41

NMO on 8420 kcs. 1844 GMT. 28/7/41

No.9. For W/T operator BRINKMANN. As a result of rearrangements [Text: Umdisponierung] the transfer of Leutnant MUETZE can not be reckoned with.

LUDWIG 1136.

8496   GROUP II/25

TRIPOLI to BERLIN

RSS 107/31/7/41

KNS on 12,960 kcs. 1852 GMT. 24/7/41

No.12. To ANGELO. Concerning STEFFENS who was started on the 8th July we have as yet no news at all to hand from ROME. As up to now I am still without an aeroplane I have been reduced to the "People's car" for the FEZZAN journey. When may STEFFENS's arrival be expected? Possibly [he will] first make journey to TIS.

WIDO.

8744   GROUP II/29

CYRENAICA to BERLIN

RSS 930/7/8/41

NEL on 9300 kcs. 1840 GMT 5/8/41

No. 29. For Major RITTER. Particulars of account sent off by courier. Please confirm reception.

BRINKMAN, Uffz.

8900   GROUP II/29

BERLIN to CYRENAICA

RSS 189/11/7/41

NMO on 8420 kcs. 1520 GMT. 9/7/41

No.4. Ref. your W/T message No. 18 of 8/7/41. Training can begin immediately. Give more detailed report concerning FIESELER-STORCH fracture [Bruch].

For Commanding Officer, Dr. THORAN, Major 341.

8919   GROUP II/29

BERLIN to CYRENAICA

RSS 825/17/6/41

NMO on 8450 kcs. 1840 GMT. 13/6/41

No.3. Car transformer [Autotrafo] must first be obtained. Duration about 3 or 4 weeks. Paper is dispatched via Courier FIGI. Anodes not in stock. Can normal 90 volt anodes be used? If so, immediate dispatch is possible.

KLAPPER.

8920   GROUP II/29

BERLIN to CYRENAICA

RSS 975/30/6/41

NMO on 8430 kcs. 1235 GMT. 27/6/41

8. Urgent. Hptm. Von ALMASY and Oblt. BLAICH are to be dispatched to BERLIN without intermediate halt. Report to TIRPITZUFER 80, telephone extension 1818.

RITTER, Major.

8938   GROUP II/25

TRIPOLI to BERLIN

RSS 107/31/7/41

KNS on 12,960 kcs. 1852 GMT. 24/7/41

No.9. To ANGELO. After establishment of direction for v. STEFFENS's official activity, please hold ready Gefreiter HEINZ FRITSCH, STAHNS DORF. Details with RITA.

DOWI.

8994   GROUP II/29

CYRENAICA to BERLIN

RSS 279B/13/8/41

NEL on 9310 kcs. at 1834 GMT. 11/8/41

No.30. For LUDWIG. Private effects of Major RITTER left here to-day by courier.

WAHRLICH.

9205   GROUP II/25

TRIPOLI to BERLIN

RSS 937/16/8/41

TTS on 12950 kcs at 1732 GMT. 14/8/41

No.16. To ANGELO. After departure on Friday evening [of] ILLU from NUT, WIDO [will proceed] with STEFFENS on Monday to "OASE" for a few days. Then without a break the journey to FEZZAN [with or of] HOLZBRECHER and STEFFENS, which can no longer be postponed, [will be made]. WIDO can be reached in TRIPOLI at his departure on Friday through GUDRUN, during Friday and Saturday through STEFFENS c/o GUDRUN, TROLI. HOLZBRECHER [will undertake] service flight to ANGELO [to discuss] technical and equipment questions. After the return of WIDO and STEFFENS from "OASE" report will immediately be made through GUDRUN, TROLI. Until then direct GUDRUN traffic is suspended.

WIDO.

12268   GROUP II/42

BERLIN to ?

RSS 779/7/10/41

PMK on 8420 kcs. 1919 GMT 6/10/41

No.3. For ILLU. Employment of SCHRUMPF as an agent [V-mann] in EGYPT is not possible. More express information is necessary as to whether it may possibly be desired that he stay for a short time with N B O. In the case of a negative reply SCHRUMPF will immediately return to his ambulance [text: SAN] formation.

No.F 1349/41

ANGELO.

12270   GROUP II/42

BERLIN to ?

RSS 935/8/10/41

PMK on 8420 kcs. 0620 GMT 8/10/41

[No.4.] For ILLU. SEMMEL communicates:-

1) Plan for journey, with points* has been despatched.

2) Fahrtdienstleiter [? = officer in/c journey] will issue further detailed instructions next week.

3) Passengers E and S in MUNICH, are being trained and fitted out with clothing. Can be sent for at any time.

4) WEBER is not suitable for the operation planned.

5) DIETRICH has arrived.

6) RAMSES finally settled

No.F/1355/41.

ANGELO 129.

12276   GROUP II/42

? to BERLIN

RSS 155/9/10/41

DKU ? on 8050 kcs. 1929 GMT 6/10/41

24556   GROUP II/25

TRIPOLI to BERLIN

RSS 28/8/4/42

ZGA on 11,950 kcs. 1615 GMT 7/4/42

No.5. To ANGELO.

1) Ref. your 10. Send 1 copy of each English novel to ADOLF, the rest here.

2) When does the money asked for PIT and PAN arrive ?

3) Could Amtschef's special plane bring DARLING?

SAMMLAARA.

25015   GROUP II/25

TRIPOLI to BERLIN

RSS 166/3/4/42

? on 11,980 kcs. 1614 GMT 2/4/42

No.29. To ANGELO. In SALAM's absence I confirm receipt of message 6 [?] 13.

SEPP.

25041   GROUP II/25

BERLIN to TRIPOLI

RSS 293/16/4/42

WPA on 8430 kcs. 1635 GMT 14/4/42

No.9. Also for SALAM. Ref. your W/T messages 10 and 11 of 13/4. ZF can supply either 3 cases of tobacco or 1 case and 5 packets of tobacco in gold for PIT and PAN. Which is preferred?

ANGELO. No 331.

25061   GROUP II/25

TRIPOLI to BERLIN

RSS 227/16/4/42

FEJ on 7800 kcs. at 1745 GMT 15/4/42

No.14 to ANGELO. Books received. Has 1 of each been sent to ADOLF ? Please send 3 cases of tobacco in paper; I should like to leave on the 20th.

SALAM.

25062   GROUP II/25

BERLIN to TRIPOLI

RSS 98/16/4/42

WPA on 8410 kcs. at 1759 GMT 15/4/42

No.12 for SALAM. DARLING left today with RITA 72.

ANGELO 382.

25063   GROUP II/25

BERLIN to TRIPOLI

RSS 127/17/4/42

WPA on 8415 kcs. at 1652 GMT 15/4/42

No.13. For SALAM. Running expenses sent off today by RITA 73.

ANGELO. 416.

25064   GROUP II/25

BERLIN to TRIPOLI

RSS 126/17/4/42

WPA on 8415 kcs. at 1656 GMT 16/4/42

No.14. For SALAM. In accordance with ZF, withholding of 42.08 RM from EPPLER's pay because of telephone charges is requested.

ANGELO. 419.

25164   GROUP II/25

BERLIN to TRIPOLI

RSS 13/18/4/42

WPA on 8500 kcs. at 1652 GMT 17/4/42

No.15. For SALAM. Ref. your message of 14 of the 15/4. One copy of each was sent from our end to ADOLF on the 14/4.

ANGELO 445.

25274   GROUP II/25

BERLIN to TRIPOLI

RSS 79/10/3/42

OWN on 13300 kcs. 1612 GMT 4/3/42

No.1. For SALAM. Deduct Rm. 65.03 from payments to MORITZ, and Rm. 107.69 from payments to MAX for bills found in apartment. Statement following by courier. Account will be cleared by ZF.

ANGELO. 81.

25275   GROUP II/25

BERLIN to TRIPOLI

RSS 127/6/3/42

OWN on 13300 kcs. 1604 GMT 5/3/42

No.2. Service message. Is Sonderkommando Hptm. BLAICH known at your end? If so, please forward following message: "possibly via Heeresfunkstelle TRIPOLI to Gefr. WICHMANN. Officers and complement of Betriebstelle send heartiest congratulations on decoration received."

TRAUTMANN, Major.

25283   GROUP II/25

BERLIN to TRIPOLI

RSS 102/15/4/42

WPA on 8430 kcs. 1645 GMT 14/4/42

No.8. For SALAM. Ref. your message no.10 of 13/4. English books dispatched on 10/4 by RITA no.71. "DARLING"* follow as soon as they arrive at this end.

ANGEO 320.

[* Evidently plural].

25309   GROUP II/25

TRIPOLI to BERLIN

RSS 44/6/4/42

ZGA on 11980 kcs. 1620 GMT 5/4/42

No.3. To ANGELO. English key books from ATHENS requested from your end on the 14/2 have not yet arrived here. Request dispatch to our end by flying courier of 6 copies of PENGUIN, ALBATROSS or TAUCHNITZ, as they are unobtainable here.

SALAM.

25330   GROUP II/25

BERLIN to TRIPOLI

RSS 162/3/4/42

WPA on 8500 kcs. 1618 GMT. 2/4/42

No.1. Also for SALAM. Amtschef will arrive by special aircraft in TROLI about noon on 10th April. WIDO and SALAM are to present themselves at HOFRA* office at 15 hours on the 10th., and to make a report to the Amtschef on their sphere of work.

ANGELO 6.

[* = HOFFMEISTER III F office TRIPOLI]

25331   GROUP II/25

BERLIN to TRIPOLI

RSS 27/8/4/42

WPA on 8515 kcs. 1611 GMT. 7/4/42

No.5. For SALAM. Ref. our W/T message No. 10 of 1/4. Seeing that ATHENS only had TAUCHNITZ books, 4 English novels were obtained from another source on one occasion, and 5 more on another occasion. Please radio at once whether we are to send them all to your end.

ANGELO. 134.

25332   GROUP II/25

TRIPOLI to BERLIN

RSS 46/20/4/42

FRJ on 7870 kcs. 1643 GMT. 19/4/42

No.17. To ANGELO. Request as soon as possible information about transport of FORD car promised from NAPLES. Try to obtain urgent shipment order for shipment station [Verladestelle] NAPLES from competent authority.

SALAM. WIDO.

22/4/42 ISOS 25418 – 25436

25422   GROUP II/25

BERLIN to TRIPOLI

RSS 149/21/4/42

WPA on 8580 kcs. 1612 GMT 20/4/42

No.16. For SALAM. Ref. our W/T message 445 of 17/4. [ISOS 25164]. Has ADOLF to be given further details from this end ?

ANGELO No.524.

23/4/42 ISOS 25495 – 25524

25498   GROUP II/25

BERLIN to TRIPOLI

RSS 138/12/4/42

WPA on 8420 kcs. 1606 GMT 11/4/42

No.6. Also for SALAM. Ref. WIDO message No. 7 and No.5 point 2. [ISOS 24556] Wish of PIT and PAN has no foundation in agreements to hand at this end. Discuss matter further with Oberst. MAURER.

ANGELO 209.

25499   GROUP II/25

BERLIN to TRIPOLI

RSS 78/23/4/42

WPA on 8415 kcs. 1620 GMT 22/4/42

No.17. Ref. your W/T message 18 of 19/4. HAECKEL probably arriving 10th May. Exact date to follow.

ANGELO No. 590.

23/4/42 ISOS 25662 – 25687

25664   GROUP II/25

TRIPOLI to BERLIN

RSS 80/23/4/42

DNZ on 12925 kcs. 1644 GMT 22/4/42

No. 23. To ANGELO. Please complete dispatch of FORD car from NAPLES if possible at the latest by 10/5. Until then security of transport guaranteed by actions of the 10th Fliegerkorps. Details concerning this matter are to be ascertained from the competent Stellen in BERLIN.

WIDO.

28/4/42 ISOS 25855 – 25876

25857   GROUP II/25

BERLIN to TRIPOLI

RSS 169/26/4/42

WPA on 8490 kcs. 1650 GMT 25/4/42

No.19. Ref. your W/T messages 17, 23, 25. Despatch of car will take place when missing tool has been obtained.

ANGELO. No. 682.

1/5/42 ISOS 26121 – 26145

26122   GROUP II/25

BERLIN to TRIPOLI

RSS 166T/30/4/42

WPA on 8405 kcs. 1610 GMT 29/4/42

No.22. As 5 cars were ordered originally, 5 are now also to be loaded after their arrival in NAPLES. Urgency was made clear and arrangements made accordingly [?].

ANGELO no.772.

4/5/42 ISOS 26310 – 26324

26310   GROUP II/25

TRIPOLI to BERLIN

RSS 38/3/5/42

KVG on 8160 kcs. 1621 GMT 2/5/42

No.1. To ANGELO. Ref. your 27. Libyan SIM has persuaded Amtschef to arrange for British prisoners captured by the Panzerarmee to be interrogated by the Libyan SM as well. Before the decision was made in SCHLOSS I had pinted out in W/T message 02374 that I have learned from an unexceptionable source that British prisoners are made to talk by coercive measures contrary to international law at the Libyan SIM. I considered this warning to be necessary because the result might possibly be retaliatory measures against German prisoners of war in English hands.

DIWO.

4/5/42 ISOS 26385 – 26398

26386   GROUP II/25

BERLIN to TRIPOLI

RSS 80/21/2/42

CWN on 13300 kcs. 1603 GMT 20/2/42

No.7. Wachtm. VON STEFFENS left for ROME on 18th February with 5 W/T operators, all drivers, and a great quantity of equipment. Arrival in ROME on 20/2 assured. Immediate transport to TRIPOLI has been arranged. STEFFENS has assignment to use the air-route with MAX and MORITZ and W/T set. Inform ALMASY of this.

ANGELO 557.

26497   GROUP II/25

TRIPOLI to BERLIN

RSS 134/4/5/42

KVG on 8170 kcs. 1655 GMT 29/4/42

No.29.In re FORD car. Ship at once. Will collect tools at this end; send your tools by courier later on. Present moment favorable for shipment. Car urgently required at this end.

WIDO.

26524   GROUP 0/153

? to ?

RSS 38/7/4/42

HGS 8930 kcs 0811 GMT 27/3/42

No.2.[?] I.C. [=Intelligence Officer] vehicles ready in about 9 [or 10] days. Shall arrive at the forward position [verne] in my own car on Monday or Tuesday. Has SPRIT gone to GIALO [?] Please obtain 2 Identity Cards [sic anglice] of Egyptian origin.

SALAM.

26525   GROUP 0/153

? to ?

RSS 258/12/4/42

HGS 8930 kcs 1412 GMT 2/4/42

In enciphering take only the outside letters. The indented ones are omitted. Had to ask for repeats of both W/T messages yesterday. Cannot hear anything on frequency 1 or 2 but great interference. Why have you not transmitted for 2 days [?]

26885   GROUP II/25

TRIPOLI to BERLIN

RSS 47/9/5/42

KVG on 8150 kcs. 1626 GMT 8/5/42

No.4. To ANGELO. Contact established with SCHULZ-KAMPFHENKEL on 8/5.

WIDO.

27100   GROUP II/25

BERLIN to TRIPOLI

RSS 34/12/5/42

WPA on 8500 kcs 1612 GMT 11/5/42

No.7. Leutnant HAEUSGEN at I c of the Panzerarmee has assignment to establish contact with WIDO at next opportunity. HAEUSGEN has taken over as successor to HOESCH. Please report approximately when HAEUSGEN is to establish contact with WIDO.

ANGELO. 271.

27252   GROUP II/25

BERLIN to TRIPOLI

RSS 17/14/5/42

WPA on 8500 kcs 1605 GMT 13/5/42

No.8. Ref. SALAM.

1) ADOLF has only the W/T traffic plan sent over by the Panzerarmee AFRICA. It contains only the frequencies, call signs and transmission times for traffic between SALAM, SCHILDKROETE, and OTTER. ADOLF has not been provided for in this plan and cannot undertake traffic by it. ADOLF has only received the English books.

2) Request therefore dispatch by return of the necessary instructions. For reasons of camouflage in several W/T messages if possible.

Who are SCHILDKROETE and OTTO ?

ANGELO. No. 300

27253   GROUP II/25

BERLIN to TRIPOLI

RSS 72/14/5/42

WPA 8500 kcs 1747 GMT 13/5/42

No.10. Agent [V-Mann] BRETON carefully trained, is intended for employment [as an agent] dropped by parachute in the CHAD area. HECKEL wishes to see the operation through. Previous acclimatization essential. Agent [V-Mann] has worked as a missionary in EQUATORIAL AFRICA for 10 years. Please inform me immediately as to when BRETON can arrive at your end.

ANGELO. No.320.

27401   GROUP II/25

BERLIN to TRIPOLI

RSS 21/15/5/42

WPA 8450 kcs 1625 GMT 13/5/42

No.9. Ref. SALAM. Please inform me immediately by W/T whether it has already been possible to establish connection with SALAM.

ANGELO. 301.

27443   GROUP II/25

TRIPOLI to BERLIN

RSS 96/16/5/42

KVG on 8150 kcs 1643 GMT 15/5/42

No.10. Service message to ADOLF. With regard to the supervision of SALAM. W/T traffic undertaking as from 12th May. Two-way W/T traffic SALAM-OTTER. 1st to 4th day, traffic times 1200, 2100. 5th to 24th day, 0700, 1430, 2100. Call signs, cipher, and frequency according to traffic plan.

27445   GROUP II/25

TRIPOLI to BERLIN

RSS 94/16/5/42

KVG on 8150 kcs 1708 GMT 15/5/42

No.13. To ANGELO. Ref. your 300 and 301. According to instructions and W/T plan no direct W/T traffic SALAM with WIDO is provided for, expressly and despite frequent consultation. WIDO is merely called in to listen to the SALAM traffic together with [us].

SCHILDKROETE, DIWO. Greetings.

27484   GROUP II/25
         TRIPOLI to BERLIN
         RSS 95/16/5/42
         KVG on 8150 kcs. 1657 GMT 15/5/42

         No.11. Continuation to No.10. Moreover OTTER will stand by to receive for 10 minutes 1st to 4th day 0700 hrs., 1000 hrs, 1600 hrs, 1900 hrs; 5th to 24th day 1000 hrs, 1600 hrs, 1900 hrs.
         SCHILDKROETE.

27621   GROUP II/25
         TRIPOLI to BERLIN
         RSS 40T/19/5/42
         KVG on 8150 kcs. 1926 GMT 18/5/42

         No.17. To ANGELO. On 17/5 Oberstltn. HECKEL and Staff were introduced to SAHARA Command in HUN*. I am flying on the 19th or 20th in an Italian machine to SEBHA. From SEBHA I am traveling via MUK** with Tenente MASSA as far as the Northern edge of TIBESTI for the purpose of "setting down" [Absetzen] and interrogating a number of TEBBU workers [Arbeiter].
         WODI.

         Note:
         *   = HON, a leading Italian SAHARA station
         ** = MURZUK

27622   GROUP II/25
         TRIPOLI to BERLIN
         RSS 39/19/5/42
         KVG on 8150 kcs. 2007 GMT 18/5/42

         No.18. To ANGELO. Ref. your enquiries "worker" [Arbeiter] BRETON. Await arrival of HECKEL in SCHLOSS.
         WODI.

27639   GROUP II/25
         BERLIN to TRIPOLI
         RSS 38/19/5/42
         WPA 8450 kcs. 1918 GMT 18/5/42

         No.11. HAEUSGEN discussion not until the 2nd half of June.
         ANGELO No.452.

27806   GROUP II/25
         TRIPOLI to BERLIN
         RSS 106/21/5/42
         KVG on 8145 kcs. 1907 GMT 20/5/42

         No.22. To ANGELO. SALAM reports arrival in GILF KEBIR.
         For C.O., HOLZ[BRECHER]

27911 GROUP II/25

TRIPOLI to BERLIN

RSS 54/7/3/42

ZGA on 11960 kcs. 1600 GMT 4/3/42

No.5. To ANGELO. I propose that if possible an aeroplane from undertaking SCHULZ KAMPFHENKEL be sent to this end now so that I may have means of moving about for long distances especially important at the moment. DIWO.

28137 GROUP II/25

TRIPOLI to BERLIN

RSS 65/25/5/42

KVC on 8170 kcs. 1654 GMT 29/4/42

No.29. To ANGELO. After more delays SALAM states today that he is ready to start. WDO.

28192 GROUP 0/161

WESTERN DESERT AREA

RSS 144/25/5/42

WEW on 7570 kcs. 0808 GMT 13/5/42

Service message. To HOL[ZBRECHER]. Please tell me whether you have [W/T] communication with SCHLOSS and ADOLF. Please answer.

Best wishes. WEB.

28193 GROUP 0/161

WESTERN DESERT AREA

RSS 142/25/5/42

WEW on 7570 kcs. 1428 GMT 13/5/42

Continuation. Besides this OTTER is to stand ready to receive for 10 minutes 1st to 4th day [at] 0700, 1000, 1400, 1600, 1900. On 5th – 24th day 1000, 1600, 1900. SCHILDKROETE

[Note. = ISOS 27494 and last half of ISK 8739]

28194 GROUP 0/161

WESTERN DESERT AREA

RSS 141/25/5/42

WEW on 7570 kcs. 0818 GMT 14/5/42

No.3. To WIDO. ABWEHR BERLIN is not informed as to the situation up to date of undertaking SALAM from here as there is no communication with SCHLOSS. It is ADOLF's or SALAM's duty to inform [SCHLOSS]. Is Ic [Intelligence Officer] listening in [mithoert] ?

28195 GROUP 0/162

WESTERN DESERT AREA

RSS 190/25/5/42

MAR on 8930 kcs. 1811 GMT 3/5/42

No.18. To Ic. Arrived safely in GIALO. SALAM.

28196   GROUP 0/162
                WESTERN DESERT AREA
                RSS 194/25/5/42
                [MAR to ?] WEB on 7570 kcs. 0923 GMT 14/5/42

No.4. Aeroplane is not to start until my return.
SALAM.

28197   GROUP 0/162
                WESTERN DESERT AREA
                RSS 193/25/5/42
                WEB on 7570 kcs. 0919 GMT 14/5/42

No.18. To SALAM. Impossible to place W/T operator in GIALO. Convert W/T link with Ic immediately to direct traffic with SCHILDKROETE, since present state of affairs is intolerable. Be sure to keep up the agreed traffic times. You must press on again with the operation [Unternehmen] with the utmost speed.
Ic. Please confirm receipt.

28198   GROUP 0/166
                WESTERN DESERT AREA
                RSS 198/25/5/42
                ETI on 8930 kcs. 1923 GMT 13/5/42

5. To Ic. Please send a first class W/T operator to GIALO with utmost despatch. Preliminary instruction in 4 watt set by WEBER.
SALAM.

28199   GROUP 0/166
                WESTERN DESERT AREA
                RSS 201/25/5/42
                IHC on 8140 kcs. 1010 GMT 14/5/42

No.3. Reconnaissance a/c have found nothing at the place reported. Please let us know your present position and further orders.
OTTER.

28/5/42 ISOS 28264 – 28289

28267   GROUP II/25
                BERLIN to TRIPOLI
                RSS 52/27/5/42
                WPA 8480 kcs. 1923 GMT 26/5/42

No.14. HAECKEL left for TRIPOLI on 23rd by 'plane. He has given appropriate orders concerning WIDO vehicles. He is, therefore, able to supply information personally about the WIDO W/T message of 23/5.
ANGELO 655.

28/5/42 ISOS 28308 – 28316

28316   GROUP 0/162
                W. DESERT AREA
                RSS 190/27/5/42
                MAR on 8140 kcs. 0756 GMT 6/5/42

No.1. To Ic. Contrary to Italian maps there is an impassable zone of dunes south-east of GIALO. After reconnoitering southwards and setting up depots I returned today to GIALO. I shall fly tomorrow with the Italians on air reconnaissance to determine a new route. Departure from GIALO accordingly will probably be on Saturday. If the entire zone is impassable I shall travel via KUFRA through territory known to me.
SALAM.

28335   GROUP 0/162/E

WESTERN DESERT AREA

RSS 189/25/5/42

WEB to MAR on 7570 kcs. 1841 GMT 2/5/42

No 17. To Ic. Departure AGEDABIA 6 [repeated] hours 3rd.
SALAM.

28336   GROUP 0/162/E

WESTERN DESERT AREA

RSS 189/25/5/42

MAR to WEB on 8140 kcs. 1606 GMT 4/5/42

Service message. To SCHILDKR. I accept your proposals with thanks. Evening reception here is almost impossible owing to 2 powerful transmitters. Best wishes.
OTTER.

28337   GROUP 0/162/E

WESTERN DESERT AREA

RSS 191/25/5/42

MAR to WEB on 8930 kcs. 1607 GMT 4/5/42

No.19. To I c. OTTER will remain in GIALO. SALAM traffic with SCHILDKROETE daily 9, 15, 2030 hrs. Starting on Tuesday.
SALAM.

28338   GROUP 0/166/E

WESTERN DESERT AREA

RSS 149/27/5/42

? on 8150 kcs. 1030 GMT 6/5/42

No.1. Flyer's report. 1230 with 2 starts no ground visibility*.
[*Note: Erdsicht, normally Boden-sicht.]

28339   GROUP 0/162/E

WESTERN DESERT AREA

RSS 188/27/5/42

MAR to WEB on 8145 kcs. 1339 GMT 8/5/42

No.2. To Ic. Air-reconnaissance established possibility of passing dune region north-east of BIRSIGEN. Am leaving GIALO on Sunday on KUFRA-track [Piste?]. Between GIALO and COT[E] 190 North-East POSTOTRUCCHI no fresh enemy tracks.

28340   GROUP 0/162/E

WESTERN DESERT AREA

RSS 192/25/5/42

MAR on 8040 kcs. 1850 GMT 9/5/42

Service message. Request traffic with WIDO daily 1830 hrs. Here frequency 1, call-sign SPY. Pass frequency and callsign WIDO.
OTTER.

28341   GROUP 0/166/E

WESTERN DESERT AREA

RSS 199/25/5/42

ETI to MIR on 8930 kcs. 1930 GMT 13/5/42

No.3. To Ic. Dune region east GIALO track impassable. One car has fallen out on account of damage to gears. Am reorganizing the undertaking via ZIGHEN and OSMWXUG CUFRA HERT [?] to the CUFRA GILFKEBIR KHARGA route known to me.

SALAM.

28342   GROUP 0/162/E

WESTERN DESERT AREA

RSS 195, 200, 202/25/5/42

WEB to MAR on 7570 kcs. 1314 GMT 14/5/42

ETI to MIR 8140 kcs. 1955 GMT 13/5/42

IMA to IHC on 8140 kcs. 1039 14/5/42

No.2. To Kommando GIALO. Have damage to gears 63km. on [line] 80 degrees magnetic from KOTE 155 of the PALIFICATA. To-morrow I shall attempt to reach Campo 3. Return possibly with 2 cars GIALO.

SALAM.

28343   GROUP 0/162/E

WESTERN DESERT AREA

RSS 196/27/5/42

WEB to MAR on 8140 kcs. 0719 GMT 15/5/42

No.6. To Kmdo GIALO. One motor-vehicle is driving from Kampo 4. T GIALO on the 15th. If it does not arrive by 16th please [send] help by air along PALIFICATA. The remaining [vehicles] are driving as far as kilometre 415 on PALIFICATA and to the east past CUFRA to-morrow. Pass what is known about the enemy at ZIGHEN without fail at 7 hrs to-morrow. Noch heute fliege Fragen [?].

SALAM.

28344   GROUP 0/162/E

WESTERN DESERT AREA

RSS 195/27/5/42

MAR to WEB on 8140 kcs. 1318 GMT 15/5/42

Service message. I propose an additional traffic period 0600 for the purpose of passing urgent message. Please answer at 2030.

OTTER.

28345   GROUP 0/162/E

WESTERN DESERT AREA

RSS 193/27/5/42

MAR on 8140 kcs. 1613 GMT 15/5/42

No.4. To German Consulate through Ic and VAA for ENTHOLT or STEFFENS. Have MANSUETI fit-up the gears of JOBISCHKA and [forward] immediately by plane to GIALO. Also [send] a charged FORD model battery.

BEILHARZ[?].

28405   GROUP 0/162

W. DESERT AREA

RSS 197/27/5/42

PEI/MAR on 8150 kcs. 0730 GMT 6/5/42

No.1. To IC. Start on the 5th at 0830.

SALAM.

28432   GROUP II/25

TRIPOLI to BERLIN

RSS 201/27/5/42

KVG on 8170 kcs. 1623 GMT 15/5/42

No.12. To ANGELO. Ref. your 300.

SCHILDKROETE is Ic Panserarmee AFRIKA.

OTTER is fuel depot SEPP[?].

DOWI.

28433   GROUP II/25

TRIPOLI to BERLIN

RSS 199/27/5/42

KUG on 8170 kcs. 1612 GMT 15/5/42

No.14. To ANGELO. Ref. your 320. Cannot answer until after consultation with HECKEL Friday earliest.

WIDO.

28434   GROUP II/25

BERLIN to TRIPOLI

RSS 135/28/5/42

WPA on 8450 kcs. 2012 GMT 27/5/42

No.16. Ref. motor-vehicles WIDO. FERI informs us to-day: WIDO's motor-vehicles were already intended for loading and have been relegated on account of present events. Until these events have run their course loading is improbable.

ANGELO. 700.

28495   GROUP 0/161

ZUARA-NALUT to ?

RSS 135/29/5/42

EAF on 8670 kcs. 1445 GMT 4/5/42

No.4. To OTTER. Calls as [agreed] with OTTER in TROLI at the time.

HOL.

28496   GROUP 0/162

TRIPOLI to SALAM

RSS 336/29/5/42

WEB on 7570 kcs. 0728 GMT 11/5/42

[No.4.] To OTTER. Calls as [agreed] with OTTER in TROLI at the time.

HOL.

28497   GROUP 0/162

? to TRIPOLI

RSS 136/29/5/42

MAR on 8140 kcs. 1314 GMT 16/5/42

No.2. Motor vehicles arrived safely. Despite inquiries to Obermdo. through ZIGHEN airmen have not succeeded in discovering anything.

OTTER.

30/5/42 ISOS 28500 – 28513

28512   GROUP 0/162/E

TRIPOLI to SALAM

RSS 335/29/5/42

WEB to MAR on 8140 kcs. 0718 GMT 11/5/42

No.17. To OTTER. Did SALAM start yesterday as planned?

I C.

28513   GROUP 0/162/E

SALAM to TRIPOLI

RSS 334/29/5/42

MAR on 8115 kcs. 1817 GMT 25/5/42

No.5. To I C. SALAM's new route via CUFRA track, 51 kms. North of CUFRA in the direction of GILF. If critical SALAM will not transmit for 3 days before and after reaching destination.

30/5/42 ISOS 28524 – 28552

28552   GROUP 0/166/E

WESTERN DESERT AREA

RSS 196/25/5/42

MIR on 8140 kcs. 1016 GMT 13/5/42

No.1. To SALAM. SEPP left by air to-day. Evening traffic by newly erected W/T station almost impossible. Change of position to-day.

OTTER.

31/5/42 ISOS 28553 – 28577

28577   GROUP 0/162

JALO to CYRENAICA

RSS 181/30/5/42

MAR on 8150 kcs. 1820 GMT 23/5/42

No.5. To Ic. Urgently need 40 drums of petrol.

SALAM[?].

31/5/42 ISOS 28608 – 28630

28630   GROUP 0/162/E

WESTERN DESERT AREA

RSS 42/31/5/42

WEB to MAR on 8140 kcs. 1323 GMT 11/5/42

Service message. I enquire whether traffic times in accordance with traffic plan and whether direct traffic between SALAM and SCHILDKROETE in accordance with message of 4th May have lapsed.

SCHILDKROETE.

28637   GROUP 0/162

WESTERN DESERT AREA

RSS 44/31/5/42

MAR on 7570 kcs. 1412 GMT 11/5/42

No.2. To WIDO. SALAM has returned to GIALO on account of difficulties of terrain. Intended to start again yesterday, after reconnoitering new route. No information about this yet.

I C.

28638   GROUP 0/162

WESTERN DESERT AREA

RSS 43/31/5/42

MAR to WEB 8140 kcs. 1327 GMT 11/5/42

No.3. To I c. 240 deposited at depot.

SALAM.

28639   GROUP 0/162

WESTERN DESERT AREA

RSS 45-6/31/5/42

MAR to WEB 8140 kcs. 0722 GMT 12/5/42

Service message. No direct traffic SALAM – SCHILDKROETE. Traffic OTTER – SCHILDKROETE at the same times as before. Please also listen in to OTTER – SALAM traffic from 12th, first day of traveling, onwards, since reception of SALAM here often suffers heavy interferences. Traffic times: 1st to 4th day 1200, 2100. 5th to 24 day 0700, 1200, 1430, 2100. In addition OTTER will be ready to receive for 10 minutes: 1st to 4th day 1000, 1600, 1900. Frequencies according to traffic plan.

28640   GROUP 0/162

WESTERN DESERT AREA

RSS 48/31/5/42

MAR on 8140 kcs. 0718 GMT 19/5/42

4. To I c. No link SALAM – OTTER since 15th. STRINGMANN and BEILHARZ left SALAM at 0700 on the 15th at Campo 5 on the KUFRA track. Reason for falling out: gear damage to leading car.

28684   GROUP 0/162 E

WESTERN DESERT AREA

RSS 189/27/5/42

EIP/MAR on 8150 kcs. 1326 GMT 6/5/42

No 1. To I c. SALAM is returning to GIALO on Wednesday evening with 3 cars and 8 men.

28685   GROUP 0/162 E

WESTERN DESERT AREA

RSS 47/31/5/42

MAR to WEB on 7570 kcs. 1311 GMT 17/5/42

Service message. Message [of the] 15th evidently misunderstood. I meant 0600 in the morning. Best wishes.

OTTER.

28686   GROUP 0/162
           WESTERN DESERT AREA
           RSS 141/31/5/42
           WEB to MAR on 7570 kcs. 1330 GMT 19/5/42

           No.2. SALAM-SCHILDKROETE communication exists. SALAM radioed yesterday evening, everything in order there. BEILHARZ is not to follow [by car] under any circumstances, unless he receives instructions.
           I c.

28687   GROUP 0/162 E
           WESTERN DESERT AREA
           RSS 49/31/5/42
           MAR to WEB on 8140 kcs. 0725 GMT 19/5/42

           Continuation. Gears taken out [?] of BEILHARZ car, put into leading car. SALAM's new route BIRZIGHEN – 50 km. north of CUFRA – GILF – destination.
           BEILHARZ.
           [For preceding part see ISOS 28640]

2/6/42 ISOS 28735 – 28777

28776   GROUP 0/162 E
           WESTERN DESERT AREA
           RSS 151/1/6/42
           WEB to MAR on 7570 kcs. at 1315 GMT 18/5/42

           No.2. To OTTER. News of whereabouts of SALAM urgently requested.
           I c

28777   GROUP 0/162/E
           WESTERN DESERT AREA
           RSS 231/1/6/42
           MAR to WEB on 8140 kcs. at 1837 GMT 25/5/42

           [possibly continuation of ISOS 28513]
           Cont'd. BEILHARZ assignment: to bring back car which has broken down to GIALO after it has been repaired and on SALAM's return set up petrol dump [at] Campo 5. Duration of SALAM's journey from 15th about [?] 16 days there and back. If there is any incident SALAM will ask for aeroplane.
           BEILHARZ.

2/6/42 ISOS 28787 – 28807

28807   GROUP 0/161
           WESTERN DESERT AREA
           RSS 228/1/6/42
           WEW on 7570 kcs. 1435 GMT 20/5/42

           No.4. To WIDO. [In a] message of 14/5 SALAM reports that one motor-car has dropped out owing to damage to gears. He is re-routing the enterprise via ZIGHEN, since the dune region east of GIALO is impassable.
           I c.

28834   GROUP II/25

TRIPOLI to BERLIN

RSS 44/2/6/42

SCH on 8120 kcs. at 1910 GMT 31/5/42

No. 27. To ANGELO. Can we count upon SALAM vehicles, after his return, on account of the great shortage of vehicles. For the moment [I] consider this to be the only solution. If vehicles are not completely ready for service please give me a WAKO voucher for TUNA in order to have 2 suitable vehicles purchased with the Purchasing Commission YORK there.

WODI.

29025   GROUP II/25

TRIPOLI to BERLIN

RSS 24/4/6/42

BHR on 8140 kcs. 1921 GMT 30/5/42

No.25. To ANGELO. From today continuing journey with the "GUDRUN-Stelle" as far as MU[RZU]K. After having given notice HOLZ will travel on with a view to revising the "GUDRUN-Stellen". WIDO will participate in a motorized and camel Patrol to RAI* and South-West towards TIBESTI for the purpose of utilizing the SENIOR-Service. Inform A D** that WIDO can be reached via MUK with the help of the Italian GUDRUN – Stellen, from where [messages] will be forwarded as required. WIDO can further be reached via own*** GUDRUN-Stelle with the assistance of Italian GUDRUN-Stellen which may be interpolated [eingeschaltat].

Signed DIWO.

* Probably an abbreviation like MUK.

** Probably Aussenddienstelle ROME under Obstltn. HELFFERICH who passes GUDRUN messages to BERLIN.

*** Eigene: WIDO's or HOLZBRECHER's? It is possible that when messages are signed with an anagram of WIDO that they are sent in his absence.

29026   GROUP II/25

TRIPOLI to BERLIN

RSS 26/4/6/42

BHR on 8140 kcs. 1943 GMT 30/5/42

No.26. To ANGELO. [I] propose that you send secretary LANG off to NAPLES at once to put through shipment of vehicles. At the moment completely dependent on Italian help, which is detrimental to the SENIOR service.

WIDO.

29084   GROUP II/25

BERLIN to TRIPOLI

RSS 57B/5/6/42

WPA on 8480 kcs. 1911 GMT 4/6/42

1. SALAM returned to starting-point on 28th, assignment carried out. Can be reached through Consul at TRIPOLI.

ANGELO. 111.

29269   GROUP II/25

BERLIN to TRIPOLI

RSS 56/5/6/42

WPA on 8480 kcs. 1916 GMT 4/6/42

No.2. SALAM arrived on 2/6 at the consul's in TRIPOLI. Please establish contact at once by W/T. Confirm that this has been done.

ANGELO. 115.

29397   GROUP II/25

BERLIN to TRIPOLI

RSS 56/5/6/42

WPA on 8480 kcs. 1916 GMT 4/6/42

No.3. Contact is to be established at once with SALAM at the German Consulate TRIPOLI. You are to make sure with SALAM that W/T communication is taken up with CONDOR immediately also from the WIDO GUDRUN end. SALAM is to go immediately to Battle H.Q. Panzerarmee I C with W/T operator and set to report and take up W/T communication with CONDOR from there. Stellenleiter NIESE with HAEUSGEN must place himself at SALAM's disposal in order to start traffic with CONDOR working. SALAM and NIESE must see to it that terminal frequencies and callsigns for ADOLF-CONDOR traffic are sent to ADOLF. Report must be made when this has been carried out.

ANGELO. 153.

29834   GROUP II/25

TRIPOLI to BERLIN

RSS 114-14/6/42

TKN 7740 kcs. 2031 GMT 8/6/42

No.7. I separated from WIDO on 3/6. WIDO is on reconnaissance patrol, while I myself are in HUT [or: HAT]. GUDRUN to WIDO via Italian army W/T station. SALAM-WIDO communication possible during journey only through German army W/T stations TROLI and MUK. Please [pass] messages for SALAM to army W/T station TROLI, as I myself have no GUDRUN wth TROLI. GUDRUN with KONDOR not possible until after journey.

HOLZ. To ANGELO.

30172   GROUP 0/161

ZUARA to DERNA

RSS 190/16/6/42, 134/22/5/42

EAF on 8700 kcs. 1442 GMT 10/5/42

No.3. To I C. Ref. our FS 1 of 2/5. Is the present whereabouts of SALAM known at your end?

WIDO.

30713   GROUP II/25

ZUARA to BERLIN

RSS 258/21/6/42

? on 8670 kcs. at 1910 GMT 21/6/42

No.11. To ANGELO. After conversation with HAECKEL and consultation requested with Italian SAHARA Kommando, WIDO probably arriving TROLI on 21/6.

WODI.

30715   GROUP II/25

BERLIN to ZUARA

RSS 259/21/6/42

WPA on 8495 kcs. 1941 GMT 21/6/42

No.6. Ref. WIDO message 27 of 31.5. [ISOS 28834] Armistice Commission communicates. Liason officer TUNIS has radioed that purchasing commission is no longer working, as it has been dissolved, and therefore provision of car[s] through it is ruled out, particularly since the French would also no longer allow car[s] to be exported now that the work of the purchasing commission is over. Issuing laissez-passer for WIDO therefore does not arise.

ANGELO. 602.

30870   GROUP 0/162

GIALO to DERNA

RSS 196/18/6/42

? on ? ? GMT 15/5/42

Service message. To SCHILDKR[OETE]. Accept proposal with thanks. Evening reception here rendered almost impossible by 2 powerful transmitters.

Best wishes OTTER.

30871   GROUP 0/162

DERNA to GIALO

RSS 182/18/6/42

? on ? ? GMT 15/5/42

Service message. To OTTER. Keep to the following traffic times until further notice: 0630 and 1830.

SCHILDKR[OETE].

30872   GROUP 0/162

GIALO to DERNA

RSS 176/18/6/42

? on ? kcs. 1548 GMT 17/5/42

No.2. Motor vehicle arrived safely. Despite inquiries at Oberkdo. Airmen have discovered nothing about ZIGHEN.

OTTER.

WESTERN DESERT AREA

Note:- The following messages are uncertain as to date. They are believed, however, to have been sent in the main in the following order.

30873   [GROUP 0/162]

Probably on or before 4/5/42

From OTTER. Propose additional traffic time 0600 for passing urgent messages. Request reply.

30874   [GROUP 0/161]

Probably between 12 and 14/5/42, inclusive.

From WIDO. I listen only to SALAM during journey and only when I am not busy myself.

30875   [GROUP 0/166 via 0/162]

Probably between 12 and 14/5/42, inclusive.

From KONDOR. Please keep to 0900 and 1500 hours as constant traffic times, so that we do not keep losing each other.

30876   [GROUP 0/166 via 0/162]

Probably between 12 and 14/5/42, inclusive.

From SALAM. Tomorrow at 1500 hours SCHILDKR[OETE]/SALAM traffic. Call for 10min. Frequencies: SALAM 6457, SCHILDKR[OETE] 6410. SALAM CAR, SCKILDKR[OETE] SLK.

30877   [GROUP 0/166 via 0/162]

Probably between 12 and 14/5/42, inclusive.

From KONDOR. Am leaving today at midday. Shall not wireless before arriving at destination. Cross your fingers.

30878   [GROUP 0/166 via 0/162]

Probably between 12 and 14/5/42, inclusive.

From KONDOR. 048 VATERUNSER [?] traffic is to remain always as it is at present. Day-time traffic at 0900 hours TRIPOLI time. [Corrupt]. Only on journey call me in day-time as above. [Rest corrupt].

30879   [GROUP 0/162]

Probably on 14 or 15/5/42.

Service message. To OTTER. Enquire whether I should take up evening traffic with SALAM and forward any messages for OTTER at the end [of traffic period] as was done today. During supervision I can hear that SALAM – OTTER traffic is going very badly. Please answer 1800 [hours].

SCHILDKROETE

30880   [GROUP 0/162]

Probably on 15/5/42 or later.

If you are in touch with SALAM please pass at once that if [W/T] contact is not established, messages are to be sent blind. Similarly when calling [indication] is to be passed as to which frequency is to be answered on.

30881   [GROUP 0/162]

Probably 15/5/42 or later.

To OTTER. Agree to proposal. If and when you have any messages for SALAM let us have them for forwarding.

30882   [GROUP 0/162]

Probably 15/5/42 or later.

To SALAM. In the interest of the undertaking I am taking over direct traffic with SALAM. Have observed when listening in to SALAM – OTTER traffic that communication is very bad. 4 messages from yesterday OK. Have passed them on to OTTER.

30883   [GROUP 0/162]

Probably 15/5/42 or later.

To SALAM. I hereby acknowledge receipt of traffic-plan and 2 books. Thanks for letter.

30884   [GROUP 0/161]

Probably on 15/5/42 or later.

To WIDO. Have you communication with SCHLOSS and ADOLF? Please answer.

30885   [GROUP 0/161]

Probably later than 15/5/42.

To SALAM. Please use frequency I. SCHILDKROETE will also send on frequency I.

30886   [GROUP 0/161]

Probably later than 15/5/42.

To WIDO [?]. To HOLZBRECHER. Please keep to times 1000 and 1600 hours until cancellation so that we do not lose each other. Have you fixed [W/T] connection during the journey or you just "listen in" ?

30887   [GROUP [?]]

Probably later than 15/5/42.

To SALAM. Please inform SALAM's W/T operator that his "handwriting" shows room for improvement and that he still needs practice in taking down from interception, because traffic of this sort is cruelty to animals.

30888   [GROUP 0/161]

Probably after 15/5/42.

To WIDO. I hereby confirm receipt of the new frequency. Please [permit] main frequency as drawn up. Frequency 1 times days at 1600 until traffic is working properly. I shall transmit on frequency 6 7560, call sign WEW.

30889   [GROUP 0/[?]]

Probably after 15/5/42.

To SALAM. Request test traffic with SALAM today, both ends transmitting frequency 2 as in [W/T] traffic plan. Call-signs as proposed. Test traffic with OTTER today at 1800 in accordance with traffic plan both ends frequency 1. Call-signs thus: SALAM MAR, here WEB. Please stay till traffic is satisfactory.

25/6/42 ISOS 30982 - 30986

30984   GROUP 0/161

DERNA t o ?

RSS 183/18/6/42

? on ? kcs. ? GMT 20/5/42

No.3. To OTTER. Consul in TRIPOLI reports departure of ENTHOLT and STEFFENS for Germany. I have had the gears taken down. Will be dispatched in a few days together with the battery to GIALO.

I c.

30986   GROUP 0/162

GIALO to DERNA

RSS 206/18/6/42

- on -kcs. - GMT 15/5/42

Service message. Propose additional traffic time at 0600 hours for forwarding urgent messages. Please answer [at] 2030.

OTTER.

27/6/42 ISOS 31202 - 31216

31214   GROUP II/474/E

STUTTGART to LIBYA

RSS 2/22/6/42

FLG on 8490 kcs. 2001 GMT 20/6/42.

For Oblt. NIESE. According to circumstances only listen in to traffic with KONDOR. Take greatest care where you are. Await further orders from this end.

RAS[EHORN]. 618.

31250   GROUP 0/161/E
RSS 189/18/6/42
? on ? kcs. ? GMT 19/5/42

No.5. To WIDO. SALAM reached GILF KEBIR on 18/5. Please keep ANGELO informed, since according to a message just received ADOLF is not listening-in.
Ic.

31253   GROUP 0/162 ?/E
RSS 167/18/6/42
? on ? kcs. ? GMT 30/5/42

No.5. To Ic. New route SALAM via KUFRA track 51 km. north of KUFRA, making for GILF. Territory known to SALAM. If things become critical SALAM will not use his wireless for [a period of] about 3 days before and after [reaching] objective.

31254   GROUP 0/167/E
RSS 197/18/6/42
? on ? kcs. ? GMT 14/5/42

No.18. To SALAM. No enemy reported [at] ZIGHEN.

31255   GROUP 0/167/E
RSS 186/18/6/42
? on ? kcs. ? GMT 19/5/42

No.19. To SALAM. For ALMASY. Consul TRIPOLI communicates:- ENTHOLT and STEFFENS have left for GERMANY. I Iave had gears dismantled. Leaving within the next few days together with batter [for] GIALO.
I c.

31256   GROUP 0/167/E
RSS 179/18/6/42
? on ? kcs. ? GMT 24/5/42

No.5. To I c. I urgently need 40 cans of petrol.
BEILHARZ.

31258   WESTERN DESERT GROUP
RSS 190/18/6/42
? on ? kcs. ? GMT 19/5/42

Dismantling of gears. BEILHARZ' car [is being] used [as] leading car. New course SALAM BIR ZIGHEN – 50 km north of KUFRA – objective GILF.
BEILHARZ.

31319   GROUP II/474/E
LIBYA to STUTTGART
RSS 98/27/6/42
LKJ on 8920 kcs. 2003 GMT 14/6/42.

For RUEDIGER. Forward via SONJA to RASEHORN. No clear conception at our end of sets employed. Set with Oblt. HAEUSGEN missing. W/T operators apparently captured. Prepare 2 good W/T men, not Uffz. BUSCH. I am all right. Greetings.
NIESE.

31320   GROUP II/474/E

LIBYA to STUTTGART

RSS 71/27/6/42

LKJ on 8920 kcs. 1957 GMT 17/6/42.

To SONJA. For Major RASEHORN. Forward at once. SCHILDKROETE has been captured with set and documents with emergency cipher. KONDOR not manned. Cannot work with them as documents presumably in enemy hands. Request instructions.

NIESE. Oblt.

29/6/42 ISOS 31365 - 31371

31367   GROUP II/25

ZUARA to BERLIN

RSS 64/28/6/42

GRM on 8100 kcs. 2004 GMT 27/6/42

No.18. To ANGELO. WIDO arrived ZUARA with Leutnant ROTHERT, for the purpose of direct communicaton DORA – WIDO – BRUNERO. Preferable that DORA undertaking be taken up with competent Italian Dienststellen; there are high, well founded hopes of close cooperation in the SAHARA with common exploitation [of material].

DOWI.

30/6/42 ISOS 31460 - 31464

31460   GROUP II/25

BERLIN to ZUARA

RSS 26/28/6/42

WPA on 8490 kcs. 2029 GMT 27/6/42

No.10. Ref. WIDO message No.13, of 25/6.

1) All SALAM vehicles will remain at WIDO's and are at his disposal.

2) Mother informed.

3) 200 DARLINGS for SALAM sent to consul [at] TROLI, remainder at ANGELO's.

4) Radio whether SALAM can be reached through WIDO and when SALAM is returning. SALAM's return in the near future is not very urgent.

ANGELO. No.820.

31461   GROUP II/25

ZUARA to BERLIN

RSS 63/28/6/42

GRM on 8130 kcs. 1942 GMT 27/6/42

No.17. To ANGELO. Ref. your 602. Entire WIDO car problem would be solved by SALAM's cars being handed over. As however spare parts and tyres cannot be obtained, a suitable vehicle would have to be for disposal for dismantling [zum Ausschlachten] also. In our opinion dispatch of NAPLES vehicles is not to be counted on for a long time if suitable and energetic steps are not taken by ANGELO Dienststelle. The Quartermaster at Ko[mmando] Rueck [waertiges Armee Gebiet] cannot understand delay in dispatch [from] NAPLES, as there must be space available for these few vehicles if insisted on with necessary energy.

DIWO.

31462   GROUP II/25

ZUARA to BERLIN

RSS 24/28/6/42

GRM on 8100 kcs. 2006 GMT 27/6/42

No.19. To ANGELO. 2 SALAM vehicles taken over, the other 5 are being repaired. Presence of SALAM in TROLI no longer required. However SALAM intends to remain in TROLI for about another 10 days. Radio if this is in agreement with your order about SALAM's making report in SCHLOSS at once.

WODI.

31463   GROUP II/25

ZUARA to BERLIN

RSS 25/28/6/42

GRM on 8100 kcs. 2012 GMT 27/6/42

No.20. To ANGELO. On taking over SALAM material [it has been found that] STEFFENS telescope is missing. Please investigate and ascertain.

WIDO.

31464   GROUP II/474/E

LIBYA to STUTTGART

RSS 97/27/6/42

LKJ on 8920 kcs. 2010 GMT 14/6/42

Am working with new set of OTTER's for ALMASY. Apply for new operator from BERLIN. After [his] arrival I shall return.

NIESE Obltn.

1/7/42 ISOS 31529 - 31564

31530   GROUP II/25

ZUARA to BERLIN

RSS 66/30/6/42

KMG on 8150 kcs. 1951 GMT 29/6/42

No. 25. To ANGELO. Gratefully welcome your decision [as to] SALAM car. Concerning the employment [Einsatz] and use [to which use it will be put] a proposal will follow through RITA. In this connection please consider that because of the lack of other means of transport and in consequence of long distances – now even almost up to the TIBESTI border – the transport of workman by own motor-vehicles is urgently necessary, therefore besides car for [my] own journey with wireless-operator, hand bag and interpreter, transport-vehicles for workmen also necessary.

WID[O].

4/7/42 ISOS 31780 - 31817

31780   GROUP II/25

BERLIN to ZUARA

RSS 111/3/7/42

WPA on 8490 kcs. 1505 GMT 2/7/42

2. Ref your message No.2. of 1/7/42. Cars remain exclusively at WIDO's disposal. Any other use is forbidden.

ANGELO. 62.

5/7/42 ISOS 31951 - 31965

31953   GROUP II/25

ZUARA to BERLIN

RSS 112/4/7/42

RMC on 8120 kcs. 1949 GMT 3/7/42

No.4. To ANGELO. Ref. your W/T message 6. Old parts forwarded to spare part depot of army M/T park TROLI, in accordance with permissions previously given. Receipt will follow through RITA.

DOWI.

6/7/42 ISOS 31966 - 31979

31977 GROUP I/474/E

LIBYA to STUTTGART

RSS 7/5/7/42

LEJ on 8920 kcs. 0439 GMT 28/6/42

162 DAIFN Schildkroetenpanzer

[No.162] For Major RASEHORN. Oblt. NIESE will arrive in BERLIN on Monday it is anticipated. KONDOR not heard to date.

OTTER.

7/7/42 ISOS 32054 - 32067

32062 GROUP II/474

STUTTGART AREA to LIBYA

RSS 121/6/7/42

FLG on 8480 kcs. at 0121 GMT 6/7/42

In a few days a representative of ADOLF will pay a visit in order to set up direct W/T traffic OTTER-ADOLF. ADOLF has been informed.

NIESE Oblt.

8/7/42 ISOS 32197 - 32208

32198 GROUP II/474

LIBYA to STUTTGART

RSS 72/7/7/42

LKT on 8920 kcs. 2234 GMT 20/6/42

For STAHNSDORF. OTTER HEIZTEIL [or: NETZTEIL?] defective. Temporarily patched up. Request delivery of a new HEIZTEIL [or: NETZTEIL?] with valves for OTTER, as valves and spare valves destroyed. Replacement is to be sent ROM to the courier stelle of OKH.

NIESE Oblt.

9/7/42 ISOS 32300 - 32321

32315 GROUP II/474

STUTTGART to LIBYA

RSS 72/9/7/42

FLG on 8450 kcs. 0032 GMT 30/6/42

To OTTER. Landed safely. Shall be in BERLIN tomorrow. If you need fresh supply of sets, please report. Best wishes to H.Q. Please transmit at 0200 hours G.S.T. only as reception is best at this end then.

32316 GROUP II/474

STUTTGART to LIBYA

RSS 73/9/7/42

FLG on 8500 kcs. 0034 GMT 8/7/42

From SCHLOSS No 6. From ADOLF No.52 for SONJA for OTTER. Wachtmeister NEISS will bring W/T and cipteh instructions ADOLF-OTTER to OTTER as quickly as possible. Until he arrives the following is to be observed:

[Contd. Not to hand]

32466   GROUP II/25

ZUARA to BERLIN

RSS 46/11/7/42

DNZ on 12,910 kcs. 0514 GMT 11/7/42

17. To ANGELO. On the occasion of impending visit to AFRICA by ANGELO please bring decorations for Maggiore BRUNERO and Tenente MASSA. Once again we are deeply indebted to both of them as WIDO is now incorporated with all plenary powers in the whole SENIOR Service inclusive of KUFRA. Please make urgent application as, apart from REVETRIA, no German decorations have so far been distributed among the SIM in LIBYA.

WODI.

32533   GROUP II/474

LIBYA to STUTTGART

RSS 108/12/7/42

LKJ on 8920 kcs. 0055 GMT 6/7/42

To STAHNSDORF for Oblt. NIESE. Present position 28 km. TOBRUK-BARDIA. New change of position pending. W/T operator and section of net-work [Netzteil] 90/40 to OQU TOBRUK. KONDOR not heard. Greetings

OTTER.

33204   GROUP II/25

ZUARA to BERLIN

RSS 75/21/7/42

RMG on 8125 kcs. 1945 GMT 20/7/42

26. To ANGELO. Which month seems most suitable to ANGELO for African journey? I again suggest that he should await development of situation in EGYPT, as he would then have far greater freedom of movement for journeys of inspection and collection of experiences.

State if in agreement.

DIWO.

33644   GROUP II/25

ZUARA to BERLIN

RSS 77/26/7/42

RMG on 8120 kcs. 1935 GMT 25/7/42

30. To ANGELO. At conversation with Inspector DEJIVE DRILLING CATANIA, the visit of WIDO to CATANIA subject t ANGELO's approval was discussed, in order to instruct the Ic air corps and air fleet there on the SENIOR situation in WIDO's area. If ANGELO approves I request the presence at it of ANGELO or Amtmann MAURER and previous orientation of FERI. Presence in CATANIA useful for WIDO also for purpose of initiating the dispatch of Ic reports at that end SENIOR to WIDO. Taking-up [Aufnahme] of GUDRUN planned. Visit arranged for 2nd half of August. If the WIDO discussion and the presence of ANGELO in CATANIA is possible I suggest that ANGELO should travel on to AFRICA and that our programme be carried out.

WIDO.

33825   GROUP II/25

BERLIN to ZUARA

RSS 33/28/7/42

WPA on 8460 kcs. 1401 GMT 27/7/42

No.11. The only possibility of getting 5 FORD cars to WIDO is for WIDO to arrange with Stab ROMMEL for these cars to be given first-grade priority and to inform the AFRICA transports section in ROME to this effect [rest corrupt].

33878   GROUP II/25

BERLIN to ZUARA

RSS 76/29/7/42

WPA on 8490 kcs. 0540 GMT 29/7/42

No.13. Ref. your message 30 of 25/7 MAURER agreed in principle to suggestion. Visit MAURER ANGELO arranged for September. Till then postpone the affair, but continue to cultivate relations with DRILLING, Inspector DEJIVE.

ANGELO. No.898..

34072   GROUP II/25

ZUARA to BERLIN

RSS 26/29/7/42

RMG on 8120 kcs. at 2004 GMT 26/7/42

34. To ANGELO. Ref. your 852. All efforts in this organisation have remained unavailing. At the moment it is more hopeless than ever. The decision made by ANGELO concerning the SALAM car has, however, solved all problems of movement with excellent effect. [Remaining 75 letters corrupt, signed]

DOWI.

ISK Transscripts

2441   GROUP II/26

BERLIN to ATHENS

RSS 65/18/2/42

GNU on 5545 kcs. 1841 GMT. 16/2/42

No.44. For AST. The Ic [Intelligence Officer] of Panzer-Armee AFRIKA urgently needs 2 novels in English, five copies of each, and containing above 200 pages. Please send such books by the next courier to Leutnant HAEUSGEN with the Ic of Panzer-Armee AFRIKA and inform us by W/T when such boks were sent.

No. F/2058 ANGELO – ANDREAS.

7165   GROUP II/26

ATHENS to BERLIN

RSS 53/1/5/42

SVA on 5685 kcs. 1922 GMT. 29/4/42

118. Urgent. Submit at once. For ANDREAS – HOEFLINGER. Ref. I H OST S 2484 of 13/4 and ADOLF-message 158 of 28/4. Telephone call requested by I H WEST Major SOELDER by telephone fruitless. Please answer by W/T as to explanation of the above mentioned affair which is not known to us, since in the meantime Most Secret 586 of 18/4 from Oberkommando AFRIKA has also arrived here with traffic plan ALMASY for undertaking SALAM. As [we have] no W/T connection ADOLF-AFRIKA direct explanation of the purpose of these [traffic] instructions which have been sent from AFRIKA was not possible.. L.I. No.161.

DISCH.

7395   GROUP II/26

ATHENS to BERLIN

RSS 23/30/4/42

SVA on 5700 kcs. 1836 GMT. 28/4/42

116. SCHLOSS for I H OST S. [a few words corrupt] Traffic plan SALAM SCHILDKROETE arrived at ADOLF yesterday. It is not possible to tell from the traffic plan for what purpose the [W/T] instructions were sent to ADOLF. Please inform at once. Ii No.158.

DISCH.

8739   GROUP II/26

BERLIN to ATHENS

RSS 85/17/5/42

YSN on 8500 kcs. 2212 GMT 15/5/42

49. From WIDO no.10 and 11. Service message to ADOLF. For supervision of W/T traffic of undertaking SALAM from 12th May, first day of travel, SALAM-OTTER traffic: 1st to 4th day, traffic times 12 hours, 21 hours, 5th to 24th day: 0700, 1430, 2100 hours callsigns, keys and frequencies as in traffic plan. Besides this OTTER will also stand by for 10 minutes to receive: 1st until 4th day, 0700, 10 hours, 16 hours, 19 hours; 5th till 24th day: 10 hours, 16 hours, 19 hours.

SCHILDKROETE.

9358   GROUP II/26

BERLIN to ATHENS

RSS 7/24/5/42

YSN on 8500 kcs. 0717 GMT 22/5/42

No.64. The I c [Intelligence Officer] with Panzerarmee Oberkomando AFRIKA has expressed the wish that an ADOLF – W/T operator should [go and] receive W/T instructions for W/T traffic ADOLF, SCHILDKROETE and OTER from Leutnant HAEUSGEN who is attached to the I c. Accordingly dispatch of a suitable W/T operator to the I c with Panzerarmee Oberkomando AFRIKA is required. Please give notice of execution of order.

ANGELO. 569.

10801   GROUP II/26

BERLIN to ATHENS

RSS 57/6/6/42

YSN on 13,280 kcs. 1142 GMT 5/6/42

10[?]. For AST. Ref. ADOLF message No.12 of 4/6. SALAM has received orders to go at once with W/T operator and set to Battle H.Q. I c Panzerarmee. Must start W/T traffic with CONDOR working himself. Inform SIEBER that he is to attempt to contact SALAM and Stellenleiter NIESE, RASEHORN's man with HAEUSGEN. SIEBER and NIESE must assist ADOLF-CONDOR and SCHILDKROETE-CONDOR W/T traffic to start working at last.

ANGELO. 154.

68010   47. For CARA. For the attention of Herr Major SEUBERT. IDA informed. There will shortly be an exchange of some Reich Germans interned in EGYPT for Egyptians interned in GERMANY. After the names have been settled by the two Governments a Check will be made here as to which Egyptian can be considered for I service. Pleae advise whether ALMASY is available for this investigation. If the investigation is successful it is intended to hand over the disposal [of the persons selected] to KO BU or KO NO. You are requested to prepare for the setting-up of a suitable reporting route with KO NO.

LUDWIG-ANSO No. 298/43 Secret.

68078   GROUP II/13

BERLIN to SOFIA

RSS 14/13/10/43

JNF on 6905 kcs 0627/32 GMT 13/10/43

48. For CARA for SCHUBERT. Report on VAN NUENSTER's assignment was sent off to VO-BUDAPEST on 12/10. PASA is asked to fetch it while he is staying in BUDA.

ANDREAS-HOLM No. 554.

69089   GROUP II/523

VIENNA to SOFIA

RSS 151/19/10/43

APQ on 7660 kcs 1326 GMT 19/10/43

25. For CARA for PASA. Book sleepers from SOFIA to ISTANBUL for 3rd-4th November for LADISLAUS VON ALMASSY, Hungarian passport no. 293486, and KURT VON PLESSING, Hungarian passport no. 46284. They will both be staying in SOFIA at the Hotel BULGARIE from 30th October and will await return of PASA.

Sgd. PASA.

9/11/43 ISK 71677 – 71687

71683   GROUP XIV/28

ISTAMBUL to BERLIN

RSS 256/8/11/43

WD on 14085 kcs 1622 GMT 8/11/43

26. ANDREAS, PROMI, BOFINGER. Ref. BOFINGER. VERMEHREN discussion. Consulate General refused entry visa for PRINZ because of AA instruction signed by RUEHLE. Reason the presence of Arab personalities and Egyptian prince MANSUR DAUD. Journey consequently impossible.

POSTER 7.

APPENDIX 3
REVIEWS, BIBLIOGRAPHY,
AND OTHER SOURCES

Review of publications on
Operation Salam/Kondor

Almásy, László Ede: *Rommel seregénél Libyában*
(With Rommel's Army in Libya), Budapest, 1943

Almásy's book was first published in 1943 and contains impressions and episodes of the desert war but on first read does not give much indication of the actual locations described. During the research for Operation Salam and thanks to detailed knowledge of the Libyan landscape the "code" for the cities and oases could be deciphered[380]. It was not too big a surprise when it was found that most of the sequences Almásy recounted in this book were related to Operation Salam. The content of this small publication was therefore integrated into the new book, particularly since it casts some light on the activities of Almásy before and after Operation Salam.

However, one has to be very careful with this book. It cannot be treated like Almásy's other writings (and as we know even in the supposedly accurate travelogues we still find plenty of "enhancements" or dramatisation). Times, places and events were changed and sometimes purposefully mixed up to be acceptable to the military censors. If one reads the chapter "Desert Patrol", actually a partial account of "Salam", one would never recognise the true nature of the operation, nor the places visited. Chapter "Commando" is based on a true occurrence, the so-called "Rommel Raid" but since the British Special Forces in reality came by submarine and not by aircraft, we can assume that Almásy has just recounted this story but was not involved personally. There was also a clear demand from the publishers that the work should be pro-German propaganda, and in many cases references like "blue-eyed blond German lads", quite alien to Almásy's regular style, appear to be the edits of a different hand.

---

380 These notes were submitted to Michael Farin who published the book in German in 2011 (Belleville, Munich).

Almásy, László Ede:
Schwimmer in der Wüste; Innsbruck 1997

The book *Schwimmer in der Wüste* is a re-publication of Almásy's 1939 *Unbekannte Sahara* (Unknown Sahara) with some additional chapters which appeared in the 1935 *Ismeretlen Szahara* (Unknown Sahara) that was the basis of the later German Edition. However the editors have not realized that *Unbekannte Sahara* was in fact based on selected chapters from two books. The missing chapters from the 1937 *Levegőben ... homokon...* (In Air ... on Sand ...) were not included, so this book is not a complete German version of all Almásy's writings as claimed.

A modest sensation at that time was caused by the first publication of Almásy's diary regarding Operation Salam and other documents which have previously never left the British archives. The editor's footnoted references to the cited documents and the diary are not too accurate, sometimes outright wrong. The mistakes in Almásy's diary were not mentioned in footnotes since they were probably not detected at that time.

While the book does not deal with incidents from the desert war, the editors do that in their foreword, mainly by quoting WB Kennedy Shaw. As is the case with the footnotes mentioned above, the foreword should be read with a certain care. They mention for example that the Italian *Compagnia Autosahariana* was established as a reaction to the founding of the British LRDG – but the Italian units existed since 1938 at the latest, two years before the LRDG. Another error is that *Sonderkommando Almásy* consisted of six independent units comparable to the patrols of the LRDG. The fact is that Operation Salam had six codenames for its W/T receivers at the various locations and that there was only a single mobile unit. The various dumps of the LRDG mentioned were in fact dumps of the SDF that was in charge of resupplying Kufra oasis. Probably more careful research could have avoided some of these mistakes but it should not be forgotten that today, more than 10 years later, additional information is available of which the editors were probably unaware.

Nevertheless, the book is very good reading; unfortunately it was only published in German.

Eppler, Hans:
Rommel ruft Kairo; Gütersloh 1959[381]

It is difficult to say if Leonard Mosley's 1958 book *The Cat and The Mice* gave Hans Eppler the idea that he could publish his story once more – but this time in his own book. Mosley's book is based on interviews with Hans Eppler and describes exactly the same story as was published again by Eppler one year later.

Eppler's book tells the story of the Operations *Salam* and *Kondor* starting with the flight to Tripoli until the two spies, Eppler and Sandstede, were set free in 1946 in Germany. For Operation Salam, it is obvious that Eppler accepted Almásy as the superior leader of the operation, but considered himself someone special and important as well. There are many occasions where Eppler makes clear statements of admiration of Almásy's skills in the desert. This is something worth mentioning since Eppler considered himself in his publications to be one of the most important spies of the *Abwehr*, and such statements clearly differ from the point of view given by Hans von Steffens in his book *Salaam – Geheimkommando zum Nil 1942*. While Eppler generally overestimates the importance of Operation Kondor and in particular his own role as a spy in the German *Abwehr*, the judgment he gives of Almásy is a quite realistic one.

Apart from Almásy, Eppler looked down on all the other members of the crew and does not introduce them in detail. The other spy, Hans Gerd Sandstede, is considered more or less as Epplers wireless operator.

Eppler describes himself as much more important than was the case. At the end he neglects to acknowledge that neither he nor his colleague achieved anything at all in Egypt, nor does he admit that it was mainly his own behaviour that brought the operation to a very rapid end.

Eppler does not mention that both of them had joined the *Abwehr* out of pure opportunism, to avoid being sent to the Eastern Front

In the chapters after his capture by the British Security Sevice, Eppler insists that he had never given any information to the enemy interrogators – however Eppler's personal file now in the British archives tells a completely different story. He gave the enemy all the information he ever had about the organisation of the *Abwehr*, his own mission and all other operations and personalities he was aware of.

The book is a good read, and does provide some otherwise undocumented episodes of Operation Salam where the preparations in Tripoli and the drive to Gialo are described.

Eppler was neither an important nor even a competent spy – but he certainly knew how to sell his story in the best possible way.

381 Eppler re-published his book in French in 1974 that was subsequently translated into English in 1977. There are some substantial discrepancies between the German and French/English versions. When confronted by Jean Howard about this, he answered:" I never imagined that somebody would be able to read both …"

Kelly, Saul: *The Hunt for Zerzura*; London, 2002

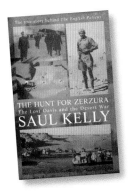

Saul Kelly was the first author who made full use of the newly released documents in the British archives and interpreted the deciphered W/T messages of Operation Salam. His book tells the full story behind the ***English Patient***.

It starts with the well known "Hunt for Zerzura" continues with episodes of behind-the-lines operations in the desert war and ends with German activities in North Africa long after the Axis forces were defeated at Cap Bon in Tunisia.

Kelly's book is based on interviews with survivors and previously unknown documentary material he found in several countries. The book reads very well and was one of the most important sources for ***Operation Salam***. Thanks to Saul Kelly's groundbreaking work the authors of ***Operation Salam***. were able to have easy access to previously secret documents. The book is a very valuable source not only about Almásy but in general for those who are interested in the exploration of the Western Desert[382]. It is very well researched and although based on texts from archives is easy to read and to understand even if one is not already familiar with the subject.

Saul Kelly's book was a breakthrough, building facts out of stories that were previously considered myths. It was one of the foundation stones of the research for ***Operation Salam***. and the authors gratefully acknowledge that Kelly has granted permission for the re-use of his research. Several chapters in ***Operation Salam***. are based on his work.

Mosley, Leonard: *The Cat and the Mice*; New York, 1958

"A true, unbelievable exciting spy story set in wartime Cairo" is written on the dust cover of Mosley's book. Mosley was a war correspondent in Cairo when Eppler and Sandstede were captured there as spies of the German *Abwehr*. After the Second World War, Mosley tracked downed Eppler, who had settled down in Neuforweiler, Saarland, Germany and was then told the full story to write this book. It is not possible to say if Eppler had his story ready when he was interviewed by Mosley, but since Mosley wanted to plot a real spy-story he brought everything into his book that such a story needs … and probably inspired Eppler to produce his own book only one year later. Since the interrogation files of the spies were still considered "secret" in 1958, it cannot be judged as Mosley's mistake that he did not consult them; but it can be doubted that he would have done so – Eppler provided exactly the story Mosley obviously wanted.

---

382 The "Western Desert" is in fact the eastern part of the Sahara. It was so named by the British who looked at it from the Nile and describes more or less the part of the Sahara in Egypt west of the Nile.

Steffens, Hans von: *Salaam – Geheimkommando zum Nil 1942 ;*
Neckargemünd, 1960

Hans von Steffens was the second to publish, after Eppler, a book about Operation Salam/Kondor. He was also the second to consider himself the most important person on the operation. He writes extensively about the preparations in Germany, the transfer to Africa and then about the setup in Tripoli. Although it is a fact that von Steffens was in service with the *Abwehr* before Operation Salam/Kondor, he was only in a relatively minor position, listening to W/T traffic in Nalut at the Jebel Nafusah in Libya. His book is quite useful to extract the activities during the preparation phase and to compare them with the statements of the other participants. Since von Steffens describes himself as the actual leader of the operation, it becomes very obvious that he had serious difficulties in subordinating himself to Almásy and dealing with the two spies who considered themselves as some sort of "precious freight" rather than soldiers who were prepared to follow the orders of a *Wacht-meister* (Staff Sergeant). The book is written as if von Steffens himself organized and prepared everything single-handedly while the others had some weeks of leisure. The fact remains that the very same von Steffens did not have much desert experience and had to leave the group shortly after they faced their first problems during the early stages in the desert – he suffered a "heart attack". The early days of planning in Germany, in which von Steffens did not take part, are directly copied from Paul Carell's account in *Die Wüstenfüchse* which had been published two years previously. The second half of the book, which deals with the stages after which von Steffens had left the expedition, is easily recognised as more or less simple copying of Eppler's book. What is remarkable is that Hans von Steffens used pseudonyms for the characters in his book, even for himself: Stetten[383]. It can only be guessed that he did this so as not to compromise the others, particularly since he was not on good terms with several of them. Nevertheless, von Steffens book is obviously accurate about the preparations in Germany and Tripoli including the testing of the W/T sets.

---

383 The various names, pseudonyms and *noms de guerre* are explained in the glossary of this book.

Bibliography

A

The Aeroplane: *Aircraft Identification, British Monoplanes*, English Universities Press Ltd, London 1942.

The Aeroplane: *Aircraft Identification, German Monoplanes*, English Universities Press Ltd, London 1942.

The Aeroplane: *Aircraft Identification, Italian Fighters, Bombers and Seaplanes*, English Universities Press Ltd, London 1942.

Almásy, Ladislaus Eduard(and others): *Militärgeographische Angaben über Ägypten*, IV. Mil.-Geo., Berlin 1942.

Almásy, László Ede: *Ismeretlen Szahara*, Franklin, Budapest 1935.

Almásy, László Ede: *Levegőben … homokon …,* Franklin, Budapest 1937.

Almásy, Ladislaus Eduard: *Unbekannte Sahara*, Brockhaus, Leipzig 1939.

Almásy, Ladislaus Eduard(and others): *Militärgeographische Angaben über Ägypten*, IV. Mil.-Geo., Berlin 1942.

Almásy, László Ede: *Rommel seregénél Libyában*, Stadium, Budapest 1943. (Published in German as *Mit Rommels Korps in Libyen*, Belleville, München 2011).

Almásy,Ladislaus Eduard: *Schwimmer in der Wüste: Auf der Suche nach der Oase Zarzura* Innsbruck (Haymon) 1997.

B

*Bagnold, Ral*ph *Alger: Libyan Sands*, Hodder & Stoughton, London, 1935

Bagnold, Ralph Alger*: Sand, Wind and War*, The University of Arizona Press, Tucson, 1990.

Bassett, Richard: *Hitler's Spy Chief: The Wilhelm Canaris Mystery*, Weidenfeld & Nicolson, London 2005.

Behrendt, Hans Otto: *Rommels Intelligence in the Desert Campaign*, W. Kimber, London 1980.

Biermann, John: *The Secret Life of Laszlo Almásy*, Penguin Books, London 2005.

Bouwer, Stefan & Thompson, Gerald: *The Aegean Pirates, the History of the 15 Squadron SAAF in World War Two*, The South African Airforce Association, Durban 2009.

Brockdorff, Werner: *Geheimkommandos des Zweiten Weltkriegs. Geschichte und Einsätze der Brandenburger, der englischen Commandos und SAS-Einheiten, der amerikanischen Rangers und sowjetischer Geheimdienste*,Welsermühl Verlag, Wels 1967.

Buchheit, Gert: *Der deutsche Geheimdienst. Geschichte der militärischen Abwehr, Paul List Verlag, München 1966.*

Buchheit, Gert: *Spionage in zwei Weltkriegen. Schachspiel mit Menschen,* Landshut (Verlag politisches Archiv GmbH) 1975.

Buchheit, Gert: *"Meisterspione" berichten* in: *Die Nachhut*, 8. Jg.(1974), H. 29/30, S. 20–24.

Buchheit, Gert: *Ein "Meisterspion" berichtet* in: *Die Nachhut*, 98. Jg.(1975), H. 31/32, S. 22–24.

Breitmann, Richard; Goda, Norman; Naftali, Timothy; Wolfe, Robert: *U.S. Intelligence and the Nazis*, Cambridge University Press, Cambridge 2005.

C

Carell, Paul: *Rommels Agenten in Kairo. Der große Tatsachenbericht von Paul Carell* in: *Kristall*, Jg. o.A., Seiten 1088 ff.

Carell, Paul: *Wüstenfüchse. Mit Rommel in Afrika*,Ullstein, Frankfurt/M 1958.

Cave Brown, Anthony: *Bodyguard of Lies,* Harper and Row, New York 1975.

Clayton, Peter: *Desert Explorer*, Zerzura Press, Corfe Mullen 1998.

Crowdy, Terry: *Deceiving Hitler*, Osprey Publishing, Oxford 2008.

Czeglédy, Gyula: *Memoirs*, ca. 1980, http://gyula.czegledi.hu

E

Eppler, John W.: *Rommel ruft Kairo. Aus dem Tagebuch eines Spions,* C. Bertelsmann Verlag, Gütersloh 1959.

Eppler, John W.: *L'espion de Rommel,* Presses de la Cité, Paris 1965 and published in English as *Rommel's Spy*, McDonald & Jane, London 1977.)

Esch, Hansjoachim von der: *Weenak – die Karawane ruft.*, Brockhaus, Leipzig, 1943.

Esposti, Fabio ; Pecchi, Carlo R.; *I Tedeschi sul Nilo (Die Deutschen am Nil)* in: *Storia Militare*, 4. Jg. (1996), H. 30, S. 27–36.

F

Follett, Ken: *The Key to Rebecca*, Penguin Books, London 1980.

G

Gross, Kuno; Chiarvetto, Roberto, Ocarroll, Brendan: *Incident at Jebel Sherif*, [self published], Switzerland 2009.

Gross, Kuno; Chiarvetto, Roberto: *The Attack on Kufra*, Books on Demand, Norderstedt 2010.

H

Hagen, Walter: *Das Unternehmen Bernhard.* Welsermühl Verlag, Wels 1995.

Höllriegel, Arnold (alias Berrmann): *Zarzura, die Oase der kleinen Vögel.*, Orell Füssli Verlag, Zürich 1938.

Höttl, Wilhelm alias Hagen, Walter

K

Kelly, Saul: *The Hunt for Zerzura*, John Murray, London 2002.

Kennedy Shaw, W.B.: *L.R.D.G.*, Collins, London 1945.

Kost, Werner: *Gebirgsjäger in Libyens Wüste*, Bruno Langer Verlag, Esslingen 1988.

Kubassek, János: *A Szahara bűvöletében*, Panoráma, Budapest 1999

Kröpelin, Stefan: *Die Wüste des Englischen Patienten – Als Saharaforscher auf den verwehten Spuren eines Filmhelden;* in Die Zeit Nr. 17, 1997

Kuper Rudolph & Kröpelin, Stefan: *Climate-Controlled Holocene Occupation in the Sahara: Motor of Africa's Evolution.* in: Science Vol. 313, 2006: 803-807

Kuper Rudolph: *Hans Rhotert 1900–1991*, in: Paideuma 38, 1992: 6 – 16

Kurowski, Franz: *Deutsche Kommandotrupps 1939–45*, Stuttgart 2004.

L

Lahousen, Erwin; *Kriegstagebuch* [See: Institut für Zeitgeschichte, München]

Lefèvre, Eric: *Brandenburg Division*, Histoire & Collections, Paris 1999.

Lucas, James: *Kommando – German Special Forces of World War Two*, Arms & Armour Press London 1985.

M

Masturzo, Andreas: *Carte per non perdersi: il deserto libico nel periodo coloniale italiano*, in *Le sfide cartografiche*, a cura E. Casti, J. Levy, Ancona, Il lavoro editoriale università, 2010

Meyer, Hans R.: *Nachts wenn der Sand singt*, self published, Heusenstamm 1999.

Mosley, Leonard: *The Cat and the Mice*, Harper & Brothers, New York 1958.

Müller, Norbert; Kaden, Helma; Grahn, Gerlinde; Meyer, Brün; Koops, Tilman: *Das Amt Ausland / Abwehr im Oberkommando der Wehrmacht,* Koblenz 2007.

Murray, G. W.: *Ladislas Almásy (obituary)*, in: *Geographical Journal*, 117. Jg., London June 1951, S. 253–254.

McGuirk, Dal: *With Rommel's Army in Africa*, Stanley & Paul Co. Ltd, UK 1987.

McGuirk, Dal: *Afrikakorps – a Self Portrait*, Motorbooks International, USA, 1992.

N

Neumann, Edu: *Nachruf für Theo Blaich*, in "Jägerblatt" Nr. 4, August 1975

Nöther, Werner: *Die Erschliessung der Sahara durch Motorfahrzeuge, 1901 – 1936*, Belleville Verlag, München2002.

O

Ondaatje, Michael: *The English Patient*, Vintage Books, New York 1993.

P

Pryce-Jones, David: *Unity Mitford, a Quest*, Weidenfeld and Nicolson, London 1976.

Piekalkiewicz, Janusz: *Der Wüstenkrieg in Afrika 1940–1943*, Weltbild, Augsburg 2000.

PRO War Histories: *Special Forces in the Desert War 1940-1943*, Public Record Office, London 2001.

R

Reile, Oscar: *Treff Lutetia Paris*, Welsermühl, Wels 1973.

Ritter, Nikolaus: *Deckname Dr. Rantzau*, Hoffmann und Campe Verlag, Hamburg 1972.

Rohlfs, Gerhard: *Drei Monate in der libyschen Wüste*, Cassel, *1875*

Rolke, Michael (Editor); Nikolaus Benjamin Richter *Unvergessliche Sahara – Als Maler und Gelehrter durch unerforschte Wüste*, Belleville, München 1999 (Neuauflage von 1952).

Rolke, Michael (Editor); *Die Karten des Sonderkommando Dora – 23 vierfarbige Croquis von Südlibyen*, Belleville, München 2003.

Rolke, Michael; *Die geladene Maschinenpistole in der Rechten, in der linken den Filmapparat*, Sammelwerkbeitrag in Flachowsky, Sören; Stoecker, Holger: "Vom Amazonas an die Ostfront – Der Expeditionsreisende und Geograph Otto Schulz-Kampfhenkel", Köln/Wien 2011.

S

Schiffers, Dr. Heinrich: *Wilder Erdteil Afrika. Das Abenteuer der großen Forschungsreisen*, Athenäum-Verlag ,Bonn 1954.

El Sadat, Anwar: *Geheimtagebuch der Ägyptischen Revolution*, Eugen Diederichs, Düsseldorf 1957.

Sansom, A.W.: *I spied Spies*, Harrap, London 1965.

Schlee, Alois: *Unter der glühenden Sonne Afrikas*, Flechsig Verlag, Würzburg 2008.

Schmidt, Rudi: *Achtung – Torpedo los!*, Bernard & Graefe Verlag, Bonn 2000.

Seubert, Franz: *Epilog zur Eppler-Story* In: *Die Nachhut*, 1. Jg.(1967), H. 2, S. 14–16

Seubert, Franz: *Der Grossmufti von Jerusalem und die Abwehr* In: *Die Nachhut*, 2. Jg.(1968), H. 4, S. 2–9.

Seubert, Franz: *L. E. Almásy* in: *Die Nachhut*, 7. Jg.(1973), H. 25/26, S. 43–46.

Spaeter, Helmuth: *Die Brandenburger – eine deutsche Kommandotruppe – zbV*, Düsseldorf 1992.

Staritz, Rudolf F.: *Agentenfunk (Schaltbilder, Stücklisten und Abbildungen deutscher Agentenfunkgeräte 1939 – 1945)*, private publication, Bamberg 1985.

Steffens, Hans von: *Salaam.Geheimkommando zum Nil – 1942*, Kurt Vowinckel Verlag, Neckargemünd 1960.

T

Trojca, Waldemar: *Küstenjäger-Abteilung "Brandenburg"*, VDM Heinz Nickel, Zweibrücken 2003.

V

The Duke of Valderano: *The Owl and the Pussycat*, Minerva Press, London 1998.

W

Waller, John H.: *The unseen War in Europe*, Random House, New York 1996.

Weis, Dr. Hans: *Die Feldforschungen von Graf Ladislaus Eduard Almásy (1929–1942) in der östlichen Sahara* in: *Mitteilungen der Österreichischen Geographischen Gesellschaft*, 132. Jg.(1990), S. 249–256.

Westwell, Ian: *Brandenburger*, Ian Allan Publishing, Hersham 2003.

Archives

The National Archives, London:

FO 141/852, Correspondence, British Embassy, Egypt

HW 19 series, Bletchley Park, RSS feeds

KV 2/86, Ritter, Personal File

KV 2/1467, Eppler, Personal File 1

KV 2/1468, Eppler, Personal File 2

KV 3/74, German Espionage in North Africa

WO 201/725, Enemy Long Range Units

WO 204/12095, Individual Case Reports (von Griesheim)

WO 208/1562, SIME Security Summary, Middle East, No. 157, 22 November 1943

WO 201/2139, Enemy Intelligence Units, Operation Claptrap

WO 208/5520, Eppler/Sandstede, Interrogation

The Imperial War Museum, London:

Arch.Nr. LRDG 11/1; Ladislaus Eduard Almásy

Arch. Nr. 4/5; WBK's Papers concerning the Almásy Commando

The Churchill Archives, Churchill College, Cambridge:

Bagnold Papers (correspondence with Jean Howard)

Das Bundesarchiv/Militärarchiv, Freiburg:

RH19 VIII – 47; Tätigkeitsbericht der Abteilung Ic in der Zeit vom 15.8. – 31.8.41

RH19 VIII – 47; Tätigkeitsbericht der Abteilung Ic in der Zeit vom 1.9. – 30.9.41

RH19 VIII – 47; Tätigkeitsbericht der Abteilung Ic in der Zeit vom 1.10. – 31.10.41

RH19 VIII – 65; Tätigkeitsbericht der Abteilung Ic in der Zeit vom 17.2. – 28.2.1942

RH19 VIII – 65; Tätigkeitsbericht N.B.O vom 7.2. – 28.2.1942

RH19 VIII – 68; Tätigkeitsbericht der Abteilung Ic in der Zeit vom 1.3. – 31.3.1942

RH19 VIII – 68; Tätigkeitsbericht N.B.O vom 1.3. – 31.3.1942

RH19 VIII – 71; Tätigkeitsbericht der Abteilung Ic in der Zeit vom 1.4. – 30.4.1942

RH19 VIII – 76; Luftaufklärung 3.5.42

RH19 VIII – 76; Luftaufklärung 8.5.42

RH19 VIII – 76; Luftaufklärung 15.5.42

RH19 VIII – 78; N.F.A.Kp. 621, O.U. 16.9.1942

Auswärtiges Amt der Bundesrepublik Deutschland – Politisches Archiv, Berlin

Information about Consul Gebhardt von Walter

Heinrich Barth Institut, Cologne:

Archive Kuper

Correspondence Rudolph Kuper with Jean Howard

Correspondence Rudolph Kuper with John Eppler and Hans-Gerd Sandstede

Archive Kröpelin

Eppler Photographs

Militärhistorisches Museum der Bundeswehr, Dresden, Archiv Müller

Kriegskarten im Zweiten Weltkrieg, Dr. Egger

Überblick über das Karten- und Vermessungswesen des Deutschen Heeres von 1919 bis 1945, Dipl. Ing. Theo Müller

Institut für Zeitgeschichte, München

Kriegstagebuch des Amtes Ausland Abwehr-Abt II

Landesarchiv Speyer

Nachlass Kaps Paul

Archive "Die Rheinpfalz", Ludwigshafen

Rubrik "Blick in die Zeit"/Series *"Rommel ruft Kairo – Eppler ruft Bonn"* 1972

Durham University Library, Sudan Archives

John Hatton Rolt Orlebar collection

Archive Michael Rolke

Hans-Gerd Sandstede, *memories, unpublished*, Hamburg ca. 1970

Archive András Zboray

Salam diary, corrected and annotated by Jean Howard (courtesy Jean Howard)

Mostert G.J.: Unpublished Diary, 19 January – 19th October, 1942

Photographs

In general, the sources of the photographs are given in their respective captions wherever known and as agreed with the copyright owners.

Karin and Manfred Blume provided the photographs of Sonderkommando Ritter to this project. Mrs Blume is the daughter of Nikolaus Ritter and she has kept the album of her father since he died.

The photographs of Operation Salam were most probably taken with Almásy's own camera. However, obviously not all photographs were taken by him but also by other members of the mission. What happened with these photographs afterwards is not entirely clear since they did not survive the time in an archive but in private hands. A set of these photographs was kept with Franz Seubert, who was the overall leader of Operation Salam. It is not clear how many photographs were with Seubert – most probably only part of the complete set. His son, Ottokar Seubert, copied them, before the Franz Seubert papers were handed over to the Bundesarchiv Militärarchiv in Freiburg and made available to one of the authors in the 1990s[384].

Dal McGuirk, an enthusiastic collector of Afrikakorps memorabilia from New Zealand in the 1980s, obtained 135 original photos from an unknown source. McGuirk used two of these photos in one of his publications but was not aware of their origin. When he was contacted by one of the authors he immediately joined te project, providing the photos for this book.

A third incomplete set of photographs is with an Italian collector. He owns 171 photos of Operation Salam, largely overlapping with the McGuirk collection. Unfortunately, despite several approaches this collector declined to support this project. About 30 photos are not included in the sets of Seubert and McGuirk – a few of them would have been important for a complete illustration of the mission, the remainder are mostly of scenes taken from a slightly different angle than photographs available in the other two lots.

A total of about 200 photographs were made during Operation Salam, it is both surprising and fascinating that a good portion of them were not relevant to documenting the operation, but only "tourist" snapshots, some in a rather bad quality.

Maps and sketches used in the book

U.C.I.P.I. – Tripolis, 1939, *Tripolis, Stadtplan* (Citymap) 1:8'000

TNA, London, KV 1467, Hans Eppler,
Interrogation Files, 1942:
   Assiut, sketch without scale

Survey of Egypt, 1:500'000, 1943:
   10 Uweinat

Carta Dimostrativa Della Libia Scala 1:400'000, Istituto Geografico Militare, 1938:
Foglio 12 Agedabia

384 Unfortunately, the Franz Seubert papers seem no longer to be available anymore at the Bundesarchiv Militärarchiv in Freiburg. It is not clear, whether they have been lost or perhaps even destroyed.

Carta Dimostrativa Della Libia Scala 1:1'000'000, Comando Superiore Forze Armate S.A., Ufficio Topografico, 1938:
>   *Foglio VI Gialo-Giarabub.*

Army Map Service (AMS) Geographical Section, General Staff (GSGS), Libya 1:500'000, 1943:
>   *3-9 Misurata,*
>   *10 Uwenat*

Deutsche Weltkarte 1:500'000, Afrika, 1941:
>   *NH 34-SO Audjila*

Deutsche Weltkarte 1:100'000, Afrika, 1942:
>   *Agheila*

Luftnavigationskarte in Merkatorprojektion, 1:2'000'000, 1942:
>   *Nr. 2425 Mittleres Mittelmeer*

Gen. St. d. H. Abt. f. Kr-K. u. Verm. Wes. (II)
>   *Übersichtskarte von Nordost-Afrika 1:5'000'000, 1941*

Co-ordinating Council for Welfare Work in Egypt, 1943:
>   *Service Guide to Cairo, City Map*

Related movies and documentaries

Almásy's enterprises and *Operation Salam* in particular were the subject of several movies and documentaries. The most famous was the *English Patient* which unfortunately has drawn a rather incorrect picture of Almásy.

Fahmy, Hekmat: *Almotasharida*, Egypt 1946.

Schleif, Wolfgang: *Rommel Ruft Kairo*, Deutschland 1958. With Adrian Hoven, Elisabeth Müller and Peter van Eyck.

Llevellin Moxey, John: *Foxhole in Cairo*, United Kingdom 1960. Again, as in the German movie of two years previously, Adrian Hoven and Peter van Eyck in the same roles.

Moustafa, Houssam Eddine: *Hekmat Fahmy the Spy*, Egypt 1994; Nadia al-Guindi in the role of Hekmat Fahmi.

Mingella, Anthony: *The English Patient*, USA 1996, Ralph Fiennes, Juliette Binoche and William Dafoe in the movie based on the novel by Michael Ondaatje.

Mayer, Kurt: *Schwimmer in der Wüste*, Austria 2001. Mayer follows the traces of Almásy based on original film material belonging to his father who joined Almásy on an expedition in 1929.

Matzek, Tom: *Gipfelstürmer und Wüstenfüchse*, Austria 2009. TV documentary, which includes, beside contributions from German explorers in South America and the Himalayas, a further part about Almásy's Operation Salam.

Glossary

Ia	First general staff officer, responsible for organisation, combat command and training
Ib	Second general staff officer, normally listed as QM as he was responsible for Logistics.
Ic	Staff officer responsible for military intelligence gathering in German units.
A/A	Anti aircraft (gun)
Abteilung	Department
Abwehr	German Military Intelligence
Abwehrstelle	Offices of the Abwehr
Ägypten	Egypt
Alam	Pile of stones erected as waymark
Alamat	Plural of Alam
AM	(It) "Amministrazione Militare" (Military Administration)
Amt Ausland/ Abwehr I H West	Oberkommando der Wehrmacht, Auslands-Abwehr, Fremde Heere West, Abteilung I under the command of Oberst Maurer and his deputy Major Seubert.
AST	Abwehrstelle
Aufklärungs-kommando	Reconnaissance unit
Bimbashi	"Commander of the 1'000" is a rank of Turkish origin and the equivalent of a Major in the Egyptian and Sudanese Armies
Campo (di Fortuna)	Italian98 emergency landing grounds located in the desert, mostly along air-routes from one oasis to the other.
CMP	Canadian Military Pattern. Trucks manufactured in Canada by Ford and Chevrolet for the British army
Comando Supremo	Italian High Command
CSDIC	Combined Services Detailed Interrogation Centre
CSM	Company Sergeant Major
Dahabeah	Type of boat on the river Nile
Djinn	Benign Spirit
Dolmetscher	Interpreter
Dreimächtepakt	Contract between Germany, Japan and Italy. Concluded on Hitler's initiative on 27 September 1940.
EGP	Egyptian Pound (currency)
Bab el-Misr	The gateway to Egypt
Esbah	Farm (Egypt)
ETA	Estimated Time of Arrival
Fallschirmjäger	Parachutist in the German Airforce
Feldwebel/ Wachtmeister	German NCO, Sergeant
Fellah	Egyptian farmer (Plural: Fellahin)
Fliegerkorps	Air Corps
Flitzer	German nickname given to the captured smaller CMP trucks and Jeeps.
Führerhauptquartier	Hitler's Headquarters
Fustificata	(It) Pista fustificata. Italian desert track marked with empty fuel drums ("fusti") in distances of about 1 kilometre

Gap	Clayton noticed "The Gap" of the Gilf Kebir from the plain in 1931, but it was Penderel who recognised its true nature from the air in 1932. The 1933 Almásy – Penderel expedition was the first to enter it on the ground. Almásy calls it the "Great Break" or "Great Rift", but Clayton's earlier name is the one that took hold.
Gara	Flat topped rocky hill
GBP	British Pound (currency)
GC&CS	Bletchley Park – officially called the 'Government Code and Cipher School'
Gebirgsjäger	Mountain troops
Gefechtsstand	Tactical Headquarter
Gefreiter	German enlisted soldier, Lance Corporal (with 6 months total service)
Generalfeldmarschall	German officer, Field Marschal
Generalleutnant	German officer, Lieutenant General
Generalmajor	German officer, Major General
Generaloberst	German officer, no equivalent in British ranks (Brigadier General is possibly the closest)
Geschwader	Group (brit.)/Wing (am.)
GeStaPo	Geheime Staatspolizei (Secret State Police). The organisation was under the administration of the SS.
Ghaffir	Watchman
Ghibli	Hot wind from the south, carrying loads of dust.
Ghibli	Italian airplane, Caproni Ca.309
GHQ	General headquarters
GHQ ME	General Headquarters Middle East
Gruppenkommandeur	Group commander
Hauptmann	Captain
Hauptmann/ Rittmeister	German officer, Captain
Heer (WH)	Army
Heeresplankammer	Topographical Department of the army
Hirashif	Fissured, eroded ground
HQ	Headquarters
ISLD	Inter Services Liaison Department
ISOS	Intelligence Service Oliver Strachey
Kampfgeschwader	Combat Wing
Kampfgruppe	Battle Group
Kommando	Command/Commando
Kraftfahrzeug (Kfz.)	Motorized vehicle
KZ	Konzentrationslager (Concentration Camp)
Leica	German manufacturer of photo-cameras
Leiter	Leader
Leutnant	German officer, Second Lieutenant
LG	"Landing Ground". The Italian "campi di fortuna" between Gialo and Kufra were renamed by the British as LG.1 to LG.8.
LRDG	Long Range Desert Group
Luftflotte	Air Fleet
Luftwaffe (LW)	German Airforce (GAF)
Lungomare	(It) Seaside Promenade
Maggiore	Major (Italy)
Major	German officer, Major
Mamur	Headman, head of administration (Egypt)
Marine (WM)	German Navy
Markaz	Seat of the local government (Egypt)
Meharisti	(It) Camel Riders in the Italian Army
MEIC	Middle East Intelligence Centre
Messerschmitt	German aircraft manufacturer. In this case it was probably the Bf 109 fighter plane.
MI5	Military Intelligence, Section 5. The United Kingdoms secret service for counter-intelligence
Muhafizz	Officer in command of the garrison (Egypt)
NBO	Nachrichtenbeschaffungsoffizier (Intelligence Gathering Officer)
NSDAP	Nationalsozialistische Deutsche Arbeiterpartei or literally: The Nazis

NSGr	Nachtschlachtgruppe – literally "Night Harassment Group"
Oberfeldwebel / Oberwachtmeister	German NCO, Staff Sergeant/ Colour Sergeant
Obergefreiter	German enlisted soldier, Senior Lance Corporal (with two years total service)
Oberkommando der Wehrmacht (OKW)	Supreme Command of the Armed Forces
Oberkommando des Heeres (OKH)	Army High Command
Oberleutnant	German officer, First Lieutenant
Oberschütze	German enlisted soldier, Private (with 6 months total service)
Oberst	German officer, Colonel
Oberstleutnant	German officer, Lieutenant Colonel
Palificata	(It) Pista palificata. Italian desert track marked with iron poles ("pali") in distances of about 1 kilometre
Palo	(It) Iron pole of the pista palificata
Panzer	"Tank". Note that the plural of 'Panzer' is not 'Panzers' but as well 'Panzer'.
Panzerarmee Afrika (PzAA)	Panzer Army Africa
Panzerdivision	Armoured Division
Panzergruppe Afrika	Panzer Group Africa
Pengo	Hungarian currency
POW	Prisoner of War
Presidio	(It) Short form of Comando di Presidio (Garrison Command). In cases as Gialo, the term was used for the building itself as well.
PzAA	Panzerarmee Afrika (Tank Army Africa)
RAF	Royal Air Force
Regenfeld	"Rain field". A location in the sandsea named by the German explorer Gerhard Rohlfs.
Reichsmark	German Currency
Rittmeister	Equivalent to Hauptmann in Cavalry units
RSS	Radio Security Service
S-Boot	Schnellboot (Speed boat)
SAAF	South African Air Force
Sarti	Luigi Sarti & figli, a firm with a plant in Bologna producing liquors and spirits.
S-Boot	Schnellboot (Speed boat)
Schmalspuroffizier	Sonderführer
Schütze	German enlisted soldier, Private
SD of the RSHH	Sicherheitsdienst of the Reichssicherheitshauptamt
SDF	Sudan Defence Force
Serir	Serir is a totally flat and featureless form of the sandy desert.
Shabura	Sand haze
SIM	Servizio Informazioni Militare (Italian Military Intelligence Service)
SIME	Security Intelligence Middle East
Sonderführer	Function in the Wehrmacht equivalent to the rank of an NCO or an officer (depending on the cathegory). This function was given to persons with a specialised civilian knowledge but without the required military experience needed to become a regular officer.
Sonderkommando	German term for 'special task unit'. It does not necessarily have to be a unit comparable to the better-known British 'special forces' but could also be an administrative unit.
Spitfire	Supermarine Spitfire. British fighter plane.
Stabsfeldwebel/ Stabswachtmeister	German NCO, Regimental Sergeant Major – created 14th Sept 1938 for NCO's re-enlisting after 12 years service.
Stabsgefreiter/ Hauptgefreiter	German enlisted soldier, Lance Corporal – but with 5 years total service. Used from 24th April 1942 to 9th May 1945 for those not fit for NCO rank.
Staffel	Squadron
Storch	Fieseler Fi 156; German STOL aircraft
Stuka	Junkers Ju 87 "Stuka" (Sturzkampfbomber), divebomber
Taifun	Messerschmitt Bf 108; German one-engined four-seater liaison plane
Tommy	German nickname given to British soldiers

Tommy guns	Nickname for the American made Thompson M1928A1 submachine gun.
Trucchi/Trucchi Track	Civillian Italian transport company supplying the oasis of Kufra along the "Trucchi Track" from Agedabia via Gialo to Kufra.
Unterarzt	Doctor, German rank, equivalent to 1st Lieutenant
Unterfeldwebel	German NCO, Lance Sergeant
Unteroffizier	German NCO, Corporal
Verbindungsmann	Liaison Person (see: V-Mann)
Vertrauensperson	Trusted Person (see: V-Mann)
V-Mann	Vertrauensperson or Verbindungsmann. An informer to a secret service or the police.
Volksdeutsche	Ethnic Germans
W/T	Wireless telegraphy
Wadi	(It. Uadi) dry river bed
Wüstennotstaffel	Desert Rescue Squadron
WWI	This term is generally used to describe World War One (instead of Great War)
WWII	This term is generally used to describe World War Two